ON FOOT

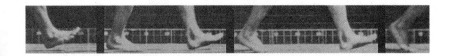

NEW YORK UNIVERSITY PRESS *New York and London*

JOSEPH A. AMATO

A HISTORY OF WALKING

foot

NEW YORK UNIVERSITY PRESS
New York and London
www.nyupress.org

© 2004 by New York University
All rights reserved

Library of Congress Cataloging-in-Publication Data
Amato, Joseph Anthony.
On foot : a history of walking / Joseph Amato.
p. cm.
Includes bibliographical references and index.
ISBN 0–8147–0502–2 (cloth : alk. paper)
1. Walking—History. I. Title.
GV1071.A63   2004
796.51—dc22   2004013674

New York University Press books are printed on acid-free paper,
and their binding materials are chosen for strength and durability.

Manufactured in the United States of America

10 9 8 7 6 5 4 3 2 1

Contents

ON FOOT

Introduction

Walking Is Talking

 IN his *Theory of Walking,* nineteenth-century French writer Honoré de Balzac wrote, "Isn't it really quite extraordinary to see that, since man took his first steps, no one has asked himself why he walks, how he walks, if he has ever walked, if he could walk better, what he achieves in walking ... questions that are tied to all the philosophical, psychological, and political systems which preoccupy the world?"[1] I hope here to answer Balzac's questions as well as the questions that prompted me to write this history of walking.[2]

My questions focus particularly on modern society. I ask who walks now, and how and why do they walk? Do they on the whole walk less? And when they do walk, do they do so as a matter of necessity or choice? I question how changes in the history of walking relate to issues of social class and status, as well as to the increasing control of government over city, countryside, and nation. How are the displacement of walking as a necessary activity and the birth of walking by choice—be it promenading and strolling, romantic walking and country hiking, window shopping, urban pedestrianism, or commuting—tied together? In what ways was walking displaced and differentiated by successive revolutions in transportation, industry, commerce, and urban life? Having examined the creation of the modern city and of marching national armies, the automobile, paved roads, and suburbs, I reflect in conclusion on a single question: What do we make of walking and this new humankind, which in the last two centuries sits, rides, and drives ever more, walks less, and walks more by choice than ever before in its entire history?

Approximately six million years have elapsed since our ancestors took to bipedal locomotion. Only in very recent times did truly extraordinary numbers of humans—first on horses and in carriages, then on trains and bicycles, and finally in cars, trucks, buses, and airplanes—begin to sit and ride rather than walk.

In the last hundred years, walking, which I will treat in most instances as synonymous with going on foot, has become increasingly segmented, circumscribed, and limited. At the same time, it has become a matter of choice, involving questions of health and recreation, as well as an assertion of individual lifestyle and social philosophy.

This revolution—inseparable from the triumph of seats and wheels, roads and smooth surfaces—marks a change in the use of the human body and mind. In the West, people do less physical work, and consequently they work less in the outdoors, stand, squat, and lean less, and do these things in fewer ways. People also climb, clomp, and stomp less as the need to walk on steep, uneven, and nonfirm surfaces disappears. At the same time, the revolution alters conceptions of space, distance, motion, movement, and the amount of energy necessary to invest in travel. It not only involves the story of feet and legs and the history of dress and footwear but also raises questions about roads, transportation, communication, cities, suburbs, and cultures.

The act of going on foot is joined to a time, condition, society, and culture. Walking belongs to the gender, age, class, ethnic and national group, and even race of the walker. The shoes, clogs, cleats, stilts, and clothes that are worn shape the walk. The loads that are carried, led, and pushed, and the way this is done, determine the walk and its appearance. The surfaces and distances the walker traverses also shape the walk, and the weather—sun, wind, rain, and even types of snow (deep and soft, brittle and crusty)—determines stride, gait, and pace, and can even dictate the need to crawl and climb. The reason why the walker travels informs his or her steps from beginning to end.

An army instructs its troops on how to march, tells them when and where to march, and even determines when they can break ranks. Other groups, usually of higher status, also teach their members how and where to promenade, stroll, and window shop—and to move as much as possible as if they are oblivious to or above certain conditions or distractions. Cities likewise, though less explicitly, put their signatures on their own pedestrians and commuters, determining their pace, willingness to give way, and even willingness to stop and help, as well as their manner of moving on sidewalks, on roads, across intersections, and in and out of public transportation. Working-class and peasant folk cultures also produce their own steps and gaits, which often have corresponding dances, such as the clomping dances of wooden shoes. Subgroups on city streets produce their own struts and saunters, which are often joined to a manner of dress, a type of footwear, and ways of standing, leaning, and looking. Tennis shoes today form voices of contemporary walking.

As rich as it is in variety, walking does not compete in status and attention with movements of hand and mouth. Inseparable from the foot and the earth it treads, walking is taken to be mundane, ordinary, pedestrian, and even besmirched and polluted—and thus in all ways worthy of being overlooked or disdained. Walking often even goes unconsidered for other reasons. It is camouflaged in the context in which its occurs. It often melts into the clothing, animal power, technology, industry, and transportation that determine and mutate walking. Furthermore, walking is joined to the rich world of human gestures and nonverbal communications. Walking, that is, is not perceived independently from the person it carried or carries. It always comes in the form of a particular body shape and movement. Fast tends to radiate importance and status. The glare of the eyes, countenance of the face, turn of the neck, movement of arms, straightness of back, projection of stomach, and rotation of hip identify and distinguish a walk and provoke a series of judgments about the walker. Likewise, the speed, stride, flow, and balance exhibited by the walker constitute the gestalt of a walk. Needless to say, walkers are known by the company they keep.

All this suggests the notion that underpins this introduction: walking is talking. It can be understood as a language, having its own vernacular, dialects, and idioms. Expressing intentionality, walking conveys a wealth of information about the walker's identity, importance, condition, and destination. Onlookers attribute their own meaning to the walker, seeing in a walk a statement of purpose or a declaration to be heeded. They also can be baffled by mixed or ambiguous messages of walking. An onlooker might not be able to suggest why a friend is on foot, or whether a change of gait is a result of illness, medicine, or weariness. Nevertheless, walking is a clear revelation of identity, as proven by the fact that radar recently developed for the United States Defense Department's battle against terrorism can identify 85 to 95 percent of individual walks as if they were personal signatures.[3]

A primary body language, walking always communicates something. Like waving, smiling, and greeting, walking belongs to the history of gesture.[4] Composed of separate actions involving not just the extension of leg and foot but also posture, arms, elbows, hands, and fists (clenched or unclenched, thumb out or tucked in), walking is taught from one's first steps. Like eating, drinking, carrying, washing, defecating, birthing, or making love, walking assembles a miscellany of movements into a whole. It presents the walker to the world. It declares who walks, how, why, in what spirit, under what conditions, and at whose volition he or she walks. Walking expresses itself with varying speed, stride, gait, and associated posture, company, dress (especially shoes but also leggings and socks), place, load, condition, and occasion.

Walking manifests health, sickness, and deformity. Not to walk constitutes living a different life.[5] Individuals may display a hobble, limp, sway, or even a lean from a lifetime of work. Arthritic knees, shoulders, backs, and elbows testify to years of carrying buckets of milk and water that pull people's arms permanently down at their sides. With varying degrees of subtlety, a walk announces or discloses a person's feelings and moods. It signals a pedestrian's vibrancy, energy, and enthusiasm, or lassitude, fatigue, and dejection. Even though observers can mistake a walk, for instance confusing a sufferer of Parkinson's disease with a drunk, they most often intuitively read the meaning, character, and intention of a given step. Human eyes read legs and feet to decipher meaning.

Along with marching and dancing, which express at once personal styles and group solidarity, individuals move differently according to mood, physical condition, and circumstances. They have multiple walking styles for different inner thoughts and feelings and myriad situations and occasions. Individuals can even effect a hobble or limp. Accompanying posture and body gestures, along with slightly averted eyes, a tilted head, projected elbows, clenched fists, or an exaggerated swing of one arm, form distinct signatures distinguishing one walker from another.

Anatomy and conditions differentiate individual walks and make them emphatic over a lifetime. The plane of the foot, the length of the stride, or other mechanics of bipedal locomotion distinguish toddlers almost from their first solo jaunts. They mark out youth as they parade across the stage in a graduation ceremony, and still distinguish the old who are still capable of pacing the halls of their nursing homes.

Orthopedists, podiatrists, and physical therapists are among our primary and most literal interpreters of human bipedal locomotion, that singular system of movement that amounts to going forward by falling from foot to foot.[6] Even in our sedentary society, an average person takes almost nine thousand steps a day. Five percent of the United States population has ingrown toenails or other foot problems, and according to the American Academy of Orthopaedic Surgeons, there are nearly four million annual visits to the emergency room in the United States for knee, ankle, and foot and toe injuries. (This is nearly three times the number of visits to a physician for other reasons.)[7] Trained in the biomechanics of walking, those who specialize in feet and walking are quick to perceive and use technical language to describe walking defects, which until a generation or two ago were known by popular phrases such as "clubfoot," "a clawed foot," "flat feet," "toe walking," or "heel walking." Experts now know that walking problems can be mechanical or vascular. They might arise from being overweight, improper posture, ill-fitting shoes, or prolonged standing, or they may have their sources in the brain, inner eye, or nervous, respiratory, or circulatory system. Likewise, problems can be directly traced to the inner ear, back, knees, tendons, ankles, or the feet themselves, in which reside one-quarter of the body's 206 bones (there are 27 bones in each foot).

Language itself commits humans to an interpretation of walking. Each synonym for going on foot offers a description and brings an interpretation with it. Passing people are said to slink, slither, stalk, shuffle, slog, trudge, hike, stroll, strut, swagger, promenade, gallivant, jaunt, mosey, wander, peregrinate, amble, or saunter. Analogies are also freely drawn from the animal kingdom. This walker is said to waddle like a goose, strut like a peacock, or resemble the high-stepping crane, while that one moves like a cat, scurries like a fleeing dog, or wobbles like a newborn colt. The Greeks called man "a featherless biped" Ἄνθρωπος ἐστί ζῷον δίπουν, ἄπτερον.[8]

The speech of walking is rich in all languages and has generated a dazzling array of English verbs of motion.[9] Walkers prowl, perambulate, sidle, ambulate, roam, take a constitutional, gad about, lumber, parade, or prance. And the vernacular has the walker going on shanks' mare, hoofing it, or mucking about. Nor do we lack for adjectives. Walkers are variously characterized as toddling, tottering, lurching, or limping—as being knock-kneed, pigeon-toed, hobbled, or lame.

The English word *walking* itself has a history that conforms to the notion that all living things can trace their origins to the sea. The eleventh-century Anglo-Saxon word *walking* meant "to roll about and toss" as the sea does.[10] Moving from shore to land (as earthly travel so often does), by the thirteenth century the word broadened to mean "to move about" or "to go on a journey." At this time of emerging commerce and expanding pilgrimages, it acquired its contemporary meaning of "going on foot."

Words associated with walking also have a rich etymology. *Marching,* which came to mean "to walk as soldiers do," derives not insignificantly from the deeper etymological sense "to trample down." *Promenading* has it origin in the French notion "to go for a walk" and the Latin "to drive forward." The curious word *saunter* in the seventeenth century referred to a self-reflective form of walking. It had its origin in the Middle English word *santer,* which meant "to muse."[11] *Amble,* "to move slowly and even leisurely," has its source in the Latin verb *Ambulare,* "to go." *Peripatetic,* which meant "to walk around" and was aptly derived from a school of Greek philosophers who walked as they philosophized, came to refer to itinerant traders and travelers.[12] *To stamp,* which in its original German form meant "to pound with one's foot," became in nineteenth-century American English *stomp,* which in the following century came to mean "a dance," "a fight," "a heavy gait," "thick shoes," or any "beating of the feet."[13] And then there is the nineteenth-century English verb *to hike,* of unknown origin, which first meant "a long and disciplined walk through the countryside" and now also can simply mean "to take a walk."[14]

Rich connotations go with such phrases as "walking the carpet," "walking a chalk line," "walking the plank," "walking on water," "walking through fire," and "walking on air."[15] An array of expressions tied to the word *step*—found in such phrases as "first step," "final step," "stepping in," "stepping out," "step on it," and "step to it"—suggests how much being on foot forms the core of human experience and is an important source of speech and metaphor.

The foot itself embeds walking in a trail of metaphorical language.[16] Aside from all the associations to be made with the clubfoot, the six-toed foot, the dirty foot, the big foot, and the callused and worn foot, the word *foot* simply means "down" or "bottom." The king's foot was literally the first measure of distance in the kingdom. While *foot* describes the bottom of a bed, the base of a hill, or the foundation of a building or bridge, *foot* can be used in an array of expressions such as being on "equal footing," "having one's foot on someone's neck," "finding one's footing," "losing one's footing," or "having one foot in the grave."[17]

Like other major bodily movements, walking is inseparable from the language of cultural interpretation. Walking, which presents itself encapsulated in balance, stride, gait, posture, and appearance, invariably expresses something about the walker. Walking can reveal strength, sociability, gender, and age, and it manifests, or is seen to expose, character and intentions.[18] Observers from within and often even from outside a culture intuitively understand the walks they observe. For this reason, playwrights, directors, and novelists draw on the universal language of walking, relying particularly on the feet themselves (think of the large, hairy feet of the Hobbits!), type and condition of shoes, and a character's first steps to introduce their creations' personalities and situations. Audiences don't have to be primed to laugh instantaneously at the jittery, antic steps of Charlie Chaplin any more than they have to be taught to tremble at the sight and sound of the tottering, thudding clomps of Frankenstein's monster.

Whether pinched or full, hesitant or bold, every walk articulates a specific type of energy and emotion. The proud take big, loud steps, especially when wearing boots, while the timid tiptoe around or "pussyfoot about." Novelists exploit our inevitable tendency to equate walks with characters when, for instance, Joseph Conrad described his protagonist Little Fyne in his novel *Chance* (1913) as an aggressive walker who marched with crashing boots—to see his walk was to hate him, we are told.[19] In *Journey to Italy* (1829–1830), German writer Heinrich Heine carried his characterization of *walk*'s expressive power to enunciate religious states of mind when he wrote, "A Catholic priest walks as if Heaven belonged to him; a Protestant clergyman, on the contrary, goes about as if he had leased it."[20]

Entire cultures interpret and value walking in different ways. The Japanese, to take a single example of the prescriptive power of culture to determine human movement, walked differently from Westerners until the Meiji era (1867–1912). "The traditional posture of the Japanese population, which consisted mostly of peasants, was that of a stooped back, with the chin thrust forward, and four limbs bent. Even while walking, the knees were kept bent and there was no counterbalancing swinging of the arms."[21] When the Japanese were instructed to swing their arms, which served the purposes of their new army, they would, with constriction, move right arm and leg forward at same time, and then move left leg and right arm forward. This special style of marching called the *namba* had been traditionally taught at home.[22] In this century, the Japanese exhibit "a richer variety of walking styles than Westerners."[23]

Greeks established the fundamental evaluation of Western walking, which is the primary focus of this book. They classified and valued forms of walking.[24] Powerful warriors, Homer prescribed, must be long striding. The slower gait, later Greek writers concurred, displayed an aristocratic background and a deliberative nature, and even indicated a man of great soul. Yet, they cautioned, men must guard against strolling too slowly, lest they be considered effeminate or lackadaisical. Women who wiggled too much when walking on the streets ran the risk of being judged courtesans, while a wag-tail male would be titled *sauloprokitao* (lizard butt) for what they took to be his effeminate stroll.[25]

Walkers were interpreted not just by how and with whom they walked but also by what they carried and how and why they carried it. At one time, of course, walking almost universally meant carrying things, which activity could be as different and differentiating as holding such precious objects as a gold chalice or a long spear, or hauling, as the great majority did, such diverse encumbrances as logs, sticks, bales, buckets, and ropes.[26] In older cultures, like the Egyptian, in which women, according to Herodotus, carried things on their shoulders while men carried them on their heads, human transport was vital.[27] It was an important reason to own slaves and it was essential to make use of their heads, shoulders, waists, and backs for carrying rather than simply using their arms and hands, as unencumbered contemporary walkers do. Material cultures afforded yolks, shoulder harnesses, poles, baskets, and pots for carrying and instructed people how to transport water, wood, grain, animals, sick humans, and babies.[28] Bearers, whose individual strength and collective inferiority was measured by the load they bore, learned how to lift, shift, and transport things passively. (The word *rock,* which is so important to American popular music, English urban commentator Peter Hall proposes, "derives from the old tradition of rocking and staggering to lighten the weight of loads carried by black burden bearers, roustabouts and longshoremen, who brought traditions from black Africa where there had never been wheeled vehicles or animal transport.")[29]

Shoes themselves express their wearer's ways, conditions, and status. A pair of peasant shoes, philosopher Martin Heidegger observed, voices a distinct relationship between the wearer and the earth.[30] In more prosaic terms, my local shoemaker in rural southwestern Minnesota explains how a shoe's wear reveals the occupation of its owner: farmers, for instance, wear smooth the part of the sole that touches the metal ladder on which they enter and exit their tractor cab.[31]

Cultures draw elemental distinctions between those who can walk and those who cannot, and they even speak of imminent death as being on "one's last legs." Until recent times, those who could not walk well, or at all, were negatively classified. Those who were seriously impaired or unable altogether to stand, move, work, and travel formed the lowest ranks of humanity. They needed the help of others to do what humans must do. With distorted bodies, they moved, if at all, slowly, clumsily, or, in the worst instances, like an animal, crawling on their stomach or swinging along on their knuckles. Literally lower than others, they were contaminated by being in more intimate touch with the netherworld of waste and decomposition. Sharing these negative views, Greeks exposed the lame at birth and Old Testament Hebrews prescribed against them becoming priests. The Greeks and Romans attributed defective character to the bowlegged. The inventive Italians, calling them *storti,* took them to be quarrelsome, while making their word for lame, *zoppo,* also mean unsound, defective, and imperfect.[32]

Hierarchies of class and status were commonly built out of and around walking. Those who could walk—the strong and able bodied—stood, so to speak, head and shoulders above those who couldn't walk, who as a consequence were closer to the ground, couldn't as easily express their will, and were often dependent on others. In turn, across the ages those who had to walk and stand were judged to be inferior to those who were privileged to ride and sit. The latter literally or figuratively had the power and money to move on the back of the former or of an animal. Those who were required to traverse long distances on foot, encumbered with goods—such as itinerant merchants or even armies—were inferior to those like king and bishop, emperor and pope, and the greatest merchants, who need not go out into the world. As the highest and most powerful, they were seated in court or city and the world was brought to them. The highest of them—occupying royal thrones and holy seats, radiating earthly and heavenly power, existing at the very juncture of society and nature—needed only to process in ceremonies, in which they might be carried on litters, or to stand on the altar before the sacrificial table. On knees with bent heads and lowered eyes, not daring to stand fully erect or make eye contact—all approached these holy sitting ones as inferiors and all retreated in the same way, bowing and walking backwards, endeavoring not to insult by appearing to depart abruptly or show the lord their backs. The very notion of worship, at least etymologically in one sense of the Greek verb for worship, *proskunes,* means to prostrate oneself in oriental fashion before king and superior.[33]

As we see through history, those who had to walk formed the legions of the inferior and less powerful. They went on foot because they couldn't ride. They were compelled to walk because of the force of circumstances or at the command of others. Walking out of necessity rather than by choice, they literally inherited the inferiority of the foot, which fastened them to the soiling earth. Walking belonged to feet and legs, which lacked the dexterity of the hand and the elevated position of the mind. Those compelled to walk suffered "the travail of travel," two words that were etymologically joined by ages of painful movement on foot. Those who had to walk belonged as well to the inferior kingdom of the working foot. Once immensely vast, that kingdom was home to the bootblack, the shoeshine boy, the footman, legions of pages, porters, bearers, doormen, messengers, waiters, street walkers, and infantrymen who came and went on foot at the command of their superiors. It also contained the despised boot licker, foot smeller, and street sweeper, along with the *footer,* eighteenth-century British English for an idle, worthless person.[34]

Even though nomads and wanderers were often envied for their freedom and the simplicity of their lives, they were viewed through the ages as inferior to members of sedentary (sitting) society, for they were compelled to move and they sat and ruled nowhere.[35] Medieval law defined vagrants as nuisances and even as threats. The homeless, beggars, and the lame, all of whom live primarily on foot, have long been seen as bringing with them disease and disorder. Still today whether one walks or sits and rides continues to be an elemental marker of relative status. The numbers of miles of paved roads in a given country, along with the numbers of cars and trucks per capita, are key in differentiating developed societies from underdeveloped ones. By this measure, Africa remains a dark continent because the great majority of people still travel on foot.

Going barefoot, which could in different contexts be a sign of humility, mourning, or intimacy, has for ages almost universally been understood as a confession of poverty and inferiority. Wearing coarse and unkempt shoes is a sign of indigence.[36] In the early part of the twentieth century, at least among the increasingly well-heeled, emerging middle class that now owned a variety of machine-made shoes, wooden shoes and shoes in poor condition immediately evoked a negative judgment. The wearer of peasant or run-down shoes was presumed to possess only one pair of shoes, to need to work in dirty places, and to have to travel considerable distances over rough and filthy surfaces. As affluence has increased in the West, the majority of people have come to own different types of footwear to express a variety of activities and even attitudes. Ill-kept shoes can express disdain for the mundane activity of shoe care, while wearing cheap sandals or workers' boots allows well-off youth to assert, with their feet, their affinity for the people. In effect, the abundance of footwear brought to an end the era when young schoolgirls feared crossing their legs lest they reveal the hobnailed shoes their fathers had made for long wear.

Shoes, of course, are implicated in a more complex culture discussion because of their ever-so-close association with the foot, which functions as a symbol of death and sexuality.[37] The foot evoked sexuality and fecundity in both Europe and Asia.[38] In sixteenth-century Spain an aristocratic woman's foot was neither to be seen nor to be touched. The Comptesse d'Aulnoy, for example, locked her door to put on her stockings. She claimed she preferred death to having a man see her feet.[39] China, where the appearance of women's feet was given priority over their use, crippled its women for a thousand years. Courtly women were kept in seclusion "as far as possible from the street."[40] Foot binding of the female child, which began at age seven, satisfied the nation's sexual preference for small feet and ensured that wives wouldn't run away from home. Matchmakers reportedly asked, "How small are her feet?" and contended that "poorly bound feet are a sign of laziness."[41]

Western courtiers, who wore jeweled and precariously high-heeled shoes, wished not to have callused and wide feet lest they be taken for earth-bound peasants, who their ancestors in fact may have been. Having small and slender feet assured superior footing over those who laboriously trod the earth. The long-lasting prejudice of the foot-gliding and -sliding court, and the urban middle classes, that evolved in

the seventeenth and eighteenth centuries against the stomping inhabitants of the countryside is captured in part by twentieth-century Bre-
ton writer Pierre Jakez Hélias. In his memoir of the early
twentieth-century countryside, he describes the country walker that
city pedestrians criticized.

> In town the peasant goes at his own pace, that is, with his daily rhythm.
> He does not travel the pitted paths, the worn earth, the prairie itself
> underfoot like a city sidewalk. . . . The peasant in the city is a wanderer
> and gazer, a type of tourist. . . . His slowness, this admirable economy
> of body, which isn't heavy or clumsy, is imposed by the rhythm of his
> work.[42]

The prejudice of city walker against country walker as slow and
clumsy is still perpetrated across the world. Hmong mountain dwellers
in Laos, for instance, are immediately identifiable when they descend
to the lowlands, as a visiting Western doctor among them recently observed. "Accustomed to frequenting steep, rocky paths he [the peas-
ant] would forget he was walking on a smooth, flat road, and he would
raise his foot too high with each step, as if he were climbing a staircase. On the plain, a Miao (a tribe of the Hmong) was as much out of
his element as a sailor on dry land."[43]

Discoverers and settlers noted that Native Americans, who have diverse traditions of running and body movements, walked in different
ways than the Europeans. The Canadian fur trader and geographer
David Thompson, who explored the whole of the Columbia River
system during the early 1800s, admiringly interpreted the gait of the
Black Foot Indians (the Piegans).

> Their walk [is] erect, light, and easy, and may be said to be graceful.
> When on the plains in the company with white men, the erect walk
> of the Indians is shown to great advantage. The Indian with his arms
> folded in his robe seems to glide over the ground; and the white peo-
> ple seldom in an erect posture, their bodies swayed from right to left.[44]

The formation of new North American society staged an encounter of diverse walking styles. In *The Reshaping of Everyday Life,*

1790–1840, the historian Jack Larkin notes one of the elusive yet mostly taken-for-granted aspects of everyday life in nineteenth-century America: "New Englanders moved heavily. The immense physical demands of pre-mechanized agriculture gave men a distinctively ponderous gait and posture. Despite their strength and endurance, farmers were heavy, awkward and slouching in movement" and walked with a "slow inclination from side to side." Already in the 1830s black slaves—perhaps in no rush to get to another man's work—showed "a preference for rhythmic rather than rigid bodily motion." At the same time, American city dwellers, who moved to the quicker pace of commerce, were distinguishable from heavy, slouching farmers attuned to slow seasonal rhythms.[45]

Offering one of many comments on the difference between country and city walks, American novelist Larry McMurtry remarks that to this day in his native Archer County, Texas, the descendants of the Germans who settled there more than a century ago have not lost their old country walk. "Their posture . . . was different from that of the cowboys and oil field roustabouts I knew. . . . I can spot [one of them] by their more measured, more deliberate way of walking, and also by the extreme concentration they bring to their work habits."[46]

Today, as comfortable sitting and convenient riding increasingly dominate Western society, walking still continues to take new forms. Walkers, though more and more sedentary at work and even in leisure, learn as pedestrians born in the era of mass transportation to travel sidewalks and to obey traffic signs. Already in the late nineteenth century, armies, parades, and demonstrations instructed people how to march in mass, as other institutions, including schools and businesses, taught them the etiquette of public walking and movements. They took up their newly learned stepping on the same smooth surfaces and sidewalks, utilizing the same transportation and communication systems, on increasingly shared schedules. With considerable idiomatic variation, walking, thanks to uniform material conditions, has come to speak a common language.

At the same time, as wealth and leisure spread, window shoppers, mall walkers, park and zoo strollers, recreational hikers, bird watchers, and ambling tourists become identifiable groups of walkers. In the twentieth century, to ever larger audiences, art, photography, and especially film and television, principal agencies of mass culture, show the contemporary world how to go on foot. French anthropologist Marcel Mauss pointed out that already by the late 1920s and early 1930s Hollywood films were starting to teach French girls ways to move and walk.[47] As spreading affluence permitted the poorer to imitate the richer, high fashion offers the rich luxurious and shocking clothes to distinguish themselves from "the aping poor." With origins in nineteenth-century Paris, high fashion, just as aristocratic culture from centuries before did, promotes nonutilitarian clothes, distorted bodies, and even the exaggerated catwalk of contemporary fashion halls to flaunt wealth and superfluousness.

Before I formally embark on this history of walking, I must affirm that this book is not a story of great and monumental walks, which every age had. Also, it is not a collection of unique trips on foot across the ages, although many such walks and trips are mentioned here. Rather, it is intended to be a narrative of human walking through the ages, the story of its major forms and transformations.

Leaving an examination of non-Western and traditional peoples' walking to the anthropological and historical work of others, I have principally devoted this history to a narrative of walking in the Western world. I believed that any attempt to integrate into my work world history or microcosmic investigation of types of walking in traditional groups and transitional societies would prevent me from writing a coherent narrative of walking. Furthermore, by keeping essentially, though not exclusively, to the main trails of Western history—those of European and U.S. history—I took the easier and in fact only route possible for me: I would remain, as best I could, faithful to my own knowledge and skills, which were derived principally from the study of Western history.

By choosing to construct a narrative of the main stages of walking in the West, I intended to make the topic of going on foot and of human movement a creditable subject for subsequent material, social, and cultural studies. By specifically charting the displacement of walking as a necessity and its emergence as a choice, I sought to develop this irreversible alteration in Western walking that occurred in the last two centuries. This, in turn, should define the significance of ongoing revolutions in contemporary society's relations to space, speed, motion, travel, locality, and community. And insofar as the West sets the direction and pace of the world, I hope to offer a consideration not just of the plight of walking in a sitting and riding world but also of the fate of a bipedal creature who sits more, walks far less, and does so increasingly by choice.

I hope to recount as an overarching theme how walking went from occupying the center of human life to assuming a much-diminished place in it. I intend to show that, like so many other human activities, such as running, swimming, hunting, and fishing, it passed from the realm of necessity to that of leisure and choice, from the commonplace and ordinary to the occasional, eccentric, and symbolic. Offering a general history of human movement, I illustrate the universal history of the foot's dethronement, with specific reference to the histories of shoes, walking sticks, chairs, horses, carriages, courts, roads, cities, cars, suburbs, and many other subjects.

A critical narrative of walking must ultimately be more evocative than comprehensive given the impossibility of writing a complete history of anything, much less a subject that at every step, so to speak, is joined to the entire history of humanity. Nevertheless, a critical history can, with reference to class and place, suggest who walked, when, why, how, how much, and under what natural and social conditions. By classifying types of walking and distinguishing specific periods of walking, the historian assigns a place to walking in human experience and, thus, records stages of humanity's altered relationship to its own body, as well as to space, community, society, and the world.

Walking constitutes a continuous and changing dialogue between foot and earth, humanity and the world. There can be no full history of this rich conversation, which, as shown in chapters 1 and 2, extends from bipedalism to Roman roads and legionnaires, and thence to medieval peasants, mendicants, craftsmen, scholars, and pilgrims—all of whom played out their destinies on foot. Walking begins to become more stratified by class and status in the seventeenth century, when upper classes, the subject of chapter 3, began "to put their best foot forward" and to make much of their promenading, strolling, and traveling as matters of pleasure, education, poetry, and even self-discovery. Increasingly, the carriage rides of aristocrats and the bourgeoisie ended with fashionable promenades on garden pathways, in parks, on large boulevards and refurbished city ramparts, and on palisades. Tourism, which originated as a necessary ingredient of an upper-class education, began over time to serve middle-class recreation as improvements in principal roads, bridge building, and policing occurred. As seen in chapter 4, walking met the multiple needs of the Romantic spirit and the pens of such figures as Jean Jacques Rousseau, Johann Wolfgang von Goethe, and Alexander von Humboldt. More than convenient, going on foot was a way to sing a song of self and countryside and explore inaccessible ruins and nature, while defying the conventions of riding society.

During the nineteenth century, as the European and the American countryside became populated, foot, horse, boat, and train travel increased as industry, commerce, cities, and migration grew. In this context walking, especially in the new and expanding urban centers, was transformed from being a condition of material survival into an activity of choice and self-enhancement. The Sunday leisurely amble, the ramble in the woods, and the long-distance and strenuous hike took their place in the expanded horizon of middle-class recreation.

For Thoreau, the quintessential American romantic, walking constituted a means for ongoing religious, aesthetic, and scientific explorations. As he circumambulated Walden Pond in the 1840s and 1850s, walking took fresh forms and moved at invigorated speeds in expanding urban centers, where pedestrians moved amidst increasing traffic. Concentrations of population, unprecedented construction, and the development of urban and interurban travel created the new urban walker, discussed in chapter 6 with a particular focus on London, who was transformed, city by city, region by region, into the pedestrian we know today: the traffic-imperiled biped. His steps would be regulated to fit the routes of omnibuses, trams, cars, trucks, and buses, and the accelerated pace of the expanding urban world. Not only would the dangerous and menacing urban crowds have to be policed, ordered, and regulated, as well as educated, sanitized, and socially integrated, but they would also have to be taught—as argued in chapters 7 and 8, with particular reference to Paris—how to get in step with democratic national society. They would have to learn to stand in lines, pass through doorways, march in civic and military parades, and attune their steps and movements, at work and play, to mass institutions.

In the aftermath of the Second World War, in response to new economic, technological, and demographic orders, the majority of Westerners, as shown in chapter 9, learned to sit and ride. The car became a common mode of locomotion. The wheel—put under everything humans or animals once pushed or pulled—eclipsed the foot. Sidewalks, cement surfaces, and roads reshaped city and countryside. People sat more, went on foot less, and carried little, while walking played a dramatically diminished role at home, on the farm, and at work. Curtailed, segmented, minimized, or displaced altogether, as illustrated in chapter 10, walking—a poor competitor among such appealing sports and leisure activities as running, tennis, swimming, mountain climbing, bicycling, skating, and skateboarding—lost its claim to set the standard and ruling pace of human movement. Reduced to the ordinary and truncated tasks of shopping, exercise, and vehicle-supported tourism, walking today increasingly seems largely superfluous and antiquated, a mere adjunct activity in a sitting and riding society.

Yet, to anticipate my conclusion, precisely in this diminished and relegated condition, walking still mutates to fit new technologies, conditions, and environments. While it increasingly becomes a matter of choice, it also assumes a powerful symbolic role as a means of protest and develops an enhanced potential to evoke alternative worlds and experiences. Indeed, walking, variable yet coexistent with human history, still holds a key to where we have been and where we are headed.

🚶 1 🚶 In the Beginning Was the Foot

Walking from the Origins of Bipedal Humanity to Marching Roman Legions

SINCE time immemorial walking has been the primary mode of human locomotion. Since the very beginning, walking and being human have coexisted. On foot humans crossed the earth, experienced life, and defined their relationship to the environment. On foot they carried their children, supported their old, hauled their tools and goods, and herded their animals. Similarly, they fled, chased, and killed, hunted and gathered, sought food, water, fuel, and habitat, traveled, played, courted, and enacted, often with the elaborate and fancy footwork of dance, their defining rituals. For millions of years, our proximate and distant ancestors moved across history on foot, rendering truth to the notion that we have walked our way to our being.

With as much as half of human time and bodily energy dedicated to walking and other supporting modes of locomotion such as running, jumping, crawling, and climbing, changes in the conditions of walking altered lives and societies. Many such changes occurred in the vast period of prehistory, reaching from the first steps and early migrations of our first bipedal ancestors to the agricultural revolution and the emergence of sedentary river-valley civilizations of ten thousand years ago.

These civilizations in the Indus, Tigris and Euphrates, and Nile river valleys marked a profound transformation in elements of human walking. Hallmarks of these civilizations—a fixed place, an annual food supply, domesticated beasts of burden, specialization in tool making, storage, utilization of the wheel, command of a river, and dominance of major trails and routes—were all factors that shaped how, why, where, and who went on foot. The first and dominant lines of status and class were drawn between those who sat, received goods and offerings, and commanded, and all the others of the kingdom, who walked, worked, carried, traveled, fought, and served principally on foot.

Of all early civilizations, the Roman empire, at the apex of its thousand-year history, reached furthermost in space. Its roads, built principally to project its army's power and state authority, formed a system of movement that identified walking with smooth surfaces, increased carrying capacity, and unified routes of travel. Its system of land travel, which utilized oxen, horses, and carts, but was based on and principally required walking, was not surpassed in Europe until the eighteenth century. If walking set the common but variable standard of local human locomotion, the marching speed and distance of Roman's legionnaires set the upper limit of prolonged land travel and defined an order of domination unrivaled since humanity first trod this earth.

"In the beginning was the foot," wrote anthropologist Marvin Harris.[1] The earliest hominid species walked on two feet from two to four million years before a subsequent hominid species made tools, and from four to six million years before Homo sapiens, our kind, appeared about a hundred thousand years ago.[2] "Anthropologists and evolutionary biologists are now agreed," science writer John Noble Wilford recently wrote, "that upright posture and two-legged walking—bipedality—was the crucial and probably first major adaptation

associated with the divergence of human lineage from a common ancestor with the African apes."[3]

Biologists and anthropologists dispute where and when a bipedal
species abandoned its arboreal habitat and got up and off its knuckles.[4] Using only patchy material evidence and conjectures based on
the molecular clock of genetic change, anthropologists writing the
narrative of bipedal humanity struggle to determine when our African
ancestors abandoned the forest for the prairie. Scientists have yet to
explain when our earliest ancestors emigrated from the African plains
or to establish connections among tool making, meat eating, and increased brain size. Earlier hope of finding a single, featured actor in this
multimillion-year narrative has steadily faded as a growing consensus
has emerged that until the unexplained disappearance of Neanderthal
man thirty thousand years ago, the earth was home not to a single
species but to multiple bipedal hominid species.

Bipedalism produced and depended on an anatomy that differentiated human from ape.[5] Being anatomically vertical and going on two
feet altered the human pelvis and limbs. The thickness of the pelvis set
limits on the size of infants at birth, which resulted in longer postna-
tal nurturing and the development of family life. The freeing of hands
opened the way for human tool making. Upright walking required
hominids to dedicate a considerable portion of their muscle and torso
to balance rather than to forward thrust. Integral parts of the balanc-
ing act of walking, human shoulders and arms, formed a marvelous
system of extension in the service of ever-grasping hands. Bipedal locomotion also facilitated humans' capacity to walk and talk simultaneously.

This form of locomotion, which arguably saved as much as 35 percent more calories than knuckle walking and allowed humans surplus
calories to supply their brains, which, even at rest, demand a "whop-
ping 20 to 25 percent of adult energy," nevertheless has a considerable
cost in pain and effort.[6] As science writer Jay Ingram puts it, "Each
stride of normal walking involves a cascade of little tricks that we perform unconsciously."[7] It requires spending three-fourths of one's time
on one foot or the other. As one strikes the ground with one stiff leg
after another, all of one's weight is set against a descending heel, only
to be transferred to the big toe as one rotates hips and redirects the

plane of foot and leg. (One tightens the buttock to keep erect when climbing.) In effect, humanity has tortuously walked across the ages on two feet with a skeleton designed originally for four-legged travel. Flat feet, swollen feet, distorted toes, blisters, bunions, hammer toes, trick knees, herniated discs, and bad backs, not to mention hernias, hemorrhoids, and other maladies associated with our bipedal loco-motion, remain the price of standing proudly erect.[8]

Human history also carries another energy cost; we must forever lug children who have not yet learned to walk or cannot keep up.[9] Young children are always falling behind and must be goaded to keep up or must be picked up and carried.

Psychologist Robert Provine speculates that bipedalism permitted hominids to make fuller use of their breath and vocal cords, enabling them to issue more complex and diverse sounds than their sniffing and panting cousins did. Or, more vernacularly, they had to walk before they talked and laughed.[10] Perhaps song and rhyme evolved to sustain them on their long marches across landscapes as well as to help them identify and commemorate special places along the way.

Afoot, humans could carry myriad objects across immense dis-tances, especially as they learned to make use of their heads, necks, shoulders, backs, and waists. With daunting effect, they could hit and throw, smash down, and kick. They also could reach and pick more ef-ficiently, especially as their species developed a thumb that could be used in opposition to the index and middle fingers. Free hands en-abled them to examine objects, make and utilize tools, and start, set, carry, and control fire—the latter a discovery presently credited to Homo erectus. Each of these functions supported and reinforced one another.[11]

Humans sacrificed an arboreal life to become bipedal earth dwellers. Afoot, humans could better exploit the environment, climb-ing hills, traversing wetlands, wading ponds, and fording streams, plus—weather and terrain permitting—traveling, as walking human-ity perennially has, up to three miles per hour. Able to transport sig-nificant quantities of food, water, and goods, they could sustain themselves over considerable distances. This mobility, which included the ability to carry children, haul tools, transport provisions, and, later, lead animals, gave humans great migratory powers.

Liberated hands played leapfrog with the use of tools and the shaping of the environment. In *The Hand,* neurologist Frank Wilson postulated that the brain's development followed rather than preceded the use of tools. Arguably, Homo erectus completed the remodeling of the hand, which opened "the door to an enormously augmented range of movements and the possibility of an unprecedented extension of manual activity" as well as to "the redesign, or reallocation, of the brain's circuitry."[12] In turn, sometime during the last fifty thousand years, human thought permitted a great revolution in control over the environment, allowing our species a choice of the paths we would travel and the places we would inhabit.

With a rotating periscope head, strong legs, and unbounded dreams, the walking species became ruler of the earth. A mean and glorious microcosm, it stood between earth and heaven, among dust and stars. Walking provided its first hold on space. At the same time, walking was the evolutionary foundation of a dominant eye, hand, and brain.[13] Subsequent complex historical cultures that crossed great seas and dreamed of flying did not acknowledge the humble feet on which they stood and the modest gait by which they proceeded. Free of aches and pains, humanity unthinkingly relied then, as it does now, on its trusted feet.

More than climbing and crawling, running was crucial for escape and attack. It was vital to hunting and herding. Runners—couriers, whose root is the Latin *currere,* to run—delivered important messages. To run fast over great, even extraordinary, distances—like a hundred miles between sunup and sundown—is a skill that still survives today in the running traditions of Native Americans and Kenyans.

The place of dance in primitive life also escapes our present comprehension. Dance, which can be considered illustrative walking, formed the spine of ritual and ceremony. Arguably, myths had their origins in describing the meaning of dance. Articulate, dramatic, rhythmic footwork could bring to life what eluded even the glib and liquid tongue. Engaging whole bodies, it could imitate and express what hands and words could not. Capable of limitless forms and multiple functions, dance imitated nature—the hesitant steps of the stalking crane, the burst of the charging lion. It dramatized first experiences, it initiated novitiates, celebrated hunt and harvest, declared who was ready to marry, and recognized who had married. Ecstatic, fanciful, and calculated, dance steps melded meaning and joined participants and observers. As walk preceded mind, so dance could well have preceded language.

A recent theory suggests that Homo erectus—the walker, the direct ancestor of our own species—emigrated from Africa at least 1.8 million years ago, spreading all the way to China and Indonesia.[14] No single theory, however, explains why or where human groups migrated any more than scientists have yet to offer a single accounting for bird migrations. Walking upright did not require travel. It did not dictate paths and destinations. Movement, migration, dispersal, and colonization each constituted separate phenomena, which did not follow a uniform pattern or have one source. Archaeologist Clive Gamble argues in *Timewalkers* that "large brains, proper feet, nimble hands, fire, stone tools, and a range of feeding patterns" were in place before humans moved in any significant numbers from Africa to midlatitude Asia and Europe between one million and two hundred thousand years ago.[15]

Wherever they settled, humans altered places to fit themselves and themselves to fit places. It is hard to imagine early peoples wandering or strolling, which activities require specialized places for leisurely walking. It is just as difficult to picture them marching, for that involves the numbers, homogeneity, and coordination that come with organized society. Only civilization affords the leisure to meander and the regimentation to march. Primitive peoples lacked the squares, gardens, and public places to promenade and the weapons, logistics, and maps to form disciplined armies. Primitive tribes shaped their walking to the landscape, terrain, climate, and objects they carried.

Adaptation can be seen in the recently discovered Ötzi man. This fully preserved frozen Alpine walker and his five-thousand-year-old clothes, weapons, and tools reveal an experienced snow traveler. According to anthropologist Konrad Spindler, his clothes, including a grass cloak, were surprisingly warm and comfortable. His shoes were remarkably sophisticated: Waterproof and quite wide, they seem designed for walking across the snow. They were constructed using bearskin for the soles, deer hide for the top panels, and netting made of tree bark. Soft grass went around the foot and in the shoe and functioned like warm socks.[16]

Since this ancient European walker was well equipped for his icy journey, we are left to wonder what unexpected event overtook him.

Small bands of humans moving on foot were pushed by necessity and attracted by abundance across the ages. Changing weather patterns, increased and diminished forests, and advancing and retreating glaciers moved them over periods of thousands of years. Over shorter periods, they responded to the availability of plant and animal life, the changing seasons, the scarcity of mates, and growing and diminishing populations. They took to their heels to flee flood, fire, or enemy. Migration was related to food gathering, tool making, pastoralism, and slash-and-burn agriculture. Neither humanity nor its environment was static. Walking was shaped to place and place was shaped to walking.

Early human cultures turned on the changing of seasons and the migration of animals. Similar to the early human, the contemporary Mardudjara aborigines of Australia survive by scouring their landscape for plants, animals, and, especially, water, and this keeps them on the move. In contrast to the Kalahari of Africa, who typically occupy a camp for many weeks before they "eat themselves out of house and home," the Mardudjara, according to anthropologist R. A. Gould, "eat their way into a camp by first exploiting all the food resources near the outlying waterholes before settling at the main waterhole. Then they consume staples between a five- and ten-mile radius of that waterhole before beginning the trek toward (but always *directly* toward) another reliable waterhole."[17] Women, who gather 60 to 80 percent of the food from reliable sources like vegetables and small game, mind the children as they go. Frequently they remain separate or trail behind the men, who often socialize with other groups and hunt alone or in pairs. Hunters require great skill to stalk and spear skittish and easily panicked desert animals.[18]

Whenever food and water sources permit gathering, Mardudjara aborigines seek sociability. "Despite the fluidity of their nomadic life," writes scholar Robert Tonkinson, "they are not rootless wanderers who lack territorial attachments. As individuals and group members, they maintain strongly felt and enduring bonds to stretches of territory, and within their home area, to particular sites of totemic and religious significance."[19] Male initiation involves a trip on foot that, among other things, serves "to acquaint the novice with the totemic geography of distant, hitherto-unknown territories."[20] The need to be mobile, which alone can provide life-giving water and food, finally trumps sentiments of care for Mardudjara elderly and infirm.[21]

Early peoples, in truth, could not go as far as their legs would carry them. Anthropologist E. Adamson Hoebel suggests that forest dwellers could not become pastoralists, and dwellers in grasslands and deserts could not readily become gardeners. "In dry grass and steppe areas," he adds, "men on the lower levels of economic development may be collectors or hunters. If they move on to higher levels of economic development, they must become herders. Only when civilizational techniques produce the plow can agriculturists successfully move into the more favorable semiarid regions."[22]

Animal trails and prominent geographic features defined the early hunters' landscape. Indeed, for generations the first immigrants to the Americas followed animals across the frozen Bering Sea and down the continent. Early North American horses, big-horned bison, camels, mammoths, and mastodons not only offered large meals but also made trails that led to water, food, protected valleys, and salt licks, as well as through mountain passes. White explorers and settlers used the same trails in their move west. "Daniel Boone," anthropologist Peter Farb wrote, "followed a bison trail in laying out his Wilderness Road across the Cumberland Gap, and many railroad beds through mountains followed routes pioneered by bison."[23]

Domestication only extended prehistoric groups' oscillation between the two poles of movement and settlement.[24] Animals—chickens, ducks, pigs, water oxen, donkeys, camels, sheep, and the like—allowed people to stay at home. These animals increased the supply of natural materials, and they supplemented humans' diet. At the same time, animals required their keepers to seek out good pastures. Agriculture itself provided the surplus food that allowed groups to tame many animals and allowed the privileged and powerful to take up a sedentary life. In river valleys, with available water and renewable soils for sustained agriculture, select groups and castes specialized in religious ritual, war making, building, crafts, and manufacturing. They could stop walking, sit down, and develop their hands and minds, counting on other members of the social body—the workers, peasants, and slaves, with strong backs and sturdy legs—to supply them with indispensable labor. With a distinction common to contemporary life, inferiors were those who by definition carried out the painful, repetitious, and onerous duties (like walking and carrying) attendant on domestic life and accompanying all social undertakings.

Occurring exceptionally late in human history, domestication further superimposed human footprints on animal footprints. Primitive peoples, who consumed and milked their animals and made use of their hides, hair, feathers, and bones, also learned to ride their animals and use them (as North American Plains Indians utilized their dogs) to carry and pull their things.[25] Walking would never be the same again once a person climbed onto an animal's back. However infrequent the ride or slow the pace, regardless of how bony the animal's back or how much maintenance the animal required, to go on other feet relieved one from going on one's own. Ownership of an animal conferred prestige. The person with one working animal was superior to the person with none, and the individual with two animals, especially for riding, was superior to the individual with only one. Imagination might race ahead to riding Pegasus, the winged horse, but even if imagined wings did not lift human feet from the wearying and degrading earth, humans could walk more erectly and with far greater ease thanks to their working dogs, horses, donkeys, llamas, camels, elephants, and oxen.

Starting ten or so millennia ago, diverse peoples integrated animals into their diet, work, and exchange of goods. They eventually transformed many of their animals into powerful engines that, displacing considerable human walking and work, lifted, carried, and pulled things and drove mills. Subsuming animal power to human wants and passions, animals relieved humans of tedious and trying work, formed another order of servants, peasants, and slaves, and allowed their owners to conjure new dreams of flight and conquest. Especially the strength and speed of the horse, when supported by ample grain and good travel surfaces, served the dream of the conquest of distant lands. The great mounted horse warriors, appearing as men who never walk, came off the steppes of Asia and confronted the world with lightning orders of speed and conquest. Changing the nature of warfare in much of the world, the mounted warrior first defined the nobility as a horse-owning and horse-riding class in early medieval Europe.

Pastoralism, which has made people the servants of animals and animals the servants of people, is, according to economic anthropologist E. Adamson Hoebel, "preeminently an Asiatic-African economic complex."[26] In the New World, only the Navajos became real pastoralists—and then only with sheep acquired from the Spanish—while the Comanche and plains Indians, whose herds could number in the thousands, used their newly acquired horses principally for riding, trade, and war. The Sioux of the high plains, equipped with horses by Europeans in the eighteenth century, gave themselves over to the pursuit of the buffalo. They became perpetual migrants. They owned nothing that could not be carried by a person, dog, or horse.[27] The horse made them the lords of the plains and prairies. Everywhere, flat, open grassland, with grain for feed, provided highways for mounted warriors. Walking and walkers fell under the shadows of their overwhelming presence.

TRAILS, PATHS, AND ROADS

The history of travel and trade has until recent times significantly depended on human locomotion and haulage.[28] Home and migration form the ever-recurrent tides of human existence. Destination and movement define the poles of the human narrative. Until the introduction of domesticated animals, boats, and ships only several thousand years ago, humanity made its memorable treks on foot. And still today, journeys off road into remote interiors of the continents require foot travel.

A tidy definition would put animals on trails and humans on paths. However, long before human language, traveling humankind confounded this distinction as it fused paths and trails in its search for passable ways and good surfaces leading to water, food, salt, and wildlife. Animal trails proved to be the most efficient way (even by caloric measure) to ascend or descend a hill. They also provided the best way to cross a terrain, furnishing routes through high and low lands, swamps and wetlands, and identifying fords for river crossing while securing their walkers water and food en route and shelter from wind, cold, heat, flood, avalanche, mud slide, and other dangers.

However, trails and paths, which conjoined animal and human ways, contrast with modern roads. The former belong to villages and tribes, the latter to societies and nations. Although select trails and paths can serve transhumance, staking out lengthy seasonal and regional routes of migration, they most commonly are local and circling. Singularly or as a set of interlocking circles and arcs, which often converge and diverge at a spring, riverbank, or watering hole, they form the grid of a people's diurnal comings and goings. The local walker not only is accustomed to them but also, over seasons and years, accommodates his walk to the environment they access.

Roads are altogether different from paths and trails. Wider, longer, straighter, and smoother, roads had their origin in the quest of highly organized societies for speed and dominance. They did not build roads for walkers and walking per se but for dominating armies, speeding messengers, and carrying wheels. Although often constructed over trails and paths, roads were built at a fixed point in time for specific purposes. As trails and paths belonged to our biology, habits, and imbedded cultures, so roads—contrived and engineered—arose out of political, military calculation. They sought efficiency in space and time in crossing the countryside landscapes in the service of kings, their temples, hegemonic gods, and cities, which first sprang up in Egypt and Mesopotamia. And although they most often moved across the local landscape indifferently to its interests and special places, they—especially with their open and smooth shoulders—proved a boon to distance walking with their relatively straight, direct, and secure pathways. They well served pilgrims, scholars, merchants, adventurers, and wanderers.

In contrast to omnipresent paths and trails set down by millennia of plodding feet, paved roads were few. Some were found in Egyptian and Mesopotamian cities, others served as Hittite processional routes about 1200 BC.[29] Most were narrow, rutted, and washed out, and came to abrupt ends at mountains too steep to grade and rivers too wide to bridge. This made all the more poignant the command of the sixth-century BC Hebrew prophet, Isaiah: "Make straight in the desert a highway for our God . . . and the crooked shall be made straight, and the rough places plain."[30]

Truly, the road was the royal way. It delivered the king's summons to the whole land. It called the people together for the kingdom's census. Roads let the court and the army enter the countryside and brought back to the court captured slaves and scarce and coveted goods—incense, amber, olive oil, pomegranates, bronze daggers, and salt. And roads, which formed routes tying east to west, north to south, supported monks in their efforts to spread the word of their gods.

Along the road, walking humanity crossed paths. Those with bark-hard bare feet met those wearing sandals of reed, thongs, and slippers of hide. (Sandals apparently were worn in Palestine from the earliest times, while in Syria and Mesopotamia diverse footwear—including a platform sandal with a covered heel and a high-laced boot—was worn, though ordinary people went barefoot.)[31] Burdened porters gave way to persons of rank. However, occasionally, proud nobles like Oedipus and his father, Laius, refused to concede the right of way and collided.

On the roads of Egypt the mighty rode in a litter. It consisted of a seat with a canopy. It was carried on the shoulders of twelve or more servants. Other servitors walked alongside with long fans, cooling the noble rider, while another carried a skin jug of water for refreshment.[32] And, later in Egyptian history, a young warrior in a chariot had right of way over any walker, local cart driver, or even the odd horse rider. Like a river, the road brought together humble and mighty, local and foreign, and invited a *journey,* which, defying its etymology, was rarely ever finished in a day.

Roads, especially before the Roman Empire, were more easily praised than traveled. Walkers, particularly those who did not move in armies or large retinues, put their fates in the hands of the roads they traversed. They exposed themselves to hunger, thirst, disease, the vicissitudes of the weather, and all the other mishaps and dangers involved in a trek across strange lands. In seventh- and sixth-century BC Babylon and Assyria, assyriologist Georges Contenau contends, roads were not truly the conductors of commerce: "Apart from a few great roads between important centres—and we do not know what they were really like—there were no roads in the modern sense, but only tracks worn by the traffic which created them and virtually dictated by the nature of the ground."[33]

Technology and logistics did not dispense with walking. The step and stride of the foot still determined the pace, capacity, and distance of land transport. Able to travel only where the wheel and hoof could take them, carts and their animals functioned best on flat and firm surfaces. Cart travel in all cases depended on the walker who could dismount to lighten the load, to guide and goad the animal pulling it, to find a pathway, or to push, pull, or repair the cart. Without strong beds, suspension system, or developed harnessing, carts were small—barely larger than the chariots that delivered elite warriors to the battlefield and hauled their booty back—and they carried little. In contrast to the horse-drawn wheeled chariot, the sure-footed donkey and heavy-load-bearing camel (still key to certain zones of Near Eastern commerce today) made single-file caravans the preferred mode of haulage.[34] Caravans were the spine of military and commercial expeditions, especially in terms of carrying vital materials such as wood. Composed of donkeys and, later, camels, caravans traveled at the speed of the walkers who guided them.[35] The most advanced civilizations of antiquity still measured space and time by the three-mile-an-hour pace of the average adult walker. Walking in effect defined the condition and labor of land travel.

Classic Greek historian Xenophon confirmed the limits of earthly travel. In the *Anabasis* he described the lengthy retreat of ten thousand Greek mercenaries across Asia Minor that started deep in the Persian Empire at the juncture of the Tigris and Euphrates Rivers and led across Armenia and Bithynia to the eastern coast of the Mediterranean. The army crossed fifteen hundred miles of hostile territory. Constantly harassed and without a road to travel, they traversed trackless deserts, forded rivers, and climbed mountains, encountering the traveler's worst enemies: hunger and cold.

Parties of the enemy were always following, and carried off disabled animals, and fought over them together. Men were also left behind who had been blinded by the snow or lost their toes by frostbite. It did some good to the eyes if men marched holding something black before their eyes; for the feet, to keep them moving without rest all the time and to take off their shoes at night. But if any slept with shoes on, the straps worked into the feet and the shoes froze; for the old shoes were gone, and they had to make them of raw leather from untanned hides newly flayed.[36]

Alexander's extraordinary 334–324 BC campaign to conquer the Persian Empire—which took with it geographers, surveyors, architects, botanists, zoologists, astronomers, scientists of every sort, and a share of diviners—survived on human legs and feet. The ratio of six infantry to one cavalry characterized the forty-three-thousand-man army he took east. (Even though Alexander made more use of cavalry than had his father Philip, his army otherwise resembled the one he had inherited from him. It depended on a core of loyal, tenacious, and senior foot soldiers, with a protective core of cavalry.[37])

Alexander's two-thousand-mile campaign to the east led across appalling roads and open country from Macedonia down to Egypt, then across the entire Persian Empire to the Indus River and down to the Arabian Sea. His troops endured all: mountains and deserts in which wheels sunk up to their axles, water, sand storms, poisonous snakes, biting insects, and toxic plants. Alexander's army, which did not escape defeats, sought to return west to the Persian Gulf from the mouth of the Indus River across the desert of Gedrosia in southwestern Pakistan, which no previous army had ever before successfully accomplished. For almost two months, a virtual city on foot of eighty thousand people, comprising soldiers, camp followers, and wives and children acquired en route, moved along the north coast of the Indian Ocean through the arid wastes of Gedrosia. Before this itinerant camp reached safety in Carmania, thousands had died, including most of the soldiers' families, who were swept away, together with their possessions, in a flash flood.[38]

The army's final catastrophe came in the form of "a violent sandstorm, which obliterated all landmarks so that even the guides lost their bearings and took a path which led farther and farther away from the coast." In the end, "a ragged column of gaunt, sun-blackened, weary men," they arrived on foot at Pura, the Gedrosian capital.[39] Their losses from the two-month crossing were appalling; only twenty-five thousand of the original eighty-five thousand that started the desert crossing survived. Horses, pack animals, stores, and equipment—all were gone. The entire army, marched beyond its limits, was reduced to foot travel, as defeated armies almost always are.[40]

Alexander's plan had been based on the hope of obtaining relief from the sea. Water and sea travel had long ago superseded land transport in its capacity. Already in the third millennium BC Egyptian monarchs turned to the Mediterranean. Having learned to sail their ships on the Nile, they tried their hand on the open sea. They discarded their boats of reed for ships made of planking from the firs, pines, junipers, and cedars of Lebanon and Syria. By the middle of the millennium, with sails, masts, hawsers, and triple steering oars, they learned to travel and trade in the eastern Mediterranean.[41] And so with the Greeks, given a choice, sail and oar overshadowed foot and road as the preferred mode of travel and transport.

ALL ROADS LEAD TO ROME

Empire meant roads. Roads—which could be thought of as interior rivers and sea lanes—were the first and most fundamental land connection between central power and interior peoples, culture, and resources. Though largely dependent on the speed of the human foot and the strength of the human back, they formed the skeleton and arteries of a kingdom. Subordinating interior lands and peoples to ports, capitals, and central administrative, political, and commercial power, roads invariably prove, over time, to be two-way routes. Reaching across localities and cultures, roads transported troops, messages, authority, and goods.[42] They imposed an order of control and taxes on what were once disconnected places, while enticing imagination to reach to the most distant land to which feet could travel. Yet, everywhere, travel dreams exacted a painful toll of traversing bumpy, muddy surfaces, spending nights in the open, experiencing unexpected events, and being exposed to wild animals and robbers. In societies as diverse as ancient Rome, Egypt, and Japan, one started and completed a long journey paying tribute to the "road gods."[43]

Egypt and Babylon had used roads to disseminate their armies and traders, composed of walkers and riders, to far-off lands. Between 500 and 400 BC, Persian roads connected Persia's far-flung provinces to its capital, Susa, with one of its principal roads, a spine of Near Eastern foot and camel travel, spanning fifteen hundred miles. China, too, had its famous walkers (Confucian scholars and melancholy poets among them), who traveled the kingdom's roads and the banks of its canal system. (The Chinese government carved the banks of its all-important Yangtze for its walking trackers to haul boats upstream against the current.)[44]

However, as a road builder and civilization built by roads, Rome surpassed all other civilizations up to its time, a distinction it would hold until the eve of the twentieth century. Its roads established a direct and efficient line, first for its fast marching armies and then for its long-distance merchants. Providing an unrivaled basis for colonization, its roads unified diverse races and cultures. The Republic expanded them first in Italy and then in every direction into Europe, Asia, and Africa. Utilizing diverse layers of pebble and sand covered by slabs of stone, the best Roman roads could be built along a hillside, embanked, supported by ditches, and even cambered to drain water. For speed, distance, and predictable surfaces, and for certain and secure routes, Roman roads provided an unrivaled walking environment. As never before, it invited the known world to venture afar and afoot. It bifurcated, for European and Mediterranean history thereafter, local and distance walking.

Rome's military strategy was built on the speed and concentration of its marching infantry. Its military success, thus, depended on the efficiency of its roads for foot travel. Built first and foremost around the tactical advantage of its infantry's foot speed, Roman roads were comparatively steep and straight. Tunnels and bridges enhanced the road system's ability to deliver troops, messages, and authority rapidly. While the Roman army had a cavalry and used animals for logistics, its real strength rested on the feet of its infantry.[45] Trained to traverse and encamp on alien territory, the infantry's power depended on the alacrity of its march, the cohesion of its ranks, its maneuverability, and its capacity to fight in close quarters.[46] As is the case with armies today, discipline and execution depended on how well recruits were drilled. They were trained to cover twenty Roman miles in five hours or, at full pace, twenty-five miles in the same period, carrying weapons and objects estimated to weigh about sixty pounds. (Given the shorter Roman miles, this equaled the three-miles-per-hour, day-long pace achieved by the contemporary British army.)[47]

From the beginning, the success of Rome's infantry depended—according to its own writers—on its ability to form, close, and circle ranks and to move in unison up and down even on the most broken and hilly terrain on attack and retreat.[48] Aside from learning "the military step," recruits also practiced running, jumping, swimming, and carrying heavy packs. Taught to be ferocious in attack, they had to be trained to move as one at all times. "For nothing," wrote Vegetius, "should be maintained more on march or in battle than that all soldiers should keep rank as they move. The only way that that this can be done is by learning through constant training to maneuver quickly and evenly."[49]

As song and dance had unified primitive groups in rhythmic motion, the march—itself a rhythmic walk—distinguished Greek, Roman, and subsequent European armies from other societies' fighting forces, according to cultural historian William McNeill.[50] The march made the army civilization's most powerful organism. As with the slaves in its galley ships, Rome harnessed humans and turned them into engines. Like a giant centipede, the legions on march cut a giant swathe across the landscape as they exploited the countryside to feed its troops and animals.

The army's power depended on an unrivaled network of roads—which formed a dense capillary system that extended from the British Isles, Gaul, and Spain south into Africa, reaching from Morocco to the Nile Basin, east into Balkans, and across Persia into northern India. Along with ships, roads allowed Rome to deliver significant numbers of troops anywhere in the empire with an extraordinary precision.[51]

Over several centuries, roads transformed Rome and its suburbs into a single metropolis. Roads led west to ports, Portus and Ostia, while the Appian Way, whose rutted stones and cedar-lined ways we can still stroll, went south and east to Taranto and north to Brindisi. The Via Clodi, Via Sataria, and Via Tiburtina came down from eastern hills paralleling the aqueducts that furnished an ever-needed supply of water for the metropolis's reservoirs and baths.[52]

In its heyday Rome had a million residents, of whom the great majority lived out most of their days going of foot, squatting on their haunches, or leaning and sitting as best they could. According to Italian historian Jérôme Carcopino, Rome was jammed with people who suffered from distresses of overpopulation similar to those experienced by contemporary urban dwellers.[53] By the second century AD, Rome was "largely an apartment-dwellers' city with a generous sprinkling of shops, taverns, restaurants, workshops."[54] Superficially, the city was attractive, full of public buildings, palaces, and large apartment complexes, and characterized by picturesque balconies, portico-covered shops, and abundant decorative flowers. Yet many of the buildings were constructed on insufficient bases and were constantly being razed and built anew.[55] Worse, fires were frequent. Water supplies, never reaching above the first floor, were increasingly scarce. And the absence of a central sewage system—despite the great *cloaca maxima*—made Rome a place in which no one escaped foul smells and potentially lethal filth.

Indoors offered little relief. Cramped spaces, scanty furniture, which made for uncomfortable sitting and lying, poor lighting, and lack of heating made staying home onerous. For much of the year, a dweller's no-win choice was between keeping the cold or light out, or permitting them in, along with street dust and insect-filled winds. Hence the great majority spent most of their waking lives up, out, and on their feet. Depending on the distance between work and home, and daily needs for food, water, and fuel, it is possible to imagine typical Romans walking three and four hours a day, not counting time spent on their feet, standing, leaning, rocking and swaying back and forth, and sitting on their haunches. Certain workers like barge haulers, messengers, and litter bearers, who depended on their feet for their very livelihoods, like peasants in their fields and orchards, could have easily spent eight or more hours a day on their feet. Only the rich had ample beds, generous chairs, and sufficient pillows for sitting and lying at home.[56]

Romans found little on the city's streets to comfort them in their pursuit of fortunes and fate. A great majority of the inextricably tangled net of some sixty miles of city streets were narrow and dirty. Indeed, of the innumerable streets, lanes, and alleys in the city's center and fourteen outlying regions, only about twenty deserved to be called roads—*viae,* which permitted two carts to pass each other— and their widths varied from approximately sixteen to twenty-four feet.[57] On them Roman pedestrians regularly encountered impossible traffic conditions and were even menaced by falling pieces of buildings and collapsing buildings.

Although Julius Caesar banned wheeled traffic from the center of the city during the day, he failed to furnish clean and orderly streets. Pedestrians got neither the paving, the sidewalks (*margines, crepidines*), nor the right of way that he also promised. Salesmen, beggars, hawkers of goods, tinkers, and cooks blocked the streets. People bumped into and stepped on one another as they tried to move along.

Even the highest ranks of Rome were not exempted from the woes of city walking. Furthermore, upper-class women degraded their reputation by appearing on the streets. As a consequence, those of means left shopping and delivering messages to their servants. When they did venture out, they usually went in a litter, escorted by a bodyguard. Those who ventured out on foot returned from their treks like everyone else—with mud-caked legs. At nights, when most Romans wisely stayed indoors with their shutters drawn and chained shut, those who dared to go out were accompanied by slaves carrying torches and were reliant on the protection of neighborhood guards. First- and second-century Roman satirical poet Juvenal complained that night's incessant traffic condemned the city "to everlasting insomnia" and declared that at night Rome was more dangerous than the forest of Gallinaria or the Pontine Marshes.[58]

It is easy to understand why those with means often left the city and its swarming masses. In the spring, nobles escaped from the crowded and noisy capital to the cooling breezes of the shore to refresh themselves by swimming, bathing, boating, and strolling in the country. In the summer they escaped the sweltering heat of the malaria-ridden city for cooler uplands. Wherever Romans went on vacation, once there they availed themselves of their feet. Regular strolls structured their relaxation. Aristocratic Pliny, at his retreat in the Tuscan hills, regularly recorded three walks in the daytime and one after his evening meal.[59] There is some evidence that considerable numbers of Romans even climbed mountains that gave them, according to historian J. Donald Hughes, a better view of the land, a deeper understanding of nature, and a sense of feeling closer to the dwelling place of the gods.[60]

Romans frequently left the capital for favorite spots in southern and northern Italy and throughout the Mediterranean.[61] Under the protection of Roman law, they traveled for diverse reasons—family, friendship, patronage, business, and government. They also sought medical care afar, took pilgrimages, attended special festivities such as the Greek Olympics, and, as illustrated by Christian St. Paul's three great journeys by ship and on foot, engaged in religious proselytizing. In the wandering and inquisitive spirit of the classical world's most famous traveler, the Greek historian Herodotus, a small number of Romans followed curiosity beyond the rim of the Mediterranean. No one is sure whether Roman travelers made it all the way to China, to the upper reaches of the Nile, or down the western coast of Africa, but they surely reached the staging points for such remarkable adventures.[62]

Wherever Romans went, travel never proved easy and often required a long trudge on foot. It always extracted pain and chanced hazard. Despite the putative glory of Roman roads, they were usually unpaved, narrow, and uneven. Even the Roman emperor could not command the straightening of every path, much less escape the vicissitudes of weather, the affliction of local tolls, or the ravages of brigandage. Rivers, of sinister and fickle currents, and shifting and uncertain bottoms, inevitably had to be crossed. Rain brought slippery and engulfing mud, and road-destroying mud slides characterized winter and spring travel. Packs of dogs and wolves attacked travelers.

No wonder sojourners augured auspicious days to start out on their journeys and, on return, voiced thanks to protective gods.[63]

Preferring to ride rather than walk, wealthy Romans journeyed in a variety of types of two- and four-wheeled vehicles. None had comfortable or spacious interiors or springs to buffer riders against perpetual swaying and bumping. Seeking to escape the lurching and jolting of cart and carriage, Rome's elite travelers preferred riding in litters. Often covered by a canopy and outfitted with curtains for reasons of weather and privacy, litters were carried by six or eight stout walking men or suspended by poles between mules and donkeys. Travel in a litter involved the constant swinging and jostling caused by changing terrain and the unevenness of the litter bearers. At best, litters carried by walking men or beasts traveled only fifteen to twenty miles in a day, and frequently produced so much jostling and swaying that their occupants, verging on motion sickness, preferred to get out and walk, proving not for the first or last time that the rights and privileges of riding did not always equal the convenience and comfort of walking.[64]

Roman foot travelers equipped themselves for their journeys. They carried money in a sack around the waist or neck. They took the ever-useful and multipurpose walking stick, which, transformed in the ceremonial hands of kings and priests into nonutilitarian staff and scepter, has great symbolic power.[65] They carried a miniature guidebook to show the way when signs and advice failed. Romans also took many "changes of clothing, as well as special wear adapted to the rigors of the road: heavy shoes or heavy sandals, a broad-brimmed hat, and a selection of capes—a short light one for milder weather, another for rainy days, still another for cold days."[66] (As if to make themselves a moving household, the well off additionally encumbered themselves with bedding, towels, kitchenware, tableware, and even couch and commode.) Travelers, in all cases, had to outfit themselves as best they could for the wear that goes with days of walking, along with cold, hunger, sun, wind, and sleeping outdoors when unable to find accommodations or to make their destination before nightfall.

The ordeal of land travel accounts for what historian Lionel Casson judges to be Romans' preference to travel by sea rather than land. In sharp contrast to Odysseus in his mythic adventures, the Roman merchant marine fleet crisscrossed the Mediterranean with a predictability and regularity unequaled by their European heirs until the eighteenth century.[67] Although inescapably victims of fickle winds and storms, ships provided the fastest and most direct route to the coveted East. Even their crowded quarters proved less taxing than the ordeal of land travel.

Even though the underlying local measure of travel remained the distance a person on foot could cover between sunup and sundown, Roman sea and land routes transformed space and time into interdependent coordinates.[68] In effect, the combination of roadways and sea lanes unified the known world, providing Mediterranean cultures a common calendar and map. With maps and itineraries, roads and sailing routes, unprecedented orders of travel, trade, communication, and transportation were realized. (Soldiers, merchants, and rulers could chart out trips that spanned years, like Emperor Caracalla's 214–215 journey to Egypt. Entire road systems could be examined, as Emperor Diocletian [284–305] did when he listed 372 main roads covering fifty thousand miles.)[69]

Even when Rome collapsed in the West, the memory of its achievement retained its hold on people's minds. Its surviving roads and roadbeds determined much European experience throughout the Middle Ages. They often defined medieval jurisdictional boundaries and pilgrimage routes, while Roman road stations accounted for the location of castles, markets, and inns. Long after it perished, Rome still drew medieval pilgrims and emperors alike south, contining to fuse foot and faith in search of a governing order and individual, religious, and political renewal.

However far in time and distance medieval walkers might be judged to be in their everyday rural lives from Rome's walking cities and marching armies, they were ultimately closer to Roman roads than the migratory trails of the early human walkers. Indeed, once medieval people left, on foot or in imagination, the circling paths and trails of village, they rode on Roman shoulders. They commonly walked on old Roman roadbeds and bridges and followed Roman routes to former Roman sites. In some sense, all roads continued to lead to Rome.

𝕏 2 𝕏 Along the Road

Medieval Pilgrims, Beggars,
Mounted Warriors, and
Early City Walkers

Fᴏʀ most of the thousand-year medieval period from 500 AD to 1500 AD, there existed no alternative to walking for the vast majority of people. The necessity of going on foot, as had been the case since time immemorial, was not in dispute.

Except in church processions, court rituals, select pilgrimages, or a singular act of travel, walking carried with it the negative connotation of simply being part of humankind's perennial attachment to the earth and the inescapable pains and burdens that went with moving and carrying. In the course of the Middle Ages, walking, as we will see, took on additional negative connotations. Each meeting with a passing horseman—the primary engine of epochal warfare—reminded the medieval walker of his position as subordinate to those who sat and rode. An occasional ride in heavy, lumbering, springless carts or on the back of a donkey did not end walkers' status as inferior to the mounted warrior who gave a first definition to nobility's place and power on the landscape.

In towns and cities, which sprang up and flourished near the end of the Middle Ages, walkers—beggars, peasants, workers, and others who went on foot—also discovered their own inferior standing. Regulations and supervision guided their movements day and night. Grandiose palaces, behind whose thick walls sat those to whom the goods of the world were delivered, only reminded the foot-bound majority of society how life was inseparable from walking, itinerancy, and insecurity.

THE MEANINGS OF THE WAY

Despite the appearance of the horse and the later development of town and city, medieval life was, no differently than in the Roman countryside, principally played out on foot. Nothing humble, nothing great was accomplished without walking. Mounted armies always depended on infantries and the legs of grooms and porters, and decisive battles were won by foot soldiers. Welsh archers with long bows gave Edward III a considerable advantage in the Hundred Years War, and Flemish communal infantries of pikemen defeated the cavalry of Philip IV of France at Courtai in 1302, after which they hung seven hundred pairs of French spurs in a church to celebrate their victory.[1] The monks and scholars, kings and bishops warmed their bones, prayed, and hatched schemes while strolling. Common people—peasants, shepherds, crofters—depended on their feet and legs to carry out their work, much as their local and agriculture-bound ancestors had for the preceding ten thousand years and their heirs in considerable numbers would throughout the Middle Ages into the eighteenth and even nineteenth centuries. Sending the country person outdoors, except during the worst weather and most severe sickness, were that rural dwellings remained (if houses at all instead of caves, cellars, lofts, etc.) almost uniformly small, dark, damp, and crowded. Beds were often uncomfortable and shared; there was a scarcity of chairs, furniture, walls, rooms, heat, and light. Life in villages and towns was mainly lived outdoors and on foot. While differing places, times, and conditions produced exceptions, common medieval humanity was perennially on foot to work, play, and travel—and so things remained until recent times.

Afoot, medieval people participated in church processions for Christmas, carnival, Good Friday, Easter, and other occasions.[2] Villagers conducted their festivals and delivered their dead to their final resting place on foot. Sometimes they wandered away from their villages when it no longer made sense to stay; at other times, they ran away from them for the sake of their lives. Children (as they have done until recent years) played out their childhood on their feet.[3] Tag, walking on stilts, hide-and-seek, follow-the-leader, and "blind man's bluff, which medieval children knew as hoodman blind," formed—as we catch a glimpse in Brueghel's painting *Children's Games*—an abiding part of the repertoire of their play.[4]

Medieval people dressed to be outdoors. Leggings, clogs, hoods, and cloaks were part of the walker's apparel.[5] "A prelate who wished to disguise himself as a peasant," according to medieval scholar Theodulf of Orléans, "dressed in a hooded headdress [useful for wind and weather], a shirt of rude linen, and a loose garment. He wrapped his legs in narrow strips of cloth and shod himself with heavy shoes." Monks, who dressed more or less like peasants, received two shirts, two cloaks, and a vestment to which a hood was attached. "In addition, he had four pairs of stockings, two pairs of drawers, a belt, two cloaks falling to the heel, wooden shoes and sheep skin mittens for winter. Annually . . . each monk received three tunics . . . two pairs of boots, three pairs of pants, two pairs of stockings, gloves, two mantles."[6]

Medieval people easily lent their imaginations to the walking and peregrinations represented in the Old Testament and New Testament as depicted in sermons and painted on church walls. Realizing how much life singularly depended on having a place on good land (of one's own or a just lord's), they grasped the importance of the Jews' long-wandering search for a homeland. Living with the dangers of travel and the difficulty of finding lodging, they readily empathized with the plight of Joseph and pregnant Mary, who, summoned to Bethlehem, were forced to take refuge in a stable. They intuitively grasped the holy family's flight to Egypt, for they, too, had, or could easily imagine having, to flee fire, plague, flood, a marauding army, or the ire of an angry father and lord.[7] Knowing that a king merited a wide, open, and even way, they understood John the Baptist's call to prepare the way of the Lord, by making level his path.[8]

A lifetime afoot well prepared medieval believers to grasp the three-year peregrination of Jesus, who, preaching as he went, zig-zagged across Judea, which extended approximately 130 miles from Sidon and Tyre in the north to Jerusalem in the south.[9] They felt a kin-ship with Jesus no riding person could, grasping that he was a perpet-ual stranger among people and condemned to a lifetime trodding the road:"Foxes have holes, and birds of the air have nests; but the Son of man has nowhere to lay his head."[10] His very message sprang from his peregrinations. On the road he met his disciples and encountered the Samaritan woman at the well. He told his parables of the prodigal son, who had to leave home to be found, and the good Samaritan, who kindly treated the robbed and beaten stranger he found alongside the road as if he were a brother.

Christ called his disciples to the road. According to the Gospel of Mark, Jesus commanded that they "should take nothing for their jour-ney save a staff only."[11] In the gospels of Luke and Matthew, Christ de-nied them even a staff:"Take nothing for your journey, neither staves, nor scrip [a small leather pouch], neither bread, neither money; nei-ther have two coats apiece."[12]

Christ's day of glory occurred when he rode into Jerusalem astride a borrowed donkey along a path blanketed with palms. On his day of humiliation he walked the Way of the Cross, which led from judgment to crucifixion. Crowned with thorns, weighed down with his cross, and spat on, he stumbled his way to Calvary, making his followers for-ever sojourners on this earth.[13]

Medieval people easily incorporated into their folklore stories of travelers, magic journeys, and the myth of the wandering Jew—who was condemned to travel afoot until the Second Coming for having taunted Christ on his way to Calvary.[14] Powerful metaphors about travel, roads, feet, shoes, footprints, walking sticks, knapsacks, sandals, cloaks, and crossroads haunted the medieval mind. A clever stranger in one medieval tale wins a bet with a king by proving that there is a foot uglier in the kingdom than the king has seen sticking out of the bed.

He wins his wager by sticking out his other crippled foot, from which two toes are missing. Before it was refined into a cane, and then a mere clothing accessory in modern times, the walking stick saw symbolic duty as the bishop's staff and the king's rod, served as the defining icon of the pilgrim, and provided the shepherd with an all-purpose instrument. The walking staff perennially supports the walker on uneven surfaces, helps him feel his way while crossing water, moves brush and branches out of the way, and can be a useful cudgel for beating off dogs and robbers.[15]

Crossroads held, so to speak, a *crucial* place in medieval iconography. The crossroad was where people congregated and erected altars, obelisks, stones, inscriptions, altars, crosses, chapels, shrines, and gallows. Marking the transition from one kingdom to another, and a parting of the ways, it resonated with great power. It indicated that one was moving on to different soil, into the realm of another people, and into the presence of another set of gods. At the crossroads restless spirits of the dead gathered to harass the passerby, and surely that was where good spirits, fairy godmothers, saints, and Our Lady appeared.[16]

The medieval walker could summon a whole stable of helping saints, who would care for his feet, direct his wanderings, protect him on pilgrimage, and assure him of hospitality. Gertrude of Tramontana, Sicily, helped believers' leg problems. Crispin and Crispinian were patron saints of shoemakers. As Christ had cured the lame, so did St. Peter, who (in Acts 4:2–9) cures a man "lame from his mother's womb. . . . And he took him by the right hand, and lifted him up; and immediately his feet and anklebones received strength and he leaping up stood, and walked." Christopher, the patron saint of travelers and sailors, still decorates the dashboard of an occasional contemporary Catholic's car. In one story, the anonymous child he carries across a river grows heavier and heavier with each step. When the distant bank is reached, the child reveals himself to be Christ and tells Christopher that he has been carrying the weight of the world on his shoulders. As a sign, Christ tells Christopher to plant his staff in the ground, and the next day, like Aaron's rod, it blossoms and bears fruit. The equally powerful legend of St. Julian the Hospitaler also played itself out on a riverbank. Having slain his own parents, mistaking them in his bed for his adulterous wife and an unknown lover, Julian sets out with his wife to seek forgiveness, finding it only years later when they build a house for sick and wayward travelers at a river crossing.

A CIVILIZATION ON FOOT

Medieval Europe worked, warred, traveled, explored, played, romanced, and carried out its religious processions afoot. In the early Carolingian period, especially in the early seventh, eighth, and ninth centuries, conditions were turbulent. Mounted and pedestrian warriors fought for land and control, at the same time that Vikings invaded from the north, Moors, from south and west, and mounted Magyars, from south and east. There were no secure social niches. Land and home had to be secured not just against nature and invaders but also against swarms of roaming tribal people from the woods who—to borrow a contemporary description of the Bretons—"inhabit the forest and make their beds in the thickets. They live by rapine, like wild beasts."[17]

The Carolingian court, establishing a model for subsequent medieval courts, frequently and regularly transformed itself into a moving village. Composed of walkers, riders, and carts, the itinerant court moved continuously from palace to palace to maintain its authority.[18] A place left unvisited was a place relinquished. Essential for implementing orders, arranging alliances, and even fighting skirmishes and wars, travel was always arduous.[19] Its maximum speed was determined by the pace and number of its walkers, by the need to provision them and their beasts and to repair equipment, and of course by weather and terrain. Describing the English court of a later and more stable time, historian J. J. Jusserand wrote, "There were few places in England where the sight of the royal train was not familiar. . . . The itinerary of King John (1166–1216) shows that he rarely passed a month in the same place; most frequently he did not even remain there a week."[20] The court officers, especially those in charge of royal travel or involved in the administration of justice and taxes, understood that authority meant constantly traveling a circuit. Litters, horses, mules, and carts did not spare even the mightiest traveler from going on foot to ford rivers, to cross steep and rocky terrain, to unburden vehicles stuck in mud and wetlands, or to escape the constant, grueling jarring of ruts and uneven road surfaces that made riding in cart or on horse painful and often dangerous.

Although many Roman roads were still partially in use as pathways by riders and walkers, they had largely decayed from centuries of inadequate maintenance, leaving their stone foundations covered by a thick layer of soil.[21] Medieval historian Jacques Le Goff contends, "In this ruin of antique trade network the first victim was the Roman road. The medieval road, which, in material terms, was more of a lane, was to be something different and emerge later."[22] Elsewhere, he notes that medieval people mainly abandoned straight Roman army and administrative roads, which were created for speed over great distances. Walking and carrying goods, leading animals and small carts, the medieval walker was intent on local trade, and he preferred "lanes and paths and a network of diverse routes which rambled about between certain such fixed points as town, fairs, destinations of pilgrimage, bridges, fords, and mountain passes."[23]

Although they supplied multiple routes, medieval roads, which were little more than a complex of trails and pathways, commonly sent their users on long, circuitous, unmarked, and errant journeys. Roads in no sense were uniform, wide, or level. Unpredictable fords made for risky crossings. Bridge building did not begin on any significant scale until the twelfth century.[24]

With the human foot and animal hoof being far superior to the wheel and cart in crossing most terrain, pack animals played a decisive role in medieval transport, as they continued to do in rural and especially mountainous Europe well into the nineteenth and even twentieth century.[25] Led by walking men, pack animals, though they could carry less than they could pull, had less difficulty than wheeled vehicles coping with ruts and moving across rocky ground, cave-ins, streams, marshland, and the gooey mud that came with rainy season. However, even the use of pack animals, with their sharp and tender hooves, did not circumvent the profound ordeal that greeted human and animal when crossing mountains, rivers, deserts, vast wetlands, or hostile territory, or yet lands covered by snow, debris, and mud slides.

For messenger, groom, porter, and serf, travel meant walking, and walking involved lifting, carrying, pushing and pulling, and bearing up against the weather. And all this equaled testing work. Serfs, like those of the monks of St. Vanne in Lorraine in the eleventh century, were obligated to carry grain "for six miles on their shoulders, or rather the napes of their necks, as the Latin text says: '*cum collo.*'"[26] Thread mills, harnesses, carrying poles, wood yolks, straps, ropes, baskets, and containers of every sort converted the walking human—his or her head, shoulder, arm, waist, leg, or entire body—into a source of energy and power for turning, pushing, pulling, lifting, and carrying. A walking person was a mobile power and portable engine.

Human portage was an indispensable engine of transport and construction in the Middle Ages, as it had been since the most remote periods in human history. On foot, loading, carrying, traveling, and unloading cargo of nearly every and shape sort, medieval people achieved great building projects of castles, cities, and churches. The great cathedrals, whose heights and volumes were not equaled until the construction of skyscrapers little more than a hundred years ago, depended not just on pulleys, winches, windlasses, and capstans but also on treadmills, operated by one or two men walking like squirrels within them.[27] Supplemented by levers, ramps, pulleys, and ropes, medieval workers lifted, pulled, and pushed objects into position.

All transport pivoted on human walking and strength. Humans supplied motion and direction to their cargoes, vehicles, and animals. With carts limited in bearing power and capacity and animals too few in number and too small in size, human walking and carrying was a requisite for everyday work. Human power, driven by feet and legs, literally built civilization. While the common classes were always expected to walk and carry—there was no other way to support life—in one instance from the twelfth century, the need for human leg and back power even put noble men and women in harness. "[They] bent their proud and swollen necks to harness themselves to the wagons and draw them with their loads of wine, wheat, oil, lime, stones, wood and other products necessary to sustain life or for building churches.'"[28]

In the early Middle Ages, from the sixth to the tenth century, lives, at least those exempted from invasions, pillage, and plague, were local and static. It was illegal for serfs to leave their place on the land, and those who ventured from home exposed themselves to every sort of danger. However, starting gradually in the eighth century, settlements sprang up in ports and along rivers as a consequence of the revival of European commerce and the abandonment of Roman roads. By the end of the eleventh century, water and land traffic again flowed, trade flourished, agriculture intensified, populations multiplied, and kings and feudal powers granted political independence to nascent towns, to which beggars, soldiers, outlaws, and the ambitious flocked to improve their lot.[29] In increasing numbers, villagers joined on the road swelling streams of immigrant students, scholars, pilgrims, craftspeople, artists, herbalists, itinerant peddlers, jongleurs, minstrels, and charlatans of every sort.

The first group of medieval walkers, however, was the peasants, who almost by definition never went to town. Comprising 90 percent of the population of Western Europe, they lived out their lives at home.[30] The peasant and the village, interdependent creations of the Middle Ages, belonged to the land and the path, not the city.[31] Unless visiting an adjacent town, or making occasional trips on foot to the regional fair, peasants saved their legs for their fields, where, as one medieval jingle describes,

> His stockings hung down his legs,
> All splattered with mud, as he followed the plough.
> He was mired in mud, almost up to his ankles.[32]

Peasants traveled a lifetime on narrow paths. They charted their ambling by familiar features and the rising and setting sun. Like the falcon tethered to his gyre, peasants, on the way to and from their fields, nearby streams and woods, market, and church, perpetually circled their own villages. They rarely ventured beyond the shadow of the local chateau or beyond the ringing sound of the parish church bell. To do so would have been to enter a wild place, a no man's land, where they would have lacked identification and protection.

PILGRIMS

The pilgrim proved to be the age's emblematic traveler. From the beginning of church history, Christian pilgrims traveled to Rome and Jerusalem.[33] Indeed, as early as the fourth century pilgrims on foot flocked to Rome, which over time erected increasingly elaborate churches atop the tombs of church martyrs.[34] According to medievalist Pierre Riche, "From the seventh century on, the quest for Roman relics, [and] the prestige of the Roman See . . . favored the multiplication of pilgrimages to Rome. All Christians went to Rome as to a second motherland; they desired to go there at least once in their lives and even to die there."[35]

The notion of making a penitential pilgrimage on foot arose early in the early Middle Ages—and it remained a fixture throughout the era.[36] Although the graves of local saints motivated ordinary pilgrimages, walking to Rome or journeying on foot or by ship to Jerusalem attracted only the most serious, and in most cases the wealthiest pilgrims. The quest for greater miracles and extraordinary forgiveness required longer and more arduous journeys. Exempted from taxes and protected as best king and church could protect them, pilgrims set out on their missions. While it can be conjectured that religious motives dominated, it also can be supposed that some traveled to escape religious vows, to find adventure, or even to fleece their fellow sheep.

In sharp contrast to today's therapeutic walking, the desire to be forgiven and the ordeal of the trip itself, an immense act of penance, constituted grounds for readmission into church and village. The greater the distance a pilgrim traveled, one could compute, the deadlier the sins involved and perhaps the greater the pilgrim's means to travel.[37] In fact, from early on, Le Goff contends, "pilgrimage was not what men wished to do, but more an act of penance. . . . [After all] wanderers were wretches and tourism a vanity."[38]

As society grew and became more mobile in the twelfth and thirteenth centuries—an era of colonization, expanding frontiers, and migration—pilgrims constituted an ever-greater segment of the traffic.[39] The church paved the way for the walking pilgrims. The Benedictine Rule instructed that every guest must be welcomed as if he or she were Christ himself,[40] and Cluniac customs from the eleventh century onward welcomed those who came on foot, but charged those who arrived on horseback.[41] Many saw the pilgrims as an economic opportunity. Boasting icons and relics fresh from the Holy Land, or from counterfeiters' workshops, cities and churches transformed themselves into attractive sites for Europe's first tourists, the pilgrims.[42] Towns such as Tours, Reims, and Brioude became prosperous, catering to the needs of the devout who sought healing from the relics of St. Martin, St. Remy, or St. Julian.[43]

Offering a curious alternative to going on pilgrimage, certain popular preachers encouraged an odd pedestrian penance. They called forth spontaneous groups of itinerant flagellants who wandered afoot, from place to place, beating one another as they went. Some preachers went so far as to suggest that flagellants might win the full plenary indulgence, which removed the penal consequences of sin and was offered to the pilgrims who attended Pope Boniface VIII's first Roman Jubilee of 1300.

The actual need to undergo the rigor of a pilgrimage diminished in the later Middle Ages.[44] The church increasingly allowed believers to substitute for pilgrimage penance done vicariously by others or indulgences won by prayers, masses, almsgiving, or local trips. In this less hearty and more settled age, the church understood that walking was hard work, took time, could be treacherous, and required leaving home unprotected. So why go on a pilgrimage, if one didn't have to?[45]

On the eve of the Reformation, a Strasbourg preacher calculated for a prisoner confined to his cell an indoor walking penance equivalent to making a pilgrimage to Rome for the 1500 Jubilee. Offering a kind of spiritual pedometer, he proposed that a prisoner could walk his cell for forty-two days and then devote himself to prayer for seven days to win an indulgence. This equaled the actual time required to get to and from Rome as well as the time spent visiting its holy stations. Erasmus scoffed at this kind of calculation. He suggested that by walking about his house, going to his study, checking on his daughter's chastity, and so forth, he too was doing his Roman stations.[46]

Nevertheless, in their heyday pilgrims popularized foot travel. Lengthy journeys required them to say their farewells, write their wills, and even agree with spouses when they could remarry if they did not return. They often set out at their priest's instruction and with the church's blessings. Many even carried a sealed license from the king, certifying their peregrination in an age preoccupied with the social threat of vagabondage. Pilgrims commonly enjoyed immunity from civil suits, and feudal duties and taxes were suspended. Before leaving they were instructed to make a sincere confession and offer amends to all they had wronged and owed.[47] Carrying a walking staff with a metal toe, the pilgrim wore a long, coarse tunic and sported a pouch strapped to his waist that contained his food and money. In the thirteenth century pilgrims began to dress distinctly in "a broad rimmed hat, turned up at the front, and attached at the back to a long scarf which was round the body as far as the waist."[48] With every sincere pilgrim expected to travel in poverty, the most zealous went barefoot and left their hair and beard untrimmed. In the course of time the church invested the pilgrim's uniform with symbolism. The pouch stood for the pilgrim's dependence on charity. The staff, so useful for beating off wolves and humans, represented beating off the snares of the devil. Also, as the pilgrim's third leg, it symbolized a commitment to the Holy Trinity.

Over three hundred years, between the eleventh and thirteenth centuries, the towns of southern France—one of Europe's most important centers of pilgrimage and associated tourism—erected a magnificent "legacy of churches, cathedrals, abbeys, and pilgrimage routes."[49] Located along Europe's principal routes to St. James of Compostella in Spain—the third most important site in Christendom after Rome and Jerusalem—the towns flourished as pilgrims sought out the grave of the martyred St. James.[50] The Compostella trail, served by four major routes from north to south, led the pilgrims across France to Spain.[51] In 1130, Pope Calixtus II commissioned a travel guide that recounted miracles, indicated routes in detail, cautioned pilgrims about local inhabitants, and directed their steps to where water and lodging could be found. Abbeys and hospices offered free lodging for the walking pilgrims, while Cluniac hostels, placed a day's journey apart, were complete with barbers and the all-important cobbler.[52] At other places along their route, camping grounds were provided.[53] "Pilgrims to Compostella acquired a characteristic costume—large-brimmed hat, cape, mantlet, *bourdon* or staff, a cockleshell (*coquille*) as a sort of medal . . . a gourd and mess kit, and a canvas bag for passports and papers."[54] Returning pilgrims joined the popular Confrérie de St. Jacques association.

Although pilgrimages could be softened by evening song, drink, and entertainment, they were ordeals. *The Guide for Pilgrims to Santiago,* summarized by Jonathan Sumption, cautions,

> In Galicia there were thick forests and few towns; mosquitoes infested the marshy southern plain of Bordeaux where the traveler who strays from the roads can sink up to his knees in mud. Some of the rivers are impassable. Several pilgrims had been drowned at Sorde, where travelers and their horses were ferried across on hollowed-out tree trunks. Other rivers were undrinkable, like the salt stream at Lorca, where the author of the Guide found two Basques earning their living by skinning the horses who had died after drinking from it.[55]

There was always the problem of procuring food, water, and, for those who rode, fodder for their animals.[56] Tolls were a common nuisance and frequently served as a pretext for a shakedown. Unpaid tolls could even result in brutal beating and death. Despite a continuous flow of secular and church ordinances to secure the safety of travel and prohibit the accosting of travelers, some unscrupulous lords, country folk, and entire villages (especially in Italy during the Jubilee to Rome in 1300) took advantage of travelers. Innkeepers and alehouse owners frequently fleeced, and even murdered, the pilgrims, disregarding local laws and customs of hospitality.[57] Sumption notes, "One observer believed that half of the pilgrims who set out for Rome in 1350 were robbed or killed."[58]

Pilgrims—slow and on foot, without horse or armed retainer, and often ignorant of where they trod—made easy prey for suppliers of food and feed, crafty beggars, itinerant quacks, and hermits who conveniently placed themselves alongside the road. (Indeed, the Knights Templars were formed in 1118 to protect pilgrims headed for Jerusalem during the Crusades.)[59] Bandits, freebooters, and outlaws abounded, as mercenaries and crusaders metastasized into brigands and even marauding armies.[60] For example, Sir Gosseline and his two-hundred-man gang—mounted and disguised as friars—forced early-fourteenth-century King Edward II to pay him and his highwaymen their due.[61] In an era when kings, princes, merchants, and church-men did not enjoy immunity from highwaymen and neither the Tale of Gamelyn, from the mid-fourteenth century, nor the better-known Robin Hood ballads displayed men with much reluctance about maiming and killing a passerby, what protection would a pilgrim enjoy?

Sometimes, pilgrims themselves proved to be wolves in sheep's clothing. In addition to outright imposters, some pilgrims were cor-rupted by the road itself, as happened to some worldly monks and er-rant crusaders. Being on the road—romantic notions aside—did not assure innocence. Being away from home could license travelers to cross boundaries they did not dare to traverse at home. "Pilgrimage," in the words of Jacques Le Goff, "could turn into errantry or vagabondage."[62]

ROVING MENDICANTS AND DANCERS

The church, too, flooded the roads with members of its own orders, though it prudently cautioned against the pitfalls of itinerancy and begging, rebuking those who would trust their sure feet and the gen-erous hands of others to lead them to Christ. In his Rule, St. Benedict pejoratively identified "the gyratory monk": "During their whole life they are guests, for three or four days at a time, in the cells of different monasteries . . . always wandering and never stationary, given over to the service of their own pleasures and joys of the palate."[63] In the eleventh century, reformer and Italian monk Saint Peter Damiani wrote, "We have suffered in fraternal love over the brothers who are restless and sinking into their ruin through the vice of roaming about." As if driven by "the most evil driver," they are returned to "the vanity of the world," and turn "away from seizing the path of true salvation."[64]

Peter Valdes, founder of the Waldensians, was "a rich merchant from Lyon who gave up his wealth and position in the late 1170s to become a wandering preacher, living a life of Apostolic poverty."[65] The Castilian nobleman and priest Dominic Guzman, who founded the Dominicans, also preached mendicant poverty. Dominican friars, unlike earlier mendicant groups, were not permitted to have property and had to beg for food. Dedicated to preaching and learning, they spread the Dominican message on foot to the premier university towns of Bologna, Paris, and Oxford. Dominican Thomas Aquinas, who wrote twenty-six books, is estimated to have walked more than nine thousand miles on his intellectual peregrinations across Europe.[66] By walking, Aquinas followed his order's rule of poverty.

Medieval intellectual life, in fact, was composed largely by transitory academics.[67] "I journeyed," wrote philosopher and logician Abelard, "through the provinces, disputing wherever the art of logic was flourishing. I finally reached Paris."[68] Following their itinerant teaching masters and becoming more accustomed to the ways of country roads than the halls of universities, circumambulating students often degenerated into beggars and thieves.

St. Francis was the premier walking monk of the road. The son of a rich merchant who as a young man briefly served as an armored and mounted soldier and was a bon vivant lover of the troubadours and their music, Francis renounced his pleasurable youth and his calling as a mounted warrior and denied father, family, and inheritance. In a decisive moment, he publicly defied his father's last claim to him by stripping nude and returning his clothes to his father.[69]

Barefoot, Francis walked and preached Christ's words: "If thou will be perfect, go and sell what thou hast, and give to the poor, and thou shalt have a treasure in heaven: and come and follow me." He challenged those who would stay at home and guard their things: "It is easier for a camel to go through the eye of a needle, than for a rich man to enter into the kingdom of Heaven."[70] Francis took his message to the people, first wandering afoot through the Umbrian countryside around Assisi and then carrying it to Italy, France, Switzerland, Spain, Dalmatia, Syria, Egypt, and the Holy Land itself.

Although Pope Innocent III accepted Francis's rule as the basis of a new order, Francis himself adamantly resisted the institutionalizing of his teaching and his society of itinerants. Francis accepted ordinary lay people as fellow travelers. Impelled by the era's new individualism and spirituality, many were attracted to Francis's ideal, which held vocation above increasingly available luxury and security. Yet, in the words of Julien Green's *God's Fool,* Francis's "barefoot beggars" posed the mystery of righteous and joyous homelessness to the majority of people who encountered them along the way. Onlookers asked, according to Julian Green,

> What mysterious force drew men to that little group they saw passing by, singing in the streets of the hill towns of Umbria or wandering through the fields and woods? Barefoot, dressed like paupers, with a robe resembling a sack and a cord for a belt, but joyful like children, they seemed to have come from another world where sadness didn't exist. Could one own nothing and live happily on this earth?[71]

Subsequent groups also took to the road for different reasons, none as distinctively as those affected by the contagion of frenzied dancing called tarantism, which first appeared in fourteenth-century Europe.[72] This specific dancing mania of the late Middle Age, which appeared first in 1374 at Aix-la-Chappelle, may have had its origins in the Black Death and contemporary extensive flooding. Undoubtedly, it expressed the social disintegration of the period. Ultimately taking its name from the tarantula spider, whose bite was supposed to cause it, the contagion spread through the Netherlands, into Germany, and south into Italy. A description of a single instance of this phenomenon portrays a procession of German men and women arriving at a town square, forming into a dancing circle, and working themselves into a frenzy until, foaming at the mouth and contorting their bodies, they fell down exhausted. With madness feeding madness, fever-bitten dancers moved through the agitated populace. Emptying villages and shops, tarantism ultimately dispersed thousands of homeless itinerants throughout medieval Christendom.[73]

CRUSADERS AND MOUNTED WARRIORS

Mendicants, beggars, the dispossessed, and the poor, the walking people of the road were not easily distinguished from one another, especially when they disguised themselves in religious garb. However, what stood forth to every traveler was the contrast between walkers and riders. No contrast was sharper than that between the pedestrian and the horse-mounted warriors of the Crusades, who, with ever more elaborate armor, utilized the roads of Europe for long-distance travel for a three-century period starting in 1095, when Pope Urban II announced the First Crusade. During this time, popes and preachers called for crusades, which sought to affirm religious and social control over a militant and revitalized Europe. To these appeals, kings and knights principally responded for spiritual and political reasons and for the sake of travel and adventure. However, adding to the turbulence and movement of Europe, which saw even peasants and children set off on foot to free Jerusalem, country roads and Italian ports swelled with mounted warriors, accompanied by foot soldiers and the large and cumbersome retinues that supplied armies on the march.[74]

From beginning to end the church sought to control the Crusades.[75] Yet the church, having, so to speak, let the knights out of the bag, could not reign them in. Kings and nobles fought among themselves and dominated the population that went on foot. With a marauding cavalry and pillaging armies, they commanded the landscape.[76] En route to the Holy Land, ruthless mounted warriors and armies accustomed to living off the land deviated from their routes to massacre Jews and overrun towns—even such great cities as Antioch and, during the Fourth Crusade, Byzantium itself, the very bulwark of Christianity. Huns, Saracens, Magyars, and now Europe's own knights left no doubt in the minds of walking society that the riding orders of mounted warriors ruled.

Besides expanding European geographical horizons and helping birth Western travel literature, the Crusades marked the emergence of the war horse and the mounted warrior in Western society.[77] To be seated on a horse was to be paramount and prominent among those who went on foot. Medieval mounted warfare, which had been prefigured by the arrival of the Huns in the fifth century AD and displayed in the contest between the knights of Europe and the mounted Moors of Spain, marked a dramatic change in European society. It drew a profound class and status line between those who went on foot and those who rode.[78] This distinction deepened, expanded, and finally endured until public transportation and the automobile displaced horse and carriage at the start of the twentieth century.

However, never the warriors that romance stories idealized them to be, the armed soldiers of the early Middle Ages came from all classes of society. Only with the wide availability of horses in the high Middle Ages, the twelfth and thirteenth centuries, did mounted warfare become an exclusively aristocratic pursuit, and even then armies headed by cavalry were still principally composed of crowds of men on foot.[79] Furthermore, knights themselves frequently joined battle on foot when their mounts failed them.[80] In the spring of 1097, knights of the First Crusade were reduced to walking. Historian Morris Bishop graphically describes their plight in the Near East:

> Accustomed to the abundant water supply of their homelands, many had not even provided themselves with water canteens. Knights marched on foot, discarding armor; horses died of thirst, lack of forage and disease; sheep, goats, and dogs were collected to pull the baggage train. A part of the army crossed the Anti-Taurus range in a flood of rain on a muddy path skirting precipices. Horses and pack animals, roped together, fell into the abyss. Continually [with hit-and-run tactics] the Turks attacked the column.[81]

Between the eleventh and the thirteenth centuries, under the spur of the Crusades, chivalry became "the most important element in the military culture of the West, at a time when the energies of the Western aristocracies were almost wholly directed to making war."[82] On the importance of the medieval horse for warfare and agriculture—and the attending need for pasturage and oats—French medievalist Georges Duby succinctly wrote, "After all, the aristocratic civilization of the Middle Ages in Western Europe was primarily a horseborne one."[83] Developing the integral connection of horse and chivalry, Michael Prestwich wrote,

> The concept of chivalry is not easy to define. Its horsiness needs to be emphasized; entry to the chivalric world was confined to those who could be expected to ride, fully armed in war, and who at least aspired to knightly status. "It is best that chivalric things should be done on

horseback, not on foot," was the advice that the constable of Norham, Thomas Grey, gave to William Marmion.[84]

The French word for knight, *chevalier,* the source of the English word *chivalry,* has its origin in the French word for horse, *cheval* (It. *cavallo,* and Lt. *Caballus*). It reveals the inseparable link among horse, knight, and aristocracy; and it carries with it the implicit relegation of the pedestrian to the inferior ranks of those who go on foot, being without sufficient power and wealth to own horses—or the weapons, saddle, boots, fields, grain, stable, and, later, carriages that go with horse ownership. With the mounted warrior went the prestige of war and armaments, a growing panoply of identifying symbols, coats of arms, flags, and other heraldic devices, and the ideological accouterments of defending homeland, defeating infidel, and being noble.[85] Additionally, the owner of horses had access to fodder to feed his horse and labor to serve his mounted expeditions. It required as many as two or three servants, who doubled as infantry, to serve the lordly cavalry. In the twelfth century, knights approached aristocratic status "as the military equipment of the mounted warrior and the training and practice needed to master its use were so expensive and time-consuming that they were out of the question for ordinary people."[86]

Synonymous with the aristocracy, riding on horseback came to constitute the most prestigious mode of travel.[87] The knight rode rather than walked. He rode with the presumption that he was superior. He sat still, perched above the heads of trudging walkers. His horse helped make the muck in which they walked. It pushed pedestrians to the side of the road and filled them, rightly, with fears of being knocked down or kicked. The mounted man left pedestrians behind—trailing in his dust and muck—and even conscripted them to feed and care for his horse, as well as to have their fatigue appeased by receiving the chance to sleep in the horse's quarters. Inadvertently or on purpose, the arrogant mounted man could trample the gardens of the humble walking peasant. With a powerful engine between his legs, a sword or lance in his hands, and expensive armor on his back, the knight was in all senses preeminent. The status of going on foot took back seat to the high and mighty business of going on horseback.

Of fourteenth-century England, Jusserand wrote, "People of any worth journeyed on horseback."[88]

The speeding and elevated knight made others seem earth- and foot-bound. They became ordinary pedestrians—or to use words etymologically tied to the word *foot,* they became "peons," the origin of *peons* being *pedos,* medieval Latin for "a foot soldier." Those who served the horseman were, to use the Italian, *pedisseuqo* ("servile") or bootlickers. While common humanity stumbled along on foot, weighed down by life's necessities and driven by its most basic needs, the knight pursued a higher calling. Valorous in the service of fair maidens and setting the first terms of long and still-enduring high-class horsey culture, he played at warfare in tournaments. Though the church condemned tournaments, and the lower classes both imitated and mocked them with battles using tubs, buckets, and clubs, tournaments went on anyway, propelled by the passion of men flexing their muscles and displaying their war horses.[89] In any case, the knight gave the wandering troubadours, minstrels, and emerging poets something to sing about until the fourteenth century, when the accursed crossbow required ever heavier armor and left the dismounted knight "a poor crustacean and an easy prey for the common foot soldier."[90] In the coming age of efficient marching town infantries, the knight became Don Quixote. Meanwhile, the mounted warrior, with large horse and stirrup, saddle, lance, and even armor—the best of new technologies—cast a shadow of inferiority by speed, power, and wealth over all others—peasants, journeymen, local merchants, clerics, and beggars—who had to travel on foot and had to barter and ask for things rather than take them.

MERCHANTS AND CITIES

As the mounted warrior juxtaposed the superiority of those who went or could go by horse to those who out of necessity had to go on foot, so the medieval city defined new forms and ways of walking. Considered perhaps the great innovation of the later Middle Ages, the city or town as "a self-governing, dynamic entity belongs to the thirteenth and fourteenth centuries."[91] Its reemergence, which can be traced back to the tenth century, is inseparable from the steady ascent of trade.

In 1300, the year of the Jubilee pilgrimage to Rome, walking staff, cloak, knapsack, and a good pair of shoes still proved a walker's best friends. Even though river and sea travel had increased dramatically, the use of animal power had intensified, and the number of roads had multiplied, travel, whether on foot or on horse, still meant vexation, peril, accident, and possible death. Darkness, as always, confounded the surest step, and rocky, sandy, wet, slippery surfaces and steep inclines doubled the foot's labor and lengthened a trip. Travel still took travelers through vastly diverse communities, with myriad laws, manners, and languages.[92] Outlaws—who might be local authorities—still found roads relatively easy pickings; waves of brigands and armies continued to ravage the countryside. The quality of roads still depended on the whims of landholders and the onerous *corvée,* the feudal obligation that compelled serfs annually to spend a given number of days repairing roads. It is true that in fourteenth-century England all proprietors were forced to watch over the condition of roads, and even religious houses had to satisfy the public weal with bridge repair, which was crucial in river-bountiful Europe.[93]

Although it was safer to travel in groups, not all travel companions were honorable. Roads and ferries charged exorbitant fees. Road signs and markers were not universal, nor uniform, nor dependable. Measures of distance and time were highly imprecise in an age when weights and measures were not standardized. The foot, to take but one measure, estimated not just lengths, amounts, and roads but also human proportions.[94] Although the king's foot constituted the era's first measure of length, not all kings had the same size foot, nor did they take the same length stride.

Yet significant improvements in travel had occurred. Road systems expanded and were stimulated by the growth of trade. Linking villages, towns, expanding cities, and prosperous regions, connecting roads formed the sinew of a more active society and mind. Italians spoke of *camminare,* "to walk the *cammino* (the road)," while the English spoke of *wayfaring,* "traveling by road" and later added to this lexicon *waylay, wayside, wayward, waywarden, waywise,* and *halfway.* Road and river travel became increasingly interdependent and even interchangeable. Where rivers, principal arteries of travel, and roads met—especially at fords, the heads of estuaries, and ports—settlements and networks of towns and cities sprang up throughout Europe.

The revival of Mediterranean trade routes increased the commercial traffic of Europe, accounting for a dramatic growth in the number and size of cities. This, in the words of medievalist Henri Pirenne, "marked the beginning of a new era in the internal history of Western Europe" and unleashed a two-and-a-half-century "Commercial Revolution" between 1100 and 1348.[95] Matched by a revolution in population, by 1300, towns, consisting of from ten to fifty thousand people, constituted whole new self-contained environments for walkers. They sprang up in populated western Germany, the Netherlands, southern England, northern France, and, of course, Italy, which stood at the heart of the revival of long-distance trade. At the same time, seats of transportation, administration, human learning, architecture, manufacture, and commerce, such as Venice, Milan, Florence, London, and Paris, reached and exceeded populations of a hundred thousand, creating new walking urban environments.[96]

Merchants and their families moved to Europe's growing towns and cities.[97] They shared roadways with the rest of medieval society: "monks and nuns on errands for their community; bishops bound for Rome . . . wandering students, entertainers, pilgrims, papal postmen, discharged soldiers, tinkers, craftsmen, seasonal workmen, serfs, troubadours, quacks, and shepherds driving their sheep and cattle to market."[98] A common nickname for commercial travelers, *pieds poudreux*—"dusty feet"—suggests that all merchants shared the onerous business of walking roads. Traveling with packs of merchandise strapped onto their backs, yoked over their shoulders, or affixed to their bodies in other ways, peddlers—a type of merchant—formed a common sight on the roads. The more prosperous merchants, loaded with goods and intent on a distant destination, preferred to travel in convoys or caravans, "with sword on saddle according to an ordinance of the Emperor Frederick Barbarossa."[99] Travel oaths bound them to a travel company—resulting friendships endured long after the company's trip was completed.

According to historian Morris Bishop, "Merchants, who traveled countless miles on foot, led a long train of pack animals, which were tended by hostlers and muleteers; it took about seventy beasts to carry the contents of a modern ten-ton truck." Merchants camped at night where their animals could graze. Their destination was usually one of any number of specialized fairs, the most famous of which were annually held in the small cities of Champagne, where the king guaranteed safety and the church permitted the temporary use of a moderate usury rate.[100] As their business increased, the upper sectors of the merchant class turned sedentary and took up loftier and more comfortable places in town, leaving the more arduous and common labor of walking and carting to others. It found it could manipulate the world, like an established king, by sitting at home.

Commercial travel, conducted principally on foot and by ship, carried the city to the world and brought the world back to the city. No contemporary went further than Venetian Marco Polo.[101] Returning to the East with his father and uncle, young Polo walked much of the length of the Silk Road. Traversing the length of Asia, he crossed at a walker's pace "the desert of Persia, the flowering plateaux and wild gorges of Badakshan, the jade-bearing rivers of Khotan, the Mongol steppes, cradle of the power that had so lately threatened to swallow up Christendom, the new and brilliant court that had been established at Cambaluc."[102] Marco Polo became the personal representative of the great steppe and horse lord Kublai Khan.[103] For nearly two decades Polo took immense journeys on ship, on animal, and on foot. His stories and recollections, written down when he was a captive in a Genoese jail, made Asia the object of the most ambitious and far-reaching European commerce.

CITY STREETS

Many factors brought people out of the countryside to town and city. War, famine, and debt drove people there; opportunity and the quest to be free led them there.[104] (Any serf who managed to live one year and a day in a town was released from any claim by lord and estate.) Columns of barefooted paupers, unemployed, itinerant workers, vagabonds, pilgrims, students, scholars, all on foot, and wandering monks, or *gyrovagi,* against whom synods and councils legislated in vain, cast their fortunes with the road, which invariably led to a town.[105] The dispossessed and banished, the injured and ill, all wanted to put their empty hands in fellow travelers' full purses. Beggars, who accented their bare feet, limp, or amputated legs as grounds for begging from those who could walk, took up places at crossroads, in front of churches, at alehouse doors where traffic passed. The most hardened beggars deformed their own children's legs or feet to touch their clients' hearts—or would hitch their fortunes to a blind or crippled child, as did the resourceful wandering rogues of the sixteenth- and seventeenth-century picaresque tradition.[106] Legions of the crippled and lame, who were represented in the art of the day as beggars on crutches or with a peg for a leg, filled out the crowd.[107] One fourteenth-century manuscript describes "a very deformed cripple, whose means of locomotion is furnished by wooden clogs attached to his hands and knees by straps."[108] Finally, the tides of war sent waves of part-time soldiers, marauders, and criminals of every sort across the land.[109]

Royal and local authorities were usually not successful in their attempts to halt these swells of ambulating human flesh. In some towns, they rounded up vagabonds and even punished those who harbored them. They passed laws limiting the numbers of days and nights one could have guests, none of which made much difference to the tides of roving humanity. Laws against loose and errant people issued by Richard II sought futilely to enforce the provisions of Edward I and Edward III against itinerancy.[110] On the verge of developing a national poor law, Richard even extended his constrictive laws to wandering scholars. Known to beg, poach, and plunder on their academic peregrinations—*pereginatio academica*—scholars added to medieval foot traffic. As Oxford records corroborate, wandering students were required to carry what became in subsequent centuries in Europe and North America the common testimonial letter, which in their case was signed by their school chancellor.[111] Crowded roads dumped more indigent and itinerant travelers on roadside monasteries than could be fed and sheltered, or even divided into the deserving and undeserving poor.[112]

The cities, to which roads delivered hordes of people traveling on foot, were not welcoming. Conditions were much as they were in urban Rome and would be until the eighteenth century. Mazes of un-paved and twisting paths, lanes, and alleys led traffic to congested roads. Roads themselves were often blocked with herds of animals, en-tourages of mounted horsemen, moving households, litters, carts of diverse shapes and dimensions, outdoor workers (who were in the majority then), and stacks and piles of materials and goods. Garbage, litter, and refuse, overflowing cesspits and leakage from manure stored around dwellings, barns, and buildings flowed into streets. Without gutters, drains, or sidewalks (for which Europe would wait until the eighteenth and nineteenth centuries), slippery and treacherous streets forced walkers, especially in rainy season, to travel at their own peril. Many streets and roads became droveways, unenclosed lanes for driv-ing cattle and other animals through town. An individual neighbor-hood had its distinct smell and sound, depending on its dominant crafts and trades. A combination of narrow, rough, and crowded streets generated a roar of noise denying the wearied pedestrian rest even at home.

Dissatisfied workers, opposing factions of the people and the mag-nates, and rival clans (which produced fractious towns with hundreds of fortified towers), constituted abiding threats to safety on medieval Italian streets. In addition to groups peacefully gathered out of cu-riosity, rumor, or a local grievance, crowds could spontaneously mu-tate themselves into angry mobs. Ward, parish, and guild festivals and processions, as well as celebrated weddings and funerals, had the po-tential to spark widespread fighting.[113] Without an articulated munic-ipal government, organized police and fire fighters, or even a steady source of income derived from property taxes, residents of medieval towns and cities were often at the mercy of the vicissitudes of nature and the unpredictable anger of crowds. City life was largely lived out on foot.

Cities fostered ghettos and nurtured crime, making walking unsafe night and day.[114] Aside from plays and highly contested horse races, like Siena's Palio, often cruel entertainment attracted pedestrians. In one 1450 case, a Parisian impresario offered a pig as the prize to the winner among four blind beggars who fought one another with sticks.[115] Students, young and perennially tempted, frequently took to the dark side of the city life, visiting taverns and the bathhouse, which commonly functioned as a brothel. Despite their rectors' pleadings, students roved about town on foot begging, stealing, and finding what fun they could. One Oxford University law penalized students for night walking twice as severely as for shooting an arrow at a teacher.[116] Raises in rent and food prices could periodically turn students into angry mobs and make certain city streets and bridges predictable sites for ritualized conflict between town and gown. Students fought to death among themselves, as well. In one instance in 1314, two large bands of students fought on Oxford's High Street, leaving many dead and wounded.

Medieval cities, alone or in conjunction with the king, did what they could to battle these multiple ills and assure the well-being and safety of their residents. They regulated work hours by ringing bells, imposed curfews at dusk, and, besides caring for the poor and unemployed, they sought to control behavior and appearance in accord with class and status. To put a page in the book of Calvin's Geneva or colonial Boston, they controlled dress and appearance on city streets. For instance, Sienese women, according to social historian Mark Girouard, were "forbidden from wearing silk clothes . . . , which accentuated the curve of their body." The Signoria of Florence, conversely, accepted as its everyday dress "a toga of red damask, with a silk hood bordered with fur, and velvet slippers." As if to reveal the fate of every married woman, Florence went so far, Girouard additionally notes, as to pass an ordinance that a "bride could ride to church on horseback, but had to return on foot, under pain of a fine."[117]

City authorities strengthened their gates, imported grain, assured the water supply, built bridges and quays, and sought to prevent fires.[118] Not indifferent to their pedestrian population, they concerned themselves with building codes, draining, widening, and straightening streets, clearing roadways of encumbrances, and even lighting them, as well as with enlarging squares.[119] Medieval cities resorted to primitive ordinances to improve streets and traffic flow. Aside from controlling wandering animals and requiring road repair, cities, to improve traffic, began street paving, which Paris started in 1185, Prague in 1331, Florence in the mid-thirteenth century, and Bruges and select German cities during the fourteenth century.[120] In fourteenth-century Paris, householders were made responsible for cleaning the street in front of their house and carrying their wastes out of town. At the same time, the city took over cleaning especially dirty streets.[121]

Vagrancy, which had been proscribed since the early Middle Ages, unabatedly nagged at European society and continued to do so through modern European history. Trouble literally came on foot. Especially during bad times it came from the surrounding countryside in the form of straggling, destitute individuals and whole downtrodden families carrying all their worldly possessions on their backs. More terrifyingly, threat wore the face of independent armies, roving bands of peasants, and bandits intent on sacking the city.

Thickened walls and enforced gates, laws, regulations, and intermittent purges were the clumsy instruments by which cities sought to repel and to evict unwanted itinerants. In 1359, London authorities ordered the country laborers, who had taken to walking and begging in their city, to leave.[122] In sixteenth-century Holland, where insistence on urban order may have been the highest and the fear of begging and vagrancy the most pronounced, "the standard sentence for vagabonds convicted of begging or petty theft or relatively minor affrays was banishment.... During a brief period at the end of the sixteenth century, the Dutch (imitating Venice) banished its vagabonds and unworthy persons to be galley oarsmen, whose rates of mortality made banishment equivalent to a death sentence."[123] Committing one's problems to the sea evoked an older medieval tradition of Europe's northern ports: the unwanted would be rounded up, placed in captainless barges, and consigned to the outgoing tides—of such episodes was born the notion of "the ship of fools." However, maritime banishment proved to be a frail measure against rural vagrancy. When people truly needed something, they took to walking, and neither king nor city could effectively stop them.

Vagabondage gave going on foot its most pitiful and abject face. It suggested the most extreme division between the class and status of those who walked out of need and even desperation and those who most often walked only when and where they wanted. Increasingly, the mounted and riding nobility defined one side of the road and the walkers, especially those driven by desperation and homelessness, demarcated the other. While the vast majority of medieval people continued to move on foot on rural trails and paths, the most privileged owners of horses created courts and palaces where they could put themselves and their horses on display.

City streets, too, constituted new and special environments for walkers. For despite crime, filth, chaos, and riot, cities provided unique freedom and spectacles for walkers. Their immensity, vitality, and novel sights, along with different neighborhoods, active markets, diverse processions, and explosive carnivals, made city walking far more entertaining than going on foot in the dull, repetitious, sparse, and burden-laden countryside.[124] The city offered the great marvel of human works.

There was so much to stop and marvel at. One could walk the ramparts of newly expanded city walls or travel the newly built quays along the river. One could walk the central and covered markets, thread one's way through the changing commercial districts, or admire the palatial homes of nobility and merchants. City dwellers might find the end of their patriotic circumambulating at the central cathedral whose towers and spires, crowning generations and even centuries of building, soared to dizzying heights. Looking past the extended hands of huddled beggars and after giving way to bunches of clergy, crowds of pilgrims, and well-shod escorted ladies of discreet comportment, cathedral visitors would pass the threshold into the sanctuary itself. There, with as quiet and respectful step as possible (even though their loud-echoing clogs might betray their class and status as common travelers), they would walk on smooth stone floors. With their visit finished at the foot of central altar, where the bishop himself kneeled, processed, preached, and sat, they could begin their retreat with customary backward steps and self-effacing bows before returning to the church square.

In this way, city and church suggested new forms of walking for processing, traveling, and, in rare instances, even sightseeing. These ways were in good measure exempted from the shadows of inferiority of class and status horse and rider had cast on walking. In the centuries immediately after the Middle Ages—the sixteenth, seventeenth, and eighteenth centuries—kings' and nobles' courts and thriving merchant cities articulated and refined fresh forms of walking. With etiquette, formal dance, and public manners, they taught the aristocracy and upper levels of the middle class distinguishing movements of foot and body. Opulent courts, lavish country homes, city squares, wide boulevards, and spacious gardens furnished ample space and smooth surfaces for superior people to promenade and stroll, to see and be seen.

$\overset{\text{\normalsize\textbardbl}}{\text{\textbardbl}} 3 \overset{\text{\normalsize\textbardbl}}{\text{\textbardbl}}$ Put Your Best Foot Forward

The Rise of Upper-Class Promenading and Strolling

 EUROPE flourished in the eighteenth century after the fierce battles of the Reformation, the horrid and engulfing Thirty Years War (1618–1648), and the wars of Louis XIV (1685 to 1715). With warfare diminished, improved agriculture, and population again growing, central states increasingly focused their attention on fostering trade, improving transportation, and organizing and taking control of society. With its stress on reason, natural sciences, practical arts, and reform, the eighteenth century was identified as the Age of Enlightenment. In this period, people in the upper classes walked and traveled more, did so more by choice, and, at court, in city, and in surrounding countryside, did so with more style and fashion.

The transformation of public life in the eighteenth century, however, did not end the rivalry of classes. To the contrary, it accelerated and exacerbated the three-cornered struggle among land, commerce, and government, which tore apart the Old Regime. Increasing opportunities for wealth and office, and power at home and abroad, spawned rivalries not just between governments (such as, most notably, that between France and England over North America) but also within and between the aristocracy and an emerging middle class. Aside from having possessions for their intrinsic pleasure, they used their possessions to display opulence, which signaled privilege and legitimacy.

Goods, privileges, and rights confirmed superiority on their owners—and with them came the obvious means and right to sit, to ride, and to walk only by choice and, then, only among special people, or just alone with oneself. Horses, footmen, and carriages (as golden and ornate as royal money could make them), along with smooth surfaces, special gardens, courts, and balls made such exclusive riding and select walking possible. Wealth allowed, and to a degree dictated, that it owners command their inferiors and servants to walk, carry, wait, bow down, and care for the tired feet and soiled shoes and boots of their superiors.

There is little wonder that nobility, and the aspiring upper middle classes, made etiquette, manners, and walking into a show of distinction. Abundant and comfortable chairs were not available; sofas had not yet been invented for sitting. And, more, with neither sitting nor lying in bed serving as good ways to display a full person, much less two or three, the nobility understandably used carriage, posture, and comportment to establish, so to speak, their social standing. At the same time, they utilized the grace, balance, and line identified with them to declare their unbridgeable difference from the common lot of dirty, working, foot-trudging, ill-shod, and barefooted humanity. Proper self-presentation, control, and behavior, which manifested itself as discretion in step and word, bolstered the status of the truly superior against the loud, brash, and aggressive upcomers from the middle class, which equated worth not with inherited rank but with activity, work, and money. People of innate superiority and true refinement would not deign to compete on the dirty streets and thoroughfares of city and business. Rather, in diametrical opposition to the rest of humanity, which walked when and where life, work, and lord commanded, they promenaded and strolled where they pleased. Fashion, which has dictates of its own, proposed that they show a noble presence, in the private gardens on exclusive estates and at special places in and around the city where their carriages delivered them.

As in so many other things, the court led the way in upgrading and civilizing the all-too-common act of walking. Elegant walking was among the first conditions of noble and upper-class refinement, which the French court and the British upper classes defined with etiquette, gestures, and manners. From the sixteenth to the nineteenth centuries, setting the fashion for the West, the French and English taught anyone who was someone, or anyone who aspired to be someone, how to put a best foot forward. In this way, they defined the walker and shaped walking, especially in the forms of strolling, processing, and promenading as a select, chosen, and refined activity.

During the sixteenth century, the planet's five hundred million or so individuals made their way through life on foot.[1] Only a small percentage rode on the backs of animals, in carts, or on sledges. Few yet rode in carriages, which first appeared in sixteenth-century Europe. A small but nevertheless growing number of the upper classes in Europe went on foot by choice. Yet this elite would dramatically expand in the subsequent two centuries as the upper middle class learned to ride, promenade, and stroll. As we will see, they transformed the very act of going on foot, and during the nineteenth and twentieth centuries, multitudes came to follow in their steps.

Historian Fernand Braudel estimated that in the sixteenth century, a century during which world population doubled, the Mediterranean region reached sixty to seventy million people.[2] This burst in population, in conjunction with economic opportunities and improvements in ship building, navigation devices, map making, horse breeding, and other craft and technological improvements, accounted for a boom in travel and transportation. The estimated value of goods transported by sea exceeded that of goods transported over land by three to one.[3] The wide dispersal of goods, plants, ideas, and religions, as well as the biographies of merchants, confirms widespread travel during this century.[4]

Migration, which remained greatly dependent on the human foot, took many forms. Emigration occurred among the populous regions along the Mediterranean basin, where sea travel was facilitated by abundant ports, and thriving cities lured mountain peoples to them. The Jews expelled from Spain in 1492 resettled in Europe and around the Mediterranean.[5] Italian merchants and craftspeople began to populate the Mediterranean lands and Europe while Spanish colonizers occupied New Spain, and French immigrated into Spain.

However, to conceive of the sixteenth century as an era of universal movement would be false. Walking principally served short journeys. Men and women, Braudel points out, "still lived under the tyranny of distance"; space couldn't be circumvented.[6] A posted horse did not always displace the foot messenger. On a trip of any great distance off the road, the horse gave way to the walking person. Furthermore, horses were scarce and expensive everywhere. In the famous horse-breeding regions of Naples and Andalusia they were jealously guarded treasures.[7]

Many factors inhibited the speed of travel. Weather and darkness could form an impenetrable screen. Vast stretches of wild lands and wasteland flatly defied human crossing. Forbidding mountains, dense forests, swamps, jungles, grasslands, and vast deserts inhibited the movement of people, goods, and ideas. Broken roads, rivers, tolls, and frontier crossings also reduced speed. Other social and geographic forces fastened humankind to a locality that they had known since birth, where they had home, work, and language, and where the circling paths and trails they knew by foot and heart formed a way beyond which they would struggle to imagine. The vast majority belonged to a fixed and hierarchical society. They truly only were familiar with the places they had walked. Samuel Johnson, for instance, said of one such region in the Scottish highlands in the eighteenth century, "The numbers who are barefoot [are] sufficient to show that shoes may be spared," and he described the area beyond Aberdeen Scotland as a country "where we could have hired no horse" and "upon which perhaps no wheel has ever rolled."[8]

Except when dancing or courting, no one could spare foot or leg for beauty or delight. Always short on carts, oxen, and horses, the walking people of the European countryside—no differently than in the countryside of the rest of the world—dedicated their bodies to work and haulage. Even the technologically advanced Chinese, who invented the wheelbarrow (to which they at times ingeniously mounted a forward sail) had to depend on human lifting strength whenever they lacked a smooth and firm surface for their weight-bearing wheel.

The world offered few level, even stretches of road. Even the best roads—like those engineered in the mountains of Fujan province in fourteenth-century China—quickly deteriorated without upkeep. Except on those selective routes where commerce and government conspired to protect traders and armies, road conditions were poor. In fact, the word *road* misleads us. Most of what existed for travel were mere foot paths and trails, walking lanes, and droveways along which herds of animals moved. Often the actual course of the roads fluctuated hundreds of yards from one side to the other depending on seasonal conditions. Throughout the year, foot and wheel encountered ruts and bumps, boulders and washouts, steep grades and abrupt ends, sinking sands and grasping clay. Roads were often unmarked or mistakenly marked.

Travel then was mainly foot travel. Historian John Croft reminds us that in seventeenth-century England even nobles, who had the means to ride, required their footmen to dismount to seek out places to break hedges and avoid "deep and dangerous ways."[9] They did not hesitate to leave the roadway and redirect their drivers through fields if a short-cut could be found. And when conditions forbade one route, they simply initiated another across adjacent lands. Indeed, the need for serviceable roads argued against the enclosure of lands—and agricultural communities' interest in improved roads arose not from their desire to travel but from their desire to keep pedestrians, horses, carts, and carriages out of their fields. Confirming the difficult conditions of carriage travel, which often reduced those who rode to walking, Croft noted that a widening circle of mud and misery "insulated the capital from the country as a whole. A hundred miles from London they were still living in the fifteenth century; two hundred miles away they were hardly out of the fourteenth."[10] In short, the roads of the sixteenth to the nineteenth centuries commonly resisted and even openly defied travel by carriage. Their surfaces typically permitted only travel by

hooves and on feet and frequently, in bad weather and conditions, forbade human and horse as well.

THEY BARELY TOUCHED THE GROUND

In Europe, the aristocracy and eventually the grand business class were
delivered by horse and carriage to and from chosen sites, where they
strolled, processed, promenaded, and put themselves—and their
feet—on display. As the upper classes tamed the physical world around
them, so, trained by Catholic liturgy and processions in solemn gestures and walking, they shaped their bodies, body language, and walking, in particular, to express solemn and ponderous things about
themselves and their actions.[11] Increasingly intent on displaying their
wealth, establishing their superiority, and declaring their legitimacy
and authority—which were perennial interests and increasingly pressing matters for throne and nobility in an age of an expanding middle
class and even incipient democracy—they trod the earth as if they
were not of this earth. They sought to be pleasing in each other's eyes
and respected and legitimate in the eyes of others.

The elite left the drudgery, filth, and pain of going on foot and carrying to others. Even when they hunted, they rode when they could.
They let servants do the mundane business of shopping and delivering messages. The elite would have no truck with the tedious and
time-consuming activity of long-distance walking and haulage. After
all, nobles presumed to bear the precious cargo of themselves. They
took themselves to be chosen vessels of word, thought, tradition, and
authority. With this higher mandate, they would not, if possible, soil
themselves with sweat and toil, wade into the dirt and muck of ordinary life. Preoccupied with their own comportment and status, relationships, pleasures, and feelings, they would let their servants go out
onto the streets to care for ordinary and trivial things. In public they
would walk and move in ritualized ways, on special surfaces, and for
particular occasions. They would not move by need, by necessity, or at
the behest of others.

Having learned the meaning of kneeling at the foot of his or her
king, a member of the court knew it to be an honorable thing to sit,

to be given things, to be carried, or, if required to walk, to have one's way cleared. Nobility (originally composed of traditional nobility of sword and land and later composed of appointed nobility of government and the highest orders of commerce) belonged to a cultural hierarchy of position, motion, manners, behavior, and gestures that were meant to express superiority. If one could not ride in a luxurious sedan chair, then it was next best to ride in a horse-drawn carriage, which became increasingly bountiful for the upper classes in the seventeenth and eighteenth centuries with spreading wealth and the availability of horses. Even though being chauffeured in a carriage was less than comfortable and even unsafe, it did relieve one from traveling on the sweaty flanks and hard saddles of a bouncing and fickle horse. Between the sixteenth and nineteenth centuries, in conjunction with ever increasing numbers and breeds of horses, carriages multiplied in number and type and improved in speed, comfort, size, design, and ornamentation.

The number, quality, and training of one's carriages, horses, and drivers constituted conspicuous displays of wealth—and elaborated the distance that separated those with means and those without.[12] Leaving the driving to someone else implied prestige. Riding liberated the mind from paying attention to the senseless and numbing road and its insistent demands. And a carriage meant having servants, footmen, lackeys, and footstools to accommodate one's tedious journey.

The fanciest high stepping started in the Renaissance court. As part of their effort to consolidate their authority, rulers gathered formerly decentralized nobility about them in the court to teach them refined behavior and loyalty. Functioning as the first and final arbiter of manners, the court taught its residents to walk and talk, to ride and dance, to stand, sit, rise, and greet. Having learned to imitate the king, these nobles disseminated their courtly ways among the lesser provincial nobility. In turn, the nobility became a model for the bourgeoisie. In this way, over several centuries, with considerable variation for place and influence, especially between Western and Eastern Europe, the ways of higher courts passed to lesser courts, to the palaces of notables, and eventually right out into the streets of the kingdom.[13]

Manners required control of voice, hand, head, leg, and foot. Kings and queens, purportedly perfect, were in fact often not exemplary.

Their behavior could lurch out of control: they emitted odd noises, with several, such as Henry IV of France, being notorious stinkers; their hands grappled where they shouldn't; and their very odd and misshapen legs did not always provide a firm and steady footing for etiquette. Queen Anne's bowlegs inspired a furniture style. King Henry VIII suffered chronic dropsy, diagnosed today as edema. Although he loved to dance, corpulence overtook him and his enormous legs were covered with painful, festering ulcers. Eventually weighing more than four hundred pounds, Henry did not keep his wives by fancy footwork.

No courts played a greater role in consolidating European aristocratic manners than those of Louis XIII and Louis XIV. "Starting in the second half of the seventeenth century," writes cultural historian Peter Rietbergen, "French court culture became the dominant factor in Europe, to remain so till the end of the eighteenth century."[14] The pedagogic instrument of Louis XIV was his court at Versailles, a spectacular fusion of palace and garden. There power, control, and image leapfrogged one another, as the king sought to teach, and thus tame, the nobles of the kingdom with manners and deference. A great hall covered by seventeen huge mirrors, a huge garden graced by fountains and pools, all reflected unrivaled glory. Immense spectacles, theatrical performances, balls, and ceremonies formed almost a constant pageant aimed at continuously dazzling the court, France, and the entire world.[15] The well-adorned foot, the carefully extended leg, and the long, trailing dress all played their part in turning space into stage at this "'theatre of power.'"[16]

Royalty everywhere in Europe emulated the French. German principalities enhanced their courts à la Versailles. In England, Poland, Sweden, and elsewhere, nobles built country palaces and town mansions in the French manner and ate and dressed like their French peers. To appear at their best, Rietbergen wrote, "They even behaved as the French nobles did, aping the intricate court manners of Versailles in the way they walked, bowed their heads, and so on."[17]

Surrounded from the moment he awoke until his evening return to his splendid canopied bed—from *levée* to *couchée*—the Sun King had no privacy. Caught in the net he cast, Louis, body and soul, belonged to his court. He worked several hours a day under the direction of a dancing master.[18] With multitudes looking on, Louis was at the center of great ballets and operas set to stately music by such composers as Jean–Baptiste Lully.[19]

On elaborate outdoor parade grounds and squares, of which Louis had his share, royalty and nobility asserted their prominence with ceremonies and processions.[20] For standing occasion or specific event, of state or church, to celebrate, commemorate, or mourn, with or without music, processions featured royal, noble, military, and clerical groups, dressed in their full regalia, moving in the most pronounced manner. Organized by rank, often carrying or featuring objects, processional walkers and riders moved at a measured and a solemn cadence, making their movement anything other than everyday walking. At the court military officers put themselves, their marching legions, and their choreographed prancing horses on display.[21] Military parades, which had their immediate origins in the drills of the eighteenth century, conveyed the unmistakable message of the power radiating from armed men moving in unison. They put feet, arms, and weapons in synchronized movement, displaying to the awe of the onlookers the singular capacity of the throne to concentrate fighting men and project its power. Marching men—armies stepping in unison—displayed the king's ability to organize society.[22]

While the cadence of song and beat have been used across the world to facilitate pulling, lifting, and other forms of work, marching provided the military with its distinctive movement. Drilling turns individual men into fighting units with *ésprit de corps*. As the Greeks and Romans knew, it produces in soldiers an ecstasy of feeling they belong to a moving and invulnerable entity. The highly trained foot soldier, in fact, made the modern European army an awesome machine—an articulated organism of which each part responded to impulses from above.[23] The well-drilled marching army—inspired by the Swiss legions, brought to perfection by Frederick William I—made for an imposing parade and set the standard for the best-drilled, most athletic, and most highly coordinated armies.[24] The goose step—the Prussian *Paradeschritt* or "Parade March"—was one the most severe and expressive movements ever conjured. With toe pointed upward on every beat, legs with unbroken knee extended to horizontal, arms swinging like cantilevers, and jutting jaw protruding, the goose-stepping soldier was an imposing sight.[25] Powerful stomping boots, joined to carefully synchronized steps, displayed a highly trained and obedient army. It was clocklike in its movement. It was the remorseless state on parade.

Before Frederick William I, Louis XIV grasped the connection between military march and drill and the creation of prescribed forms of dance and movement as complementary means of imposing control and securing social order. In Louis's court, the birthplace of modern ballet, its members were coordinated and synchronized with continual rituals, dances, military displays, and orchestrated ceremonies.[26]

Promenading and strolling—civilian counterparts of marching— also required the correct place, the right occasion, and the proper surface. The court, the garden, or the newly rebuilt squares were the right venues for one's select walking. Inaugurations, balls, wedding, victories, or funerals provided the proper celebration for the discreet display and prominent strutting of oneself. Elaborate marble floors, spacious stairs, or finely graveled garden paths, the very opposite of the narrow, filthy, congested, rutted, mundane lane or common street, fit the movement of the proper and privileged. The path of somebody of importance had to be open, dry, firm, clean, safe, perhaps elevated, and as free as possible of obstacles, stomping and awkward peasants, foul crowds, and other unsightly and intrusive things.

Away from the court, special people who came in the course of the prosperous eighteenth century, whether by inheritance, wealth, public office, or a measure of self-selection, to consider or wish themselves to be counted among the nobility developed a distinct way of walking. They operated according to the illusionary but enduring social truth: you are what you are seen, said, (and whispered) to be. To escape the eyes of others, they found privacy, walking along quiet, pleasing, and solitary garden paths. There they could flirt or even harvest the fruit of flirtation. There they found chances to think of themselves as free of all pervasive others and to believe, as if Eden or even Arcadia were to be found in the garden, that they had singular natures especially worthy of the era's newfound claim of happiness.

Aristocratic and wealthy middle-class families, who naturally owned a horse and carriage, or two, or many more, as well as respectable clothes, shoes, and perhaps footmen, also engaged in fashionable walking and strolling, which fused recreation and sociability. Their Sunday and holiday outings often involved promenades in carriages to the ramparts or surrounding hills, where with vistas of the town below, they would stroll, confident that they were at the their best among the best.

WALKING AMONG ONE'S OWN KIND

From the Renaissance until the closing decades of the nineteenth century, the royalty, the high aristocracy, and then the upper bourgeoisie furnished Europe with a remarkable array of places for the superior classes to display their fancy dress and steps.[27] Fashion historian Alicia Annas wrote,

> The motion of walking was so admired in the eighteenth century that all fashionable people spent a portion of each day publicly promenading in a park where, while nonchalantly strolling and conversing, they could display themselves and observe others displaying themselves to best advantage. Since walking began with the feet, the costume item that most influenced this movement was the shoe. . . . One was expected to maintain the same elegant carriage standing in walking as standing still.[28]

With chairs not yet bountiful or comfortable and sitting not yet "an acquired art even at the court," grace and fashion most often stood and moved on foot.[29] It was important, lest one act like peasant, worker, or rude social inferior, not to lean, slouch, get down on one's haunches, or sit and lie on the floor. Thanks to improvements in carpentry and stonework, the richest people of Europe gracefully glided across opulent floors of inlaid wood and tile. On them the elite promenaded, strolled, and danced.[30] Across open expanses of ballrooms, coiffured and jeweled women (who could not and did not wander the street) could spin and twirl in syncopated movement. From the middle of the sixteenth century, this select group left stomping dances to the vulgar people. They need not be reminded of clomping feet—and clapping, cracking, shouting, and yelping. They left the waltz to their earthy inferiors. Instead, they dedicated their gracious steps to more disciplined, refined, and cerebral group dance until, under the influence of the French court, they took to the minuet à *deux*.[31]

Already by the seventeenth century humanists credited dance, which in the preceding century was tied to both military display and social success, with an educational value similar to that held by horseback riding and skill with weapons.[32] Dance lessons and classical ballet remained compulsory for French officers into the nineteenth century.[33] One had to bow and click one's heels to earn the hand of one's partner and proceed to the floor on which all—two by two—were on display. The way a couple danced—the way their feet moved—revealed who they were.

Magnificent staircases, which we identify with Mannerism and the Baroque period, also displayed dress, foot, and social status, as well as testified to the wealth, leisure, and social cohesion of the upper classes. Great stairs suggested power and status; long, curving staircases offered a chance for their elite users to accent their practiced effortlessness and gracefulness. On them courtly women arrived and disappeared like heavenly apparitions. Flowing stairs transformed those who walked them. With protocols designed to assure social status, one entered on a solemn stage on the wide and balustraded staircase. On it one announced oneself and one's companion fully by dress, walk, and movement. At the pinnacle of society, Louis XIV gloriously ascended the Rheims Cathedral staircase to his coronation. The great staircase at Versailles, Escalier des Ambassadeurs, magnified visitors' ascent to the Sun King. Staircases like that of the Chiswick House in London, the Pommersfelden in Germany, and the Belvedere estate in Austria architecturally highlighted luxurious balconies, ceilings, gardens, and the users of the stairs. The foyer staircase in the nineteenth-century Paris Opera (to choose one of many outstanding staircases in early modern and modern Europe) formed a magnificent showcase for audiences in attendance.

Gardens, often entered and exited by a bifurcated staircase, also set off the displayed and chosen walking of the rich and powerful from that of the rest of humanity, which went on foot as life required, work demanded, load necessitated, and experience accustomed. They constituted the entrance to and exit from an enchanting environment distant from the hurly-burly life of town and the dull, dusty countryside. Geometric and sweeping paths—surfaced with fine gravel or paved stone—smoothed the lord and lady's way, making their stroll a kind of mannered dance. Gardens, and cemeteries modeled after gardens in the second half of the eighteenth century, did not support rough and irregular rural paths identified with the countryside.[34] Many gardens included a fountain, edged a reflecting pool, traced out a labyrinth hedge, or drew the walker to a statue, a decorative temple, or an overview of the surrounding countryside. Serene and immaculately ordered, gardens also proved useful places to bare one's soul, to play conversational peek-a-boo with true feelings, or to find an Arcadia ideal for practicing solitude.[35] Walking here became a leisure activity—and one that enhanced the self.

Walking in gardens consumed large portions of polite European society's leisure.[36] Indeed, the English garden (developed but differentiated from the Renaissance Italian and the seventeenth- and eighteenth-century French geometric garden) was made for walking, with grass lawns and gravel walks laid across open and asymmetrical, but not rough or wild, terrain.[37] With choice and placement of vegetation, English garden designers projected "the undulating line as natural." They went so far as to disguise the border of the garden and surrounding landscape "with the use of the haha, or sunken fence." Joining garden and surrounding countryside led to an expanded desire to shape "the country without" and had the effect of transforming much of England itself. Spearheaded by a tree-planting rage on the part of English nobility, England became a land of "new parks, traversed by rides and avenues that primarily were conceived as visual extensions of the garden paths."[38] In some profound but ironical way, the English garden, which invited walking, had the effect of defining wilderness as a place in which humans never set foot.[39]

The walk through the garden, which provided the training ground for the romantic traveler, constituted a sustaining ritual for those who inhabited and visited a country home.[40] For those privileged with wealth and leisure, which included those of great inheritances, secure income, and servants, who could avail themselves of the garden experience, walking became a pleasurable activity.

The early modern city—the Baroque city—also constituted a new environment principally for upper-class walkers. Serving the courtly ideals of magnitude of scale, ostentation, and display, it produced a distinct order of movement and exhibition. Leaving the lower and working classes walking their medieval lanes, alleyways, and narrow, congested streets or forcing them to move in the backwater or along the edges of the new straight and broad avenues and boulevards, the Baroque city was opened up to serve parading armies, personal carriages, and sumptuous urban residences. It afforded leisure opportunities for promenades, strolls, processions, and even pleasant shopping. It built straight and sweeping thoroughfares in the service of dignified and official urban traffic. Establishing garrisons, parade grounds, and esplanades, which served power and its displays of marching and mounted troops, it also constructed parks, gardens, and squares, which offered great vistas and produced ample stages for those who needed to stroll among their kind.

Rome was the epitome of the Baroque city. The Counter Reformation Pope Sixtus V, who completed the dome of St. Peters, built long avenues and great piazzas dominated by ancient Egyptian obelisks. The popes, according to urban historian F. Roy Willis, became stage designers, and Rome was their theatre.[41] In Paris, Willis wrote, "bureaucratic absolutism tried its hand at design. Royal edicts created a riverfront lined by grandiose facades, and expanded the courtyard of the Louvre and linked it to the tall pavilions of the Tuileries palace and the controlled vistas of the regimented gardens beyond."[42] In Russia, Peter the Great established a new capital for himself at St. Petersburg. Built on a swamp at a phenomenal cost of human life, the city was distinguished by its monumental buildings and wide avenues.

Urban critic and historian Lewis Mumford depicts the Baroque city as producing a new order of traffic. It was designed at the expense of the community and pedestrians to serve the movement of wheeled cannons, which were indispensable to the destruction of walled castles and independent cities in the countryside. It also served the carriages, which publicly advertised their occupants' importance on the way to conduct business, parade, and stroll.[43]

Clearly, the Baroque city had military purposes. Enhanced urban fortifications formed corsets into which people, homes, and multistory buildings had to be squeezed. Esplanades defined an open space between town and fortification, making that space a perfect killing field for lethal fusillades. The need to billet troops led embattled monarchs to erect barracks. Squares and fields, like the Champs de Mars in Paris, the white, sandy grounds behind Whitehall in London, or even Boston Common, furnished training grounds for marching troops and cavalry. Wide avenues, testifying to the era's increasing dominance of space and wish to control speed, permitted the rapid deployment and movement of troops and wheeled artillery. Centuries in advance of nineteenth-century urban architect Baron Haussmann, who used wide and connecting boulevards to open and neutralize the narrow, sinister, and revolutionary streets of medieval Paris, Alberti—"the chief theoretical exponent of the Baroque city"—recognized military uses for wide and open roads. He called them *viae militares*.[44]

Where the Baroque city did not transform medieval and Renaissance urban Europe with its widened avenues, enlarged squares, new churches, and immense, multistoried residences, it left traditional neighborhoods, lower- and working-class life, and traffic patterns unaltered. While not free of curfews and codes, the majority in city and countryside, as the Roman working classes and peasants did before them, lived out their lives, weather permitting, outdoors and on foot. Walking, the majority daily sought water, food, and fuel, worked, pursued entertainment, and suffered life's misfortunes and maladies, lamenting, quarreling, rioting, and rebelling.

At the kaleidoscopic heart of the city stood beauty and the beast. Butted up against beautiful buildings, fine clothes, cultivated gestures, idle strolling, and the haughty elegance of the *beau monde* flowed lanes, alleys, and streets that, flooding over with filth, crowded with beggars, drunks, syphilitics, and idiots, home to whores, retired footpads (highway robbers), and pickpockets, were likely to spawn a mob at a moment's notice.[45] At the meeting points of these old lanes and the era's new avenues, medieval Europe, still on foot, gave way to mounted authorities and the riding, parading, and promenading upper classes of modern Europe. Walkers got out of the way of horses, lumbering carts made way for lighter and speeding carriages, and all moved to the side rather than be run over by a rushing military cavalcade. With foot surrendering to hoof and wheel, traditional pedestrians, as seventeenth- and eighteenth-century paintings reveal, became groups of anonymous onlookers, an audience for public ceremonies, passing processions, and privileged promenading in carriage and on foot.

The Baroque city, above all, was designed to serve and to feature the prominent. It hosted the parades of the well-wheeled and well-heeled. Driven by ambition to shine in the eyes of others, they vied for attention with their multiple and opulent carriages, the prestige automobiles of eighteenth-century elite.[46] Mumford quotes from Mercier's eighteenth-century *Tableau of Paris*:

"Mind the carriages!" [he] cried, "here comes the black-coated physician in his chariot, the dancing master in his *cabriolet,* the fencing master in his *diable*—and the Prince behind six horses at a gallop as if he were in open country. . . . The threatening wheels of the overbearing rich drive as rapidly as ever over stones stained with blood of their unhappy victims."[47]

Mumford notes that "in France the stage-coach, introduced in the seventeenth century, killed more people annually than the railroad that followed it."[48]

Shoppers, too, were on parade in the Baroque city. Going shopping showed the world that one owned a horse and carriage, had money to spend, and assembled one's life out of one's choices. Along the way, one, with no malice intended, might show his or her superiority by splattering with muck the lowly walker. To shop, one no longer needed to enter the dark, turbulent, and populous quarters of the medieval city. Instead, the shopper could find adjacent to the new boulevard stores often shielded by arcades and fronted by glass windows. Window shopping—a principal form of twentieth-century recreation involving ever decreasing amounts of walking—constituted a type of stop-and-go promenading. The early eighteenth-century writer Daniel Defoe was shocked at such a waste of time. "I have heard," he wrote, "that some ladies, and these persons of good note, have taken their coaches and spent a whole afternoon in Ludgate Street or Covent Garden, only to divert themselves in going from one mercer's [textile dealer's] to another, to look upon their fine silks and to rattle and banter the shopkeepers, having not so much as the least occasion, much less intention to buy anything."[49]

CIVILIZING THE SELF, CULTIVATING THE FOOT

To the degree that the highest classes chose, shaped, and refined their environments, they also cultivated themselves. Multiple words, ranging from *manners, fashion, good taste,* and *etiquette* to the distinctly French *civilité, politesse,* and more comprehensive *honnête,* described an expanding upper-class control of body and gesture that occurred from the sixteenth century onward.[50]

Since beauty and manners are mainly skin deep, style and fashion fluctuate between covering and uncovering the human epidermis. The steps toward elegance in Europe involved many human artifices. They included perfumes and makeups (powders) of one sort or another and a wardrobe of ornate clothes, headdresses, canes, umbrellas, and—not least—footwear and other walking apparel. Indeed, the slick slipper and the high leather riding boot defined the feminine and masculine poles of noble perfection. Indeed, the woman had to glide according to the constraints of her clothes and slippers, just as the man had to adjust his stride to his boots.

The feminine body was both shaped and constricted in a hundred ways. The graceful woman pinched her steps, altered her gait, drew in her stomach, and curved her shoulders back to realize the era's prescribed image of beauty at rest and in motion, and to accommodate the clothes she wore. Corsets, stomachers, crinolines, hoops, trailing skirts, rising embroidered collars, garters, gloves, fans, parasols, elaborate wigs, bonnets, and even preposterous hats supporting exotic plumage or model ships all played their part in giving birth to Venus and setting her in motion with a stiff neck, stilted posture, and restricted walk. Not only did corsets, hoops, long-trained dresses, and layers of skirts and petticoats weigh her down, shorten her stride, and diminish her maneuverability, especially in the face of doors and entrances to sedan chairs, but they also offered proof that she was beyond manual work and that her father or husband had servants to do such work. If we look at French fashion from 1500 to the French Revolution, which was increasingly restrictive and elaborate, we see that it held the walking, standing, and sitting woman in stern bondage.[51]

Footwear served nobility's ascendance.[52] Literally elevating upperclass women above the mud and muck that engulfed contemporary country and city lives were pattens—clogs of one sort or another whose heels raised them a foot or two off the ground.[53] As late as the nineteenth century, pattens sounded on city streets. At one point in *David Copperfield,* their sound returns Dickens's theater-struck protagonist to the reality of the surrounding "muddy, miserable world."[54] Indoors, however, nobles dared not wear their loud and clumsy pattens, lest they be like the lower-class hobnailers, whose heavy, awkward shoes made their very name a synonym for a boorish and churlish individual.

With their shoes as important to the impression they created as the elaborate language they spoke, the hat they doffed, the ringed hand they extended, or the cane or the parasol they carried, those who mattered indeed put their best-shod foot forward. Whether attired in light, jeweled cloth or embroidered slippers, adorned with ornate, hand-made shoes, or precariously balanced on heels located at the center of the shoe, the affluent walker advertised wealth and high standing with his or her shoes. This was done not just by the cost of the footwear but also by its obvious incompatibility with the hard work, carrying, and long-distance walking that made up everyday life for the majority. Conspicuous refinement and extravagant ornamentation ruled in the seventeenth century with the wearing of silk-soled shoes, mules with floral or silver embroidery, and silk ribbon latchet shoes with silver embroidery. Shoes were further refined in the eighteenth century, with the use of shaped heels, buckles, and printed leather.[55] And in a pinch, one could always speak of the exclusivity of one's shoemaker or, better yet, casually refer to one's very own private shoemaker. Inadvertently, these fancy shoes also testified to a simple fact: up and out of mud and up and off rough surfaces, they were meant for smooth and even surfaces. The transformation of Cinderella's original leather shoes into glass slippers suggests how far polished and inlaid wood led the imagination away from bumps and filth, rock and stone of common ground. And even those noble officers—who rejected slippers in favor of big, black, shiny boots—did so to call attention to their higher and dashing calling in the service of king and sword.[56] Boots also declared ownership of a horse and stable and a servant to shine one's boots.

The evolution in early modern history of the stylized cane (the British walking stick), whose origin,[57] as discussed earlier, is the staff, also reveals that travel by foot occurred for upper urban classes in a tamer environment and on more negotiable surfaces. In aristocratic hands the diminished and stylized cane—made of ebony or sturdy oak, which still retained lethal potential to strike human or animal—replaced the taller, stronger, homemade walking staff.[58] The light bamboo cane first appeared around 1500, no doubt a product attained by foreign trade. Its development—including the use of ivory, ebony, and whalebone, as well as highly decorated and jeweled knob handles—depended on the increasingly regular surfaces of court and city.[59] Though still used to prop up the gouty, arthritic rich or draw attention to a war wound, the cane—with rare decorative samples being made in glass—principally served as a clothing accessory. However, it also could disguise a gun or sword, store a pen and paper, provide medicine, conceal a drink, or serve the peregrinating walker in other ways.[60]

The umbrella also underwent a transformation, and in some periods doubled as a cane.[61] Having disappeared in the Middles Ages, it reappeared in the sixteenth century in Italy, in the seventeenth century in France, and in the eighteenth century in the rest of Europe, when it took the form of the fashionable colorful parasol of the upper-class stroller, became an important dress accessory, and lost any significant use as a club or stick. It remained a standard element of women's fashionable outdoor dress through the nineteenth century.[62] An early symbol of heavenly sovereignty and a preserver of fair skin that courtly beauty claimed as its own, the shading parasol punctuated promenades with twirling and flirting colors. Waterproofed in the late seventeenth and early eighteenth centuries, the umbrella developed a second utilitarian use for the walker: having long served people against scorching sun, it would now shield them from drenching rain. By 1800 this plebeian cousin of the fashionable parasol became the common companion of all urban pedestrians—to the consternation of London carriage drivers whose views open and raised umbrellas blocked.

Unfortunately for its aspiring owners, the umbrella offered a kind of prima facie evidence that its owner walked and, thus, lacked a carriage or means to take one. Yet the fish peddlers of France took the possession of an umbrella, which proudly unfurled, as a claim to equality with ladies of nobility.[63]

APPROPRIATE STEPS FOR AN ISLAND AND AN EMPIRE

If the French taught the eighteenth-century Western world proper ways of walking and talking, the British upper classes proved themselves to be the most adept students and disseminators of French ways.[64] Popularized among the nineteenth-century Victorian middle classes, English etiquette—shaped by French manners—was readily adopted by respectable folk throughout the British empire.

The teachers of manners linked carriage (whose original fourteenth-century meaning was connected to transport and haulage of goods rather carrying self) to behavior, action, and words. As John Essex expressed in his *The Young Ladies Conduct* (1722), "What I say of good Manners is in relation to the Moral Behaviour, as good Breeding is in the Civil or Ceremonious Deportment of the Body; the last is useful, but the first is absolutely necessary."[65] What Essex and his kind fashioned for the enlightened century became the rules of conduct for prospering merchants and industrialists that emerged in the late eighteenth and early nineteenth centuries. New money dressed itself in courtly ideals and gave itself the social savoir-faire found in Lord Chesterfield's letters. Elevated beyond the barefoot and roughshod working classes, well-heeled politeness became the hallmark of the civilized person in nineteenth-century business, school, and society.[66]

Indeed, nineteenth-century British manners could be described as distilling and consolidating six centuries of European instruction on correct appearance and behavior.[67] Heir of Italian and Spanish teachers of manners and French courtly ways, the English culturally adjudicated the proper expression of emotion, the appropriate gesture, and the correct body posture or movement. Etiquette prescribed walking on the correct side of someone, or going ahead or staying behind. It instructed its practitioners in bowing, doffing a hat, kissing a hand, wearing clothes and shoes, waving a fan, and when to kneel on one knee and two knees. The lists of prescriptions regarding deportment, poise, respect, and carriage treated walking directly and implicitly. At all times, etiquette required one to stand erect and move decorously.

Free of leggings and boots—at least when off his horse and inside the court—the noble used fancy stockings and knickers, with lace, to show his leg. (Manners further advised him to pull up his long hose to avoid wrinkles.) Also, he was instructed to stand still and solemn. "An unintentional shuffling gait, bent knees, or pigeon toes distract the audience's attention from dialogue and situation"—and made him appear like a rude peasant or a fishmonger.[68] There were general proscriptions against standing splayfooted or with quivering legs. Italian cleric and poet Giovanni Della Casa, who wrote a sixteenth-century book on etiquette, advised that readers should not flay their arms as if sowing a cornfield, or make as much noise as a cart by stamping their high-heeled pattens on the street cobbles.[69]

Amidst the hustle and bustle of the market, English ladies, who did venture into the streets, had to learn to form a sedate and secluded island, moving with "restrained deportment." Women on foot were to offer the illusion of grace, poise, and cleanliness that everyday life denied the rest of miry mankind. American John Adams, serving as an ambassador in Europe at the time of the Revolution, stated the era's ideal of grace as well as an aristocrat could, when explaining why he declined to engage in fashionable skating. "It is not simple velocity or agility that constitutes the perfection of it, but grace," which he apparently lacked. Of skating, riding, fencing, and dancing, he added, "Everything in life should be done with reflection."[70] With grace's burden falling principally on women, their movements were the most restrained and difficult, especially when they were forced to venture out on foot in town or country. Traveling the street women often suffered misfortune, like being splashed by mud from a passing carriage or losing a boot to the sucking muck of a water-covered lane.[71] In Paris, to trust John's wife, Abigail, the streets were appalling. Despite the city elite's obsessive concern for fashion, the splendor of its buildings, and continuous parades of thousands of carriages on display—singularly and by rows, coursing fashionably in and out of town—on foot one encountered a dark and dirty town. The stench was more than she could bear, pathways were heaped with mounds of goods and piles of rubble, everywhere one saw women degraded to prostitution, and "the people themselves were the 'dirtiest creatures' she had ever laid eyes on."[72]

Once indoors, men and women were to discard their coarse apparel and protective high pump overshoes, and study dance in their heelless satin, velvet, silk, cloth, or leather slippers.[73] The dancing master drilled his pupils in the correct manner of standing and walking: the lady was to be taught "to put her feet close to one another, the toes slightly outward . . . in a straight line because that makes you stand firm, easy, and graceful."[74] One early-sixteenth-century dance master insisted that dancing was "one of the best exercises that a Noble man can learne in his young yeares, and that fasioneth the bodie best." Yet he emphasized that one should not emulate one of "those Ordinarie Dauncers . . . who appear to be druncke in their legs . . . in shaking alwaies their feet." Further, he advised, "have good grace in the carriage of your bodie: this is the principal, and without the which all the rest is naught."[75]

The eighteenth-century categorical imperative, which fell on all who wished to move in accord with the higher rotation of the heavens, was that the step be moderate in length, and the heel touch the ground first. "The knee of the leg which moves forward should be straightened just before the foot touches the ground to receive the weight of the body; the whole leg, from the hip, turned slightly outward without strain or effort."[76] Of course, all of these minute regulations governing movement, walking with companions, and address and comportment toward social inferior and superior were aimed at producing solemn, dignified, and yet natural movement and gesturing, whose intent was the discretion, control, and grace that made a visible distinction between social superiors and inferiors.

The eighteenth-century English aristocracy and upper middle class, confident in self and certain in manner and etiquette, prepared to greet the world on their own terms. Correspondingly, they traveled farther and more frequently than their predecessors had. Opportunities, education, and prestige beckoned them from afar. British commerce and politics opened the world to the English upper classes.

Already in the seventeenth century the upper classes had engaged in a combination of the diplomatic and educational trip that formed "a phenomenon that could be called a cultural constant: the Grand Tour."[77] Focused primarily for the English on France, western Germany, and especially Italy, the Grand Tour constituted by standing agreement a fitting finale to class and cultural education. Targeting select social and historical sites, the tour allowed youthful travelers to look at themselves in the continental mirror of their own kind. Relying on carriages, servants, and retainers, the trip excluded all unnecessary walking, carrying, or any other activity (like cleaning and shining boots or loading or unloading goods) that would soil hands, constitute degrading exertion, or cause one to do what one's servants and workers have to do. A genteel rite of passage, it trained one in how to move gracefully about at home and abroad.

By the end of the eighteenth century, suggesting how much travel had been popularized, the Grand Tour became the petit tour as English men and women of far less means started to take trips across the channel for brief stays. Instead of visiting significant peoples and have-to-see places, they pursued their own pleasures and curiosity. Some sought fun in the sun, while others indulged in the shadowy delights of night. Still other travelers began to search off the road for out-of-the-way places. On foot, by horse, and in rented carriages, they sought out the highways and byways of provincial Europe. Some of the upper classes, from nobility and the upper reaches of the middle class, who will be treated in the following chapter, found a source of poetry in walking the back ways. While they discovered by going on foot nature, historic places, and native people, they passed the trudging and carrying people of the countryside.

Considerably improved roads and ships encouraged British travel. Abundant numbers of carriages, now sporting improved springs and roomier interiors, made trips more comfortable and speedier. By the end of the century, a restless spirit (perhaps the same spirit that drove Samuel Pepys a century earlier to make impulsive fifty-mile daily trips on horseback) now pushed young men in their racing phaetons to make weekend visits up to a hundred miles from London.[78]

Other factors stimulated increased travel. London's surging population, which went from 675,000 in 1750 to 865,845 in 1801, exerted increasingly powerful centripetal and centrifugal forces on all of England. The labor and housing demands of the dawning Industrial Revolution set society in motion in the last decades of the eighteenth and first decades of the nineteenth century.[79] In turn, dramatically increased production in shops, mills, and factories accounted for a mounting circulation of goods. An astronomical growth in construction also drove the development of a transportation system, which was notably enhanced at the end of the eighteenth and start of the nineteenth century by the development of canal systems and the invention of the train, iron bridges, and macadam roads. The last, by the prescription of its founder, Ayrshire roadsman John McAdam, required setting three layers of fifty-millimeter crushed local stone, with drainage on both sides, to build a road with a hard, solid, load-bearing surface.

A corresponding acceleration in the movement of people and things in and around London and throughout the kingdom produced what George Eliot called "the rush of everything."[80] Villagers and peasants, in accelerating numbers, tromped on foot, as individuals and whole families, out of villages to nearby towns and distant cities in search of work. High- and lowbrow folks, well-to-do revelers, ordinary pleasure seekers, and commoners filled with uncommon ambition trekked roads even to distant ports. Improved transportation and roads increased walking, having opened the countryside to the idea and the very possibility that migration might improve one's condition.

A society in such motion drew moral commentary. Deploring the increasing homogeneity of manners, dress, and dialect in England during the late eighteenth century, John Bying wrote in his journal, "I wish with all my heart that half the turnpike roads of the kingdom were plough'd up, which have imported London manners, and depopulated the country. I meet the milkmaids on the road, with dress and look of strand misses; and must think that every line of Goldsmith's 'Deserted Village' contains melancholy truths."[81] The Marquis de Bombelles noted, "One does not travel anywhere so much as in England, nowhere has one so many means of departing."[82] "The duc de Lévis thought the English practice of living in a suburb while working in town an example of the '*déplacement*' of all classes."[83] While it eventually took Americans to invent the word for this phenomenon, *commuting,* the English were already by the mid-eighteenth century its quintessential practitioners.[84] Unrecorded, the lower-middle, working, and poor classes continued to take journeys, long and short, on foot.

"A TAMING OF SPACE"

The bustle of England—particularly London—was also felt elsewhere in Western Europe. In increasing numbers, Europeans traveled for reasons of government, business, religion, and culture.[85] And for many others with means and leisure by the second half of the eighteenth century, travel passed from being an obligatory activity to being an elective one.

Tourists in Europe found a world that was more hospitable to travel than the one that preceded it. As in England, in regions of Western Europe, principal roads—a select set of internal arteries of a kingdom—were widened and expanded. Canals, which multiplied in France, Spain, and elsewhere in Europe, facilitated barge travel. Bridges were built, and governments suppressed beggars, brigands, and ruffians as best they could. Riding became more common as the number of horses and carriages increased, and the popularity of horse racing—the quintessence of land speed until the advent of the train—grew.[86]

Travel time between major cities such as London and Edinburgh or Paris and Bordeaux was significantly cut between 1750 and 1790.[87] Confidence in regularity of land and sea travel so transformed European expectations that by the end of the eighteenth century companies could expect contracts to be fulfilled rather than nullified, as they had frequently been previously, by appeals to unpredictable happenings, acts of God.[88] All this constituted what historian Eugen Weber termed "a taming of space," which had the profound effect of setting society in motion.[89] Upper and middle class more and more took to the roads on their horses, in carriages, and in stagecoaches. Farmers and haulers put yet more carts and goods on roads while peddlers, day laborers, journeymen, seasonal workers, and so many others from the middle and bottom ranks of society set out on foot.

Improvements in transportation were far from universal. Local travel still prevailed in the countryside, where the foot still set the pace of the land. The walker still best have trusted company on his travels and still best remain leery of strangers. The majority of eighteenth-century European roads still remained unpaved paths and trails. They were still far more easily traversed by animal hooves and human feet than rolling wheels. Their walkers had to walk with their heads down to watch their step. Often they found themselves moving parallel to a set of ruts, which seasonally transmogrified into barely distinguishable pathways across the landscape.[90] Roads were not marked, weather could catch travelers without refuge, and the walkers who didn't carry what they needed on route soon discovered that food and water were not always accessible. If darkness fell before their destination was reached, ditches, haystacks, or warming manure piles might be the only beds available. If the traveler fell sick along the way, care was essentially a matter of luck.

Travel over considerable distance required calculating one's itinerary in relation to fickle seasons and nebulous frontier and border crossings. Wild animals, chasing dogs, running pigs, bandits, and wind and weather, all of which plagued medieval and Roman traveler, exacerbated the unsteady and risky nature of journeys on foot. No matter the quality of one's carriage and retinue, the chance of accident caused by weather, darkness, uneven surfaces, collapsed bridges, sick horses, collisions, and the like made every wheeled trip an ordeal and an adventure. Until the middle of the eighteenth century and even well into the nineteenth century, walking remained for the many the surest mode of travel. There of course existed a hearty breed of walkers like Jonathan Swift, who could walk thirty miles or more in a day and found strenuous movement necessary for his well-being. ("He would rise at intervals from his secretarial work and run up a hill behind the house and down again—half a mile each way.")[91]

What historian Thomas Macaulay wrote of seventeenth-century travel in England remained true of the next century in much of England and Europe:

> Of the best lines of communication the ruts were deep, the descents were precipitous and the ways often such as it was hardly possible to distinguish, in the dusk, from the unenclosed heath and fen. . . . It was only in fine weather that the whole breadth of the road was available for wheeled vehicles. Often only a narrow track of firm ground rose above the quagmire—coaches stuck fast until a team of cattle could be procured to tug them out of the slough.[92]

Writing of his travels in 1770, Arthur Young confirms Macaulay's observation and explains why every trip on carriage was likely to involve going on foot at one point or other along the way.

> To Sudbury. Turnpike. . . . Ponds of liquid dirt, and a scattering of loose flints just sufficient to lame every horse.
>
> To Wigan. Turnpike. . . . They will meet here with ruts, which I actually measured four feet deep, and floating with mud only from a wet summer; what therefore must it be after a winter?
>
> To Newcastle. Turnpike. . . . A more dreadful road cannot be imagined.
>
> Oxford to Witney. . . . Called by a vile prostitution of language a turnpike.
>
> From Chepstow. Rocky lanes full of hugeous stones as big as one's horse.[93]

Almost everywhere in the European countryside, the foot remained the most reliable mode of transport, especially on low-lying, rocky, sandy, and steep surfaces, or when rain, snow, or powerful winds swept the landscape. Even in mid-eighteenth-century France, which at the time had the best roads in Europe, travel by carriage in midcentury averaged only two to three miles an hour.[94] The fastest journeys covered twenty-five miles a day.[95] Despite advances in bridge and road building, space still prevailed over human will.[96] Even long-distance travelers didn't universally travel by horse and carriage. As in the preceding century, they rode asses, used mules for transport, traveled in litters, and rode in rough carts. They walked whenever need or wish arose.[97]

In France, composed of approximately thirty-six thousand parishes, local routes were still by far the busiest ones. A collection of footpaths, mule paths, and local roads serviced a world of pedestrian peasants who rarely ventured further than four or five miles from their village. Every village had a link to the neighboring *bourg* and market. This link took the form of a *sentier* (single-file footpath), a *carrière* (open to carts in single file and roped animals), or sometimes even a true *voye,* theoretically sixteen feet wide. (Road names commonly reflected their specific functions. There were salt and contraband paths, fish-cart roads, vineyard tracks, sheep trails, cattle routes, or even potters ways.)[98]

Even the king's highways that carried long-distance traffic did not offer smooth and level travel. First developed at the end of the sixteenth century for couriers of the post (on which the king held a monopoly from the time of Louis XIII), these royal routes also became important in the seventeenth and eighteenth centuries for wheeled vehicles and especially mobile artillery.[99] Even though only a few main roads (significantly called *strada di carri,* "carriageways") were even paved, the majority still had narrow dirt surfaces, frequently crisscrossed rickety wooden bridges, lacked signs or light posts, and imposed onerous tolls. Despite servants and money, with axles breaking, horse legs and hooves shattering, and carriages tipping, the well-to-do travelers of main roads remained unable to cushion their trip with comfort. Intermittently, they took to their feet to relieve dizziness, aching bones, and sore buttocks.

Travel conditions worsened as one went south and east from England and France—and so the likelihood that one would end up walking increased. Travel in eighteenth-century Italy brought "extreme discomfort."[100] Carriages—as uncomfortable, according to Goethe, as old-time litters—overturned frequently and turned riders into long-distance walkers. Small-town inns offered walkers and travelers third-rate conditions or, in the south, simply didn't exist at all. Even in tidy, brick-paved Sienna, eighteenth-century traveler and writer Father Labat, O.P., "preferred to sleep on a table wrapped in his cloak with his valise for pillow rather than in a bed full of bugs and fleas."[101] As soon as English agriculturist and travel writer Arthur Young entered Italy, he began to curse its filthy inns and noted roads so bad that coachmen refused to travel them.[102] As elsewhere in Europe, travel held the possibility of encounters with every sort of vagabond, thief, con artist, and beggar.[103] And one's trip was to be punctuated by many long walks.

Conditions deteriorated the farther south and east travelers went. Eighteenth-century noble Lady Mary Wortley Montagu, traveling in 1716 in a chaise, with guards, described the frightful precipices dividing Bohemia from Saxony and remarked on the travelers' cadavers that she saw floating in the Elbe.[104] The early-nineteenth-century French travel writer Marquis de Custine scattered instructions to future travelers throughout his *Empire of the Czar* based on what he had learned during a three-month trip through Russia in 1839.[105] On the quality of Russian roads, he told the rider to expect to be a walker, if he or she were lucky. He reported that the drivers were daredevils and the springless coaches uncomfortable, even dangerous. The roads, normally full of irregularities in surface and varying immensely in width, were in places engulfed in sands into which horses plunged above their knees, losing their wind and breaking their traces. At other spots they were covered by "pools of muck, which conceal large stones and enormous stumps of trees that were very destructive to carriages. Such are the roads of Russia," he concluded, "except during the seasons when they become absolutely impassable."[106]

Almost everywhere in the eighteenth century, travel, however conducted—in carriage, on horseback, or by foot—remained, as its etymology indicates, travail. Yet despite its burdens, ordeals, pains, and dangers, travel steadily expanded throughout European society, especially among the upper classes. Government, trade, commerce, education, and curiosity promoted it; means, leisure, and needs permitted it. Correspondingly, conditions and security on main roads improved, as government built highways and battled highwaymen. Land transportation systems, thanks to more horses, better vehicles, and even select stage runs between main cities, increased. Ships, canals, and roads, as an ensemble, rivaled and surpassed Rome's transportation system. The more money and goods circulated and the more representatives of the established classes traveled, the more society as a whole was set in motion, which meant more and longer movements on foot for urban and rural working classes. Walking remained the most convenient and only affordable way for the vast majority. On foot one hauled goods or wares, or guided one's cart, pulled by ox, donkey, or mule, to local markets. Walking either in bands or groups, country laborers followed, as they did into the twentieth century, seasonal paths of migration for other regions and towns. On foot country folks bade farewell to a place they knew too well in favor of a place, which except for promising words from a relative or friend, they didn't know at all.

As walking remained the common, ordinary, and undifferentiated mode of locomotion for everyday life, it was replaced by riding and selectively refined by the upper classes. Differentiated into promenading and strolling, walking became a vehicle for social identity and display. There even emerged from the upper classes, during the last decades of the eighteenth century and early generations of the nineteenth century, new breeds of walkers. Some, as we will see, left the smooth and safe surfaces of court, garden, city square, and the main routes of the Grand Tour to explore nature, discover hidden pasts, and encounter nations' native peoples. Others, whom we will identify broadly as romantic walkers, sought in walking a means to find and express their real selves and often did this in conscious defiance of those who rode.

⚡ 4 ⚡ Mind over Foot

Romantic Walking and Rambling

B Y the last half of
the eighteenth cen-
tury, those with means
and leisure chose pleasant places to ride and then
stroll. Carriages and coaches had begun the integration of city and countryside in the most
prosperous and populous parts of Europe. Gardens, parks, city walls, and nearby riversides,
forests, and villages all afforded a place for fancy
and recreational footing.[1] In this period walking
went from being a leisure activity of the aristocracy to a popular pursuit of the upper middle
classes. Originally done in carriages (*Promenaden
en Carosses*), promenading on foot grew in popularity.[2] Increasingly in Germany, men and
women began to see their public strolls as a
means to health, wholeness, and community. In
this way walking moved from indoors to outdoors, from tailored garden lanes to tree-lined
avenues, from ramparts and city overlooks to the

surrounding countryside. (Revealingly, the German words *Spazieren* ["walking"] and *Wandeln* ["wandering"] remained synonyms until the 1830s, when walking in the city and hiking in the countryside, differentiated in fact, went their separate linguistic ways.)[3]

Starting in the last decades of the nineteenth century, Romanticism offered a new definition of walking as it directed walkers towards solitude, on the one hand, and communion with the countryside and nature, on the other. With its defining aspirations for feeling, expression, and union with self, nature, and others, as well as its simultaneous preoccupation with the unique, singular, and historical, Romanticism opposed the Enlightenment's quest for order and control. Articulated by a range of thinkers from German Georg Wilhelm Friedrich Hegel (1770–1831) to American Ralph Waldo Emerson (1803–1882), Romanticism in its philosophical form of Transcendentalism sought by metaphor and vision to overcome the limits and categories imposed on thought by Aristotle and Kant. Its underlying hope, with variation of statement, was to find communion, whether it be through spirit, nature, or community, with the ultimate source of being.

Diverse and conflicting in its impulses and forms, Romanticism outfitted the minds of nineteenth-century Western walkers, especially hikers, mountain climbers, and countryside ramblers, with uplifting reasons for setting out on foot. With feeling, sentiment, passion, and nostalgia, romantic walkers could idealize their walks, rambles, and hikes as means to attain direct contact with nature and natives. A sweeping cultural revolution, which influenced the writing of history, literature, and philosophy, and the making of arts and fashions, Romanticism changed walking. It took it from being a lower-class necessity and an upper-class select activity, and transformed it for those with means and a certain subjectivity into an elevated vehicle for experiencing nature, the world, and the self.

These poetic pedestrians of the upper classes left off strolling in courts, squares, gardens, and places where promenading carriages assembled, and they took to walking alone or in small groups, in out-of-the-way and even sublime places. Romanticism encouraged walkers—in early generations as individuals and in subsequent generations as groups of adventurous tourists—to venture into remote landscapes and forgotten places where they would ramble and explore. For romantic natural scientists, walking, in fact, was the best means to study the earth up close.

Casting themselves in opposition to the sedentary and fixed confines of court and city, romantic walkers made going out on foot an act of repudiating those who strolled and promenaded. They used their rambling, hiking, exploring, and even mountain climbing as means to encounter unique landscapes, to make contact with traditional peoples, or to connect with popular and democratic society, which lived and went on foot. Walking for them expressed their feelings and uniqueness.

NECESSARY CONDITIONS

Significant material, social, and cultural changes had to occur and coalesce so that walking could be perceived as something other than a largely undifferentiated matter of necessity for the many and a refined activity and diversion for the few. In order to be positively differentiated from riding in a carriage and going on horseback, it had to be given intrinsic worth as a unique way of experiencing and knowing the world. In effect, walking had to be transformed into an indispensable "poetic" mode of locomotion offering a sense of communion and an elevated state of mind. Romanticism did this.

This transformation also depended in its origin and especially its popularization on the existence, at least in some measure, of safe and controlled spaces in the countryside. It depended on improvements in transportation, which allowed trips on foot to be taken at desired locations without one having to walk to and from them. It was contingent on walks that at least did not entail the high probability of the misfortunes of robbery, murder, and starvation. In effect, Romantic idealizations and enactments of walks in the countryside were predicated on an improved—if far from fully articulated or truly developed—system of transportation, more effective government control, increased policing, better roads, and more and better carriages and horses.

Beyond these conditions, walking and travel, as we have already in part seen, had to be idealized and popularized as instrumental in forming a new self, art, and science. Romanticism, the agent of this change, had to validate the countryside and nature as fresh sources of human feeling, knowledge, and experience. It had to lure walkers' curiosity and sympathy beyond class and locale. Associated with the early nineteenth-century origins of folklore and anthropology, it had to lead the countryside rambler to encounter diverse peoples and their customs and beliefs and embrace them as expressions of the same nature and God. It had to depict—as romantic artists did so well—nature as beautiful, rich in variety, and awe inspiring. It had to entice the walker with the promise of elemental, sublime, and even religious experiences.

Romanticism, in turn, had to mutate the subjectivity fostered at the backs of gardens and along the edges of promenade grounds, and set hearts imagining and longing for more distant places. Even if walkers could count on walking better roads and finding more dependable transportation, Romanticism had to convince the potential walker that going on foot was a true way to experience self, nature, and truth as one.

WORDS ALONG THE WAY

Romantic thinkers argued for walking as a way to free the captive self from the artificial, urban, and mechanical world and to connect with one's true inheritance.[4] Already in the 1770s, Flintshire naturalist Thomas Pennant, Britain's first great tour guide, left the main roads to discover "the authentic natural-born Briton," the descendants of the earliest tribes that had survived "the onslaught of modern civilization."[5] Those bored by the Grand Tour and in search of the real Britain now had at their disposal turnpikes that cut in half travel time from London to Chester or Edinburgh. From there, donkey, ferryboat, and foot delivered true adventurers to lakes, mountains, and precipices and true encounters with the wild, the picturesque, and the awe inspiring. By going on foot they could enter the heart of enduring Scotland and Wales, where resonated ancient lyrics and epics. By walking one swore one's allegiance to the past. To be a true patriot one went on foot.[6]

English romantic poet William Wordsworth sealed his devotion to the country by walking incalculable miles in the Lake District of England and in Europe. Affirming his allegiance to place, step by step, verse by verse, he affirmed the local and rural character of England's true life.[7] For Wordsworth, as for his fellow romantics, walking revivified the path and commons that gave life to the English landscape and its traditional customs. Starting in the sixteenth century, enclosure—the three-century process of land appropriation by commercial farming—culminated, according to its critics, in the middle of the nineteenth century by taking control of more than 50 percent of the nation's fields and closing a corresponding number of commons and walking ways.[8]

Wordsworth's poetry formed the trailhead of a tradition of poetic pedestrianism that reaches from English Romanticism to Americans Whitman and Thoreau to the Japanese poet Basho. Wordsworth's poetry disencumbered walker of polite and mannered self. He substituted country freedom for courtly stricture and urban constriction. An aesthetic vagabondage, his walking was on a continuous pilgrimage. It promised to heal the self's broken relationship with the world. His artful wanderings offered an alternative to congestion and untamable change. He fostered a romantic ideology that set paths against roads, countryside against city, walker against rider.[9]

Wordsworth's pedestrianism, however, did not follow from a universal elevation of walking from the realm of necessity to that of choice. On the contrary, his type of country walking, so dependent on having means and leisure, occurred at the end of the eighteenth and the beginning decades of the nineteenth century, when the great majority of people in the West still walked because they had to, not because they chose to. Like the vast majority of peoples of the entire world, the British common folk were without money to own horse and carriage or to travel, even if they were available, on barge or on train. They still walked to gain their daily bread, and to travel meant to go on foot. Wordsworth's poetry predated at least by fifty years the full transportation revolution, which made fast and cheap travel available and, thus, dissolved walking's perennial association with necessity, poverty, and vagrancy.[10]

Country walking in general did not need to be free of its associations with the working and lower classes for it to be practiced for exclusive pleasure and exotic leisure by those with means. Cultural historian Robin Jarvis identifies a long parade of people who traveled on foot—by choice and for pleasure—even prior to Wordsworth's 1798 *Lyrical Ballads,* a manifesto for romantic poets. William Coxe traveled the continent on foot in the 1770s and 1780s, in the same period Foster Powell engaged in all sorts of record-breaking athletic pedestrianism and William Bowles carried out a walking tour of the continent that started in the north of England before progressing to Antwerp and going down the Rhine.[11] John "Walking" Stewart, who became a kind of holy walker ("an Indo-Scottish *saddhu*"), topped all romantics in the pedestrian ordeal he attached to his search for the inner truth. He hiked from India via the Arabian desert, France, and Spain back to England in the 1780s.[12] Carl Moritz, a German pastor who persisted in walking through southern England on foot in 1782, did so to the befuddlement and amusement of those who rode past him and of inn keepers, who were not easily convinced that a walker had the means to pay them or the sanity to restrain himself from doing something else that was crazy. Radical orator John Thewell, a son of the working class, made his narrative of walking, *The Peripatetic,* written in 1793 during the heart of the French Revolution, a pedestrian's view of differences between the downtrodden and the elevated.[13]

Tourism, on foot and on horseback, was well established in Wordsworth's very own Lake District by the 1790s, when he turned walking into poetry.[14] Simultaneously, popular romantic foot travel occurred in Wales in the 1790s. There it attracted Wordsworth's friend Samuel Taylor Coleridge, who stepped out the beat of his verses, while making a walking tour of more than six hundred miles in the summer of 1794.[15] In 1798, *Monthly Magazine*'s semiannual review of literature noted, "We are happy to observe an increasing frequency of these pedestrian tours: *to walk,* is beyond all comparison, the most independent and advantageous mode of travelling."[16] In effect, already by the 1820s, considerably in advance of the establishment of a new public transport network, walking had become a preferred form of travel among small and romantic segments of the educated and leisured middle class. They did this on the condition of not having to carry a considerable load or having to walk to or from their principal route. In effect, they did on occasion and by choice what the majority carried out daily as a matter of course. Their rambles in the countryside were begun at a time when walking still expressed the condition and stereotypes associated with physical work and social inferiority.[17]

In his *Instructions to Pedestrian Tourists* (1821), writer Robert Newell made an argument for walking as "the safest, and most suited to every variety of road; it will often enable you to take a shorter track, and visit scenes (the finest perhaps) not otherwise accessible; it is healthy, and, with a little practice, easy; it is economical."[18] Stressing health, recreation, and aesthetic purposes, writers like Newell pitched walking to the professional classes. By the early nineteenth century, walking in part replaced the Grand Tour, which had already been dramatically downsized in the eighteenth century, as increasing numbers drawn from the middle class traveled for shorter periods simply for pleasure, and which had been completely decapitated by the French Revolution and Napoleon.

Although improved material and social conditions fostered the development of the walking tour, its increased popularity depended far more on Romanticism and the cultural fashions it spawned. It launched people on outings into the countryside. There they saw picturesque landscapes, walked places steeped in history, and met the authentic inhabitants. Indeed, people of means and leisure were set in motion well before "the golden age of coaching," which didn't dawn until 1820–1836.[19] With no concern for the majority of humanity's onerous dependence on its feet, romantically inspired walkers took to the road by choice. They did this to the bewilderment and disdain of those who walked out of necessity. They carried little, often used a well-crafted walking stick, which they may have even nicknamed, and wore what they idealized as appropriate dress—which obviously set them apart from the folk they idealized and, arguably, essentially invented.[20] Inwardly, the romantic walkers followed a subjective path. Rejecting the desire of the privileged upper classes to parade before and shine in the eyes of one's own kind, they sought a more ethereal goal: they would distinguish themselves by being true to themselves, nature, and membership in greater spiritual communities.

No one better delivers us to the origins and heart of romantic walking than eighteenth-century French writer and thinker Jean-Jacques Rousseau, the father of romantic pedestrianism in Europe and North America. He was born into the working classes in 1712, and much of his early life "was that of a wanderer, an adventurer, the life of a hero of a picaresque novel."[21] Viewing himself as a perpetual outsider even in his recognized but never prosperous years in Paris from the middle 1740s to 1750s, and plagued especially in the final decades with restlessness fed by growing paranoia, Rousseau was a determined and deliberate lifetime walker.

"Of all writers known to history," Will and Ariel Durant write, "he was the most devoted walker."[22] Rousseau himself acknowledged his indebtedness to walking in *The Confessions,* declaring, "I can only meditate when I am walking. When I stop I cease to think; my mind only works with my legs."[23] His very road to Damascus, so to speak, occurred on one of his frequent six-mile walks in 1749 from Paris to Vincennes to visit his imprisoned friend, Denis Diderot, editor of the great Enlightenment literary project, the *Encyclopédie.* On route the inspiration came to him that won him a prize for his response to the Academy Dijon question about the relation between the nature of progress in the arts and sciences and its nature in the field of morals. His response that a reverse relationship existed between progress and morals resulted in his *Discourse on the Sciences and Arts,* which established him as a serious light in Paris.[24]

However, for most of his life Rousseau went on foot for the same mundane reasons his working-class contemporaries did. Walking proved the most available and only affordable way to change places in the world. Notably, when Rousseau did walk, he was forced to move on his heels because of corns. On occasions, when he rode in a carriage, thanks to the generosity of employer or patron, he was not spared pain from his ailing kidneys that severely bothered him from his twenties on.

Rousseau's earliest journeys on foot led him from Geneva to Turin to Annecy to Lausanne to Neuchâtel to Bern to Chambéry to

Lyons.[25] On one count, his extensive travels across Switzerland and France resembled those of novice touring guildsmen, members of the *camponnage,* who as apprentice craftsmen annually circled France on foot like their medieval predecessors.[26] On another count, his life reads like a bizarre adventure, beginning with his flight from his native Geneva at sixteen to escape a life of plebeian engraver's apprentice and his finding refuge as a Catholic convert in Savoy. He then made his own way as a footman in Turin, a student in a choir school in Annecy, a lover of a baroness in Chambéry, an interpreter to a Levantine mountebank, an itinerant musician, a private tutor, and then a secretary in Venice. He did all this before establishing himself in Paris when he was still in his early thirties.[27]

Where the need for material security did not force him to go, his ambition and quest for inner peace drove him. Inner contradictions that never let him feel at home for long always tempted him to take to his heels. With an active but repressed sexual drive, he experienced companionship and the sense of home with older, rich, and mothering women—whom, over time and with much verbose strolling in garden and countryside (a common and inexpensive means of courtship), he transformed into lovers.[28]

Rousseau trusted his walking feet not only to secure him opportunities and to cure his wounded heart but also to set himself in moral contrast with those who rode. He believed that his class superiors, the privileged, artificially rode while the sincere, like himself and the rest of the working world, went on foot. Rousseau was certainly no friend of sophisticated and carriage-filled Paris. He repeatedly remarked in *The Confessions,* which at points reads like a spiritual *cahiers de doléance*—or perhaps the Magna Carta of romantic malaise—that he was "born for the country."[29] Under this rubric he announced themes as old as Vergil and as recent as Earth Day. "At Venice amidst the stir of business . . . at Paris, in the whirl of society," he wrote, "always the memory of my woods and streams and the solitary walks would come to distract and sadden me."[30]

In *The Confessions,* written in Paris in 1770, Rousseau depicted Paris, the pinnacle of his youthful ambition, as the antithesis of the country and the moral life to which the aged moralist repeatedly and earnestly dedicated himself.[31] He described the streets of Paris as being at the heart of his bitter disappointment upon his very first encounter with the city.

> How greatly did my first sight of Paris belie the idea I had formed of it! . . . I imagined a city of most imposing appearance, as beautiful as it was large, where nothing was to be seen but splendid streets and palaces of marble or gold. As I entered through the Faubourg Saint-Marceau, I saw nothing but dirty stinking little streets, ugly black houses, a general air of squalor and poverty, beggars, carters, menders of clothes, sellers of herb-drinks and old hats.[32]

Near the conclusion *of The Confessions* Rousseau declared, as if to issue the romantic walker's manifesto, that free and open country walking was superior to sitting, riding, or being confined in the busy city and that his own idle ambling and rambling was superior to that of society's artificial conventions.

> The idleness I love is not that of an indolent fellow who stands with folded arms in perfect inactivity, and thinks as little as he acts. It is the idleness of the child who is incessantly on the move without ever doing anything, and at the same time it is the idleness of a rambling old man whose mind wanders, while his arms are still.[33]

The inhibiting niceties of the refined drove Rousseau to praise rustic delights. He repeated in *The Confessions* how he was uncomfortable in the society of educated men, shy and wordless before beautiful women, and most happy when in the countryside. Rousseau made his determination to escape court and city a motor force of his being, and transformed his very solitary walks into an identity.

Discontented and frustrated with his relationships with Paris luminaries and uncertain whether he should return to his native city, Protestant Geneva, where he might not be able to make a living, Rousseau left Paris in 1756 for a small cottage twelve miles away in the countryside. Furnished to him by his friend and sponsor, Mme Épinay, the cottage served his needs and those of his ever-solicitous illiterate common-law wife, Thérèse Levasseur, with whom he shared a home and had three children, all of whom were turned over to the orphanage.[34] There, he "thrilled to the nightingale's song" and, reminding an American reader of Thoreau's relation to his Walden Woods, he did not leave "a path, a plantation, a wood, or any corner around his house unexplored."[35] Rousseau claimed that his place in the French countryside formed a platform, which, "not wild but solitary, transported me in mind to the ends of the earth."[36]

In his final work, *Les reveries d'un promeneur solitaire* (*The Reveries of a Solitary Walker*, 1778), Rousseau identified happiness with a consciousness free of conflicts. He sought an impossible unity between sentiment and thought, between what is seen and what is experienced, between the walking foot and the reflecting mind. In his idealized literary ambles through the countryside, Rousseau spared himself the conditions of the common rural walk. He did not carry a heavy backpack, lead a stubborn animal, fend off an attack from a mean dog, evade a guileful beggar, battle swarming insects, fail to avoid a simple fall, or experience the inevitable fatigue of a long walk. He simply sauntered to celebrate his consciousness.

Starting in 1765, fifty-three-year-old Rousseau supplemented his strolling with plant collecting.[37] "Botany," claimed Rousseau, anticipating the thoughts of many of his followers in England, Germany, and North America, as well as subsequent modern country walkers, "makes me forget men's persecutions, their hatred, scorn, insults, and all the evils with which they have repaid my tender and sincere attachment for them. It transports me to peaceful habitats among simple and good people."[38]

However, Rousseau found no magic plant to stave off his mounting psychological conflicts and his restless itinerancy. In his final years, until his death in 1778, Rousseau's inner life made him more a persecuted vagrant than a joyous itinerant. Afflicted by intensifying paranoia, he believed all of literate Europe was joined in a conspiracy to defame him as "*a moral monster*" with "*a soul of mud*."[39] With phantoms of accusations closing in on him, Rousseau walked the landscape in a spirit not dissimilar to those who pace asylums and city streets. Testifying to a sense of being under constant surveillance, he wrote, "The ceiling above my head has eyes, the walls around me have ears. . . . I am hemmed about by watchful and malevolent spies."[40]

Rousseau responded to his condition the only way he knew how—with another lengthy book, *Rousseau, juge de Jean-Jacques,* which he published in 1776, two years before his death. He dedicated it to proving that there was no great contradiction between his professed ideals and his private life. Shortly after he completed *Rousseau, juge de Jean-Jacques,* his interior crisis reached a crescendo. Rousseau took to walking the streets of Paris handing out self-printed circulars to anonymous passersby. Addressed "*To every Frenchman who still loves justice and truth,*" the circular sought vindication in the eye of the imagined stranger.[41] He sought at random the vindication that had been withheld almost from the beginning from this self-conscious walker and wanderer.[42]

A CLASSIC TRAVELER

Influenced as a youth by the contagious sentiments of Rousseau, Johann Wolfgang von Goethe (1749–1832) left the garden and the common route of the Grand Tour. One of the formulators of the German *Naturphilosophie,* Goethe sought more than an abstract and mechanical view of nature. He sought to find the underlying elements of art and nature during an extended sojourn in Italy from 1786 to 1788.[43] In accord with the great majority of his fellow European tourists, Goethe attributed no intrinsic good to walking. He made his travel as easy on himself as possible, resorting to horse and mule, carriage or litter, the *chaise-a-porteur.* He might have joined his opinion to writer Richard Pyke's assessment of the Italian leg of the Grand Tour: "One thing the traveler never did—walk. Only outlaws and madmen walked; it was considered neither safe nor a pleasure."[44] Nevertheless, Goethe was willing to walk to get where he wanted to go and see what he wished to see. On his trip to Italy, especially Sicily, Goethe walked a lot.

Interest in the sciences of geology, botany, and archeology took Goethe on foot off well-traveled roadways.[45] After a lengthy stay in Rome, whose streets he walked regularly, he was attracted by the powerful magnet Pompei, whose excavation had begun in the 1740s, as well as by Mt. Etna and Sicily. Each site in Sicily required considerable

walking and background reading. The latter was furnished by Eng-
lishman Patrick Brydone's *Journey to Sicily and Malta* (1773).[46] He also
read with a passion Prussian ambassador and German archeologist
Baron J. H. von Riedesel's *Reise durch Sicilien und Gross* (1771), writing
that it was "a little book I carry near my heart like a breviary or talis-
man."[47]

Goethe believed Sicily to be the nexus where Europe, Africa, and
Asia met; it was the locus at which the fullest crystallization of nature,
history, and art history occurred. Sicily's singular fruits did not spare
him—or his fellow romantic travelers for the next century and half—
its traveler's thorns: terrible inns and taxing hikes up steep mountain
and seaside ascents. And then too going on foot brought those continual and unmediated face-to-face encounters with the misery of the
poor and the discrepancy between them and the richest. On the
labyrinthine and revealing colorful side streets of Palermo, Goethe observed,

> A long thin gentleman dressed in a coat fit for grand ceremonies [pro-
> ceeded] with great calm and dignity along the middle of the street,
> through the rubbish. Smartly dressed and powdered, with clothes of
> silk, his hat under one arm, sword at his side, and elegant shoes with
> buckles decorated with precious stones: thus he walked along, calm and
> serious, and everyone's gaze was fixed on him.[48]

Along Sicily's main thoroughfare to the sea, a muck-laden road,
streamed "the famous carriage parade of the nobility," who toward
evening "drive out of town toward the harbour to take the air, chat
with each other, and, above all, flirt with the ladies." Inquiring about
its excessive filth and why it could not be carted away on the backs of
donkeys as in Naples, Goethe received an ironic reply. Perhaps, his
source responded, the muck covers the disgraceful condition of the
pavement, which reveals the embezzlement of public money; or perhaps the nobility "keep the streets thus because they like a soft, elastic
surface for their carriages."[49]

Goethe called Palermo's recently established public gardens "La
Flora," and there he intently strolled and observed "the most wonderful corner in the world. . . . Here [plants] grow luxuriantly and freshly

in open air; perfectly fulfilling their destiny, they make themselves manifest." Here in this beautiful garden, Goethe felt he caught a glimpse of the ancient chimera: the first plant, the *Urpflanze*.[50] Outside Palermo, Goethe surveyed the temple at Segesta, clambering the steep hill to its theater hundreds of yards above. Traveling along the southern coast of Sicily, he practiced geology and botany, while admiring the magnificence of the fallen temples of Agrigento and the rich inland valleys of southeastern Sicily. In eastern Sicily, Goethe climbed up to the amphitheater on the high cliffs of Taormina. His ascent on foot to the fiery summits of Mt. Etna was rebuffed by blustering morning winds.[51]

Goethe returned to Naples seasick, a victim of a long and perilous storm.[52] Yet he judged his arduous trip to Sicily to be of inestimable value: "Without Sicily, Italy leaves no image in the soul; [Sicily] is the key to everything."[53]

OUT OF THE GARDEN

The romantic walkers, who spiritually arose out of the upper literary classes, had their secondary and material genesis in Europe's broader control of spaces and life. This control was witnessed in court, palace, country home, and city. It grew as Europe, at home, took fuller control of its own farms and fields and, abroad, increasingly explored, charted, and mapped the world. Sovereignty, shaped by enlightened monarchs and new republics, and emboldened by the French Revolution and Napoleon, further conquered the geographical recesses of nation. Improved ship building, canal building, and boat travel, along with bridge and road construction, increasing commerce, and prospering agriculture, accelerated the conquest of space.

The garden held a special place in defining European conceptions of space and nature. It proved to be a training ground for the sensibility of future romantic walkers. A revolution occurred between the Renaissance garden and the enlarged Baroque garden, which was a cultivated landscape that need no longer produce anything more than mental, physical, and social stimulation for walkers in the seventeenth century.[54] In turn, it was expanded in the eighteenth century, while at the same time it relinquished its disciplined and symmetrical nature and its reliance on statues and monuments. As typified by the English garden in opposition to the Baroque garden, the new garden was freer in form and borders; it stood as a botanical celebration of nature's rich and spontaneous forms. Here was a place of exercise for those who didn't need to work, a private place to sit or pace, in hopes of achieving less conflicted feelings and greater happiness. Here in the garden was a place for romantic walkers to warm up for their solo flights into nature. A larger revolution of mind and sensibility spurred the walker out into the world. New conceptions of nature and improved physical sciences winged the modern walker's feet with curiosity. Geology, whose implications were debated in the press, became a popular pastime in the first decades of the nineteenth century, in Britain, Europe, and America, as did botany. Landscapes became places for painting, detailed observation, and discovery of the beginnings, processes, and ends of life. Art, emerging natural sciences, and philosophy went hand in hand in preparing the romantic sojourn into nature.[55]

The adventures of explorers like English Captain Cook, Americans Lewis and Clark, and German Alexander von Humboldt led travelers to imagine places worlds away. Foot followed expanding imagination, as the eighteenth century calculated the heavens, articulated the laws of nature, mapped the dimensions of unknown continents and boundless seas, and attributed sublimity and cosmic forces to landscapes.

For the sake of advancing science, starting at the end of the eighteenth and the beginning of the nineteenth century, amateur scholars and then academics began to travel the world. Botany and geology, profoundly associated with national economic interest, followed and preceded the flag. In the same period, archeology focused scholars on Italy, Greece, and the eastern Mediterranean, while the emerging studies of folklore and ethnography turned their followers in the direction of folk and primitive peoples.

In this same period, sensibilities ran almost as if they were untethered. They invented peoples and places, craved for freedom, and conjured revolutions. At the same time, romantic thinkers, like Walter Scott and Walter Grimm, who sought out medieval folk tales, customs, and costumes, provided peoples and nations with myths, legacies, and matching landscapes.[56]

A disciple of Goethe, the young Alexander von Humboldt grasped the power of mind not just to apprehend the environment but also to transform human understanding of nature and the human place in it.[57] Inspired by French navigator Louis Antoine de Bougainville's *Voyage autour du monde* (1771) and German naturalist Johann Reinhold Forster's *Observations around the World* (written about Captain James Cook's second global voyage), von Humboldt conducted a five-year expedition (1799–1804) through Central and South America and Cuba.[58] Setting the standards of contemporary scientific work, his observations were characterized by painstaking empiricism, remarkable breadth of intellectual interest, passion for the beauties of nature, and a commitment to a universal science.[59]

Humboldt did his science on foot. He traveled more than six thousand miles walking, leading a mule, and paddling a canoe. He explored the course of the Orinoco River and the source of the Amazon River and their connections, while ascending peaks of the Peruvian Andes, laying the foundation for meteorology and physical geography. He offers glimpses of the pedestrian ordeals required by his expedition, which—to choose but a single measure of its immensity—"collected 60,000 plants of which only a tenth were known in Europe."[60] He traveled day in and day out over the course of five years on foot. He immersed himself in jungles, climbed to mountaintops, and scoured valley bottoms. Against the daily inertia caused by the need to take meticulous measurements and engage in exhaustive collecting, Humboldt led a caravan composed of as many as twenty mules and their Indian handlers along severe and difficult slopes. The expedition experienced native attacks, sickness, and even starvation, punctuated by uplifting moments such as the one on the Chimborazo (a twenty-thousand-foot inactive volcano in Ecuador, eight thousand feet higher than Etna), where Humboldt found butterflies, "borne by ascending currents of air to those almost unapproachable solitudes, which man, led by a restless curiosity or an unappeasable thirst for knowledge, treads with adventurous but cautious steps."[61]

Echoing descriptions written by Goethe, Humboldt reveals the passion that animated romantic travelers, scientists, and poets. His evocations of the whole of nature in its constituent parts made him not just the defining voice of natural science, the arch-poet of romantic explorers, but also, one might say, the spiritual founder of ecology.[62] Humboldt's journey, so important to the story of American walking, inspired the partially simultaneous 1803–1806 Lewis and Clark expedition to the Pacific Northwest. His example brought Swiss natural scientists Louis Agassiz and Arnold Guyot to explore the United States. On foot, Agassiz from Harvard and Guyot from Princeton defined the young republic's science and its preliminary knowledge of the West.[63] His influence sparked Ralph Waldo Emerson's and Henry David Thoreau's turn to nature on foot, and inspired the young John Muir to walk the world in pursuit of nature. In 1867 Muir quit a promising job in Indiana and set out on his famous thousand-mile walk, which carried him from Indiana to Florida, where a life-threatening bout of malaria interrupted his goal of reaching Central and South America, where his beloved Humboldt had trod two generations before.[64] Humboldt's work inspired the young Charles Darwin, an intent observer of life in the pond in the back yard of his childhood home. In this way, Humboldt shaped the passionate intellect that directed the ever faithful foot toward nature on a pedestrian journey that took alternate steps between romantic awe and scientific knowledge.

TOWARDS NATURE

Other cultural currents joined the influence of Humboldt and the sciences in leading walkers out of their gardens and cities in search of nature. Already in the late seventeenth century, before Romanticism, there was a corresponding shift of mind that transformed the general perception of nature and its mountain- and seascapes. An array of religious and aesthetic thinkers began to think of nature in a way no peasant or farmer could: independently of its ability to supply food and subsistence. Even in the barren and sterile, they espied the sublime and the presence of God. Turning away from the conventional view of mountains as dreary and forbidding places, they started to see them as beguiling wild domains that invited climbing adventures, inspired art, and even promised transcendence.[65]

Dawning Romanticism, in turn, elevated mountains into subjects of awe and beauty.[66] European landscape painters such as Salvator Rosa and Claude Lorrain depicted European mountain ranges, as John Ruskin put it, as "the beginning and the end of all natural scenery."[67] Aesthetics shaped the sensibility of Europe's explorers and climbers, while permitting Americans (desperate to distinguish their new nation as a place of singular beauty) to view their mountains proudly "as the freshest representatives of God's handiwork."[68] Transforming mountains and other landscapes into stylized images for cultural consumption, artists and writers defined for future generations where foot would step, what eye would see, and why heart would throb.

Among the developments stirred by these images and sentiments was mountain tourism and then mountain climbing, the most exclusive, expensive, and athletic test. Starting with hiking in the late eighteenth century, it took mature form with actual climbs in the Alps in the 1830s, 1840s, and 1850s and with the 1857 formation by the middle class of the British Alpine Club, which resembled the scientific and geographic societies that proliferated in the first half of the nineteenth century.[69] Mountain climbing was influenced by the development in English public (that is, elite private secondary) schools and universities of muscular Christianity, which joined faith, vitality, individual conditioning, and strength.[70] Although romantic in its essential themes of heroic struggle and humanity against the elements, in its origins mountain climbing was fused to British militarism, patriotism, and empire. With English climbers the prime teachers of this lofty act of strenuous and dangerous walking, British-like climbing clubs quickly sprang up elsewhere in Europe and America. With the declaration in 1852 that Mount Everest was the tallest peak in the world, the race to its top was on.[71]

Appealing to the young, bold, leisured, and rich (especially when the most distant and challenging expeditions were in question), this most rigorous, selective, and expensive form of walking and hiking amply rewarded its successful practitioners—the ones that it didn't kill. It gave them not just a sense of the highest distinction of human exertion but also the feeling that they had taken risks for the delivery of the whole world at their feet. "Alpine travel," in the opinion of Swedish anthropologists Jonas Frykam and Orvar Löfgren, was a way of buying hardship for the middle class and carrying out, in the eyes of the local mountain peasants, "work without a purpose."[72]

Wild beaches and rugged coastlines underwent a less dramatic but similar transformation in the late eighteenth and nineteenth centuries. Romantic artists metamorphosed them from untamed and infertile places that generations of earlier travelers had avoided into sites prized for their simplicity and solitude. The collective desire to go to the shore arose in the period from 1750 to 1840. Ocean coasts began to appear as a refuge from teeming and sullying civilization. It was where walkers and numbers of romantic writers experienced first hand the infinite and awe-inspiring terror of the raging ocean.[73]

Showing a more benign and popular side to beach walking—and sitting and lying by the end of eighteenth century—Germans, Scandinavians, and Russians—ever in search of sun—were imitating the British aristocracy, which turned the beaches of Italy into mandatory stopping-off spots. While the early and dramatic romantics made the seaside a place for self-knowledge, by the middle of the nineteenth century direct railroad lines gave easy and quick access to scores of European and American beaches. Along them sea resorts and cottages sprang up, allowing groups to install themselves in places that matched their tastes and means. Beaches were used for their supposed healing waters and curing fresh air.

Southern England's Brighton beach drew London society. Its popularity with the upper and middle class was tied to medical prescriptions for exercise and a belief that healing could be found in bathing in and drinking salt water.[74] Beaches, which brought people to the edge of nature, also served as getaways, hosted family reunions, often involved a lot of food and drink, and provided a chance to shop, to mope about, or simply to sit and read. The beach offered choices to its walkers. One could walk for solitude or to keep company, travel the entire length of the beach or hike nearby dunes or cliffs. Walking on the sand or in the water, one could exercise or comb for shells, wade into the water to battle the surf or even swim. Weighed down by heavy bloomers and moral strictures, women entered water at risk of life and reputation. Boardwalking at the beach, which at Brighton's Styne was done to music, put strollers desirous to see and be seen between human structures on one side and nature on the other.[75]

Romantics fashioned the aesthetics of places, which subsequent waves of serious tourists imbibed. In search of self and nature, "artists and writers," as Frykmann and Lögren succinctly state, "became the vanguards of the new tourism."[76] Their select peregrinations led away from the more immediately accessible and productive lands of the thriving economy and toward more remote historic places such as Sicily, Sardinia, and Greece, or wherever nature existed in the form of "rugged and exotic landscapes."[77]

The first nineteenth-century guidebook writer, German Karl Baedeker (1801–1859), described the enriched experience walking gave the traveler, frequently using the phrase "*sich (etwas) erwandern*"— to get (something) out of walking.[78] As early as the 1830s, tourist entrepreneur Claude François Denecourt, a veteran of Napoleon's army, responded to the increased popularity of the weekend walk. Frykmann and Lögren offer this synopsis of his early efforts to get Parisians out into the countryside:

> During the 1830s Denecourt transformed the king's forest around Fontainebleau outside Paris into a popular destination. He was inspired by the romantic cult of the woods, but his ambition was to make the wilderness user-friendly. Thus he developed [with the use of blue paint and a system of arrows] the nature walk. . . . In 1837 he could offer visitors a number of *promenades solitaires*. The blue arrows led you along rambling paths, which were equipped at suitable distances with attractive sights. . . . This was something far more adventurous than the park promenades, and thanks to the newly established railway between Paris and Lyons, a rapidly growing number of Parisians made the expedition to Fontainebleau, in order to walk eight to ten miles.[79]

Romantic voices, which shaped values emergent in the early nineteenth century, also reinforced the choice of pedestrian tourism. They asserted an imperative of nascent democracy: members of the same society should get to know one another. By roving the countryside on foot, one practiced a kind of "landscape patriotism." You could "walk yourself Swedish," as the author Carl Jonas Love Almqvist put it.[80] While commercial, civic, and national interests drove tourism and travel as an industry, individuals traveled for new experiences and identities.[81]

Much of this pedestrian tourism—commercial, recreational, nationalistic, and romantic—might anachronistically be judged by hardcore walking advocates as mere recreational pap, especially in comparison with the arduous tests that went with serious nineteenth-century hiking and climbing.[82] However, as literary critic Paul Fussell remarked, "the terms *exploration, travel,* and *tourism* are slippery."[83] What we would call *exploration,* writers in the middle nineteenth century called *travel,* and what we call *travel* (in phrases like "travel industry") should, by measure of exertion, be reduced to *tourism.*[84] In any case, tourists of the nineteenth century, far less likely to catch a ride or be spared a hike or a climb, often faced physical ordeals and did considerable walking as a matter of course.

In a walking classic, *Shank's Pony,* Morris Marples offers some insights into those who walked for pleasure and travel. "During the second half of the nineteenth and the early years of the twentieth centuries," he wrote, "walking for pleasure was associated particularly with the intellectual classes. Dons, parsons, public school masters, and higher civil servants, members of that intellectual aristocracy . . . tended to include walking if not climbing, among their principal relaxation."[85] Cambridge churchman and scholar of eighteenth-century English thought, Sir Leslie Stephen (1832–1904), furnished an extreme example of dedicated pedestrianism. Aside from race walking, he supplemented his lengthy daily walks—which were a form of speed walking—with at least thirty miles of walking on his regular Sunday outings, which included bucking the ferocious winds in the fens north of Cambridge.[86] Among regular walkers Marples distinguished two basic forms of elective walking. First, there were those who "walked, for exercise and relaxation, in the intervals of their work, either daily or at week-ends"; and second, there were those who, often moved by romantic impulses and destinations, spent their vacations on walking tours.[87]

Hunger for knowledge and adventure, which took people beyond the confines of civilization, delivered them to places where ships and roads came to an end—and wilderness began. In the wild, walking, supplemented by climbing, crawling, wading, and other means of human locomotion, was required for travel and survival. Such superhuman pedestrianism was exemplified by American Arctic explorer Robert Peary, who reached the North Pole in 1909, thanks to an ingenious use of sled dogs and a remarkable tenacity of spirit. Explorer Sir Ernest Shackleton, in his failed 1914–1915 expedition to the South Pole, offered another example. His and his crew's successful escape from cold, ice, sea, mountains, and starvation testified to human ingenuity and will, while it also attested to the indispensable importance of a strong body and legs.

Indeed, in the twenty-first century, even when laboratory, microscopes, computers, and remote sensors carry out and gather so much scientific information and metamorphose so many scientists into sedentary creatures, the need and the romantic impulse to enter into nature on foot still survive. Amateurs and professionals trek on foot across the world to see and gather the earth's rocks, plants, and animals.[88] Going on foot still remains, as it did for Humboldt, the first means for students of nature to gather it in their embrace.[89] Harvard University entomology curator, Philip Jackson Darlington, a collector of extraordinary prowess, exhorted the young naturalist Edward O. Wilson to go out on foot and

> [D]on't stay on the trails when you collect insects. Most people take it too easy when they go in the field. They follow the trails and work a short distance in the woods. You'll get only some of the species that way. You should walk in a straight line through the forest. Try to go over any barrier you meet. It's hard but that's the best way to collect.[90]

A BREED OF MODERN WALKERS

Walking, then, under the tutelage of the romantic mind, thought, sensibility, and sentiment, took new forms in the nineteenth century. As the great majority walked out of necessity and the upper classes strolled and promenaded for pleasure, the heirs of Rousseau, Wordsworth, Goethe, and Humboldt rambled, hiked, mountain climbed, and explored on foot.

For amblers, excursionists, or, to use a word poet Wordsworth coined in a 1791, *pedestrians,* one type of romantic walking is inevitably about the self and words.[91] Another breed of romantic walking appeared in the form of the ethnographer, hiker, or explorer who seeks to contact forgotten peoples or enter unknown places. These walkers, who inevitably saw themselves leaving burgeoning industrial society, abandoned highways and roads for paths, lanes, tracks, trails, towpaths, and bridleways.[92] Their treks retraced the journeys of ancient peoples and the paths of migrants and pilgrims.[93] Traveling from northern to southern Europe, they sought out ruins, which revealed the spirit of antiquity, and followed on foot common medieval routes of beggars, peddlers, highwaymen, pilgrims, and crusaders.[94] Walking a day in the Umbrian countryside enrolled the romantic walker into the pedestrian order of St. Francis. Nineteenth-century British historian Thomas Babington Macaulay believed that by walking he could revivify the seventeenth-century places and battlefields of which he wrote.

Walking provided the romantic walker a way out of the complex society into a simpler and more basic time.[95] If only in imagination, which in truth often matters most, the foot's labor could serve as a poetic, metaphorical, or even ideological means to refashion communities divided in the contemporary world between work and land, city and countryside. Twentieth-century French thinker Paul Valéry declared that walking reactivates the triangular relationship existing among "world, mind, and body."[96]

In the nineteenth century, however, the romantics were not alone in redefining walking. In fact, emerging urban and industrial society, which romantics criticized at almost step, gave rise to new forms of urban walking. There was the urban pedestrian, who, far from Wordsworth's poetic pedestrian, learned as matters of need and work to travel in great cities. He moved on its sidewalks, through its congestion, across intersections, and under police supervision, with a mass of fellow city walkers. Also, later in the century the commuter, whose genesis is in the city, came forth. Another form of urban walker, commuters intermixed walking and evolving public transportation systems, crossing the city according to work hours and time schedules. Also, there appeared in cities the window shopper who, with style, strolled and purchased as he or she went. And finally the sophisticated *flâneur,* born in Parisian bohemia, constituted a type of an urban stroller who, strutting, posing, and lingering at fashionable places, sought interesting angles on the humanity of the city dweller.

However much romantic walkers in the majority directed their steps out of the city into countryside, they perceived the coming of unprecedented orders of transport and society—and didn't like what they saw. As much as any romantic walker, American thinker Thoreau, who was a keen reader of Wordsworth, Rousseau, Goethe, and Humboldt, stood in opposition to the world being formed in Boston on the eastern periphery of his home in Concord, Massachusetts. Across decades, he daily walked, crisscrossing Walden Woods and circumambulating Walden Pond. And never far from his mind were encroaching Boston and the passing railroad. He conceived that, already having transformed much of the east, the new national order of power and commerce was moving west at accelerating speeds. Thoreau knew all too well that he walked along the side of the widening road down which the expanding republic drove.

⟨ 5 ⟩ North American Walking

Exploring the Continent on Foot

Eearly colonial Americans clung to the seacoasts. The towns were, in truth, rural townships developed around fishing, agriculture, and lumbering, or some combination of these. At the end of the seventeenth century, chains of prosperous towns and fishing villages, constituting the colonies, girdled a great interior wilderness.[1] Major commerce and travel was done by ship. However, even though the first settlers brought cattle with them—and horses in following generations—most inland travel was done on foot.

Like their fellows in Europe, who were much like their medieval predecessors, the inhabitant of the colonies moved, worked, and survived on foot. Travel was principally local. Followed paths were narrow, uneven, and inconsistent. They circled ponds and wetlands, detoured steepest cliffs and rocky slopes, and led to safe places for fording streams and river. With impenetrable forests on every side, bountiful bogs and wetlands, and rocky and sandy surfaces, colonialists followed established Indian and animal trails. As settlement expanded, their own cow paths, skid lanes, and enhanced paths and trails were walkers' only alternative to trail blazing. Long trips were in every sense daunting. Travel at night was difficult; in extreme weather, perilous; and in winter and spring, with deep snows and rain-drenched soils in which human feet and animals' hooves sunk, at times altogether impossible.

The haulage of things on land depended largely on human legs and backs and what colonists could harness or yoke to their cattle, oxen, and horses. Carts never ran easily on steep, rocky, or soft lands, and their effective usage depended on relatively level, smooth, firm, and dry surfaces. Wheeled, horse-driven road traffic in the countryside was far more dependent on local conditions than it was in the following three decades in North America.

The defining means of locomotion, foot travel measured distance, effort, time, and, thus, the cost of transport. Walking was calculated in the payment of American revolutionary soldiers. Distances among fields, mills, towns, and ports determined place of settlement as well as the price of land and goods. Deciding on the location of a new church, which could double as a town hall, frequently split parishes and towns between those who could easily walk to it and those who could not. Distance, a nonreducible constant measured by foot travel, shaped settlement in the early colonial towns, which, for instance in Massachusetts, could be large—more than a hundred square miles and a half-day's walk from end to end. The ability to walk to a place, when water travel was not an option, accounted for the frequency of contact between people and towns.

The largest colonial cities were small villages by contemporary measures. Walkers easily traversed them, even when the street seriously impaired the walker. Founded in 1630 by John Winthrop and religiously homogeneous in its early decades, Boston—a center of American Puritanism—regulated its pedestrians and their behavior in accord with the Bible and church teachings. Reminding one of Calvin's Geneva or yet earlier medieval cities, which also regulated street conduct, the religious elders that ran Boston (to take one example) were intent on making its walkers see and illustrate the proper life. Indeed, a whipping post was erected in 1630 and city elders vigilantly conducted Sabbath patrols. In 1650, showing how upper-class propriety and righteousness were confounded even in these Puritan minds, the colonial court passed a law forbidding "the wearing of great boots" and other extravagant dress, "unless the wearer was worth the substantial amount of two hundred pounds."[2]

Of course, this was a hundred years before 1750, when Boston's population reached fifteen thousand, exceeded in number of inhabitants only by New York and Philadelphia. By then certain roads were paved, the first paving stones having appeared in 1674. The port, diverse industries, and various professions differentiated zones of the city. For the sake of urban traffic, cart size was regulated by length starting in 1720. Increasing numbers of horses and carriages, which also meant more money, more commerce, and better roads, already started to congest the thriving city's thoroughfares in the first half of the eighteenth century with commercial carts and promenading carriages. Squeezing walkers to the side, traffic also concerned shopkeepers with street cleaning, which so preoccupied Philadelphia's Benjamin Franklin. Vigilant about propriety and order, Boston's justices agreed in 1746 to walk the town and observe the behavior of the people. Out of fear of crowds and mobs, which soon would turn against British authorities, already as early as 1756 Boston authorities banned evening processions by the lower classes, which frequently ended in bloodshed.[3]

More than another fifty years passed before Emerson, on the basis particularly of what he saw in Boston and other urban centers, declared with a philosopher's universality that "civilized man has built a coach, but he has lost the use of his feet."[4] His generalization was far from true of the working classes of both rural and urban worlds and did not embrace those who lived and explored the American backcountry and wilderness. Nevertheless, Emerson, with uncanny accuracy, caught the drift of the upper classes that could and did ride in carriage by choice. And he raised a question, on which his student Thoreau reflected and which has been made emphatic by the last century and half of Western, even non-Western, experience. He asked for us to ponder what is not just a person but a society that has abandoned its feet for a seat? How is this sitting humanity and sedentary society at odds with walking humanity and the way of life it created? Surely a major stage of this transformation occurred in eighteenth- and nineteenth-century North America when it went from being a walking to being a riding, driving, and sitting continent.

In the course of the nineteenth and first half of the twentieth century North Americans became the leaders of a great riding revolution. Vast spaces disposed North Americans—Native Americans and European descendants alike—to ride whenever and wherever they could. With their vast grassy plains, North Americans were quick to welcome the imported horse into their lives and, from its first appearances in the Southwest and the New England colonies, to judge it indispensable for riding and, arguably more importantly, for haulage. They organized canals, along whose banks men, mules, oxen, and horses pulled, to conduct their growing inland commerce in the east, and they quickly accepted the train—the iron horse—as the principal engine for continental settlement, development, and the integration of the west into the nation. In turn Americans, whose cities adopted public transportation, were the first to mass produce the automobile and to adjust their walking lives to its dominance.

In the aftermath of the Civil War, the railroads, which connected east and west and crisscrossed individual states and territories, largely supplanted transport by foot and restricted travel by horse and wagon to the shorter hauls between field and town.[5] Annihilating space, spanning east and west coasts, and drawing distant places much closer together, the railroad connected the Great Plains—from Texas to Manitoba, from the Mississippi to the Rocky Mountains—to the rest of the nation and the world at large. Providing a smooth, interconnected, and uniform surface, the railroad integrated the nation into vast and expanding metropolitan markets more than a half-century before the arrival of the automobile and the building of paved road systems.

So walking, which once carried almost every farmer to field, merchant to shop, and child to school, and which was the most common and dependable means for travel, was superseded in part over time, first by horse, then by train, and finally by automobile. Transportation systems diminished, circumscribed, and in large measure did away with walking as the common mode of travel. Their expansion culturally re-defined walking. Aside from its use in ceremonial display, recreation, and the most immediate local matters, walking became stereotypically a mode of domestic locomotion. It served principally the servile, the poor, children, the old, and, for a long time, the majority of women—in effect all those who did not participate in the speeding and pro-gressing affairs of contemporary public life. For those with means and influence, it was largely left a secondary, an elective, an eccentric, and even a protest activity, as we will see in the conclusion of this chapter with our discussion of Henry David Thoreau, who used walking as means to bemoan the passing of pedestrian country life and to protest emerging riding society.

With no beasts of burden other than the dog, the first occupants of the North American continent traveled on foot, and their capacity to carry things with them was severely limited.[6] They strapped their goods to their backs or pulled them on toboggans and travoises, a primitive sledge used by Plains Indians that consisted of a platform of netting supported by two trailing posts attached to dog or, later, horse. On foot Indians, resembling their most ancient bipedal ancestors, hunted, went to war, and maintained long and complex networks of trails for exchanging goods from coast to coast. They traveled in short and long moccasins, using leggings to protect their legs on rough ter-rains.

Being dependent on foot travel, Native Americans established di-verse traditions of distance running, jogging, and fast walking. They often took the measure of one another and whites in terms of how far they could walk and how fast they could run. On more than one oc-casion, Indians and Europeans accepted walking as a means of staking out ownership. Pennsylvania colonial authorities used a lost treaty to prove that the Delaware Indians ceded to William Penn a tract of land at the junction between the Delaware and Leigh Rivers. It extended forty miles in depth, which the Indians, using their traditional meas-ure, estimated to be the approximate distance a man could walk in a day and a half.[7] When offered in 1737 the chance to buy a Delaware tract of land equal to a day's walking, Thomas Penn—William's son—abused this tradition by clearing paths and engaging expert walkers.

They covered more than sixty miles in a day. The Delaware objected; Penn responded by inviting the Iroquois to remove the Delaware, who in turn allied themselves with the French.[8]

Indian trails were often animal paths. Native Americans followed bison, mountain sheep, and other animal routes through mountain passes, forests, wetlands, and prairies. These trails, which often followed land along waterways, shed water in rainy seasons and blew clear of snow during winters. Unmarked until European settlement, these Indian trails usually proved to be the quickest routes to water and the easiest routes over steep and rough terrain. Modern highway builders adhered to a number of these efficient trails when laying out the roads we still drive.

European explorers and settlers brought horses, oxen, mules, donkeys, wheeled carts, elaborate pulleys and roping systems, and a tradition of boat and ship building to facilitate their explorations of and advance on the continent. Nevertheless, they had to depend on their feet, as well as local knowledge and hospitality, especially during the sixteenth century, when horses were scarce and costly to feed. Indeed, walking was frequently the sole means of inland travel passage, even though walkers found no inns to welcome them or maps to guide them. Going on foot was the principal means of the traveler in the backcountry. And guides, hunters, and trappers, lucky enough to have horses for carrying loads, often traveled on foot to lighten loads, move up steep ravines, traverse ice flows, follow cluttered river banks, or cross boulder-covered fields. River and cart travel also entailed considerable walking. Afoot, one climbed a tree to reconnoiter, leaped rocks, traversed muddy and snow-covered land, and proceeded against strong winds and rains. Insufficient supplies, uncertainty about sources of water, extreme weather, Indian attacks, and charges by wild animals, not to mention the necessity to cross raging rivers, traverse sandy deserts, and cut through dense thickets, constituted the hardships basic to continental travel.

The Spanish brought riding horses and packhorses to aid in their conquest of the New World. Horses allowed the Spanish to carry out expeditions from coast to coast in their search for glory and gold and to spread their religious faith. The first *conquistadores* of Mexico, who arrived led by men mounted on horse, gained the advantage of being mistaken for gods. Over time escaped steeds bred a plentiful population of wild horses that roamed the grasslands of the Southwest. Native Americans first looked to these animals for food but soon discovered the economic potential for trade and the distinct advantage horses offered in buffalo hunting and war. The ascendance of the mounted warrior over people on foot, which occurred in Europe, North Africa, and Asia, was duplicated in North America as riding warriors became dominant. In need of grazing ground, on the one hand, and capable of covering immense distances and superior in tracking buffalo herds, on the other, they drove walking Indians from the open spaces of the Great Plains before the American republic was born.[9]

Spanish explorers made a number of astonishing American treks. Alvar Núñez Cabeza de Vaca, often called the first man to walk across America, relied heavily on Indian help after he and three others escaped from Indian captivity and embarked on a six-year-long walk from the Gulf of Mexico to the Gulf of California in the 1530s.[10] Hernando De Soto led an expedition that landed in 1539 in what is now St. Petersburg, Florida, pushed north through the present-day Gulf states, crossed the Mississippi near today's Memphis, then proceeded to the site of contemporary Little Rock, Arkansas, before following rivers back to the Mississippi, where he died of "privation and fever in 1542."[11] Francisco Vásquez de Coronado's search for the fabled cities of gold led his 1541–1542 expedition from central Mexico across the Southwest to present-day central Kansas, where he found, in his words, "plains so vast that in my travels I did not reach their end."[12] In 1598 Don Juan de Oñate led a group of five hundred colonists to New Mexico to settle that region. The large retinue traveled with eighty oxcarts, two luxury coaches pulled by mules, three small pieces of artillery, and seven thousand head of livestock. A small exploration party he subsequently led traveled the Colorado River, reaching the Gulf of California in the spring of 1605, fifteen years before the Pilgrims came ashore at Plymouth Rock.[13]

French explorer of North America Robert Cavelier La Salle, who sought a navigable way to the Orient and who claimed Louisiana for France in 1682, made incredible trips on the upper and lower Mississippi and through the Great Lakes region. He proved just how grueling and myriad the pains of travel and exploration on foot were. In an expedition that historian Francis Parkman described as the "hardest journey ever made by Frenchmen in America," La Salle, facing adversity of every sort, covered more than a thousand miles in sixty-five days. He wrote of one two-and-a-half-day stretch of the journey spent crossing through the thorn and bramble thickets of southern Michigan, "Our faces were so covered with blood that we hardly knew each other."[14]

Missionary and explorer of New France Father Louis Hennepin too recorded another type of travel hardship. In 1680, while he was exploring the upper reaches of the Mississippi River, a tribe of Sioux captured him and his companions. The walking Indians, exercising their superiority over the foot-weary whites, forced the latter to complete an excruciating five-day march to a settlement on Mille Lacs, located in the center of present-day Minnesota. Beginning at sunrise and continuing until two hours after sundown, Hennepin and his men were made to walk at an exhausting pace they could not keep. Rather than letting the captives lag behind, the Indians, according to Hennepin, set fire to the dry grass behind them in order to encourage them to move faster.[15]

British colonists, occupying a 150-mile band of land along the Atlantic coast, established an agrarian local-market culture, which was leavened by overseas trade. Supported by only a rudimentary transportation system, with a relatively self-sufficient economy, in possession of few horses, and fearing thieves, hostile Indians, and an inhospitable wilderness, early colonists clung to familiar ground. The majority never ventured more than twenty miles from their home; their travels on foot took them to field, mill, meeting hall, nearby river port, or favorite hunting, fishing, or berry-picking grounds.[16] Those who did travel any distance away from home moved in small groups, on rough paths and trails. Traveling from settlement to settlement over uneven and broken surfaces, colonists, even those who rode horseback, were more likely to move at a walker's pace, picking their way across the landscape, rather than at the speed of a galloping horse. Throughout the colonial period, land transport was costly. It took time, wore down the animal, and broke carts, and even when things didn't go wrong, transport still involved considerable walking, lifting, and carrying. The transport of goods, materials, and people—like the banished and exiled Acadian, known as French Neutrals, who were given over to colonial custody on the eve of the French and Indian War in 1755—was meticulously entered as an expense in town ledgers. Attesting to the fact that the burden of the poor then, as since time immemorial, was to walk, in 1765 hundreds of the captive Neutrals migrated from Massachusetts to Québec on foot.

In the colonial South, even less emphasis was placed on overland travel because of the extensive river system along which the region's farms, settlements, and commercial enterprises were located. Anything that could be floated downstream was. However, even without good roads, many boatmen found, as pointed out by historian Val Hart in his *Story of American Roads,* they could make better time walking back upstream than attempting to row or pole against the current.[17] Travel along the Natchez Trace—a five-hundred-mile-long wilderness trail along the Mississippi that linked English, French, and Spanish settlements and grew in commercial and military importance from the 1780s to the 1930s—testified to this. Using the Natchez Trace (which connects present-day Nashville to Natchez, which was the northernmost Spanish settlement until it was annexed to the Mississippi Territory in 1798), boatmen shipped supplies and farm goods down the river. Once they arrived at their destination, they sold everything, boats included, and prepared for the return trip. Seldom having made enough profit to afford a horse to ride back on and facing difficult and robber-laden trails, boatmen would wait until they could form a small band of fellow travelers. Then they would assemble supplies and start out on their three-week journey home on foot. One of these men, known as "Walking Johnson," bragged that, walking, he had three times beaten the post rider back to Nashville.[18]

The lack of good road systems throughout the colonial world stifled commerce. However, as the economy developed and colonists' desire for goods grew, groups of "foot peddlers" (a redundancy since *ped* etymologically serves as a Latin prefix for *foot*) emerged to serve the dispersed and isolated markets. America's first walking salesmen, they were chiefly dissatisfied farmers and their sons who no longer found the wilderness as terrifying as they found an extra dollar alluring. The peddlers, with trunks full of wares on their backs, transacted commerce, moving along poor roads from towns to outlying farms and villages. Where commercial traffic grew and business prospered, a richer breed of peddler sprung up. They could afford horses to transport their wares. In the few places where decent roads existed, horses pulled carriages loaded with pots, pans, cloth, and other goods.

Not only did these itinerants facilitate the flow of goods inland, but they also served as important communication links between the settled coast and the unsettled frontier. Peddlers carried news and letters to distant relatives and served as "scouts for that great migration westward."[19] They, along with the passing settler and the circuit rider (the backcountry minister), were bombarded with questions concerning the safety and progress of settlement in the west.

In the decades just prior to the American Revolution, an increase in population prompted many colonists, on foot, to push out beyond established western borders. The Wilderness Road from Virginia through the Cumberland Gap to the Ohio Valley, opened by men working on foot and first traveled by pedestrians, was the only existing route for those wanting to cross the Appalachian Mountains. The original Indian trail had been identified in 1750 by Dr. Thomas Walker and was blazed by Daniel Boone and his crew in 1775. From then until 1796, when it was officially named, the Wilderness Trail existed only as a horse path, which despite its primitive state served an estimated two hundred thousand people on their journey west.[20]

Trails and roads were unsuitable for wheeled vehicles, so horse travel was the preferred mode. Because packhorses could only carry between one hundred and two hundred pounds, in contrast to an average covered wagon that could be loaded with one or two tons, horse trains could grow to as many as five hundred animals.[21] When such a train was traveling the narrow (often two feet wide) trails over the mountains, a leader would typically walk in front of the first horse, and each horse that followed would be tied to the one in front of it. People would be spaced at intervals between the horses to ensure that the baggage was secure and to prod any lagging horses. This mode of travel persisted well into the nineteenth century.

A common form of travel for those who had few horses was the riding-and-tying method, which allowed two separate parties to share horses. The first group would set out on foot, and the other would follow on horse. After the riders passed the walkers and proceeded several miles down the trail, they would tie the horses securely next to the trail and continue on foot. When the original walking party came upon the horses, they would mount and then ride past the other group in the same fashion. This method allowed everyone to rest, including the horses, and literally points out the degree to which North American exploration and settlement depended on the leapfrogging of two- and four-legged travel.[22]

After the United States acquired the Louisiana Territory west of the Mississippi in 1803, Thomas Jefferson selected Meriwether Lewis and William Clark to travel up the Missouri and beyond to assess the resources of the purchase and to seek the coveted Northwest Passage. Their assignment was to determine whether the Gulf of Mexico and the Pacific were linked by a river system, and in the absence of any such connection, to pioneer an overland route across the Rocky Mountains to the Pacific.[23] This exploratory mission, which embarked from St. Louis in May 1804, would test a human's endurance and the limits of contemporary water, horse, and bipedal travel. Upon the party's return, twenty-eight months later, the best route they could report contained no fewer than 340 miles of overland travel, of which 140 were quite mountainous.[24] The party, which had to split up at crucial junctures, spent almost as much time afoot as it did afloat. The shifting sandbars of the shallow, silt-laden, meandering Missouri, its opposing currents of three to four miles an hour, and the strong opposing headwinds of the Great Plains frequently reduced them to wading, tugging, pushing, and pulling their way up river.

Members of the expedition went ashore to camp, hunt, and survey the country, to reconnoiter the best route, to stockpile provisions for their return trip, and to lead the horses they bought from the Snake Indians to carry their baggage over the Rocky Mountains. They went on foot both to meet friendly and to escape hostile populations, which concerned them from their entrance into what today is South Dakota through their crossing of the Continental Divide and their arrival at the Pacific coast to their return to their starting point. Starvation and winter weather killed off the horses they attained, further increasing their reliance on foot travel. The expedition had to travel overland where the river was not navigable, at first portaging their supplies and boats until they began to build new rafts and dugouts out of cotton-wood trees.

Quoting from Lewis's journal in June of the first year of the journey when the expedition was in the vicinity of the present Tiber Dam in Montana, Stephen Ambrose wrote,

> It rained all night, "and as I expected we had a most disagreeable and restless night." At dawn "we left our watery beds" and proceeded downstream, but only with the greatest danger, because the wet clay was "precisely like walking over frozen ground which is thawed to small depth and slips equally as bad." In passing along the face of a bluff, Lewis slipped at a narrow walkway of some thirty yards in length across a bluff, made by the buffalo. He nearly went straight down a craggy precipice of ninety feet. He saved himself with his espontoon and just barely managed to reach a place where he could stand "with tolerable safety."[25]

The gravel along the slopes of the Missouri was also so wet and slippery that the men had to remove their moccasins to gain better traction. In other spots the river accumulated deep muck, which could steal a moccasin and make walking altogether impossible. Sharp rocks cut shoeless feet. Maneuvering along the banks meant trekking through cutting grasses infested with rattlesnakes and ticks, penetrating or circling thickets, and walking amid hovering crowds of mosquitoes and biting flies. It required traversing adjacent streams, swamps, and sloughs, and climbing up the steep banks of the Western Missouri. There were dramatic encounters with grizzly bears and with long, painful, and unavoidable patches of prickly pear—a hazard to the unprotected foot and leg of the walker. At one point in July of their first year, Clark's feet were "a raw, bleeding mass of flesh torn apart by prickly pears."[26] Repeatedly, the men suffered the climate and the landscape, experiencing violent colds, dysentery, injured feet, and strained and dislocated limbs.

When Lewis and Clark returned to St. Louis in September 1806, the nation celebrated an epic journey. The expedition, having lost but a single man, had traversed a continent—by combination of boat, horse, and foot—and had opened a national vista on what seemed the limitless west. They left no doubt that walking was the condition of having providence over the west. Those who would know it and have it would walk most of it.

A rapid succession of explorers, traders, and trappers converged on the west in the first decades of the nineteenth century.[27] Each illustrated the condition of walking and the epic scale of proportions of foot travel in the early nineteenth century. John Chapman, better known as Johnny Appleseed, defied easy classification. Born in Leominster, Massachusetts, in 1774, he started wandering the Midwest in 1801. Beginning in Ohio, he praised the healing powers of the domestic apple wherever he went until his death at the age of seventy-one.[28] Mystic, missionary, friend of the Indians—cutting down no tree, carrying no weapon, killing no animal—he walked, as if a type of American St. Francis, barefoot even in the winter. Hard and callus-toughened feet were a common condition of the unshod poor.

Another unusual pedestrian was gardener and botanist David Douglas, who, traveling on foot, with only a dog for a companion, crossed and recrossed the Rocky Mountains in Canada and the United States several times in the 1830s and 1840s. He sent more than fifty trees and one hundred plants to his employer, the Hudson Bay Company.[29] Surviving and earning one's living by roaming on foot described the life of many trappers, traders, peddlers, ministers, and others who populated the frontier with pedestrians.

Jedediah Strong Smith was among the hardy breed of fur traders, pioneers, and explorers whose immense wanderings included a search for a southern overland route to the west. In 1825, under the commission of the Rocky Mountain Fur Company, Smith, walking half as much as he rode, traveled from the vicinity of present-day Salt Lake City along the Virgin River to Colorado. From there, he pushed across the Colorado River and Mojave Desert, arriving to the surprise and consternation of Spanish settlers at the San Gabriel Mission on the Pacific Coast near today's Los Angeles.[30] He and two of his men successfully returned east for a rendezvous in 1827, making them the first white men, as far as is known, to cross the Sierra Nevada and the Great Salt Desert.[31] The continent was explored and prepared for settlement by walkers.

French explorer and scientist Joseph N. Nicollet and painter and explorer George Catlin (who were among the first whites to visit the Pipestone Quarries in present-day southwestern Minnesota) were early explorers of the upper Great Lakes and the northern Great Plains. The hosts and guides of the explorers were Indians and back-country people—fur traders, voyageurs, and mountain men. By foot and paddle, they and others hiked and canoed the many regions of the vast west in the late 1830s, 1840s, and 1850s.[32]

As tales of the Lewis and Clark expedition and subsequent explorers and adventurers spread throughout the young republic, settlers from north to south poured out to the frontier west. Along the Arkansas River Road, which connected Missouri to New Mexico, the number of wagons traveling the road went from 25 to 130 per year in the 1820s, to five to six hundred per year during the 1850s gold rush.[33] Between 1841 and 1859, more than three hundred thousand people made the journey. Many started and completed the trip on foot. Broken wagons, worn oxen, lame horses, buttocks sore from hard sitting, bones wearied from constant jostling and shaking, rivers to cross, rocks to move, hills to climb or descend, and many more reasons converted those who ostensibly rode into long-distance walkers. Images of horses and cowboys have suppressed the truth of how Americans settled the west on foot.

The Mormon trek of 1846 and 1847 was one such awesome pedestrian migration. Fifteen thousand believers, many on foot, some pushing handcarts, left Illinois at the start of 1846. They reached the western banks of the Missouri by the first winter, where they were stricken by cholera and black canker. Their leaders reached the Great Salt Lake Valley in July 1847. During the 1840s, nearly twelve thousand settlers traveled the Oregon Trail from Independence, Missouri, to the Oregon Valley.[34] Though the Oregon Trail in fact was no single road or route, it promised the possibility of making a wagon trip, unimpeded by mountains, to the fertile and rich west coast. With the shared promise that they take their things and goods with them to a new land, traveling communities of riders and walkers experienced births, deaths, marriages, and christenings on their two-thousand-mile journey along the trail.[35] Their pace was slow. Their wagon wheels didn't always find firm and level surfaces for rolling on. The journeyers frequently resorted to walking to prod their sluggish oxen on, to lead their horses on sharp climbs and descents, and to traverse soft ground and ford rivers.[36] Far more pioneers on the Oregon Trail drowned attempting to cross swollen streams and rivers than at the hands of hostile Indians.

Horses and oxen were indispensable when it came to packing large quantities of supplies or pulling wagons across immense distances. Even though the slower-paced ox—often a milk-producing Texas longhorn—was preferred to the horse for pulling loads, both were used. Finding water and forage along the trail was difficult—and the inability to do so reduced more than one party to going on foot. Any act threatening the safety or health of the horses was treated severely. A person caught sleeping while guarding the horses had to walk in front of his horse and lead it all the next day.[37] The well-being of their animals and horses constantly occupied the emigrants, for their loss meant their goods would have to be discarded and their children and old carried. Even before they arrived at steep and snowy mountain passes and fields of breaking ice and crusted snow, so incompatible to sharp hoofs, their hoof animals faced the uneven surface of the pot-holed prairie. Poison plants posed a great risk to the horses and livestock. In addition, feed could be incredibly scarce, especially in dry seasons and regions. A group of a thousand traveling horses needed daily the equivalent tonnage of seven acres of grass during periods of normal precipitation and around forty-two acres per day during drought.[38] The limits of horse and cart travel were magnified as one moved off the relatively flat paths of the plains up onto the desert and into the forests and mountains. The journey and speed at which people crossed the continent was still measured by walking.

As America became more populous and trade and commerce expanded in the course of the nineteenth century, the demand for roads grew louder and paths evolved into roads for carting.[39] Civic leaders claimed that settlement, profits, and statehood itself depended on more and better roads. Merchants and politicians alike agreed on the need for safer and wider trails to accommodate large wagons hauling goods behind teams of up to six horses.

Yet during the nineteenth century the call for more and better roads went largely unheeded in the countryside. Roads required the levying of taxes, and the great majority, short on money and accustomed to living out life on foot, preferred walking to paying. Going on foot was the common fate of students who traveled as far as four or five miles to school, wives who hauled water to and from distant wells, itinerant salesmen or traveling ministers of Christ who brought their wares and preachments to remote farms. Furthermore, few Americans knew how to construct a road properly, and there was no organized system for making any improvements. In the north, roads were formed over time by the same treading foot or hoof, along the same truncated paths between settlements. In the south, roads lacked any identifiable pattern and did not consistently lead from settlement to settlement. Despite the fact that commerce required improved and expanded roads, neither state nor federal government had a system in place to create them. And even though road improvements increased travel for the well off, a significant portion of the upper classes—perhaps fearful about increased taxes—remained wary of changes in the transportation system. In 1826, Indiana politician Oliver H. Smith, whose campaign trail for U.S. Congress literally led him across places without roads and bridges, with only Indian paths to move on, abandoned his carriage at one point to go on horseback for fear of being considered too haughty.[40] In this he was not unlike contemporary politicians who cater to popular sentiment by abandoning cars for buses or bikes to make "down-to-earth" populous campaign bids.

Nevertheless, road building did make progress in the nineteenth century, which simultaneously increased riding and walking by multiplying the number of accessible places. It received a large boost from toll roads such as the private Lancaster Turnpike, which joined Lancaster to Philadelphia in 1794. It offered a wide, smooth, and dependable surface on a pay-as-you-go sixty-two-mile stretch, prompting a regional public outcry for road building.[41] With successful finance and effective methods for construction, private companies took the lead in road building at the start of the nineteenth century and retained it to the Civil War. The success of these short, private roads prompted gradual improvements in longer trans-Appalachian routes. Two such routes were the Pennsylvania Road, which ran from Philadelphia through Lancaster and Harrisburg over the Appalachians to meet the Ohio at

Pittsburgh, and the National Road, which went from Cumberland, Maryland, through West Virginia and Ohio to St. Louis. Toll roads also play a significant role in the spread of improved roads, demonstrating that the public, with means, was ready and willing to pay for faster travel.

Advances in canal building, the steamboat, and the iron horse, in addition to increased availability of horses and the growing popularity of carriages, also supported the notion of the middle class that travel should be fast, convenient, and predictable. And while poor roads were the rule during the nation's first century, the first outline of a desired and interconnecting inland transportation system was being supplied by the railroad.

AN ARDENT AMERICAN WALKER

Inspired by Romanticism and antithetical to growing urban life, individual Americans thinkers articulated at the start of the new century a contrast between what they took to be the moral life in the woods and the distorted existences of the city.[42] Early American writer Philip Freneau dubbed himself "Philosopher of the Forest" in the 1780s. In the 1790s, he assumed the guise of an Indian in his "Tomo-cheeki Essays." His moral line was the superiority of the wild genius of the forest to the artificial production of art.[43] In 1800 Philadelphia physician Benjamin Rush, also identifying with the wild and the primitive, argued, intoning Rousseau, that man is not happy until he is returned to the woods.[44]

While Freneau and Rush made primitivism a fashionable topic in Philadelphia drawing rooms, New Hampshire lawyer Estwick Evans actually "walked the talk." In 1818 he donned a buffalo robe and put on moccasins and, in the company of two dogs, set forth on "a four-thousand-mile 'pedestrious tour' into the West."[45] Wishing to divest himself of the vices of civilization, Evans sought to acquire the simplicity and virtue of native feelings amidst the solitude and grandeur of the western wilds. "While traveling the southern shore of Lake Erie, his feelings welled into a romantic paen: 'how great are the advantages of solitude.'"[46]

A number of thinkers in the next generation began to take pleasure in wild country while denouncing the nation's swarming cities and continental hegemony. None equaled in passion or fame dedicated walker Henry David Thoreau (1817–1862) in articulating these themes. On his long daily walks around his native Concord he was vexed by the visible encroachment of nearby metropolitan Boston, only eighteen miles away, and he anguished over the engulfing spread west of the young Atlantic republic. As if on a perpetual picket line, Thoreau put his foot down on the side of local rural life against engulfing urban society, typified for him by "the congested, animal-filled, muddy, and dusty streets of cities like New York," where he had stayed for a short while.[47]

In a eulogy of his friend Thoreau, Ralph Waldo Emerson described him as a person who "could not bear to hear the sound of his own steps, the grit of gravel; and therefore never willingly walked in the road, but in the grass, on the mountains and in the woods." Emerson's eulogy left no doubt about Thoreau's commitment to locality: "Thoreau dedicated his genius with such entire love to the fields, hills and waters of his native town that he made them known and interesting to all reading Americans."[48]

Thoreau walked because he didn't like riding. In fact, by his own confession, he was "no friend of horses."[49] He went on foot because sitting didn't suit his active nature, and because a long walk made him more intellectually productive when he sat and wrote. Literary critic Van Wyck Brooks described Thoreau as being "tough and muscular," "with workman's hands and feet."[50] Biographer Robert Richardson wrote, "People noticed that his eyes rarely left the ground. When he did look up, he swept everything at a glance."[51] Appearing awkward, Thoreau proved a surprisingly graceful ice skater and, although he was not truly a big or strong man, he had remarkable stamina as a walker. He was also an indefatigable canoeist. He lived out his youth as walker, not hesitating on one occasion to travel eighteen miles on foot, from Concord to Boston, in order to hear Emerson speak and to walk home again after the lecture.[52]

Prior to his daily walk, which went on for as much as four hours, Thoreau took a dawn swim in Walden Pond. By character, he surely belonged to the sternest order of peripatetic monks. At the same time, moved by the spirit of his times, Thoreau could not stay at home any more than Melville's Ahab could stay ashore or Whitman could stay off the fleshy, grassy roads of dawning democracy.

Walking fused with his other consuming passion, writing. It stoked his active mind with ideas and observations. It provided, in the words of Richardson, a "link between fact and myth, which he prescribed as necessary for the nature writer."[53] Walking established a productive state of mind. One step, and his day's work was underway; gait established, his workshop was erected. He could begin collecting materials for the burgeoning notebooks that he transformed into his multiplying journals, both of which were the principal sources for his essays and books.[54]

Thoreau thought with his feet, so to speak.[55] Walking determined the form of his books, which were structured by the succession of what he observed rather than logical argumentation.[56] This mode of discourse—that of journeyer rather than that of philosopher—separated Thoreau as a thinker from his mentor, friend, and fellow Concord resident philosopher Emerson, whose writings pursued ideas.[57]

Nevertheless, Emerson identified many of the trails the young Thoreau followed.[58] He articulated the popular doctrine of transcendentalism, an early-nineteenth-century literary and philosophical movement that associated such luminaries of the young republic as Bronson Alcott, William Ellery Channing, Margaret Fuller, Walt Whitman, and Thoreau himself. Predicated on the notion that the spiritual exists behind the empirical, transcendentalism was defined by Emerson as "the feeling of the Infinite"—and in his writings, he continued to speak of nature as an immanent life spirit, "a force he alternately called the Aboriginal Power and the Over-Soul."[59] The intellectual center of this first blooming of the nation's intellectual life, Emerson assessed the value of European cultural life, declaring the primacy of contemporary German thought.

Emerson also nudged Thoreau in the direction of the emerging natural sciences, especially geology and botany.[60] Taken up by the spreading passion for gardens and "botanizing" strolls, which had already moved Rousseau, Emerson encouraged Thoreau to take an academic interest in plant taxonomy, origin, and distribution, which had been spurred on by Goethe and von Humboldt.[61]

Preaching self-reliance and embracing solitude, Emerson sought an alternative to what he described as "'this mendicant America, this curious, peering, itinerant, imitative America.'"[62] Considering the new world's travelers—ministers, lecturers, colporteurs, showmen, and hucksters—he, according to historian Lewis Perry, continually called for great men and culture to act in counterbalance to the changing world. Thoreau took Emerson's message to heart: the new individual must retreat from civilization and escape the imitations of learning.[63] A solitary walk in the woods makes a person anew. "'The tradesman, the attorney,'" Thoreau wrote in *Nature* (1836), "'comes out of the din and craft of the street and sees the sky, the woods, and is a man again.'"[64]

Thoreau's passion was to be the reborn man he and Emerson idealized. Indeed, during his two-year stay from July 1845 to September 1847 at Walden (located on Emerson's property), Thoreau carried out a trial of Emerson's prescription for self-reliance. Thoreau's book *Walden,* according to historian Leo Marx, "may be read as a report on an experiment in transcendental pastoralism."[65] It also reads as an expression of that romantic transcendentalism that runs from German idealism to English poet, critic, and philosopher (and friend of Wordsworth) Samuel Taylor Coleridge to Emerson, to Thoreau, and then to naturalist John Muir.[66]

Even though fourteen years separated Emerson and Thoreau, on many matters they traveled hand and hand. Emerson occasionally strolled the Concord woods that Thoreau circumambulated his whole life. Emerson proposed walking trips to Cape Cod, where Thoreau traveled three times. As a lecturer and scholar Emerson had traveled much of his life. In the last decade of his life, the seventy-year-old Emerson went all the way to California. He visited at Yosemite the naturalist John Muir (1838–1914), whose exploratory travels, often on foot, in Australia, India, Russia, Alaska, the American south, and California made him, next to Thoreau, America's greatest walker.[67]

Sharing similar concerns about encroaching Boston, Thoreau deeply internalized Emerson's ambivalent feelings about the coming of the railroad, which, passing so close to Concord and Walden Pond, disrupted the traditional landscape.[68] Over time, however, their positions diverged. Emerson increasingly found good in the progress of civilization and its cities and transportation, while the younger Thoreau railed against the advancing urban and national cultures. Train whistles jarred Thoreau's sensibilities. He could not find grace in expansion or complexity. Only by walking on backcountry trails, along the margins of woods and small settlements, could he observe, study, and embrace the nature he loved.[69]

The content of Thoreau's journals markedly shifted during his stay at Walden from literary, classical, and religious preoccupations to natural and scientific observation. Both stages for Thoreau depended on going on foot. Walking initially offered images and metaphors that sparked his romantic ideas about humanity's place in nature. It furnished him, as it had preceding generations of romantic writers, a vehicle for structuring his reflections on literature, humanity, and his times. This is illustrated by his "Walk to Wachusett," "A Winter Walk," and "Walking," and in his books *A Week on the Concord and Merrimack Rivers* (1849), *The Maine Woods* (1864), and *Cape Cod* (1865).

Cape Cod (posthumously published) conflates the three trips he made to the Cape. On these trips, going on foot, he traversed the length of the Cape's ocean side twice and its bay side once. He crossed between the two sides frequently. The professed purpose of all three trips was to learn of the sea, that great wilderness that every romantic poet—worth his salt, so to speak—had to encounter. "[It] covers," Thoreau introduced his book, "more than two thirds of the globe, but of [it] a man who lives a few miles inland may never see any trace."[70] However, once at Cape Cod, he focused, according to Richardson, "not so much on the ocean as on the shore, the coast, the beach, the region between the ocean and the land, a region Thoreau finds wild and strange."[71]

With his mind surging with matters of God and nature, swelled by recent readings in Coleridge and von Humboldt, and frothy with reflections on Hinduism, Thoreau arrived at Boston on his way to the Cape only to be greeted by tragedy. A handbill announced the death of 145 lives at Cohassert (on the Cape). A ship laden with immigrants from Galway had hit an offshore rock and then foundered. Thoreau and his travel companion, poet William Channing, arrived at Cohassert in the company of those who had come to reclaim their dead.[72]

This tragedy that Thoreau used to preface his *Cape Cod* did not turn the work into theological reflection, nor did it save it from being more or less a walker's miscellaneous chronicle. It recounts his plodding progression from place to place. It mixes in fresh sights and experiences with gleanings from recent readings on geography, geology, and botany. Along with recording encounters with odd characters and bits of sea lore, he notes the difficulty of lengthy beach walking. He points out how hard it is to trudge through heavy beach sands and the dangers involved in walking under the Cape's sandy cliffs, against which one could be trapped by a rising tide.

His *Maine Woods* (1864), also posthumously published, similarly joins together observations and reflections made on two separate trips to Maine. It too testifies to Thoreau's love of backcountry—the middle ground between society and wilderness.[73] While detailing the fruits of geological and botanical observations, he reports on weather, travel conditions, hospitality, toll use, canoe making, clothes, eating habits, and other manners of Indians, settlers, and lumbermen. He devotes particular attention to walking and related matters, such as maps, the care of shoes (pork fat softens them), wading streams (which soften feet and make them unsafe for walking), scrambling up sharp ravines, and the impossibility of following river banks covered by fallen timber. He openly admires the three guides who make long portages of their boats, which weighed from four to six hundred pounds, and applauds "the boys along the bank who walk on floating logs as city boys on sidewalks."[74] He repeatedly calls attention to the conditions of the small roads and paths—such as the winter roads that vanish in the summer, leaving the traveler without trace of rut to follow, and the curious log roads that loggers improvise across wetlands.

In *The Maine Woods* Thoreau does dedicate considerable passion to finding a middle ground between humanity and nature. He embraces John Locke's notion that "in the beginning all the World was America."[75] And he notes that the new exploiting nation has "advanced by leaps to the Pacific, and left many a lesser Oregon and California unexplored."[76] Thoreau repeats the familiar contention: primordial America—the one that greeted its original explorers—still lurks just off its main traveled roads. He defends settlers against the common charge that they are without culture, and suggests that North American Indians (who were of considerable interest to Thoreau) had established a more wholesome relationship with nature than avaricious and churning civilized humanity had done.[77]

On his descent from his unsuccessful attempt to climb to the top of the highest mountain in the east, Mount Katadhin, he realizes nature's irreducible inhospitality to man. He judges it "primeval, untamed, and forever untameable." There, as he had on the wreck-strewn beaches of Cape Cod, he encounters nature wearing a savage face: "It was Matter, vast, terrific—not his Mother Earth, . . . [not] home."[78] In the second part of the book, Thoreau dwells on how humanity violates nature. Base motives carry people into the wilderness. The explorer, the lumberman, paid with city money, "is not the friend and lover of pine." Civilization, he concludes, has no heart for wilderness.

The Maine Woods cultivates a lacerating contradiction. Nature is indifferent to humanity, and humanity considers itself the master of nature. Society and wilderness are not equals—no blissful union binds them together. Even the middle ground, which Thoreau most cherished in the settlements in Maine, are not free of destructive change—and for Thoreau, no God in heaven mends this rent cloth. Thoreau can only walk and observe.

SAUNTERING

Thoreau's famous essay, "Walking"—originally called "Walking and the Wild"—affords a conclusion to the inseparable relation walking had to his thought. In it Thoreau stands humanity on its feet. Walking, he begins, forms an art that only a few understand. Exploiting the unknown etymology of the word *sauntering,* Thoreau suggests it derives from pilgrims' march to the *saint terre.* He invents a second possibility: *sauntering* has its origin in homelessness—a walker who is *sans terre.* Every place is home to the homeless.[79] Identifying with walker over rider, migrant over city dweller, Thoreau jocularly declares himself a saunterer, a holy drifter, a vagabond of a sort. Taking side with the poor, inferior, yet ultimately more ancient, he declares that he does not belong to the ranks "of Equestrians, or Chevaliers—not Ritters, nor Riders," but instead to the walkers, "a more ancient and honorable class."[80] He says he was born into the family of walkers—*Ambulator nascitur, non fit.*

Although his walking tethered him to a place in the countryside that had been settled for two hundred years, in his essay Thoreau equates walking with wilderness and freedom. Thoreau would walk west rather than sail east. "I must walk toward Oregon, not Europe," he declares. From the east, expect light, Thoreau argues, but from the west, receive fruit. The west, he continues, is but "another name for the Wild." The wild houses multiplicity. While it sustains and nurtures the civilized, it also gives rise to prophets.[81]

If writing theory as he did in "Walking" entered Thoreau into national discourse, his daily walks embedded him in a locale. Concord's people and landscape formed the core of Thoreau's wordy circumambulations. Aside from oodles of books he borrowed from friends and the Harvard library, Thoreau trusted his education to his everyday steps and daily conversation. An active mind on active feet, Thoreau posited, constituted footing for knowledge of self, nature, society, and humankind.

Advancing society, Thoreau understood, jumped local places and minds by leaps and bounds. Nations overran berry patches, gardens, meadows, and rural settlements. They and their commerce sentenced his beloved Indians and landscapes to extinction. It made their ruin a subject for lament; it turned them into subjects for historical study. Intellectually, he acknowledged, at least on one occasion, that his attempt to fit the world into his microcosm, in which he himself was studying in increasing detail, was making him microscopic. He wrote in 1851,

> I fear that the character of my knowledge is from year to year becoming more distinct & scientific—That in exchange for views as wide as heaven's scope I am being narrowed down to the field of the microscope—I see details not wholes nor the shadows of wholes. I count some parts & say "I know."[82]

As localities and native peoples disappeared before advancing society, so visible nature vanished in the face of developing theoretical and laboratory science. Charles Darwin's *Origin of Species* (1859), to which Thoreau responded immediately and positively, proposed a global theory of the source and development of all life. In light of Darwin's theory, his own observations on the succession of woods or the spread of seed in the vicinity of Concord, however acute they might be, could only illustrate a global generalization. The pursuit of developing scientific knowledge, he was beginning to realize, would force him to leave traveled Walden Woods for a sitting universe devoted to theory, microscope, and laboratory.

A LAST TRIP

For Thoreau the whistling train announced the eclipse of place by a new order of commerce and speed. It marked the homogenization of space and the subordination of the local and the wild. Nevertheless, in 1861, with failing health, severe bronchitis, and an underlying case of tuberculosis, Thoreau was advised by his doctors to seek out a better climate for the sake of his health. Thoreau responded by setting out for the west, which had long evoked his curiosity as the last great reserve of the wild. Boarding a train going west he first went to Chicago, from there crossed to Dunleith, Illinois, on the Mississippi, then took a steamboat up the Mississippi to St. Paul, Minnesota. After several days of observing prairie flora and fauna, he embarked on a small steamboat up the shallow and meandering Minnesota River. The boat proceeded by fits and starts.[83] Showing the inconvenience of travel at the time, passengers often disembarked from the boat at bends and walked across vegetation-covered isthmuses only a stone's throw wide but a mile or two long. Fallen trees had to be removed from the river's course—and the grounded and banked ship had to be constantly freed by windlass and cable. Having passed young settlements at Mankato and New Ulm, the steamship eventually arrived at its destination, the Redwood Falls Indian agency.

On board with Thoreau were Minnesota Governor Alexander Ramsey, "a bevy of beautiful women and brave men," Indian agents, and a German band.[84] Several thousand Indians were assembled for their arrival and the gala event, which would mark the paying of annuities to the Sioux Indians for their land. At the agency for only a day, Thoreau took a three-mile hike out onto the great expanse of the prairie, which did not show a single tree on its western horizon. At the ceremony, Thoreau portentously identified noted Indian unrest and singled out Little Crow, who would join the young braves in a full-scale war up and down the length of the Minnesota River Valley in 1862.[85]

Thoreau died before the defeat of the uprising. He did not experience the end of the Civil War; nor did he witness the postwar industrial north concentrating its phenomenal industrial energies, covering the prairies with farms and logging off much of the forests of Michigan, Wisconsin, and Washington. He died five years before the railroads linked east to west, dictating thereafter the settlement of peoples, the movement of goods, and the grid in which future travel and walking would occur.

The closing of the frontier in 1900 signaled the eclipse of back-country people—the guides, trappers, hunters, swampers, and other forms of early American walkers. The era of footpaths, trails, and foot-bridges was all but over on the local level. Reliance on the canoe for transport was a thing of the past. The ox was displaced as a beast of burden, although the number of working horses—the first instrument, after the foot, to subdue vast American space—increased. At work in farm fields, hauling on country gravel roads (usually from railroad station to farm), and working as all-important drays on city streets, horses continued to increase in number until 1920. The conquest of "the wild" had all but occurred. The small and wild, measured by narrowing quadrants, would survive only in national parks and wilderness areas, protected from commercial intrusion, traffic, and motorized machines

Hereafter walkers would have to learn to accommodate themselves to the new grids of time and distance created by railroads, cars and trucks, highways, and, of course, cities, which increasingly gathered in the people and resources of the countryside and dispersed, in exchange, good and ideas. In cities country walkers would have to learn to become pedestrians if they were efficiently to traverse—first on foot and later with the possible help of public transportation—miles of streets between home and work. They would have to learn the wily ways of urban traffic, avoiding being hit by horse and carriage, negotiating a maze of streets, and operating as a civil pedestrian should in encounters, giving the right of way, and so on. Having learned to idle and gaze when in town, they, once they had modest sums of disposable money, would have to master the arts of punctuality, snappy walking, reading schedules, and learning to ask for transfers as they moved. They had to become commuters. Like their counterparts in London, Paris, and elsewhere in metropolitan Europe, immigrants would have to learn new ways of moving on foot and by public transportation if they were to taste the pleasures of the city. Like rural immigrants to the city everywhere, they needed to locate and shop at their favorite markets, stroll local streets, when off work, and find their way even at night to dance halls and street dances. To follow fashion, they had to pay visits to the ball field, the park, the zoo, and the beach, or even to travel out into the countryside. Doing all this meant accustoming oneself to moving in crowds consisting of strange and foreign peoples as well as learning in mass where and how to walk, stand elbow to elbow, and wait and advance in lines on sidewalks, at store fronts, on ramps, in elevators, and in street cars and buses. Indeed, the nineteenth and early twentieth centuries created whole new breeds of urban walkers.

From this perspective, Thoreau's life appears to stand at the end of American country walking. He witnessed walking—this first and principal way of American native and colonial locomotion—being displaced by horse, steamboat, train, and telegraph. Romantic walker, Thoreau circumambulated in ever tightening circles—like an archaic peasant around a church steeple—as vast systems of transportation, communication, commerce, and national power circumscribed the globe. Walking, he spun a web of great meaning out of Walden, Concord, and backcountry America, while civilization, typified by burgeoning Boston, Philadelphia, New York, and, quintessentially, London, filled the horizon.

As small and rural places were ignored, bypassed, and obliterated, it was inevitable that this romantic and articulate walker would become the patron saint of localists, ecologists, and country walkers. His books are packed in many a contemporary knapsack. Who, to ask a rhetorical question, would not wish, at the mere price of taking to foot in the countryside, to be free of the complexities of advancing civilization—its congestion, pollution, and social fragmentation? Who would not desire to experience the indisputable but not predictable ecstasy of the walker's flowing gait or have the privilege of chosen solitude? Who, of those who know the pleasure of long walks and careful words, does not wish to claim, at least at times, the patrimony of this articulate saunterer?

Yet, in truth, who would voluntarily abandon completely the opportunity-filled and kaleidoscopic urban centers? Since the Middle Ages the splendorous nervous energy of the teeming city has brought visitors to gape and gaze—and be taught fresh ways of walking and living. As much as any metropolis, nineteenth-century London created a new walking environment for the majority and instructed urban walkers there and everywhere how to step out and go on foot.

⚹ 6 ⚹ City Walking

The Genesis of the Urban Pedestrian
in Nineteenth-Century London

 ITIES fostered new breeds of walkers. The disciplined pedestrian, the speeding commuter, the idling window shopper, the elusive *flâneur,* and the organized marching groups were foremost among them. Nineteenth-century London and Paris perhaps best reveal, of all Western cities, the metamorphosis of the urban walking environment and the genesis of the gallery of contemporary urban walkers. Everywhere their creation was inseparable from the general formation of national, industrial, and mass society and the particular articulation of public transformation.

Even though a new epoch of transportation was dawning at the start of the nineteenth century along select land and water routes in England, France, the Netherlands, Germany, and the Atlantic coast of New England, the vast majority of people still traveled on foot in town and country. Indeed, at that time, Europe's urban and rural inhabitants, who journeyed further, spent as much time and energy going on foot as their medieval counterparts did.

Even nineteenth-century intellectuals, to select one group whose origins lay primarily in the middle classes, who sat a lot to read and write, relied on their sturdy legs and humble feet. They did this not just to be up and about and to create, but to move from place to place in the city and from one town to another in the countryside. Some of them went on foot to save money, others because it was the most efficient way to travel, and yet others for reasons of habit, health, recreation, and creation.

Among committed walkers, to mention some, there were nineteenth-century English essayist Thomas De Quincy, who regularly took walks of more than forty miles, and writers Samuel Taylor Coleridge and William Wordsworth, whom we have already mentioned. While English constitutional historian Frederic Maitland at least on one occasion walked from Cambridge to London, he was outdone by historian Thomas Macaulay, who regularly walked from central London to Clapham or Green, while Charles Lamb regularly walked five, ten, or fifteen miles within London, and did as much as thirty miles or more in London's northern outskirts.[1] Charles Dickens, a kind of urban counterpart to Thoreau, continually wrote about the London he constantly walked. Only walking sufficed for him to know the city up close, in detail. Unable to afford a cab in London, political exile Italian nationalist Giuseppe Mazzini, who lived on the outskirts of London, frequently arrived at his hosts' covered with telltale mud, having economized at the expense of his legs and feet.[2] In sum, these representative pedestrian luminaries went on foot much like English country people and Londoners, who as a daily matter walked five to ten, or even more, miles to and from work.[3]

These intellectuals surely would have found their match across the channel. There was ardent walker Richard Wagner, one of many composers who found walking a means to relaxation and creation. Despite his short legs, Wagner walked from Dresden to Leipzig and back.[4] Then there was radical political thinker Pierre Proudhon, who as a matter of course, economy, and efficiency told a colleague to wait for him in Paris, as he would be there in six days, the time it would take him to walk from Strasbourg to Paris.[5] Historian Eugen Weber describes the young Victor Hugo as a love-struck *bipède*.

In July 1821, a nineteen-year-old poet set out on foot from Paris to woo the girl he loved and who loved him. Her parents, who opposed the marriage of young people with no expectations, had decided that renting a summer place in the environs of the capital, as they usually did, would bring the suitor running to spoil their holiday. They rented a house in Dreux instead, then a picturesque old township some sixty miles west of Paris on the road to Normandy. A stagecoach ride that far cost twenty-five francs and Victor Hugo did not, they were sure, have twenty-five francs. But he had good legs. The Fouchers and their daughter, Adèle, left Paris on July 15; Hugo followed on the 16th. On the 19th he was in Dreux and on the 20th gained parents' consent to the courtship.[6]

Scientist Pierre Curie was another intense walker. His wife and fellow scientist, Marie Curie, wrote in her autobiography that he "loved the countryside passionately, and no doubt his silent walks were necessary to his genius; their equal rhythm encouraged his scientist's meditation."[7] She did not mention the leisure that permitted him to walk, but she did describe their walking honeymoon in 1895 as "a wedding tramp." Boasting that she kept up with him without fatigue, she confessed to "sacrificing the proprieties" by shortening her skirts a little so as to be able to walk freely.[8] Eleven years later Pierre Curie walked up the rue Dauphine to his death on April 19, 1906. He tried to cross the street, slipped, as pedestrians so frequently did on the rain-soaked pavement, and was crushed by a heavy horse-drawn cart.[9] He died under the hooves of a horse and the wheels of a cart. An uncommon mind suffered what was a common pedestrian's death.

Beyond the relatively small upper class that strolled because of leisure, money, and fashion, England, as many observers noted, was a walking nation. This pedestrian substratum endured across the nineteenth century. Even late in the nineteenth century, English literature reveals the nation most advanced in transportation to be still a walking nation. The poor villager Jude Fawley of Thomas Hardy's *Jude the Obscure* (1895), for instance, lives out his aspiring but miserable plebeian life walking. On foot he catches his first glance of his future wife, Arabella Dunn. He courts her by escorting her six miles on foot to see the glowing lights of a nearby town. Walking, he studies Latin, seeks out a divinity school, later practices his craft as a stonemason, and falls in love with his cousin Sue Bridehead, and on foot—not riding—he moves with her and their children from town to town, job to job, disappointment to heartbreak until death does him in. Especially testifying to his position in the lower working class, his fate was inseparable from walking.

Literature about the laboring classes up to and even after the First World War, whether set in rural villages or urban neighborhoods, testifies to pedestrian-based localism, which was only significantly eroded in the course of the twentieth century with the triumph of mass transportation.[10] Working-class lives were tethered to place, which meant people relied on foot for work and play. Memoirs still resonate with the close association of belonging to and walking a place. On Ascension Day in London there is "Beating of the Bound," a ritual in which the young boys of the parish, in conformity with tradition, walk and touch certain buildings, marking off the parish's boundaries.[11] As in the Middle Ages, parish, place, and walking formed a trinity of locality, the sense which Irish poet Roy McFadden captures when he writes, "Every road in Ulster veined my heart."[12]

Locality, as circumambulated space, dominated the working class well into this century. Local scholarship winners from villages, small towns, and neighborhoods of England arrived at the university entirely ignorant of where they were. They were as disoriented as any foreign tourist, and they never thought to buy or spend money for a city map.[13] Their mental map, ingrained as much as language itself, belonged to the streets where they grew up, the streets they walked. Nearby towns might have been foreign countries for them, and when they were in them they walked with the alert and hesitant step of strangers and immigrants.[14]

Decades and even generations after others took to riding, the working classes remained into the middle decades of the twentieth century attached to the village and neighborhood they traveled on foot.[15] Testifying to how much life was carried out and experienced in relation to walking, memoirist William Woodruff, born in 1916, remembered from his childhood all the foot traffic that passed his childhood home in Blackburn. He notes the scissors grinders, peddlers of such things as threads, needles, and ribbons, who cried their wares, and his favorite, the tinker, who mended pots and pans. And he recalls the morning parade of pedestrians to work: "Not long after t' knocker-up (a fellow who went around in the morning waking up the workers) had finished rattling our window-pane, a stream of wood-shodden workers began to hurry past my window on its way to work. . . . The clip-clap on the cobbles drowned out all other noises. In winter, deadened clogs meant a heavy snow; clogs that rang meant a frost."[16]

While the coming of the automobile, whose steering wheel few working-class men sat behind until the 1950s, was a common sign of the coming of modernity, another, especially in the countryside, was the disappearance of the wooden shoe.[17] It vanished with the passing of the bipedal order that had established place, village, parish, and neighborhood. Its clomp was no longer heard as the working classes now wore mass-produced leather shoes—and wandering shepherds, traveling gypsies, itinerant salesmen, perambulating tinkers, peregrinating craftsmen, and vagrant beggars disappeared from the scene. These ambulatory orders (called *los ambulantes* in Spanish), often weighed down with things or pushing or pulling a cart of sundry size, began to disappear in the expanding commercial and transportation hubs of the West after the First World War. Foot and horse traffic was banished from main roads, and wagons and trucks, capable of carrying much larger volumes, displaced them. This change is all to be seen in the making in nineteenth-century London, which more than any other metropolitan center began what, in retrospect, can be seen as a transformation of walking in England and the West.

LONDON WALKING

Historian Paul Langford notes the existence of what one editor of travelers' tales called "a craving for locomotion" and another commentator described as "a perfect mania that the English have for moving about from one place to another."[18] "One," the marquis de Bombelles commented, "does not travel anywhere so much as in England, nowhere has one so many means of departing."[19] According to

Langford, the need of the restless English to be up and about—"jaunting around," to use a phrase from the period—made them Europe's first commuters, even though it was Americans who later perfected the art as well as coined the word "commuting."[20] The English penchant for movement—be it walking in the street, riding on horseback, or parading in a carriage—all without any actual business in view, "'but simply to be absent from home,' was something on which almost all contemporary commentators agreed."[21]

As peasants everywhere equated their destiny with the strength of their legs, the urban English took themselves to be as good as the speed of their feet. Known as pedestrians par excellence, Londoners took pleasure in their walking.[22] Their brisk pace had been commonly observed since the eighteenth century and set the norm against which Cornelius Webbe in the 1830s listed such irritating foot-dragging pedestrians as "waddlers, crawlers, wallers, strutters, butters, bustlers, hustlers, saunterers, plodders, swaggerers, loungers, room walkers."[23] The main streets of London, according to Langford, were constructed and maintained for constant use, whereas those of many other capital cities were cluttered and filthy. In London the very word "pavement" came to mean the surface that was intended for those on foot.[24] And, in that period, one promenaded best in London—with its parks, squares, and even its malls, which provided sheltered walks.[25]

While London imitated Paris at the start of the eighteenth century, at century's end Paris copied London.[26] The latter, now exceeding the former with the size of its population and the activity of its commerce, now excelled Paris with its shops, with large glazed windows, and with resorts.[27] And London even superseded Paris in strolling and recreation, especially due to its public pleasure gardens of different sizes and social gradations. Vauxhall, one of the most important of the two dozen or so pleasure gardens that had sprung up around London, offered straight walks through groves of trees on the one side and, on the other, a great open space where boxes were assembled around a bandstand and orchestra. A mix of people from fine lady to prostitute, duke to city merchant to pickpocket—each group for its own reasons—walked and wandered till twilight, when the lights on the boxes and band shell illuminated and the concert began. Providing intervals for walking and socializing, the concert played until midnight and could be adjourned with walks into the dark and the trees.[28]

Nevertheless, London, with its ever mounting congestion caused by a swelling population, equally discouraged walkers. Its speedy walkers invariably were frustrated by numerous unpaved or poorly paved roads, small streets, lanes, and byways, which formed serpentine mazes.[29] Their walks required moving around carts and carriages while dodging the continuous encroachment of windows and doorsteps into traffic lanes. And even streets and roads that were paved and lit after a fashion and had posts protecting pedestrians were without curbs and involved their walkers in continuous dodging.

In truth, there were two worlds there as elsewhere in Europe and particularly in Paris, where one contemporary commentator correctly stated there is a great division between those who ride in carriages and those who walk. Indeed, the only thing that separated them was the running board, which in fact "is the point of departure from one country to another, from misery to luxury, from thoughtlessness to thoughtfulness. It is the hyphen between him who is nothing and him who is all."[30]

A 1764 report from the London Commission of Sewers and Pavements inventoried impediments to walking and traffic that remained obstacles into the middle of the nineteenth century: "Pavements were defective, even in the principal streets." Gutters in the middle of the street were "so deep as to be a source of danger to vehicles." People still threw into the street "their offal, ashes, rubbish, broken glass, and pottery, [making] the street a kitchen midden." And, the report's inventory of defects continued, streets were frequently obstructed by unloading wagons, footpaths not elevated above roads were "liable to be overflowed with mud," pedestrian posts only served to narrow the streets, and footways were obstructed by parcels, boxes, barrels, cases, casks, and building materials. Craftsmen, for reasons of light and space, always took their work to the streets. Additionally, multiplying shop signs, which could fall in high winds, blocked the movement of air, and rainspouts poured down on the heads of passersby.[31]

With the rural countryside still within walking distance, the central city's streets, allies, byways, and lanes filled and emptied with rising and retreating tides of shepherds and their animals. (One stag hunt ended in 1820 at Number One, Montagau Street, Russell Square.)[32] Carriages and carts of all kinds, accumulating in number in the closing decades of the eighteenth and beginning decades of the nineteenth century, navigated the same swelling urban sea. Noise was always present, as were refuse, dust, dirt, and manure. With just a little rain, the streets filled with mud and muck that proved useful for purposeful splashing and resentful throwing against one's superiors. These conditions were common enough to create a bountiful number of porters—sedan chair drivers for the rich—whose motto could have been, "Leave the walking and carrying to us!" Indeed, servants and footmen, who often doubled and tripled as armed retainers, porters, and messengers, jammed the streets. They were joined by fruit, vegetable, and flower sellers, and cross sweepers who broomed the way clean for passing "lord and lady." Step cleaners, finders of cigar butts, pure finders (collectors of dog dung, used in tanneries), along with prostitutes, crooks, pickpockets, blackguards, gin addicts, and drunks, swelled London's streets.[33]

Vendors, hawkers, street traders, and local craftsmen, who need to meet people, on foot and face to face, walked and sold in the streets or set up their booths and barrows, further blocking alley and street. Among the salespeople of the street, there were those of a low order by virtue of their taking care of the feet or filthy shoes of others. There was the corn cutter, who, targeting the limping pedestrian, shouted, "Your feet to mend—corns to cut."[34] Shoeblacks also thrived amid the muck and mire. Their customers were all those who wished to have their shoes shine, to appear as if their wearers had not crossed the filthy fray they had in fact crossed. Some had their shoes brushed six times a day to prove they didn't walk in manure. A shoeblack needed but to plop down his three-legged stool, his pot of blacking, and "two or three brushes, a rag, a knife, a stick, and an old wig with which to wipe off the dust or mud," and he was in business.[35] And one could always find someone to repair shoes en route in this era of handcrafted footwear. Only in the second half of the nineteenth century did shoemaking become mechanized and industrialized.[36] By then, advancements in technology, principally the sewing machine, permitting the mass manufacture of cheap shoes, and the very number of people walking, who were capable of buying shoes and found them a necessity for work or city travel, combined to call into existence the whole new footwear industry.

Street processions, whose origins could be civic or private, ceremonial or improvised, were as common as were funeral corteges.[37] Crowds gathered and stood waiting for public flogging, pillorying, and execution, which were among the best amusements of streets filled with music, entertainment, and theater.[38] London's perpetual traffic jam transformed many a rider into a pedestrian; often the best thing—the only thing—to do was simply to get out and walk.

GET A STEP ON

At the beginning of the nineteenth century, congested London streets began to see efforts toward improvement. Gates and posts, called "bollards," designed to defend places and peoples against horses, carts, and carriages, were installed, and curbs and sidewalks were elevated above the roadway. But these amenities brought pedestrians little relief.[39] If anything, problems worsened as commerce and industry increased and goods, carts, and coaches multiplied. For instance, the city's first outer-ring road, built between 1756 and 1761, which diminished "the congestion hitherto caused by the innumerable herds of sheep and cattle wending their way along Oxford Street and Holborn to Smithfield Market," only invited more traffic into the city from the surrounding suburbs and countryside.[40] Each new bridge (six road bridges and seven rail bridges were added between 1812 and 1870), each enlarged and straightened street, and each new system of transit produced a temporary solution that spawned tomorrow's problem.

These changes and expansions in London's roads were of course part of a larger transformation experienced not only in England but also across Western Europe and in North America that was caused by population growth and the building of canals, train lines, and industries.[41] At the heart of this transformation stood what historian and critic Lewis Mumford identified as the quintessential megalopolis.[42] In control of every type of enterprise, London drove vast economic forces. Worldwide lanes of ocean commerce, then railroad lines, and finally highways were the web over which flowed a vast exchange of human energy and raw materials.[43]

In tandem with urban growth came the first stage of the London suburb between 1650 and 1850. Increasing numbers of nearby country estates were converted at increasing rates into suburbs, to which prosperous London merchants retreated. As they grew, riding—at least to and from the central city—increased while walking proportionately diminished.[44] A similar pattern emerged in the contemporary United States, with upper-class suburbs springing up in Boston, Philadelphia, and New York.[45] Such places as these anticipated the continuing eclipse of the walking center by the riding suburbs.[46] As greater numbers withdrew from the city center, so distances between home and work increased throughout the metropolitan area, with a corresponding rise in wheeled traffic between the periphery and the center. This change gave birth to the riding rather than walking commuter.[47]

However, as we will see later, the commuter doesn't make a first full appearance until the very end of the nineteenth century with the development of the urban mass transport system—specifically, the mass production of the automobile in the middle of the twentieth century. Meantime, throughout much of the nineteenth century, city residents like their predecessors went afoot.

City walkers, who could be pushed along by a variety of causes and impulses, lagged and sped along, shopped and rushed to work depending on neighborhood and hour of day. They stopped and crossed streets at random; an order was not yet imposed on how they moved, stood, leaned, or squatted on their haunches, waiting in line. To lie on the ground, to lower oneself to the level of the feet of others, would have won the judgment of sickness, inebriation, or homelessness. Absent traffic signals and police, anything resembling a full system of sidewalks, and a shared sense of etiquette, walkers, as individuals and groups, were undisciplined and even unruly. At any one moment they might vary their pace and direction as they darted from one place to another, swerved to avoid a vehicle, circled to pass an obstructed walk, or made a beeline to greet an acquaintance. In contrast to promenading in parks where the well-off strutted their fashionable stuff, day-in-and-day-out ordinary city walking required its practitioners to master the art of ducking and dodging. Accommodating stride, limb, and brain to the pressing throngs, urban pedestrians developed distinct survival skills. Traversing a dangerous landscape of swiftly altering situations, amid a kaleidoscope of sounds, sights, shifting currents of people, and moving objects, pedestrians had to stay alert to save their hides.

Well into the twentieth century, workers close to the heart of London continued, like their country cousins and in contrast to riding suburbanites, to slog out their lives on foot. Walking synchronized the dominant currents that came and went with the opening and closing hours of businesses and government offices.

Aside from quiet Sundays, changes in season and weather caused permutations in city walking.[48] Winds blew up dust, which covered clothes, got in eyes, bowed heads down, and stole hats. Rain altered and mixed the flows of street and sidewalk traffic. It also made slipperier surfaces for human and beast. A fallen and injured horse caused a pitiful traffic jam.[49] Rain also produced a salute to the heavens by legions of eye-poking and head-bumping umbrellas that doubled the density of street traffic.[50] Charles Dickens caught some of this in his description of London and its foot passengers caught in implacable November weather, which prefaced his *Bleak House*:

> As much mud in the streets as if the waters had but newly retired from the face of the earth. . . . Smoke lowering down from the chimney pots, making a soft black drizzle, with flecks of soot in it as big as full-grown snow-flakes—gone into mourning, one might imagine, for the death of the sun. Dogs, undistinguishable in mire. Horses, scarcely better, splashed to their very blinkers. Foot-passengers jostling one another's umbrellas in a general infection of ill-temper and losing their foothold at street corners, where tens of thousands of other foot-passengers have been slipping and sliding since day broke. . . .[51]

Cold drove many to seek out street fires and to huddle in the warmest corners they could find. Freezing rain put all in peril. And, of course, fog's grip on London can't be forgotten. It expanded the mystery and intrigue of the megalopolis.[52] Against it the older oil lamps and even the new gaslights—first installed and demonstrated at Pall Mall in 1807—proved impotent. According to contemporaries, lights shone mere "points of flame in the swirling miasma" during the great fog that enshrouded the city and the surrounding countryside, day and night, from December 27, 1813, to January 3, 1814.[53] Few people, according to the London *Sun* newspaper, ventured out, and streets were still except for "the voices of night watchmen or the noise of some solitary carriage cautiously feelings its way through the gloom."[54] Throughout the century fog often prevented the London pedestrian from seeing beyond a foot or two ahead and occasionally proved fatal to pedestrians.[55]

The scurrying middle-class walker (often armed with umbrella and a satchel) did not walk at the same pace as the worker, who faced a full day of physical work ahead, or the newly arrived country person, who didn't know where he or she was or was intent on simply looking around. Women and men, singularly and in groups, walked differently. Old and young did not move the same. Children played, chased and darted, lolled and went arm and arm, and moved at slowing speeds as they put themselves on display and flirted. Lugging wood, water, staples, and infants, if not the family's entire belongings, overburdened mothers invariably had something to carry, which changed their stride and gait when they walked the streets. The old often hobbled, limped, or virtually dragged themselves along, paying with their feet, legs, and back the price of a lifetime of working, poor nutrition, and absent health care. Deliverers, on foot and with two- and four-wheeled carts, joined the parade, abruptly forming crisscrossing currents as they moved goods from store to store, street to building, and back, making use of stairs, early elevators, and, later, basement elevators. Street vendors worked their way upstream like feeding fish or staked themselves out on corners to feed at the confluence of two streets, where foot traffic slowed and swirled. The unemployed stopped and accosted the passersby as best they could. According to Henry Mayhew, in *London Labour and the London Poor,* published between 1851 and 1862, the streets were the battlegrounds of orange and watercress peddlers, scavengers, crossing sweepers, and so many others making a last-ditch stand against the poorhouse, where one might end in the hands of the anatomists.[56]

Sounds, sights, smells, and experiences were many on London's streets. Cobblers, coopers, wheelwrights, potters, tinkers, and knife grinders, concentrated in different neighborhoods, put out distinct sounds, while bells continued to clamor and carriages to clatter throughout London. Historian Peter Ackroyd quotes an 1837 journalist who complained that "the loud and everlasting rattle of the countless vehicles is an everlasting annoyance"—and explains how the city used wood paving—slippery when wet—on such main thoroughfares as Oxford and the Strand to soften sounds.[57] Adding to the cacophony of street sound, colorful slang and catcalls could abuse or entertain the passerby. "Who put a turd in the boy's mouth?" and "as bare as a bird's arse" could be traced back to the fifteenth century. Conversely, to be called a *walker* around 1830 was an ephemeral street pejorative lasting only a few months, which, when "uttered with a peculiar drawl upon the first syllable, and sharp turn upon the last, was used by a young woman to deter an admirer, by young boys mocking a drunk, or anyone impeding the way."[58]

Pedestrians encountered more dangers on the streets than name calling. There were ever volatile and spontaneous crowds. Altercations among pedestrians, shopkeepers, and cabbies, into which the passerby could get drawn, kept the streets alive and astir. Holidays, festivals, and fairs proved primary excuses for energetic merry making. (Bonfires characterized Guy Fawkes Day, and on rare occasion when the river froze there were "Games on the Thames.")[59] Urban crowds—not yet disciplined by police in the first half of the nineteenth century—could at times be deadly quick to constitute themselves into a cruel court, and an innocent well-dressed pedestrian or foreigner might precipitate a mud-throwing event.[60]

Night required exceptional caution, encouraging the prudent walker as in times past to carry a sturdy cane for self-defense. Night walking—*noctambulation*—couldn't on any terms be turned into safe sleepwalking. Well into the middle decades of the century streets were still lit only by limited lamps and patrolled by a mere handful of the newly constituted police. Night amblers risked theft, muggings, and even murder. Reading shadows and recognizing footsteps were necessary survival skills for Londoners whose attraction to night pleasures made them prime targets for those who lay in wait.[61]

Pedestrians had to pick their way through certain neighborhoods with great care. On the street they had to protect themselves from the omnipresent pickpockets and bevies of beggars, and—as often happened outside the gates of work—they had to avoid the confidence men, shakedown artists, and others lying in wait for the freshly paid worker. Among the unknown twisting lanes and alleyways of the older part of the city, pedestrians had to avoid getting lost or losing their children. En route, midcentury pedestrians still couldn't find water to drink or any public place to relieve themselves in an emergency, especially when struck by the era's all-too-common stomach maladies. However, if their shoes came apart en route, or a nail poked its way through their shoe bottom, they could take advantage of the near-omnipresent shoemaker, if they had a spare coin or two.

In London, as in every urban environment, there was always something to step in. Domestic animals—pigs, cows, chickens, ducks, and horses—still roamed freely. In this town of hundreds of thousands of horses manure was everywhere, even though private and later civic cleaners were employed. Waist-high posts protecting pedestrians on sidewalks and at house and building entrances endangered groins. While roads were better paved, cleaned, and lit around 1830, in truth, the way had not yet been made smooth and level for urban walkers. Indeed, to be a successful London pedestrian one truly had to be "an artful dodger."

At midcentury, the chance of riding, even by those coming in and out of the city, was still only at 30 percent, with 400,000 of a total 508,000 walking.[62] (Omnibus and train passengers combined equaled approximately 25 percent, with 140,000 passengers.) While in 1850 five thousand horse riders passed Temple Bar each day and the number of private carriages in town may have been ten thousand or more in number, things steadily changed thereafter, making by 1890 the sight of a man on horseback rare and leaving London with only twenty-five thousand carriages.[63] In the city itself the well-to-do increasingly walked in this period as congestion grew, the cost of keeping and feeding horses escalated, and public transport spread.

The modern city—be it London, Paris, Berlin, Rome, or New York—has produced the quintessential city walker: the pedestrian. The pedestrian moves as a part of traffic, walking among crowds and strangers, traversing a kaleidoscopic and mutating landscape. Over time, pedestrians collectively were taken off their feet as they traveled a growing distance between home and work and increasingly relied on urban transit systems. At some point in the last decade of the nineteenth century or first decades of the twentieth century, the city pedestrian—who still may walk to and from transit—evolved to become first and foremost the riding commuter. He or she walks ever shorter and more segmented distances in the city and in the suburb.

The story of the modern city walker, of course, does not form a linear narrative from walking to riding. Going on foot may actually have increased in the last half of the eighteenth and first half of the nineteenth century, the gestation period of modern transportation. Coupled with a steady population rise from the late eighteenth century, improved roads, canals, and trains stimulated increased foot travel as villagers in ever increasing numbers sought out larger towns and cities in search of mates and work. At the same time, increased societal migrations whetted appetites in excess of transportation systems' capacity and ability to offer affordable prices. In fact, Western Europe remained essentially a walking society until the middle of the nineteenth century and the great majority did not take to riding mass transit until the opening decades of the twentieth century.

The story of London transport offers in microcosm the history of urban travel and shows how the city walker became essentially a "riding" pedestrian and commuter. London transport started the century serving the consolidated and densely packed London area of 950,000 and the Greater London area of 1.1 million. Together this combined area, whose heart at the time lay only two miles on each side of the Thames, constituted 12 percent of the entire nation (i.e., England and Wales). It ended the century serving a region of 7.4 million people, which constituted 20 percent of the nation.[64] Starting with the horse bus system in 1829 and boasting the first steam underground in 1863 and the first electric tube railway in 1890, the London transport system involved diverse land and water transit, which included a variety of privately and publicly owned systems, and operated numerous lines and a variety of stations.[65] Geographic and class diffusion is underlined by the fact that "by 1912 working men's tickets represented about forty percent of all suburban railways journeys within six to eight miles of the center of London."[66]

London opened the first underground urban railway in the world in 1863. Contradicting predictions, it was immediately popular. On the first day thirty thousand passengers, choosing speed over sunlight, traveled between Paddington and Farringdon Stations. The journey took about eighteen minutes. In 1868, the Metropolitan District Railway opened a second line between South Kensington and Westminster. In 1884 the two lines were joined to form the Inner Circle.[67] In 1890—six years in advance of Budapest's subway, eight before the Paris Métro, and ten before New York's system—London introduced the world's first electric tube railway.[68]

Helping create the commuter, the deeper and cheaper metro tube system—made possible by a new boring machine and the use of electric traction—proved immensely popular. It stole millions of passengers from the subsurface train line in 1900, when the Central London Railway offered a flat fee from west London to the City. By 1907 the heart of today's underground system was in place. A rapid and interconnected system, with hinges at central switching and rail stations, extended several miles in every direction into the city's suburbs.[69]

At the start of the new century, Londoners were turning into riding commuters as historic, densely packed London emptied out and metropolitan suburbs grew in number, size, and distance from the center of the city. Roy Porter notes that "bus and tram journeys per Londoner increased fivefold between 1881 to 1913."[70] For a slightly different period Francis Sheppard estimated that

in 1875 the number of journeys per annum by train, tram, and bus in the London area had been about 275,000,000 m. Twenty years later it had more than tripled to 1,000,000,000, although the population had risen by less than fifty percent in the same period. . . . The number of journeys per head of the London population rose 65 to 165 per annum; and by 1911 this figure had risen to 250 journeys on all public services.[71]

Still in 1900 it appeared that congestion—which engulfed other European and world cities—appeared to be winning out.[72] Despite growth in underground travel, transit was still dependent on horse and surface travel, which made walking a speedier means than riding in a horse-drawn vehicle.[73] One source of the congestion was the city's estimated 50,000 horse-pulled buses, trams, carts, and private carriages.[74] Approximately 1,450 trams were pulled along 147 miles of track by 14,000 horses, while "as many as 690 omnibuses per hour were passing the Bank of England standing at London's commercial center, and nearly as many crossed at Piccadilly Circus."[75]

However, by 1910, a revolution in transit and traffic was underway in London.[76] An electric tramway operating on the perimeter of London penetrated the center of the city at countless points.[77] Motorcar taxis equaled in number horse-drawn hansom cabs and hackney coaches, while the gasoline-powered bus replaced the horse-drawn tram that ran on tracks.[78] With underground stations dotting the city at half-mile distances along a line, the integrated electric subway system tightly circled London and joined it to a ring of immediate suburbs—such as Aldgate to the east, Highgate to the north, Turham Green to the west, and Elephant and Castle to the south.[79] Like a great reciprocal pump, train, underground, and bus brought people in and out of the city, producing a new species of urban pedestrian and commuter, who walked (or ran) between rides. This commuter was offered the assistance of moving stairs and elevators on the way up and down to station platforms.

DISCERNING STEPS

As it developed over the course of a century, London's transport system—on land and water, in city center and periphery—exacerbated urban turbulence.[80] Despite having been built not only to improve traffic but also to clear slums, new roads, docks, bridges, metro lines, and train lines initially fueled congestion and metastasized poverty, crime, and squalor to other sections of the city.[81] While the docks and new streets evicted approximately 30,000 people in the period from 1853 to 1901, railroad construction displaced 120,000 Londoners in the same period.[82] Expelled from home, they flocked to adjacent neighborhoods, where demands for housing elevated rents, which in turn catapulted them and the poorer residents of these neighborhoods to yet more distant places, where they were without community and compelled to make on foot longer treks to city center and work.

In *Dombey and Son* (1848), Dickens vividly depicted the "wrecked industrial landscape" that was produced by the building of the London and Birmingham railway at Stagg's Garden in north London:

> The first shock of a great earthquake had, just at that period, rent the whole neighbourhood to its centre. Traces of its course were visible on every side. Houses were knocked down; streets broken through and stopped; deep pits and trenches dug in the ground; enormous heaps of earth and clay thrown up; buildings that were undermined and shaking, propped up by great beams of wood. . . . There were a hundred thousand shapes and substances of incompleteness, wildly mingling out of their places, upside down, burrowing in the earth, mouldering in the water, and unintelligible as any dream.[83]

The metamorphosis of the urban landscape added to the turbulence of Europe's first megalopolis, where it was estimated that in the 1860s approximately six hundred thousand workers lived impecuniously, and hence afoot, off daily or even hourly employment. Removed at ever greater distances from their jobs, ever greater numbers of workers, averaging an income of a pound or less a week, could not afford a daily transport fare of even six pence.[84] Walking claimed even more energy from unemployed workers. One contemporary worker described his daily search for work:

> I first went down to the riverside at Shadwell. No work to be had. Then I called at another place in Limehouse. No hands wanted. So looked in at home and got two slices of bread in paper and walked eight miles to a cooper's yard [where they made barrels, buckets, and

other wooden vessels] in Tottenham. All in vain. I dragged myself back to Clerkenwell. Still no luck. Then I turned homewards in despair. By the time I reached Stepney I was deadbeat.[85]

At the end of the nineteenth century, legislation confronting the growing distance between worker and work required lower fares that turned walkers into riders, even though only approximately one person in four from the working population took train, tram, or bus to work.[86] At the same time, transit, which had dramatically accelerated sprawl, constituted a revolutionary system of human transportation. The ensemble of the electrified surface tram (the most economical inner-city mode of travel), gas-powered buses, and the intracity train and tube system had created the commuter.

The commuter, who may have still walked to and from station, and from station to stop, and stop to work, was a new bipedal creature. His instincts were to ride when he chose to, or when he could. Walking, unless the nature of his job or particular location dictated otherwise, was no longer a destiny, a way of life, but instead a limited and chosen activity. Walking, sitting and standing, descending and climbing, waiting and scurrying, jumping and leaping, pushing, squeezing, and running, this newly spawned breed of urban walker went to work and back. He checked connections and clocks; his agile, almost fishlike travel was a matter of punctuated time and space. Crowded together in a bus, or herded together in the underground, commuters were sent hurtling through darkness and flashing images until deposited on the cement shores of a chosen stop. From there, by foot, along the margins of tunnels, up stairways, on rolling stairs, and by elevator, they were returned to the streets above, where their walking pace defined the tempo of the city's movement.

Of course, not all city walkers took up the commuter's dominant pace. Some, with extra money and time, sought distraction and amusement in a city filled with mounting attractions. They ducked into bars and coffee shops, lingered in parks and gardens, sat out the rush hour in the movies, or did their street walking at night on what were, at the end of the century, far better lit and policed streets than at its start. In London, as elsewhere in Europe and North America, humanity, thanks to electric lighting, began to live and amuse itself in what French thinker Gaston Bachelard calls "the age of administered light."[87]

As wealth and goods became more abundant, shoppers multiplied in London and across Europe and North America, forming a swelling, slowing, and even halting stream of traffic on retail streets.[88] Of course, some shoppers darted in and out of stores. With bags and packages held in hands and arms, some jammed and pushed while others made urgent and undignified rushes, forcing larger retail establishments to filter their entering and exiting customers through newly installed revolving doors. Even when the stores were closed, shoppers—especially, at first, those from the upper sectors of the middle class—learned to stroll from window to window, as if the whole world of goods were placed at their feet for their perusal.

Store owners had responded at the end of the eighteenth century to the growing taste for window shopping with larger displays and enlarged window fronts. Built between 1816 and 1818, the Royal Opera Arcade—consisting of "eighteen small shops on one side, each with a basement, a small mezzanine and a Regency bowed window"—offered uniquely concentrated shopping.[89] However, London was not quick to advance to the department store. While Paris built its first department store, the Bon Marché, in the 1860s, London kept shoppers walking to separate individual shops, continuing to rely on its arcades and bazaars.[90] While department stores did spring up to meet new shoppers and increased demand in the metropolis's smarter suburbs in the 1870s and 1880s, city stores coped with an estimated doubling of the numbers of shoppers during that period by expanding their premises and increasing the variety of their stock.[91]

By the end of the century, however, Harrods and other large-scale modern department stores had opened in London. They had huge staffs, some numbering in the thousands. Supervised by vigilant floorwalkers, company detectives of a sort, workers often slept in company dormitories and were thus harnessed to their post day and night. Electric lighting highlighted products on display. Pneumatic tubes, which were driven by compressed air, saved walking by zooming cash and orders back and forth and between the floors of the store, while Otis elevators—installed in multifloored department stores in the 1880s—spared customers the effort of stair climbing and allowed them to put the most expensive things, fittingly, highest up in the store. A lift operator, outfitted in uniform and with gloves, swinging open and closing a heavy gate, graciously whisked privileged customers up to the desired floor, where they could stroll. The escalator made its debut in London in Harrods in 1898.[92] In 1906, the London department store Selfridge's took a page from Chicago's Marshall Fields by welcoming its exploring customers with especially spacious store windows and ample interior floor space to move about in comfort.[93]

In the course of the nineteenth century, shopping took the form—at least for the prospering middle class—of a privileged and self-congratulatory ambling. It manifested having time and money. In dramatic contrast to the crammed and cacophonous working-class markets, department stores and arcades offered their customers ample room once inside, and a relaxed atmosphere. Shopping constituted a distinct type of both outdoor and indoor city walking. Customers could linger and even loiter, much as they do today in malls, walking about simply to escape the weather or to stroll arm-and-arm à deux. Now shopping fostered a type of dreamy walking—it even invited idealizations of the city itself.[94] Here was a clean, wholesome, and opulent place where deserving people of means could exercise their choice, receive the respect they deserved, and get the goods they wanted. Walking would be unencumbered, peaceful, and self-satisfying.

THE MINDFUL STEP

One last group of city walkers deserves attention—the writers, who walked the city to explore the new faces of humanity contained on its streets. Drawn to the city in droves, they were dissimilar to the city planners who analyzed the city with abstract and careful calculations, charting, often in terms of quantifiable data, the movement of pedestrians and commuters. Contrary to those who would design and engineer the city on drafting boards, writers—afoot and with words—tried often as sensitive and alert wanderers and strollers—flâneurs—to penetrate the heart of humanity and the new urban environment.[95]

The most classic effort to analyze the living city with attention to the details of the texture of everyday life was carried out by the twentieth-century German-Jewish thinker Walter Benjamin. With keen powers of reflection on urban society honed as a young man on the streets of Berlin and by a visit to Moscow, Benjamin began in 1927—as a self-exiled scholar in Paris—his thirteen-year analysis of the early-nineteenth-century Parisian arcades.[96] He saw these shopping galleries, formed by shop-lined walkways and filled with Parisians daily and nightly strolling to gaze at luxury goods, posters, and panoramas. These arcades revealed a society's evolution from one based on mutual concern to one based on commodities and material well-being.[97] A vast montage of readings, anecdotes, and insights resulted from Benjamin's continuous pondering of the arcades. Writing with a wealth of details about cafés, omnibuses, fashion, advertising, prostitution, and boredom, he wrote, "streets are the dwelling places of the collective."[98]

Through the highest conscious product of the arcades, the French stroller, the *flâneur* (typified for Benjamin by French poet Charles Baudelaire), he sought to explore the emergence of the modern mind. The *flâneur,* Benjamin conjectured, was detached from the city he walked. Because he did not know where his thought should alight or what end he should serve, his detached strolling, sitting, and reflecting, itself a type of intellectual consumption, yielded no identity. Without property or profession, in his first form he was the Bohemian (*il bohème*) of France of the 1830s and 1840s. With sufficient money, usually derived from his parents or an estate, and refined taste for his leisure, he was allied entirely neither with the middle class nor yet with the metropolis.

His reflective pedestrianism, both emotive and critical, resonated with ambiguity. He turned to the moving crowd. In its illusive, flowing, phantasmagoric images he sought the meaning of the contemporary city. At the same time, among the arcades the *flâneur* took a step into the marketplace for himself, his ideas, and the arts. There he became a shopper of his own place in emerging commercial society. Without old or new patron, without being anchored in a place or having a defined social alliance, he possessed an ambivalence that formed a distinct optics of perception. Collectively, out of the ranks of

Bohemians and *flâneurs* surfaced the intelligentsia, which prior to the Europe-wide revolutions of 1848, sided with early utopian and revolutionary ideas, schemes, and causes.[99] The French Revolution had already shown in blood what happened in Paris, when—in the city's gardens and debating clubs—disaffected thinkers came in contact with disaffected workers.[100]

Contemporary writers in the spirit of the *flâneur,* such as Baudelaire, went from Paris, and elsewhere in urban Europe, to London to see up close on its streets the modern world in the making. Following their subjectivity, these romantic city walkers pursued the city on foot along its gaudy, glaring streets, down its most narrow and sinister alleyways, and into new, opulent retail stores. By describing street scenes, they encapsulated the human condition in a single encounter, be it with an image of a child locked out of the poorhouse; a streetwalker emboldened in her trade; the exchange of life-saving favors of those with no means; or the cruel indifference of the carriage rider who will not descend into the street even to see the pedestrian his carriage has run over. Considering London to be the Rome of the modern era, these urban writer-walkers opened their minds to the streetscapes and fashioned their reflections out of and around it.

Having learned to write about the human traffic and the street figures of St. Petersburg, Fyodor Dostoevsky (1821–1881) went to London.[101] Everything he identified with Europe's economic injustice, depersonalization, and loss of spirituality he found walking the streets of London in the summer of 1862.

> One . . . night—it was getting on for two o'clock in the morning—I lost my way and for a long time trudged the streets in the midst of a vast crowd of gloomy people. . . . The populace is much the same anywhere, but there all was so vast, so vivid that you almost physically felt things which up until then you had only imagined. . . . The streets can hardly accommodate the dense, seething crowd. The mob has not enough room on the pavements and swamps the whole street. All that mass of humanity craves for booty and hurls itself at the first comer with shameless cynicism. Glistening, expensive clothes and semi rags and sharp differences—*they are all there.*[102]

The French philosopher and critic Hippolyte Taine also sketched a pedestrian's portrait of London. Amidst the prosperity, he identified those "northern men, with their athletic temperament, who need plenty of air and exercise," and "the English girl [who] covers more ground on her feet in a week than a Roman girl does in a year." London's abundant parks supplied, Taine continued, ample space for English walkers and riders. Another world poured out onto London streets—"children in rags, paupers, street women, as if a human sewer were suddenly clearing itself." Filled with fighting, drunkenness, and mayhem, "the whole place [was] alive with 'street-boys,' bare-footed, filthy, turning cartwheels for a penny." Painful creatures of all ages, most of whom were dirty and barefooted and wearing clothes that had made the rounds, appeared to "have lain down to sleep anywhere on the ground, among the feet of the crowd." Taine remarked that a recommendation was required to use the Reading Room of the British Museum, but he noticed that all sorts of people got in, even people *with no shoes on their feet*.[103]

Of all writers, foreign and British alike, Charles Dickens most tested his foot and pen on London.[104] London was his library and studio— the best place in the world to know humanity up close, foot to foot, nose to nose. Dickens was an insomniac, a noctambulist, and like Doctor Johnson a century before him, a compulsive and formidable walker.[105] He opened his *Old Curiosity Shop* (1840–1841) with an invitation to visit London. "Night is generally my time for walking . . . I have fallen insensibly into this habit, both because it favours my infirmity and because it affords me greater opportunity of speculating on the characters and occupations of those who fill the streets."[106] In *Nicholas Nickleby* (1839) Dickens, who walked, wrote of the London that rode, shopped, and prospered—"that rattled on through the noisy, bustling, crowded streets of London." Along the same streets, Dickens observed, "There was a Christening party at the largest coffin makers," and "life and death went hand in hand, wealth and poverty stood side by side; repletion and starvation laid them down together."[107]

Dickens wanted to tell one part of London about the other, to explain the half that walks to the half that rides. In more than one work he explained dark, grimy, ashen, toil-laden, hunger-filled, and foot-weary London to the glittering and glamorous world of carriages and boulevards, of selective ambling and ostentatious strolling. In an essay in "A Nightly Scene in London," in the weekly *Household Words,* Dickens described the mute homeless from whom conditions have stolen even their patter. "Crouched against the wall of the Workhouse, in the dark street, on the muddy pavement-stones, with the rain raining upon them, were five bundles of rags." When asked where they had been all day, the first of them replied, "About the streets." When given money, she offered no thanks. She simply "melted into the miserable night," adding to the legions of London's invisible walkers.[108]

Young Oliver Twist travels on foot sixty-five miles to London in seven days. Along the way cold, night, and hunger close in on him. He fears being attacked by dogs and encircled by parish police. At one point "his feet were sore, and his legs so weak that they trembled beneath him."[109] Finally the young John Dawkins, alias "the Artful Dodger," delivers Oliver to a London lodging: "A dirtier or more wretched place [Oliver] had never seen."[110] There he learns the guileful arts of street survival.

Dickens demanded that society care for its own. In this he anticipated social reformers in London and their American counterparts such as Jacob Riis in New York and Jane Addams in Chicago, who worked in the late nineteenth and early twentieth centuries to make their cities fresh, clean, healthy, and welcoming—better places for walking. For the sake of the health of urban children and the improvement of the nation, they encouraged the building of parks, took children on hikes, and delivered them to fresh air camps where outdoor walking and living would create an improved breed of humans.

Already the working classes in England, the United States, and elsewhere in the West were prompted to believe in their improvement as their conditions ameliorated in the last third of the century. They began to eat better, live longer, and get better medical care. They had means to buy beds, chairs, and furniture for their dwellings, and to taste, however parsimoniously, new pleasures of leisure and recreation. In increasing numbers they had better reasons to stay at home when they could rather than venture out onto the streets.

At the same time, other drummers were beating far different tunes for human movement. With tracks and roads reaching into the countryside and penetrating village and peasant life, government tightened its tentacled grip on society. Indeed, in the nineteenth and twentieth centuries, the state—waging its long war begun in earnest in the eighteenth century against the unruly and restless mobs, and threatening crowds that focused on city streets—took control of national pedestrian life. Ever more powerful, government and its institutions—first on the national and increasingly on regional and even local levels—defined the nature, speed, punctuality, and manner of society's movement. The success of commerce, government, and armies themselves depended on getting pedestrians, commuters, consumers, citizens, and soldiers literally in step. The century's first and most imposing test would be for France to bring revolutionary Paris to heel.

$\overset{\text{\tiny ?}}{\text{\Large 7}}\overset{\text{\tiny ?}}{}$ A New Footing for the Nation

*Taming and Cleaning Up
Revolutionary Paris*

 THE nineteenth century witnessed the transformation of the great cities of the West. Road building, sanitation, suburbs, public transport, and a tremendous increase in foot and vehicular traffic created an unprecedented urban environment and a new breed of walker for it. By controlling crowds and mobs, which had defied civic authority since the Middle Ages, the authorities and police helped give birth to this environment and the urban pedestrian and commuter. Only control of the streets could stave off the revolution, secure the expanding interests of the ruling and riding classes, and produce a new order of traffic.

The nineteenth-century struggle for the streets pitted mounted and armed soldiers and police against roaming mobs and parading crowds. Its most coarsely drawn axis followed an underlying class war that opposed upper-class property owners, who moved across the city for their affairs, promenaded in carriages, and strolled and shopped on foot for leisure, against the rest of society, which went on foot as a matter of necessity. In its most dramatic moments of revolt and revolution, this struggle became an open war between authority and crowds insisting on immediate needs, wants, rights, and even, when the intellectual allies shaped wishes, dreams of an entirely new and different society. At all times, it fell to the government to regulate the ever present divide between increasing numbers of carriage riders and those who went on foot.

Predictably, authorities chose the side of public order and private property. It was far more natural to side with the peaceful and orderly walking—graceful strolling, shopping, and commuting—of known people, their own kind, than to side with the shifting, amorphous, and ill-defined enemies in the streets. They had no doubt that the mob, the crowd, and even the whole city represented, if anything, the seething, volatile, and uncontrollable underside of society. Pledged to its own survival, authority insisted on control. It would, as best as it could, suppress vagrancy, unlicensed itinerancy, illegal assembly, rebellious marching, strikes, and other forms of threatening pedestrian behavior, which they identified with the dark and dangerous underclasses. A crowd going on foot was potentially subversive.

Also, authority had a primary stake in domestic tranquility and order. How could there be commercial interest and development amidst turbulence and anarchy, which were bred by growth itself? Consequently, civic authorities took drastic measures. They institutionalized the police, tore down and rebuilt center city zones for the sake of urban development and transportation, and made avenues wide enough for hauling cannons and shooting them against the pedestrian enemies. Across Europe, over time, civic authorities shaped rules and laws to assure crowd control and govern vehicular and walking traffic. They even regulated the movement of the upper classes' private carriages and promenades.

This transformation occurred at the very time when the city superseded the countryside, and the middle class, triumphing over the aristocracy, began to impose its ambitions, aspirations, and senses of work and efficiency on national society. This change throughout the

West can be illustrated in Paris, where revolutionary crowds on foot, in 1789, truly began the nineteenth century with the question, Can national government subdue its own society? And there, by century's end, regulations and police had turned the movement of the masses into that of citizens, shoppers, productive assembly line workers, and, in 1914, obedient foot soldiers.

Rivaling London in shopping and leisure, Paris excelled London before the revolution as a place where the nobility and upper middle class promenaded in carriage and on foot. By the end of the reign of Napoleon III (1850–1870), Paris became an open urban center. It served, as the state would have it, traffic, commerce, fashion, the movement of troops, and firing of cannons. Retracing Parisian steps sketches paths to be followed by Western urban walkers.

TRANSFORMING CITIES

The transformation of European and north American cities coincided with the mature phase of the Industrial Revolution, during which more buildings were constructed, more public projects undertaken, more goods produced and circulated, and more urban growth sustained than in all previous centuries since the time of Christ combined. The building of roads, railroads, canals, bridges, tunnels, and water and sewage systems, along with commercial agriculture, large-scale mining, electricity, factories, and skyscrapers profoundly altered urban and rural environments.[1] As never before a civilization shaped human work, play, and movement. It was inevitable that it would change human walking.

This transformation altered walking and walkers. It involved laying and paving streets and furnishing them with gutters and sidewalks. Sidewalks provided at least comparatively safe, straight, dry lanes for speedy pedestrians. (*Trottoirs,* French for "sidewalk," were for those who wished to *trotter!*) This transformation originated the production of smooth and easy-to-clean surfaces, which allowed walkers to wear lighter shoes and glide on their speeding feet rather than stomp and clomp along as their ancestors had done since time immemorial.[2] Powerful and portable engines, combined with pumps, pipes, and valves, produced a revolution in cleanliness and sanitation. This revolution brought abundant fresh water into European and North American cities—animating public fountains, baths, toilets, urinals, fire hydrants, and swimming pools in the most progressive cities—while inconspicuously shunting waste, sewage, and storm waters out.[3] Indeed, the greatest accomplishment of the Victorian era was, according to British historian Asa Briggs, the creation of a hidden network of pipes and drains and sewers "more comprehensive than the transport system."[4] All this eventually made for a cleaner walker and walking environment. Indeed, the walker could take to the streets to relieve himself or herself, to take a shower, or even go for a swim. To walk the streets no longer meant that one was necessarily dirty and foul.

Where smooth, light, and transparent surfaces triumphed, the urban world sparkled. Pane glass made a see-through world. Shoppers, whose noses and errant steps were no longer severely punished by piles of waste and mounds of decomposing materials, could stroll past inviting storefront windows and, once inside in a shop, examine the goods in a comfortable ambience filled with glass display cases. Modern lighting, first gas and then electric, became a standard measure of urban progress from the middle of the nineteenth century on. Light changed the environment indoors and out, if for no other reason than that it permitted walkers to see where they trod.[5] Ample light improved indoor activities (games, cards, reading, and so forth), providing less reason to seek relief on the streets. Outdoors, lighting provided cities with a full and safe nightlife, capitalized on by the emerging entertainment and restaurant industries.[6] The lights at Marshall Fields, the *Chicago Tribune* reported, "were resplendent, giving delight to the crowds that walked the streets."[7]

In tandem, technology and law swept cities cleaner than ever before. Cities were paved on an unprecedented scale. Imposing zoning and banning nuisances removed many of the sources of the most repugnant smells, sounds, and sights. Industry supplied homes and offices with a plethora of brooms, shovels, and brushes, while foot scrapers, vestibules, and revolving doors saved interiors from what outside air currents and shoes tracked in. In turn, cities learned effectively to dispose of dead horses and horse manure and eventually, carrying out of one of the great revolutions of modern history, to do without the horse itself.[8]

Urban congestion, with foul air and water and significant epidemics of typhoid, cholera, tuberculosis, measles, polio, and other diseases in London, Paris, and elsewhere in the nineteenth century, placed public health at the top of the rationalist-oriented progressive agenda.[9] Like a legion of sniffing and moralizing Sherlock Holmeses, public health officials examined streets, soils, and especially tenement slums for sources and vectors of disease. They scrutinized run-offs, streams, creeks, rivers, cisterns, wells, and pumps. And they did not neglect the air! Stench, fog, haze, dust, and other olfactory unpleasantnesses were scrutinized as sources of what were commonly taken to be the bad air of disease-causing miasmas.[10]

Nuisances of every sort—all that was deemed unhealthy, unsightly, dangerous, and even immoral—were increasingly swept from the streets, making easier passage for vehicles and pedestrians alike. Legislators and police removed from the street vagrants, beggars, and prostitutes, along with noisy shops, saloons, disorderly houses, and roaming animals, while licensing peddlers and other itinerant salespeople. Civic laws and rules instructed commercial agents as to when and what they could sell and solicit on the streets, and told street entertainers where and what they could perform. Requiring merchants to maintain their sidewalks, cities forbade them from setting up stalls and workshops, leaving open cellar doors and grates, storing goods or working in front of their store or in the road, or impairing traffic in other ways.

The imperative to transform the city and its traffic extended to controlling and disciplining walkers themselves. Cities now taught walkers as individuals and groups not to spit, litter, urinate, drink, act drunk and disorderly, or fight on the streets. At the same time, citizens were taught not to loiter and block streets and sidewalks, to walk on the sidewalk, to stay on the correct side, and to push and shove. Traffic laws, which were articulated in the twentieth century, instructed pedestrians how to cross streets at intersections, where they and vehicular traffic competed most fiercely for the same space. From the perspective of comparing medieval and early modern urban life with contemporary city existence, control started to take some of the vitality and spontaneity out of the street.

Urban society required that on some level the movement of humans on foot and the movement of vehicles (which went, whether by horse or motor, considerably faster than walkers) be reconciled. They separated the two between sidewalk and road, and then sought to control their intersections at street corners and other crossings to form an efficiency of movement. But beyond achieving traffic orderliness and teaching pedestrians manners, which some judged to be the hallmark of civilized life, Western governments had more enduring reasons to control their streets. Experience taught that the streets can foster unruly mobs and crowds, which on occasion threatened governments and even precipitated revolution. Authority had good reasons to be leery of restive crowds.

CONTROLLING STREETS

Despite governments' standing interest in controlling streets, they had long been essentially impotent to direct the currents of people who flowed into and collected, mingled, and moved about in the city. Since the twelfth and thirteenth centuries, major cities had been porous. It was almost impossible for premodern states to know the individuals who composed crowds, much less monitor groups, without organized police, record keeping, official documents and records, and power. Additionally, the individuals who composed mobs were hidden in the anonymity of an age when investigation was not an established craft and identities, street names, and street numbers weren't fixed.[11] Purges, massacres, and pogroms, exploited by a calculating state, alone served as the coarse instrument of expulsion of urban undesirables in early modern times, as did the abused *lettres de cachet,* which, bearing the king's signature, became grounds to put someone in prison.

Urban crowds, which composed modern Parisian history and proved to be the center of the French Revolution, often proved liquid and nearly impossible to define by number, origin, and motive. A mob—which the French tellingly call *la rue* (the street)—spontaneously assembled, sparked by an immediate incident, such as the rising price of bread or a rumor about the pending harvest or marching peasants. Actions often quickly followed, with spontaneous street justice often taking the form of beatings, killings, and looting. The crowd, quick to take up a role on its natural stage, the streets—especially the squares and open plazas—produced leaders, protests, and riots. Like a flowing river, the mob gathered, carrying power as it went, and yet it could vanish as swiftly as it appeared.[12]

Scarcity and bread prices often moved the masses, especially the women, out onto the streets. Rumors often coalesced them into mobs. Uncertainty subjected them to a volatile mix of desperation, fear, and myth. Authorities, correspondingly, reacted with their own myths and fears of the crowds they had to govern but didn't know. Indeed, an anxious government considered every street festival and demonstration potentially an uprising in the making.[13] It correctly conceived the masses as the foot soldiers of rebellion and revolution. In times of heightened alert, such as even England faced in opposing the mounting and rallying Chartist movement in the great revolutionary spring of 1848, authorities gathered police and armies and barricaded banks and property against rioting and pillaging mobs. It called officers back to service, deputized private individuals, and summoned the cavalry and artillery as they heard about countryside crowds assembling to march on the city, or striking workers gathering at the city centers.[14]

The most dramatic street episodes of early modern history occurred in eighteenth-century Paris. The French government had, like the rest of Europe, long used public execution and punishment to declare to the anonymous crowd the seriousness of its intention to enforce law.[15] Monarchy, in turn, had cut serious swathes out of Paris for boulevards, squares, gardens, and imposing palaces where it could display, parade, and promenade imposing power and wealth. But this did not suppress the city's volatility, which continued to grow in the last half of the eighteenth century for reasons well explained by historian David Garrioch in his book, *The Making of Revolutionary Paris*.[16]

In the eighteenth century, Paris's population, whose aggregate numbers we can only guess to have ranged from five hundred thousand to a million, significantly increased in the course of the century.[17] Other factors, according to Garrioch, made the Paris of 1789 very different from the Paris of 1700. This new city occupied three times the space the old one did. It was a more mobile city, augmented by population movements to and within Paris. Tourists and business travelers grew as a result of improved transportation and growing commerce. Parisians themselves multiplied their commercial, familial, and cultural connections within the city, with the adjacent countryside, and with France and Europe at large. Within Paris itself, increasingly the walking working class sought work and leisure outside of its accustomed neighborhoods.

Despite improvements, such as the opening of the riverfront and the building of new gardens and roads, the ruling plan of Paris was still medieval. Pedestrians still suffered streets that were dirty, crooked, congested, and narrow, only fifteen or twenty feet broad even when they ran between buildings six and seven stories high, such as the Palais Halles and Châtelet.[18] Paris was still plagued by intense, and now expanded, congestion of carts, animals, and teeming ambulant street groups. There was "a large number of vendors of fruit, vegetables, fish, and flowers, pushing their wheelbarrows, as well as clothes-dealers, glaziers, chimney sweeps, and water-carriers, rattling the handles of their buckets."[19] Traffic rules, ordinances, and police to control the conduct of the streets still had not been established. Nevertheless, the city's walking environment had been significantly altered. Many of its streets had been paved. They were now better lit with new oil lamps in contrast to older tallow candles. More and faster carriages and coaches moved along the streets, pushing walkers to the crowded edges of pavement or forcing them to take cover behind large stones that projected from some houses or in the common recessed doorways. As a modest consolation prize, they were offered some early sidewalks in the 1780s, which moderately protected the walkers from carriage drivers, who without a rule of road drove on left and right sides at will.

Demographic change, mobility, and turbulence weakened the cohesion of urban neighborhoods, which were composed around local customs, parishes, and crafts. Local people were more likely to walk further between home and work, while neighborhood streets were increasingly filled with strangers. At the same time, in the closing decades of the eighteenth century, centralizing government challenged local authorities. While the old order continued to underpin and shape individual Parisian communities, the city as a whole emerged. Although the population was differentiated by individual interests, class divisions, buildings, and patterns of vehicular and foot traffic, issues of freedom and justice increasingly percolated through Paris at large.

Perhaps nothing in the second half of the eighteenth century could have stopped the city from rioting or deflected the crowd's demonstrations from becoming increasingly political.[20] A rising but politically thwarted middle class continually surfaced questions about control of the city and nation. Revolts in America, Holland, and other places inspired hope for a dramatic resolution to a growing field of complaints. Parisians were ready for change. They stood, in the words of Garrioch, "simultaneously more politically aware than in the past and more helpless in the face of government."[21] The elite of parishes and trades had lost power to central government in the years preceding the revolution. At the same time, as "urban space was becoming more uniform and easier to navigate," the groups and classes in the city were more and more likely to take up and embroil themselves in the abstract issues of government and nation.

Revolt in Paris caused revolution in France in 1789. The French Revolution was long in preparation, its way having been paved by a succession of events. More than two decades of failure to achieve financial reforms—at the heart of which failure lay the inability of the monarchy to find a way to tax nobility—forced the summoning of the age's long-defunct French Estates General to Versailles. The Estates General stalemated over the issue of whether the body's voting would be by individual delegate or composing estate. The third estate, composed of those who did not belong to the church or aristocracy, responded in June by declaring itself France's National Assembly and, with its famous Tennis Court Oaths, decided it would not adjourn until it provided France with a constitution. On June 27 the king, encouraging the other two orders, the clergy and nobility, to join the third estate in the assembly, approved the formation of the new single-house assembly. Then the fervent Parisian crowd took to the streets and the course of the revolution began.

Fears of invasion of the city by ravaging peasants, rumors of a counterrevolution, mounting anger over the shortage of bread in the city, and suspicions about what was occurring at Versailles filled the streets on the eve of July 14. The mulling crowd found its target in the Bastille, the symbol of central power and a cache for arms and ammunition. It stormed and destroyed the Bastille and paraded the head of its governor around the city on a pike. So the French Revolution began, and shortly thereafter the revolutionary mob beheaded the provost of the merchants and paraded his head around town as well. The attack on the Bastille, and the freeing of its prisoners, was of utter military insignificance, but it proved a founding moment for the republic. It led the king to recognize the National Assembly and don "the red, white, and blue cockade of the Revolution."[22]

In October pedestrian Paris again directly intervened into the revolution and shaped its course. Moved by hunger and agitated by the widely accepted notion that the court was responsible for their misery, a group of seven to eight thousand women, four hundred or so men, and some ideologues set out on foot to cover the thirteen miles from central Paris to the royal residence at Versailles. By doing this, they transformed the traditional bread riot, which was commonly led by local women against the town miller or baker, into an attack against central authority. They did nothing less than take King Louis XVI and Queen Marie Antoinette hostages, bringing them back to Paris as captives of the revolution. It took seven hours to bring the riding royal family back to Paris from Versailles. Along the way the triumphant marching women, who had gone to Versailles wanting bread, returned chanting, according to Lord Acton, "We bring the baker, the baker's wife, and the baker's boy."[23] The crowd, in effect, had delivered king and queen, with the new assembly and the future of France not tailing far behind, to Paris. Those who ruled the world from horse and carriage were now in the hands of walking and parading Paris.

The crowd thereafter intervened repeatedly on foot in the course of the revolution. For instance, in July 1791, thirty thousand Parisians showed up to protest the king's attempted flight. In August 1792, with revolutionary France at war with Europe and conditions steadily deteriorating, the crowd stormed the Tuileries and slaughtered the king's Swiss guards. Next, in the notorious September Massacres, a mob took suspected enemies of the revolution from city prisons and summarily executed them after trials by hastily improvised tribunals. Justice belonged to roaming street crowds. Again and again, pedestrian Paris—

with its mobs made violent and volatile by events, scarcity, ideas, and rumors—drove the revolution where the deliberations of sitting bodies could not foresee.

What else other than a dynamic city like Paris could have provided personnel for a new elite and cadres of bountiful militants, along with members prepared to attend endless meetings dedicated to redefining the whole of society? What other source could have supplied a national guard of 116,000 in 1793 ("around two out of every three adult males in the city") and a freshly recruited group of seven thousand who scoured the countryside for grain and counterrevolutionaries?[24] What else other than a highly energized city could have sustained a network of political connections, turned out voters for numerous elections, and provided regular audiences for the Reign of Terror's public guillotining, which averaged sixty a month in 1793 and 1794? Paris was France's premier stage of revolution. On its streets and squares the quickest emotions, the basest passions, the most novel fancies and abstract ideas were literally acted out. While horses, carriages, and carts (particularly those used to haul the accused to the guillotine) were important props for the revolution, the French Revolution was acted out on foot. The face of the new democracy had to be augured in the mulling, roaming, marching, and parading Parisian crowd.

The revolution forced ruling and riding Europe fearfully to look out its windows at the streets of its own cities. The revolution's prodigy, Napoleon, magnified this fear. Having suppressed the crowd at home with "a whiff of grapeshot," on behalf of the revolution's Directory in 1795, this new young general, starting with command in Italy, went on to topple authorities, regimes, and the very notion of traditional authority throughout Europe. His popular armies of drafted foot soldiers, with their unprecedented frontal charges with bayonets, gave the revolution a bloody and democratic visage. His summons to people to rebel against the old order was as aggressive as his plans for Europe were revolutionary. Surviving and restored regimes of the post-Napoleonic era feared the mob and crowd as never before. Conspiracy, sedition, revenge, terrorism, riot, and uprising potentially lurked for them in every assembly and gathering crowd.[25] City foot traffic in the form of crowds threatened their property and order. Security required vigilant surveillance of their streets, including lodging houses, wine shops, popular theaters, brothels, and multiple other places whence violence might spring. Every urban quarter could harbor hoarders, deserters, and spies and might nurture agitators; every province might foster plots for secession and counterrevolution. The crowd had proven itself capable not just of violence, savagery, but also of turning the world on its head.

Democracy, liberalism, nationalism, and industry, which accelerated between the late eighteenth century and mid-nineteenth century, intensified the recognition that streets, walking groups, and public spaces had to be brought under control. From their saddles and through the windows of their carriages, authorities vigilantly watched the foot-bound populace, whom they saw drunk with ideas of justice and social change. They especially worried about students, groups, clubs, and associations intoxicated with causes. Fear of change pervaded European authorities, from Spain to Russia. Even the young American nation, though it had been spared the fratricidal bloodletting of the French Revolution, carefully surveyed parades and political assemblies to see that the crowds followed local, state, and federal laws of the young republic. The British government curtailed reformist gatherings and brutally suppressed mass labor's demonstrations, starting with the Peterloo Massacre in Manchester in 1819 and continuing on to Bloody Sunday in London in 1886. A pattern of conflict between pedestrian crowd and mainly riding authorities imposed itself on the century. Protesters rallied, filed, marched, paraded, picketed, and blocked streets, squares, and parks, and authorities counterattacked with sabers and horses—and pistols and rifles.

European society was plagued by revolts and uprisings in the first half of the nineteenth century and confronted with revolutions in 1820, 1830, and 1848. In 1848, the city streets of Europe echoed protest, uprising, revolt, and revolution. It all started with an uprising in Palermo in January, then spread with revolution to Paris, Rome, Venice, Milan, Vienna, Budapest, Prague, Berlin, and elsewhere. Everywhere crowds took to the streets, and with the passionate and ideological enthusiasms of students, liberals, socialists, and others, they issued manifestos and built barricades.

Again the eye of the storm settled in Paris, which teemed with new peoples, arts, and ideas. In a huge surge of growth comparable to that of London, the population of Paris, starting—it is estimated—at 750,000 in 1815, almost tripled over the next hundred years, going from one million in 1851 to more than 2,750,000 in 1911. During the same period its suburban populace grew from approximately 250,000 to more than 1,250,000.[26]

The streets of Paris were as dangerously overcrowded and congested in the 1830s as they were in the closing decades of the eighteenth century.[27] A dense population crammed itself into the city's historic center until the 1840s, when Parisians began to move in considerable numbers to the northern and northwestern outskirts. Traffic remained literally murderous—and pedestrian rights were consistent with what commentator Louis-Sébastien Mercier noted in his 1780s and 1790s sketches of Paris: "When a cab ran you down, officials determined whether the big or little wheel did you in. The cabman was only responsible for the little wheel. If you died under the big, there was no financial compensation for your heirs."[28]

Starting in 1823, municipal law required property owners to install sidewalks, but as late as 1847 many of Paris's streets were still without them. As in contemporary London and the rest of urban Europe and North America, in Paris waste, refuge, and heaps of horse manure, along with running rivulets and stench-producing puddles and ponds, made the pedestrian's route a hazardous one. The rich added to the walker's perilous path with their habit of throwing horse manure in front of their residence to reduce the noise of passing carriages. At every corner, pedestrians who could afford to care about their appearance would summon a "shoescraper" to remove muck from their shoes. Pedestrians would flick flies off their arms, especially if they found themselves in the vicinity of the meat markets located near the center of the city, where streets ran red with blood and tinted the shoes of passersby.[29]

Paris could be nominated as the barnyard of nineteenth-century Europe, but so could many other places in Europe during this era when sewer systems were primitive or nearly nonexistent, markets were unregulated, and animal cadavers often went uncollected. In Italian the word *budello,* which means "guts and intestines," also, not by accident, means "alley." Suffocating stenches, smells, and dusts, organic and industrial in origin, distinguished streets and neighborhoods, which were closely associated with each other, and whole cities. (Berlin, for instance, was known for its smell of putrid cheese.)

Other conditions threatened more than pedestrians' feet and noses. In matters of hygiene Paris was several decades behind London, according to Marchand. It took the cholera epidemic of 1832, which killed twenty thousand Parisians, to convince the inhabitants of the richer parts of town that they were not immune to the disease that savaged the poor sectors and that something had to be done.[30]

Crime also took hold of Paris, body and mind, in the first half of the century.[31] According to demographer and historian Louis Chevalier, crime became citizens' everyday worry. The rapid growth of crime, Chevalier argues, imprinted "the whole urban landscape," especially central Paris, where "slum and affluent mansion lived cheek by jowl," and endless "nooks and corners ideally suited robbery" day and night.[32]

Revolution came to Paris again in 1848. During the initial phase of revolution in February, King Louis-Phillippe abdicated and a constitutional republic was declared. The liberal middle class had won the republic of its aspirations, while the lower classes remained discontented about joblessness, taxes, slums, epidemics, high rents, miserable housing, and insufficient public transportation. The liberals sought to placate the discontented poor and working classes by establishing national workshops for relief and setting up the Commission of the Luxembourg, a kind of parliament of workers and employers dedicated to discussing common interests. Meanwhile, the forces of order in the government prepared to take control of the ambiguous situation by arranging elections, "by bringing troops to Paris [and] by taking steps to render the National Guard loyal to 'the cause of order.'"[33] By the end of June the forces of order in government and the army defeated the working-class rebellion. They crushed the workers, whose demonstrations had successfully stormed the bourgeois National Assembly and formed a provisional government. With the bloodiest street fighting Europe had seen, revolution was defeated at its improvised street barricades by General Louis Cavaignac's artillery and cavalry.

With a resounding vote, the election of December 1848 constituted a plebiscite to the presidency of Napoleon's nephew, Prince Louis Napoleon Bonaparte. Besides securing his own power, Napoleon III's most urgent task was to bring Paris and its workers to heel. While undermining the masses' voting powers, his reforms targeted the urban conditions that engendered insecurity, violence, and revolution. The most significant step Napoleon took in this direction amounted to nothing less than the rebuilding of Paris. New arteries, designed by Baron G. E. Haussmann, would link the center of Paris with its railroad stations, reducing the congestion of the latter. Other arteries would battle against congestion and poverty, while yet others would fight places where contagion and unrest were concentrated, by allowing air and armies to penetrate more easily.[34] Haussmann's leadership produced, according to historian Eugen Weber, "the city we know today with its impressive vistas, its wealth of squares and parks, adequate water supply and sanitary sewers."[35] Not dissimilar in motive to the builders of Vienna's encircling, tree-lined, ceremonial Ringstrasse (laid out between 1858 and 1864), Haussmann and his collaborators sought to increase Paris's security and government's social control over its burgeoning pedestrian and vehicular traffic. They also aimed at glamour and power by providing wide avenues useful for social parading and military access.[36]

Yet much or even most of Haussmann's work was designed to improve transit, which would facilitate traffic and increase the city's commerce. He nearly doubled Paris's roads, which in length went from 424 to 850 kilometers. He initiated a five-fold increase in the sewage system, which was augmented from 143 to 773 kilometers.[37] He also eradicated many of the mazes of alleys "where crime and insurrection bred," and he drove many of the poorer people, who could not afford high rents in the new central quarters, into the suburbs, removing the dangerous crowd to the periphery of the city.[38]

Preparing Paris to be a modern city, Haussmann strove to have traffic flow smoothly by connecting intraurban arteries to perimeter railway stations.[39] With the 1860 annexation of land beyond the old city walls, Paris more than doubled in size, going from 8,250 acres to 17,750 acres.[40] Carved into twenty *arrondissements* (districts), Paris stood ready for a new era in administrative and police control of traffic and crowds.

While there were relatively small but increasing numbers of Parisians who made use of the omnibus, in addition to boat and carriage, the great majority of Parisians still resorted to shank's mare for the sake of speed and economy.[41] Walking still remained the most efficient way to traverse a distance up to three or four miles separating work and home. It also remained the cheapest way for the vast majority of workers and middle-class people to get about given the cost of the tram, the omnibus (organized into a single company in 1855), and the Métro—the subway system—which was introduced in time for the Exposition Universelle of 1900.

As the working class relocated itself in the closing decades of the century from the expensive city center to the north and northwest center, so central Paris was sensually reconfigured for its middle-class walkers. Its streets would serve bankers, officials, merchants, professionals, and craftspeople and their families' transportation, shopping, and leisure needs. The older auditory and olfactory environments, once familiar to the Parisian walker, were removed. Familiar echoes no longer reverberated in pedestrian ears. Gone were songs and shouts urging the lower classes to buy, as only they would, used clothes, old hats, eggs, hazelnuts, cabbage, chicory, baked potatoes, almanacs, frog legs, rabbit skins, rats, guns, bullets, handkerchiefs, firewood, and water.[42]

New mixes of city walkers occupied Paris's streets, with variation by neighborhood and proximity to city center. The salaried middle class and working class grew in numbers as they formed predictable streams of workers moving between work and home. At the same time, there was in many zones an increased number of leisure walkers and strollers. There were more and more shoppers who, singularly and arm in arm, sought the amply displayed goods of the *grands magasins* concentrated on the *grands boulevards*. "Paris—one immense illuminated shop window as well as site of world's fairs in 1878, 1889, and 1900—adapted," in the words of cultural historian Alain Corbin, "to the reign of the commodity." Sidewalk cafes drew more and more spectators on the flows of passing traffic. Swelling numbers of tourists and provincials came to Paris to gape and gaze and be awed, slowing the pace of walking traffic, increasingly composed of those who walked and commuted to and from work on fixed schedules.

As slums were cleared, neighborhoods diminished, and local walkers replaced, so too the mulling and spontaneously assembling crowds of times past disappeared. Increasingly, the shouting and gesticulating crowd, even in the noisy and gathering market and ethnic and regional neighborhoods, stood, if not at odds with then at least in dramatic contrast to, the triumph of business discipline, individual autonomy, and urban control. Foot traffic, at least as idealized on drafting boards and in city design by those in control and in search of efficiency, now should flow and be directional. The street should no longer belong to crowds.

This did not mean that Parisians (like urbanites elsewhere) ceased to resort to the streets to voice their emotions and demands. However, they were more and more likely to do so not as a spontaneous decision of a neighborhood crowd but more and more in conjunction with and under the direction of outside ideas and agencies. Increasingly organized, Parisians marched and paraded at the urging and under the collective banners of new national groups and unions, which arguably used demonstrations as a forceful means to speak to those in power.[43]

Popular protest, however, did not entirely disappear. Street theater still moved on walking feet. Paris refused to acknowledge German military victory in the war of 1870, marked by the surrender of General Bazaine at Metz in October. Parisians threw up barricades and refused to surrender to the victorious Germans until a desperate hunger, which left the city eating rats, induced Paris to sign an armistice in January of 1871. In March, in opposition to the newly formed National Assembly, radical and republican Paris elected its own city government, the Commune of 1871. The troops of the Assembly located at Versailles overcame the improvised defense of the Commune in the last week of May. They culminated this infamous "Bloody Week" by visiting summary and sanguinary punishment on a large but indeterminate number of prisoners.[44]

The Third Republic, which hesitatingly emerged during the years following the war, continued to watch Parisians take their passions to the streets. They literally changed street names to accord with altering historical perspectives and mutating causes.[45] Marches and parades supplemented their local and national votes. Parisians took to the streets in 1873 to voice their support for the presidency of General Marshall McMahon, who—soldier, monarchist, and neophyte in politics—seemed to hold the promise of the restoration of a strong France. In 1888 an immense crowd gathered along the route of the procession accompanying Victor Hugo to his grave. In 1889 Parisians en masse filled the streets to support and contest conservative opposition to the hundred-year celebration of Bastille Day. On September 20, 1892, parades of troops, artillery, and marching bands wended their way across Paris to celebrate the centennial of the republic.[46] With more than words, with sticks and stones, student and intellectual Dreyfusards, starting in 1898, engaged in street fights to contest the innocence of Captain Dreyfus, falsely accused of treason by government, army, conservatives, and French nationalists.[47] Finally, multitudes of Parisians turned out to welcome another war against Germany in 1914.

But despite the great passions involved in these affairs, the spontaneity of the crowd had been diminished. As the streets in measure had been swept clean of disease and crime, so had mobs and crowds been significantly eliminated. The right of assembly had been regulated and institutionalized. Protesters were better policed and under greater surveillance.[48]

Paris—the very symbol of Europe and mother of revolt and revolution—had gotten in step with the new century. Walking and human movement had been synchronized to emerging complex, mass, industrial, national, urban society. Just as poor and working-class neighborhoods were sacrificed to this unprecedented order of transportation, so too were nobility's and the upper middle class's promenading carriages and strolls. An invisible clock and internal discipline had been implanted in gregarious bipedal humans in order that the complex organism of the contemporary city could exist. Distance and time became principal coordinates of their movement.

ON THE SUNNY SIDE

Urban traffic delivered to Paris and the world new senses of time and distance.[49] Foot speed was no longer the universal measure of speed. The railroad and the telegraph standardized the twenty-four-hour clock. At the same time, the industrial working day and week (which continued to evolve in the nineteenth and twentieth centuries) put society on a uniform calendar of work and leisure.

Collectively, industry, the railroad, and urban transportation systems—which saw at the turn of the century a sevenfold increase in use in France, England, Germany, and Austria-Hungary—got cities and nations rolling on time, moving in step.[50] They delivered millions into the city for work and business, and extracted equal millions to the surrounding countryside for vacations or to find recreation at the multiplying racetracks, fairs, golf courses, and amusement parks, or the beach.

Beyond transportation and communication, other new inventions and ways were transforming Western urban environments in the decades preceding the First World War. Light-suffused impressionist paintings, filled with walkers, offer a counterimage to the dusty and soot-filled industrial landscape.[51] Historian Eugen Weber helps us sketch for Paris the bright side of walkers' new environment at the turn of the century. By 1900 Paris boasted the creation of nearly 350,000 electric lamps, which banished a lot of real and imagined stalkers from the Parisian night. In their place, the walker commonly encountered better-dressed and better-behaved Parisians as more and more sectors of society increasingly dressed and acted to match their superiors. Spitting, a common habit until then, became less acceptable; those with handkerchiefs were expected to use them. At the same time, both sexes were less likely to use a tree, the side of a building, or the mere turn of a back as the door to their toilet. It wasn't polite to expose one's body in Paris or, soon, in any other self-respecting place.

Writer Stefan Zweig observed the same evolution of the walking environment and walker in the contemporary Vienna of his youth. He wrote in his *World of Yesterday* of a general advance in urban lighting and sanitation and a corresponding change in the comportment of city walkers. Dim streetlights were replaced by electric lights; people moved about in horseless carriages with a new rapidity; it was no longer necessary to fetch water from the pump; hygiene spread and filth disappeared. Consequently, people became handsomer, stronger, and healthier. Sports steeled their bodies. Fewer cripples and maimed and persons with goiters were seen on the street. These miracles "were accomplished by science, the archangel of progress."[52] Someone might even get it in his or her head to postulate that only a strong, proud, and pure people should walk the streets and march for the nation.

At least Zweig's own class, the upper bourgeoisie, was apparently succeeding in educating its own and, to a degree, even influencing their workers' bodies, gestures, and movements. Cleanliness, self-control, and discipline went hand in hand with the new pedestrian, commuter, shopper, and factory worker.[53] Near the middle of the nineteenth century etiquette and manners overtook the European middle class as it started to dominate the city's life and streets.[54] The middle class, which began as best it could to clean itself up and made the cleaning of its house a daily affair, began regulating its bodily behavior and appearance.[55] The bourgeoisie and, increasingly, all city folk no longer did such things as frenzied dancing or relieving themselves, as peasants still commonly did, by sitting on the communal board place on top of the farm manure heap. Disgust and discomfort became internal monitors of their public appearance and the way they presented themselves, dressed, stood, and walked. As if now aristocrats themselves, they carefully groomed their horses since they would appear in public as their surrogates.

A QUICKENING PACE

Pedestrians now moved not only under the direction of behavioral self-control and hygiene but also in relation to an internalized clock, set by business, office, and train hours and the traffic of the surrounding environment. Punctuality now became a principal virtue of the self-regulating pedestrian, whose life fell under the shadow of multiplying public clocks and time schedules. In Paris, and throughout France and the rest of the West, the pedestrian internalized the habit of "considering not just hours but minutes."[56] The success of the first Paris Metro added and testified to the accelerated rhythm and punctuality of the city's movement.

As Greenwich time—mean solar time fixed at the Royal Observatory in Greenwich, England—began to calculate standard time for the entire world, dawning technologies punctuated time, abbreviated space, induced synchronization, and helped make the pedestrian-commuter the most common and uniform of urban walkers. Usually carrying little or nothing, the pedestrian commuter established the standard of speed of walking at around the perennial three miles an hour. This sidewalk and station pace was fast and constant compared to that of the tarrying walker, browsing shopper, and the solemn moving crowd, but was dramatically eclipsed by that of speeding bicycles, racing motorcycles and cars (unless caught in a traffic jam), and the zooming airplane ahead on the horizon. The near instantaneous reach of news and radio stunned the human imagination, making the walker appear a soon-to-be anachronism or, alternatively, a point of stability and tradition in the face of the senseless acceleration of all things.[57]

Even though the cultural elite, the avant-garde, and traffic flow led the world in a new direction, continuity with the past was not shattered. Old ways and conditions still shaped walkers and their experiences. Going on foot still remained necessary and a way to save money for the working classes. In many urban settings and situations, when distances were less than a few miles, it still remained even for the middle classes the most efficient way to travel. Public transportation simply did not reach everywhere. Shopping in markets, for the poor and working classes, and in stores, for middle classes, still required walking, as did the practice of different leisure activities in town and country.

At the advent of the new century, cultural historian Eugen Weber notes by way of examples, the majority of pedestrians appeared and smelled as they always had. They didn't bathe or change their clothes regularly. Nor did they brush their teeth or visit a dentist. In effect, they continued to encounter each other as the foul-breathed stinkers they had always been.[58] Even though fashionable people had taken to wearing white shoes, the majority wore brown or black, the only pair they owned. Barefoot children now peered through shiny glass store windows at displays of machine-made shoes, which they didn't have but would like to have. Many workers and peasants still trudged their way through today as if it were yesterday, or a hundred years earlier, without a *sou* for a ride. For many of them, in contrast to the middle class, the streets were on weekdays and weekends—especially on Sundays—their sole refuge and pleasure. In city and countryside alike the majority still inhabited small, damp quarters and went without access to running water and indoor toilets. (Even hospitals still did not have an abundant supply of running water, and Paris's richest people, who had indoor toilets, had no bathrooms and only a single tap of running water on each floor.)[59] There was good reason to be up and about, which invariably meant, for common humanity, a little walk around.

Even though the slogan of the era was *tout-à l'égout*—"everything to the sewer!"—many streets remained without sewers. "By 1903 only one Parisian house in ten was connected to the [sewer] system."[60] The age still belonged to the horse and dray (a low, heavy cart without sides), which still claimed the city's manure, hauling it off to nearby suburban farms and market gardens. We easily forget that in 1900 the horse still ruled Paris, London, and North America—and the majority went on foot.

In the countryside, the walking speed of human and beast still measured the distance between neighborhoods and villages, and thus to family and friends, and determined the earning of one's daily bread. For much of rural France, where in 1891 two-thirds of the population still lived in small rural parishes of fewer than five thousand inhabitants, adjacent provinces were as remote and mysterious as other continents.[61] In contrast to their quick-footed, scurrying, and unencumbered city cousins, peasants still trudged on, doing the same chores and suffering the perennial travail their ancestors had endured. They continued to discipline their bodies and minds to the activities that keeping animals and walking the land permitted.[62] They still inhabited a world in which standing, leaning, and crouching was common and where the absence of furniture and comfortable chairs did not make sitting, which was often on the ground or where one could, at all preferable to lying down or standing on one's feet.

Darkness still characterized nighttime in rural France and Europe. Paved roads didn't reach deeply or consistently into the European or North American countryside. Sidewalks and broad, level roads had not been laid. Water and waste systems had not yet been installed. Public fountains, which flourished in Paris, were rare in small towns. Women, with the exception of those who could afford to buy the circulating water hauler, spent their mornings carrying water home from the town's single fountain or the closest well. The countryside itself afforded few places to go or see. People in the vast majority walked not according to the refinements of choice and taste but according to the dictates of necessity.

Small, dreary, provincial towns remained precisely that until long after the turn of the century. Streets were often unpaved, barely lit, if at all, and narrow and winding—"so difficult to negotiate that the last sedan chairs did not disappear until the late 1880s." There was only a small walk to promenade and a small square where a newly formed local band—a military band at that—might play on Sundays. There were few stores, little shopping, and minimal social interaction between classes. "Only market day introduce[d] a little life" into what youth found to be dead towns.[63]

Yet an essential difference existed between the old and new way. City and countryside now irrevocably belonged to the same embracing nation and its demand for conformity of thought, behavior, and control. Communication and transportation wove city and countryside into the same tapestry of space, mind, and movement.

As was particularly the case in England, Sweden, and Germany, with their growing middle classes, increasing numbers of walkers, hikers, and climbers, along with bicyclists, took to the countryside's paths, lanes, and roads on Sundays and holidays. Some even took advantage of the train to extend their reach into the picturesque countryside. At the same time, provincial folks with moderate means, who lived along main railroad lines, started to take in the city's lights and sights. Luxurious boulevards, colossal monuments, and recently created museums, gardens, parks, and zoos provided novel walking, especially for country folks.

Abundant goods created wishes that turned into wants, which over short periods of time became needs. Distant places sparked local minds. Public education and travel (often experienced with conscription or the return visit of polite and better-dressed city cousins) planted in rural minds itches and even deep hankerings to taste other places. They imagined themselves free of their own dingy quarters, stick-in-the-mud families, and smelly, stubborn animals. They dreamed of traveling smooth and wide avenues, being colorfully dressed, among bright objects and gay people. They hungered for Paris and other amazing places. They would be paid real money—perhaps as a clerk, railroad employee, or teacher—and just possibly allowed to sit in an office chair all day long and manipulate words and numbers. They would disencumber themselves of that world their parents and grandparents had hauled on their backs. In the evening and especially on Sundays they would stroll city streets in clean clothes and new, shiny shoes.

Looking across the same fence, but from the other side, city people idealized the countryside. They looked to it for relief from congestion, poor housing, noise, and crime. They had forgotten it as a place of marginal production and never-ending work, as the peasants knew it to be. It was for the middle-class country walkers, hikers, or amateur explorers of nature, who worked, competed, and aspired in town, to conceive of the country as a spiritual resource—a place where they could be fancy-free and footloose and return to their true and natural selves. It provided picturesque scenery for good photographs and painting. As Frykman and Löfgren wrote, expeditions into the countryside were "based on collecting beautiful landscapes," and actually occurred around planned footpaths, guidebook listings, and newly erected sightseeing platforms, all of which structured the enjoyment of the scenery.[64]

By the beginning of the twentieth century, city and countryside had become, at least for the reflective middle class, each other's mirrors.[65] However, more than mutual projections joined them in national life. Institutions also integrated town and country by providing citizens with similar experiences, laws, and rights, and at the same time, mass transportation and communication increasingly synchronized entire nations' movements in space and time, in city and countryside. Citizens increasingly walked and rode as part of an interconnected system. Despite immense differences between those who rode and those who walked, they began to think, feel, and, more importantly, act as members of a single nation. To the terrible disillusionment of international socialists and other pacifists, peasants and workers from different nations, as we will see, marched off in step to the same war.

⫙ 8 ⫙   Getting in Step

Disciplining the Mob and
Marching the Masses Off to War

WITH the emergence of mass, industrial, democratic national society at the start of the twentieth century, the synchronization of movement and the control of walking became vital for political authority, social order, economic productivity, and military effectiveness. It created a polarity between marching as a means of public expression and marching as a necessary element of state and military control.

This polarization could already be witnessed at the start of the century. At the very time stroller and shopper flourished in the city and hiker and roamer thrived in the countryside, the movement of *fin du siècle* pedestrian and commuter was subordinated to mass transit and urban traffic, and increasing numbers of citizens marched as organized groups to express themselves and their allegiances. In 1914, a profound gulf was opened between the chosen walking of an expanded and prospering middle-class society and the dictated marching of Western nations going to war.

The need to regulate and coordinate society's overall movement and walking became paramount by the turn of the century with the formation of mass transport, the integration of city and countryside, the maturation of capitalism, the rise of global imperialism, and the attempt to turn peoples into a single nation. It assumed life-and-death importance with the First World War, the Great Depression, and the Second World War.

By the turn of the century, government was required to do more than build sidewalks, design streets, create public transportation, and regulate pedestrians and commuters. It was no longer sufficient merely to regulate traffic, curtail mobs, and suppress rebellions. For the sake of national unity and strength, governments had to turn walkers, as individual pedestrians and moving crowds, into obedient and productive citizens and make their behavior and movement serve the nation. As we will see in the conclusion to this chapter, this involved totalitarian Italy, Germany, and Russia in efforts to achieve total control over the streets and their walkers.

OFF TO THE COUNTRYSIDE

At the turn of the century, in increasing numbers, the middle class chose country walking for leisure and health. It went into the countryside in search of alternatives to city streets and city life. It found nearby parks, idyllic and scenic places in the countryside, resorts, beaches, and even mountains to scale and jungles to penetrate.

Railroad and rural road systems in Europe and North America permitted walkers to choose where in the countryside they would walk. They could also match their shoes and apparel to the trip they anticipated, and travelers could choose from a growing literature one of many reasons to justify their trek. They could even feel superior to fellow walkers on the grounds of destination, clothes, gear, or comportment, while denouncing commercialism and conformity. The children of romantic walking, they would wrap their treks and pere-grinations in complex ideas, nostalgia, or criticism of industrial, mass society and the vulgar herd. Indeed, the most alienated of nineteenth-century European thinkers, Friedrich Nietzsche, selected walking as a way to regain his health and strength.[1] Founder of psychoanalysis Sigmund Freud chose walking for his well-being and relaxation. On summer Sundays, Freud forsook his daily brisk circumambulating of Vienna's Ringstrasse and went out into the surrounding countryside. He and his family would outfit themselves as peasants, right down to their leather shorts, and go off mushroom picking in the Wienerwald.[2]

In England the popularity of walking was considerable. Groups sporting such names as the "tramps," "vagabonds," and "wanderers" expressed the widespread sentiment that it was good to walk and be free from the city, even if only for the day.[3] The Sunday Tramps, a weekend walking group from London composed of lawyers, doctors, intellectuals, and professionals set out to the countryside for health and leisure. The group held 252 meets and racked up 5,000 miles of travel before dying out as a club in 1894, only to be revived several years later, in 1900, by English historian G. M. Trevelyan, who claimed that "his legs were his doctors."[4]

As elsewhere in Europe, especially in Germany, Austria, and Swe-den, columns of British citizens exited their towns on trains to hike the countryside. British women joined the pedestrian exodus to the country as well. Often forming their own groups, they also accompa-nied men on local hikes and long-distance walking adventures. They found freedom in the country they didn't have at home in the city.[5] To take a single nineteenth-century example, Gertrude Bell, an anti-suffragette who could walk the streets of London only with a chaper-one and her father's permission, scampered up and down the Alps with admirable proficiency. In the 1930s women in Britain joined in the enthusiasm for hiking—"the hiking cult"—at the same time they took their places in "the Keep Fit Movement, the Women's League of Health and Beauty, and the leap in popularity of Youth Hosteling and camping."[6]

Some walkers made their trekking a solitary activity. No one did this as much as well-known philosopher A. H. Sidgwick, a solitary pacer, who argued that talking and walking were not complementary acts.[7] A methodical walking master at Harrow tramped all over England at the rate of twenty-five miles a day and kept maps to show his pedestrian prowess.[8] Other Englishmen walked out different passions. In tandem, brothers R. N. and J. N. Naylor—admirers of travel adventures from Cook and Daniel Defoe's fictional *Robinson Crusoe* (1719)—took a 1,372-mile walk. They went on foot from John O' Groat's—the place on Scotland's northeast coast that is taken to be the northernmost tip of Great Britain—to "land's end in southern England."[9] Along the way, they observed nature, collected stories, legends, and pieces of local history, and offered insights about the best shoes, foot care, and the ordeal of walking in a week-long rain. They published an account of their walk, *From John O' Groat's to Land's End,* in 1916, a year in which their fellow citizens were interested in far more grim marching.

Trips of individual walks and walkers constitute a body of literature revealing a range of motives.[10] In his charming book *Travels with a Donkey,* writer Robert Louis Stevenson describes how he traveled the Cévennes—a mountain chain in southeastern France—with a donkey he purchased from a priest.[11] Turn-of-the-century English Catholic convert Hillaire Belloc confirmed his faith with a pilgrimage on foot to Rome. As if to walk himself back into the Middle Ages, he refused to travel on off roads, slept out at night, and made one uninterrupted march of seventy miles.[12]

Starting in the last decades of the nineteenth century—the high noon of European imperialism—steamships and trains began regularly to deposit travelers at places that explorers, merchants, and soldiers only decades earlier had heroically sought out. Without roads and transportation, many of these places made walking a necessity.

On safari in Africa, in 1908, the young officer Winston Churchill realized that "the white man's burden," if he were to travel ten or fifteen miles a day, was to go on native backs. "Without porters," Churchill deduced, "you cannot move."[13]

Detailing his ninety-two-day trip for self-knowledge across British Guiana in 1933, British novelist Evelyn Waugh, also showing the transfer of class differences to the non-Western world, wrote of his porters going barefoot except when traversing rocks, for which they fashioned sandals of palm bark.[14] The terrible biting cabouri flies forced

Waugh and his companions and their porters to keep walking to avoid being bitten. And worse than the harsh biting cabouri were the djiggas, which "work their way through one's boots to the soles of one's feet, where they drill holes and lay their eggs, preferably under the toe nails or any hard piece of skin."[15] Belonging, like Waugh, to the generation that was too young to have fought in World War I and having to find his adventure afar and on foot, Graham Greene took an uncharted and dangerous "200-mile trip on foot through a portion of West Africa in 1934."[16] In his *Journey without Maps* (1936), he recorded how he was ravaged by insects—great red ants, roaches, chiggers, and the worst kind of malarial mosquitoes—while internalizing his footsore journey into a "memory of the complicated delights of fear in infancy."[17]

But as far and deep as these solitary writers went on foot into the jungle and wilderness of the self, they did not escape the fact that the nation they had left behind had annexed and subjugated walking to a collective purpose. Having harnessed foot to traffic laws, it had made the most awesome adventures and journeys of the time collective acts of politics and war. Though adventurers abroad, at home these writers were regulated pedestrians whose steps were made ever more subservient to laws, thanks to the introduction of cars and trucks. Individuals and groups of walkers, too, moved under increased surveillance and curfews. Even in the countryside, walkers were circumscribed in their roaming for reasons of national security, while innocent hikes were hijacked to serve "higher ideological causes."

This can be seen starting already at the turn of the century, when walking and hiking in the countryside were increasingly given collective meanings and uses. One's rucksack was increasingly loaded with collective sentiment and big ideas. Talking was overtaking walking, even on remote paths and trails. Going on foot was increasingly made to affirm allegiance to a philosophy and a way of life, or at least it was interpreted that way by society. Perhaps this process was inescapable in era of organizing: a time that witnessed the birth of an array of causes and the proliferation of organizations, including the Boy Scouts, suffragettes, Zionists, socialists, youth and athletic associations, religious and philanthropic groups, labor congresses, and national and paramilitary movements. Aside from providing uniforms, banners, and distinct occasions for and manners of walking, such organizations, which were in need of a cheap and universal activity for its members, formed walking associations. These associations invariably dictated why, where, and with whom one should walk, hike, or march.

In Great Britain the Ramblers' Association promoted the hiking tradition as both a recreational activity and a sport.[18] Germany, where authorities used calisthenics, recreation centers, and marching to reform its youth and save it from socialism and mass society, "middle-class gymnasium students joined the small informal groups of Wandervogel (wandering birds) that hiked and sang across the countryside, thus escaping the discipline of school and family."[19] In the United States, the Sierra Club, founded in northern California in 1892, fused the era's mounting enthusiasm for outdoor recreation with a passion to preserve the wilderness. Founded by John Muir—walker extraordinaire and creator of Yosemite National Park—the University of California, Berkeley, hiking club grafted to its walks a philosophy of conservation and a tactical political goal of protecting the park against loggers, cattle ranchers, and would-be dam builders.[20]

ORGANIZING CITY WALKERS AND WALKING

In cities walkers were organized around narrower and tighter regimes. People, especially in large cities, get in each other's way when they try or are forced to occupy the same space. In the simplest things, passing in a doorway, getting in and out of an elevator, meeting face to face turning a corner, or queuing up in a line (*queue* being an old French word for "tail"), people run into each and must learn to give way. On crowded urban sidewalks and intersections, walkers, strollers, shoppers, and pedestrians encounter each other. They shove, jostle, compete, and differ from one another for reasons of age, gender, power, status, urgency, and so on. And in places like London, New York, Rome, and elsewhere, certain streets and neighborhoods, during certain periods, can have their own ways of walking and appearing, which constitute a dialect or argot if one wishes.

Gathered together by hundreds of thousands in cites and even millions in metropolises, the walking public—by force, law and regulation, and manners—must be coordinated in its everyday actions if the society is to be pleasing, productive, and even inhabitable. Issues that might seem trivial to us, who have long ago learned the ways and etiquette of city walking or rarely walk at all, surround the proper use of sidewalks, stairs, escalators, ramps, doorways, and fenced walkways. These issues include questions about who can walk them, in what ways (circling, going arm and arm, linked in a long line, or with an unleashed dog), and with what things (long poles, big swords, or big picket signs). These issues consist of matters pertaining to the right to approach, sell, and solicit passersby or stop traffic by not moving, by entertaining, or by lying down. Policies, legislation, negotiations, and armies often decide which groups can parade and march on roads, when, and under what conditions. Keeping order on the streets, a good and a necessity of civic life, engages authorities in a continuous struggle and can provoke the most serious crises.

Already by 1900, unprecedented levels of order had been achieved on city streets. Much of it derived from internal control associated with upper-class English ways and city manners, which had been disseminated across Europe and North America since the eighteenth century. In the nineteenth century the middle classes and even elements of the working class imitated the walk, dress, posture, and speech of their superiors. At work and play, citizenry became more mannered and regulated in its public behavior. On principal streets passersby were more courteous, more quick to acknowledge one another with the doff of a hat or handshake. They were less likely to turn a bump into an insult or grounds for a fight. While neither law nor police nor manners had chased away vagrants and itinerants, pimps and prostitutes, the insane and homeless, staggering drunks, organ grinders, bullying groups, or loitering crowds, a kind of polite pedestrianism ruled streets and squares in middle-class neighborhoods.

At the same time as a norm for individual city walking arose, group marching and parading—of increasing importance for public expression—took form. It was legalized, regulated, and made more orderly. Parties, unions, associations, clubs, and bands (popularly organized in Britain in the 1850s) claimed a place, right, and power in the life of emerging nations. Moving ensembles, marching and walking groups made a manifest statement of public identity and allegiance. Stretching blocks, perhaps miles, they carried with them the latent, even undifferentiated threat of turning into uncontrollable mobs or, once armed, being organized into armies. Marching groups moved with considerable variation—with or without uniforms, music, placards, and banners, going arm and arm or eight abreast, almost strolling or with a crisp and syncopated step. Moving at different speeds and levels of comportment, they could evoke a range of human emotions.

On the eve of the First World War, people established their identities by walking the sidewalks or parading the streets. On sidewalks, by dress, gait, and manners, one could exhibit his or her place, identity, and aspirations, emphatically denying for all to see that he or she was a rowdy, a bully, or a country bumpkin. On the roads, on the other hand, with the defiant groups or the law-abiding citizens, one could profess one's membership in organizations, allegiance to causes, and commitment to the nation.

In the aftermath of the First World War, which had taught so many to march and parade, paramilitary groups, political parties, and unions vied for the streets throughout the West. A succession of larger and more intense street marches between the March and November revolutions, calling for peace, bread, and land, culminated in St. Petersburg in the victory of the more opportunistic Bolsheviks. A bitter contest for control of the streets in postwar Italy and depression-ridden Germany produced regimes that recognized that their power and authority rested on the control, and even total dominance, of the streets.

INSTRUCTING WALKERS

However, authorities, ideologies, and organization were not the sole arbiters of street walking, expressing, and gesturing. Indeed, simultaneous with ideological and political efforts to shape walking, commercial and popular cultures competed to define the gestures, rhythms, and meaning of public movement.

Motion pictures grew in the vacuum left by the collapse of whole empires and moral orders of the nobility and upper middle class, which crumbled in the First World War and its aftermath. Besides furnishing a warm public place to get out of the streets, get off one's feet, and sit comfortably (even in peace and quiet and even with a chance for intimacy), movies offered models for emerging mass society to express its emotions, sensibilities, images, and identities. They provided a repertoire for participating in everyday life—stepping out, expressing choice, or yet adhering to the most recent fashions.

Movies taught their viewers stereotypes—even created archetypes—of how the rich and poor, the snobbish and humble, the stylish and gauche moved. They gave examples of the upper classes shopping, strolling, getting in and out of carriages, pushing their fancy baby strollers, and having someone pick up and carry their luggage. At the same time they showed, though much less, the lower classes trudging dusty roads, seeking work, or moving along the street in a crowded immigrant neighborhood. Moreover, movies taught their audiences how to strut, slink, and glide—how to get in and out of a car (which the majority did not yet own), how to walk arm and arm, how to hop in and out of bed, how to windowshop, or how to peruse a department store.

Aside from musicals that joined feet and legs and whole moving bodies to a public expression of feelings, movies provided a vast lexicon of walks, from that of the rushing messenger boy to that of the moseying and ambling cowboy, from those of the discouraged, beaten-down workers and quick-striding businessmen to that of the swaying and hip-rolling beauty queens. From the exaggerated gestures of silent films to the more subdued talking films, movie stars from Greta Garbo, Marlene Dietrich, Mae West, Shirley Temple, and Judy Garland to Rudolph Valentino, Douglas Fairbanks, Fred Astaire, Jimmy Cagney, and Humphrey Bogart (to mention but a few) ran the West's most popular and uninterrupted academy on how to walk, move, and gesture. At the same time, with their own distinct walks, Buster Keaton, Laurel and Hardy, and the Marx Brothers imitated the coarsest and most clumsy walks and manners of the lower classes while mocking the stiff and rigid movement of the pretentious rich.

Books on manners, including those of redoubtable stalwart Emily Post, simply couldn't hold a candle to the screen as an instructor of style and movement. Indeed, middle-class idealizations of gesture and manners propagated by books fell second to movies, which were complicit with and even formative of emerging mass and popular street culture. At train stations, amusement parks, ballrooms, and along the streets of the interwar years, the populace exhibited a freshly enhanced repertoire of walks, speech styles, and gestures and a new level of self-confidence.[21]

At the same time, there were other common, though more prosaic, instructors of pedestrian life. An array of institutions explicitly instructed people on where, in what ways, and when to move. As traffic laws regulated the movement of pedestrians on sidewalks and streets, churches, public libraries, and museums, along with theaters, businesses, restaurants, and offices taught the etiquette of movement and indoor walking, which in many instances reinforced the traffic laws of the street.

Beyond institutional instructors, there were educators and reformers who sought to work literally on the very footing of the nation. Motivated by the notion that a nation should be composed of strong and healthy citizens, late-nineteenth-century reformers in England and the United States set their sights on the human body. To straighten and strengthen the individual's body was to enhance the whole national body.

Already by the first part of the twentieth century, historian Georges Vigarello suggests, the body was first perceived as a set of forces, then as a kind of motor driving people through their days.[22] The aim of physical education was no longer to mold the human body into a classical model but to train it for the good of both the individual and society as a whole. Physical training stressed posture, which was a first expression of a healthy person and collectively a statement of a strong and wholesome nation. Accommodating the increasing need to be out in the public, especially in business and sales, it aimed at appearance. It taught the advantages of appearing to be a person in control, who had a direction, took better of care of himself or herself, and was not beaten down by work. In effect, to appear as though one was, or aspired to be, a member of the upper middle class was the first step to joining it. Men, accordingly, were exhorted to tighten their belts, pull back their shoulders, stick out their chests, and tuck in their bellies, and thus walk erect and upright. Women too were exhorted to stand straight no matter how much the long and tight rein of the corset left nearly "all women in the latter third of the nineteenth century suffer[ing] from middle curvature of the spine." Additionally, strengthening the universal call for erect posture, historian Alain Corbin notes, was the "fear of tuberculosis [that] persuaded people of the wisdom of doing breathing exercises designed to increase lung capacity."[23] Orthopedics, too, turned to exercise and training, with the support of recently developed remedial gymnastics.

Child saving "was a widely supported reform movement in the United States between 1880 and 1920."[24] Where better to save the nation than through the children of its expanding and concentrated urban centers? On the bodies and minds of the children the reformers saw the desultory effects of crowded ghettos, air and water pollution, and the nation's booming factories, unsafe conditions, long hours, and child labor. In New York City, one center of reform, there was a call for sunlight, better air circulation, and improved sanitation in worker housing.[25] New York's Outdoor Recreation League worked to create special places outdoors for children to walk and play on the grass, not simply the sidewalks.[26] Hull House (founded in Chicago in 1889 by Jane Addams and Ellen Gates Starr) and the Henry Settlement House (founded in New York in 1895 by Lillian Wald and Mary Brewster) built gymnasiums, organized children's clubs, and provided spaces for activities and games. At the national level, the Playground Association of America, advocating the need for movement and exercise, sought public resources for fun and games. Collectively, park and recreation efforts sought to save children who were physically enslaved at sweat shops, pinned down in the damp and cramped quarters of home, and confined to narrow streets and polluted neighborhoods. Reformers, perhaps in conformity with their own middle-class childhood opportunities, would have children for their own individual sake and for the good of the nation run, jump, hike—breathe in and out fresh air.[27]

Schools took up the crusade to shape student bodies. "Shoulders back! Heads up! Double file! Speed up!" were commonly heard commands, all aimed at producing uniform posture, gait, and manners. Physical education classes, though taking various forms, aimed at building strength and improving individual coordination and group movements, so important to the movement, strength, and even power of a nation, with team games and dance. Schools themselves were charged by state and national authorities to conduct health examinations that included not just eyesight and hearing but also body mechanics.[28] The tie between schools and physical education grew stronger during World War I, and it was considered essential in its aftermath, especially in Fascist Italy and Nazi Germany.[29] The obvious connection between education and physical education was the belief that a strong and coordinated nation would prove itself, on foot and in mind, superior at war.

Other public and private agencies sought to improve society's movement and muscles. Gymnastic and calisthenics associations (created originally by German and other European patriots to turn their own youth into fighting troops equal in discipline, strength, movement, and spirit to Napoleon's successful popular legions) aimed at having a stronger and healthier populace. Ethnic, student, and town hiking clubs, and town bands, with and without a military end, all taught walking and moving in unison as a way to health and esprit de corps. At the same time, labor organizations and political associations taught their members to dance in groups, sing in choruses, perform theater, and parade in processions as ways to weave them into a group that had pride in itself and public respectability.

Groups need their foot soldiers, and foot soldiers need not just to believe in their cause and organization but also to profess their allegiance in public. Historian George Mosse writes that Socialist Ferdinand Lassalle, who was instrumental in forming the first German workers' political party in 1863, saw his followers as "an army" and termed his speaking tours "army inspections."[30] Lassalle taught mass agitation as a way to establish worker presence and achieve workers' goals, and he conducted party meetings as a type of communal liturgy. Typically, choral groups greeted Lassalle at the train station with much fanfare and song. Then they accompanied him with a triumphal parade that led through city gates to the center of the city, reminding one of religious processions of an earlier era.[31] Marching, workers put themselves on display as formidable components of the nation.

Holidays were commonly transformed by socialist leaders into working-class political events. In 1889 the Second Socialist International designated May Day (May 1) as labor's holiday. It was intended by Socialists and Communists to be "a world festival," which would demonstrate the solidarity of the working class and make a "call for world peace and unity."[32] The May Day march of the workers through towns took over the streets on which the bourgeoisie strolled on Sunday and, Mosse noted, implicitly declared that the "streets, parks, and gardens belonged to the working classes."[33] There was no disputing the political and military nature of the May Day march. It said to the world that the laboring classes were equal to state and church.

Similar to past church and town processions, other newly formed groups paraded on the streets. They did so for the sake of their own internal cohesion and public recognition. Parading not only made the marchers one but also put their numbers and banners before prospective followers, contending groups, and, of course, government itself. However, the modern parade with its flags, banners, marches, and salutes, which we might roughly date with the unification of Italy and Germany and the formation of socialism in the 1860s and 1870s, was no longer a processing group, roaming mob, or, necessarily, revolutionary crowd. It now walked under a more defined organization and calculating leadership. It was more likely to follow a defined path, further a strategic or established goal, and serve an articulate political ideology. This collective marching of nationalists and Socialists unwittingly moved towards the staged and manipulated mass demonstrations of the twentieth century.[34]

Hiking associations formed in pre–World War I Germany revealed the degree to which prosaic human activities could be ideologized. The Wandervogel, for example, "was a national organization of conservative and increasingly anti-Semitic youth hikers rebelling against what they saw as the restrictive, effeminate bourgeois society of their parents' generation."[35] Pfadfinders, the German Boy Scouts, espoused a more conservative marriage among citizenship, national duty, and hiking and camping skills.[36] On the other side of the political spectrum, the Naturfreunde (the Friends of Nature), a hiking club for socialists and workers, had on the eve of the war 115 affiliates and 12,000 members.

In the English-speaking world, various organizations took up the task of improving minds and bodies and, by extension, society; their programs invariably involved an effort to shape individual thought and behavior. Two such groups were the Young Men's Christian

Association (YMCA) and the Boy Scouts. Both were conspicuous in their attempts to capture simultaneously the spirits and feet of lower-middle- and working-class youth.

Founded in 1908, the Boy Scouts of Britain was instantly popular, spreading across Europe and North America; the Boy Scouts of America was established in the United States in 1910. From its inception the Boy Scouts straddled the ideals of being a good Christian and a good citizen, while incorporating the virtues of a well-drilled soldier and a free-roaming Indian scout.[37] In good measure, the organization's composite nature is explained by the experience of its founder, Sir Robert Baden-Powell. A lifelong enthusiast of public-school Christian manliness, he was a heroic Boer War commander, the author of *Scouting for Boys* (1908), and a social reformer.[38] Boy Scouts socially functioned as a middle-class engine operating to get working- and lower-middle-class youth in step with national industrial society.[39] "The Boy Scout," a contemporary advocate of scouting wrote, "will be something different from the cigarette-smoking street-corner loafer, who diversifies his indolence by occasional bursts of hooliganism."[40] In effect, scouting was a vehicle serving as a rite of passage from youth to manhood, from one type of street behavior to another, from neighborhood to nation at large. With the outbreak of the war in the summer of 1914, many East End London scout troops, proving that the message (especially its civic and military elements) had taken, marched from their headquarters to a nearby recruiting station.

The YMCA, the Young Men's Christian Association, also had its origins in England. It was founded in London in 1844 by a young dry goods clerk named George Williams. The organization aimed to improve conditions and opportunities for young businessmen, while the YWCA was formed in London in 1855 to provide homes for working women.[41] Both the YMCA and the smaller YWCA occupied themselves with its members' physical, intellectual, and spiritual needs. The YMCA spread to France and Holland, established its first North American branches in Boston and Montreal in 1851, and arrived in China and Japan before World War I. In its 1855 annual report, the United States YMCA gave physical education a primary role in helping "the young men of our cities."[42] In American cities indoor activities such as tumbling, gymnastics, calisthenics, basketball, and volleyball were high on the organization's agenda. According to the same 1855 report, rambling clubs (also known as outing clubs) were formed to serve the peripatetic and adventurous tendencies of youth in a day when there were no automobiles.[43] These clubs aimed at scenic sights in the countryside and also featured bicycling or jogging.[44] The YMCA, which in addition to especially focusing on the needs of urban boys also targeted different social classes, diverse races, and workers from individual industries, also offered vocational courses for secretaries, physical educators, and salesmen.[45] Its salesmanship course stressed appearance, manners, and gestures. It taught that one should set one's feet firmly on the ground and walk confidently to manifest self-esteem and control.[46]

Middle-class reformers in England and the United States channeled their passion into improving the lives of slum dwellers. Earnestly seeking to improve neighborhood life, reformers sought not only to clean up the streets but also to remove from them the swaying drunk, the lurking crook, the enticing prostitute, and the strutting gang. Ardent about making over what New York reformer and journalist Jacob Riis famously termed "the other half," reformers focused on improving workers' posture, stride, speech, and gesture, which was essential to both self-confidence and appearance as respectable, competent, and participating members of society. Surely, this advice, if taken, would separate city and country cousins and the generations themselves as the self-improved young stood tall among the majority of their beaten, worn, curved, malnourished, and injured working-class parents and surviving grandparents.

Other institutions shaped public walking and appearance. Professions propagated codes of manners, which included cleanliness, good posture, proper carriage, and correct walking that conveyed the impression of good breeding and competence. (They discouraged noisy, clumsy, lumbering, waddling, excessively long-striding, and other heavy-footed manners of walking, along with tentative, hesitant, pigeon-toed baby stepping.) Sales personnel had to approach customers with a walk that was confident but not overbearing. Like personal servants of the upper classes, they were to be subdued and discreet, refined in gesture, manner, and speech, but at all times displaying that they were willing, ready, and able to serve. They were to stand tall but not too tall; make eye contact but not stare; move with a confident but not imposing stride. Their voices were to be restrained and modulated, their dress clean and appropriate, and their shoes shined. When on the road, the salesperson was to observe all these niceties and be especially conscious not to track dirt or bring noise and confusion into the client's office.

Industry, too, insisted on discipline. The need for efficient assembly lines imposed a rigorous order on workers' movements. Factory workers had to be taught punctuality—which implied that workers show up on time, move quickly, return promptly from breaks, and concentrate on the work before them. In factory towns, the factory whistle commanded that workers move in locked step with the plant's regime from day to night. Richard Arkwright (1732–1792), whose cotton-spinning machine, patented in 1769, helped initiate the Industrial Revolution, announced the discipline of the new regime: "Human beings had to renounce their desultory habits of work, and identify themselves with the unvarying regularity of the complex automaton. The new industrialist," he continued, "had to train his work people to a precision and assiduity altogether unknown before."[47]

Some industries went far beyond the norm in seeking to mold the behavior and appearance of their workers. To take a single North American example, starting in 1914 Henry Ford sought to Americanize his immigrant employees, a measure that conformed to the heightened nationalism of the period. He equated being a good worker with being a good American. Workers who enrolled in his company's English-language and citizenship classes were promised the extraordinary higher pay of five dollars a day and the chance for future promotions. Company investigators actually entered the homes of foreign workers to teach new methods of sanitation and bodily care and, at the same time, detect evidence of traces of recalcitrant ethnic cooking and manners. The graduation program for the successful workers was held on the stage of Detroit's Masonic Temple, to which Ford, as a member of a pioneer Masonic lodge in Detroit, had a special relation. The program literally had graduates enter one side of a mock giant melting pot dressed in native dress and exit from the other waving an American flag as they walked across the stage in the clothes of a typical American worker.[48]

As urban society turned walkers into obedient pedestrians and factories made workers into disciplined automatons, national armies turned young men into marching soldiers. The nineteenth century's democratic mythology elevated the status of civilian foot soldiers above that of the mounted aristocracy.[49] Drilling, as repetitious and disciplined movement, and parade marching, as national and military display, proved the principal means by which armies fashioned people into citizen infantries. They turned fresh and raw recruits—hordes of diverse strangers of various regions, languages, professions, body sizes, walks, strides, and gaits—into a uniform body. On the street, marching armies awed crowds with uniforms, weapons, and synchronized movements. With flags unfurled, trumpets blaring, and drums beating, they represented the strength and determination of the nation. Military bands had an important adjunct role in impressing the public with the nation's seriousness of purpose.[50]

Across a Europe led by Prussia, marching came to serve not only the military but also society as a whole.[51] Associated with calisthenics, gymnastics, athletics, hiking, and physical education, marching was utilized to promote national strength, health, and vitality.[52] Marching established an imposing pace and a solemn presence on modern life. The ultimate expression of a dignified and serious movement, marching expressed a nation in step with itself and moving forward.

MARCHING OFF TO WAR

Armies, which modeled themselves on the advancing industry that supplied them, never escaped dependency on the feet of the infantry. Historians describe Sherman's army of sixty thousand men—which ravaged the South, cutting in five weeks a swathe of 285 miles long and 60 miles wide across Georgia, from Atlanta to Savannah—as "a marching city." As much as modern warfare, starting in the American Civil War, turned on logistics, massive munitions, barbed wire, machine guns, railroads, and metal ships, armies still moved on foot.

In the four years of the Civil War, soldiers, who were constantly mobilized, drilled, assembled, marched and countermarched, deployed and redeployed, covered as much as twenty-five hundred miles a year on foot.[53] Expending five to six thousand calories a day, individual soldiers were loaded with as much as fifty pounds minimum. General Thomas J. Stonewall Jackson provided the outstanding example of Civil War marching, with his troops, in the 1862 campaign, marching and fighting 670 miles in forty-eight days without a loss of efficiency. On the march Jackson's troops discarded overcoats and knapsacks but retained their weapons and blankets and waterproof sheets, worn in a roll over their left shoulders.[54]

Troops often joined a battle, as a few Confederate regiments did for the second day's battle at Gettysburg on July 2, 1863, at the very end of a day-long march of twenty-five miles. Fighting itself often was preceded, as it was for Major General George Pickett's troops at Gettysburg, with a long, exposed march across an open field. At a certain point, the advancing troops quickened their pace as they left the rain of incoming cannon fire and entered a screen of whizzing bullets. Then, forsaking the pace of an ordered advance, they moved to full attack on the run with bayonets fixed. With their attack blunted and then stopped, retreat began. First the soldiers walked backwards firing, and then they ran as best they could until they found a place of defense or exhaustion reduced them to a slowing, frayed line of straggling troops. Mounted officers, the leaders of the foot soldiers, often strove futilely to return their disintegrated troops into an orderly march and speed their flight to safe ground.

Proud armies marched off to the Civil War, and defeated southern and even victorious northern troops were disassembled and disaggregated wherever they were at war's end. With the exception of an occasional organized parade, country soldiers traveled home on empty roads and worn paths, marching and in groups no more. They returned alone, in twos and threes, wearied and, many, crippled men.[55] Foot soldiers, then and throughout the twentieth century, illustrated extremes of walking. To the young and idealistic men, they offered images of heroism: the enduring glories of marching and face-to-face combat. To older and more seasoned veterans, they who walked and fought while others commanded and rode from afar were victims no Washington or hometown victory parade redeemed.

In any case, walking and standing around—legs, feet, and boots— were what the army was about. Indeed, Lee's campaigns north to Pennsylvania stripped the countryside his army passed of cattle, horses, and shoes, yet not having enough shoes was one of the reasons that may have initially brought the ill-shod Confederates to Gettysburg, which was rumored to have a store of shoes.[56] Three-fourths of Civil War wounds, of which there were millions, occurred to either arms or legs. The sixty thousand amputations performed on northern and southern soldiers—both a great cause but at the time sole cure of serious infection—became distinguishing badges of young veterans, badges that a caring government dared not overlook. Federal and state governments offered new prosthetic devices for the thirty-five thousand surviving amputees.[57]

Europeans took little heed of the bloody cost of the American Civil War, the first mass industrial war. Living in a period when the Napoleonic wars were forgotten and the most recent wars they were involved in were fought on the periphery of the continent, European societies put themselves on a military footing in the closing decades of the nineteenth century.[58] Hardening alliances, a mounting arms race, incidents provoking national pride, the successes and failures of global imperialism, and military adventures aroused intense passions. Communications and transportation advances greatly diminished the buffer of space and extended the reach of expanding navies and armies, while expanding and shifting alliances entangled European states in global rivalries. As military leaders digested the lessons of the American Civil War, the Austrian-Prussian War of 1866, and the Franco-Prussian War of 1870, generals fashioned weapons, troops, and logistics tailored for future wars.[59] They had no idea how many legs and arms of its foot soldiers industrial warfare would grind up.

European commanders did know, however, that future battles would require an unprecedented military synchronization of men and materials, which was obvious given the increased discipline and coordination of society as a whole. Thinking of speed and power, they did not conceive of a four-year stalemate—an immense violent traffic jam of armed pedestrians—on the Western front. Troop mobilization and logistics, scheduled around tight timetables and diverse calculations, integrated into complex strategies and rational plans, were expected to produce speedy and decisive victories. Beguiled by their potential for swift movement and transport and the firepower of new weaponry, generals' staffs failed to forecast a long war of attrition. Thinking of war as something still chivalric and heroic, they did not conceive it in terms of the raw number of troops and shells they could deliver to the front. They did not imagine their forthcoming heroic encounter as a dreary, ordinary, and pedestrian event that would drag on for four years and turn on foot soldiers' ability to endure bombardments, confront machine guns and barbed wire, slog through mud and holes, sleep on the ground, keep their feet warm, find a replacement pair of shoes, and go on.

The train and the truck delivered the soldiers en masse to the front. Gasoline engines, trucks, motorcycles, bicycles, tanks, airplanes, poison gas, barbed wire, the wireless telegraphy, and other new technologies gave war real killing power but only potentially a new speed. Battle, however, proceeded on foot, if not on one's belly.[60] In fact, the foot soldier—in contrast to officers who rode on horses, even bicycles, or in cars and trucks—often only got one or two good long rides out of the war: one to the front and the other, if he was lucky, alive and back from it.

"The average French soldier," military historian Alistair Horne writes,

> moved on his feet, weighed down by a kit that made him resemble a deep-sea diver; two blankets rolled up in a ground sheet, a spare pair of boots, a sheepskin or quilted coat, a shovel or pair of heavy wire scissors, [etc.].... On average, the *poilu*'s total burden weighed over 85 lbs. It was hardly surprising that tired soldiers slipping on a slimy path of the approach route to the front got up "less easily than a maybug that has fallen on its back."[61]

Once arrived at the front, armies, contemporary military historian John Keegan writes, found that the almost miraculous mobility conferred by the rail movement evaporated. Face to face with each other, they were no better able to move or transport their supplies than Roman legions had been; forward of railhead, soldiers had to march, and the only means of provisioning them was by horse [several million of which were requisitioned by the contestants at the start of the war].... Indeed, their lot was worse than that of the well-organized armies of former times, since contemporary artillery created a fire-zone several miles deep within which re-supply by horse was impossible and re-provisioning of the infantry ... could be done only by man-packing.[62]

On both the receiving and giving end, trench warfare reduced the World War I soldier to feeling inconsequential. More dwarfed than a pedestrian on the busiest and noisiest streets, the soldier lived week in and week out in dust, mud, and muck, among broken tanks and cadavers and exploding shells. Normal time was obliterated. Boredom, which came with waiting and standing, was great. Bombardment was regular and, at times, intense. The space between the two opposing armies was aptly called "No-Man's Land." It was void of civilians, vegetation, and animals, although rats flourished. While strategies of attack varied by army and circumstances, the basic prescription was to advance on foot into fire and complete one's assault with bayonet ready.[63] Assaults produced small victories and even breakthroughs, but stalemate between the two sides on the Western front prevailed.

One of the weapons that appeared on the front—on September 15, 1916, at the battle of the Somme—presaged a new form of warfare: warfare not on foot, nor on horseback, but on an armed, rolling vehicle that needed neither roads nor paths. The new revolution and mechanical device to replace foot and hoof was the tracked tank. "[It] portended to change," according to another military historian, Lidell Hart, "the face of war by substituting motor-power for man's legs as a means of movement on the battlefield and by reviving the use of armor as a substitute for his skin or for earth-scrapings as a means of protection."[64] The tank's track would cross the most bomb-broken and shattered terrain, face unimpaired withering machine-gun fire, which mowed down exposed soldiers like harvested grain, break through barbed-wire fences, scale and span trenches, and deliver decisive and winning firepower.

Nevertheless, the tank failed to break the stalemate. The bomb-devastated land produced a surface too irregular for travel by track, wheel, or even hoof. The human foot and the foot soldier—the pedestrian of war—remained the defining atom of trench warfare. Ultimately, war turned on foot soldiers, who were more agile and maneuvered far better than machine and animal on truly uneven surfaces. At a moment's notice, the foot soldiers singly or in unison could alternately crawl, climb, run, jump, hide, and bury themselves in the earth. However much armies learned to kill from afar—and they improved considerably at this in the First World War—in the end victory depended on soldiers having to close on one another to conclude a battle. Resistance had to be stamped out. Trenches and bunkers had to be searched for the enemy and one's dead. And when battles were over, officers must sit face to face to sign a truce.

As the war dragged on, riding and marching armies were mired down on a shattered landscape. With greater reserve and flexibility than animal or machine, the foot soldier was condemned to walk until killed or wounded. "Bent double, like old beggars under sacks," Wilfred Owen, who was killed at the front in the last year of the war, opened his "Pro Patria Mori," which continues as follows:

> Knock-kneed, coughing like hags, we cursed through sludge,
> Till on the haunting flares we turned our backs
> And towards our distant rest began to trudge.
> Men marched asleep. Many had lost their boots
> But limped on blood-shod. All went lame; all blind;
> Drunk with fatigue; deaf even to the hoots
> Of gas shells dropping softly behind.[65]

ON THE STREETS AGAIN

In the aftermath of the war, marching and parading were not reserved for celebrating victory. Again, they were adopted for public discourse. They announced the existence of a group, sought members, staked a claim on the nation, and even made a direct bid for taking over the government.

City streets everywhere filled up with the results of the war. The consequences of World War I were immense: about ten million dead, twenty million wounded, and countless amputated, mutilated, and lame survivors. Civilian property was destroyed in vast amounts, capital and gold reserves were depleted, authority was impugned everywhere, defeated empires were dismantled, and new nations were declared. It is no wonder that the aftermath brought crowds, strikes, and aborted revolutions to the streets of defeated and even victorious nations. While statesmen sought to balance power, build a new Europe, redistribute German possessions in Africa and the Pacific, establish governments, and restart profoundly weakened economies, civic order balanced on the outcome of revolutions in the streets of Germany and Hungary and street battles throughout Italy. Often in worn uniforms, veterans, discontent with their condition and the world to which they returned, called on morally and economically depleted governments, which verged on bankruptcy, to put society back together: to provide food, jobs, and prosperity. Anticipating the principal axis of interwar struggle between Communists and Fascists, these street conflicts involved parading workers from the prewar political Left battling a new nationalistic Right composed of ideologically motivated veterans and freshly formed paramilitary groups.

The first round of this conflict was decided in Italy. In 1922, strutting and pompous fascist premier Benito Mussolini threatened to "March on Rome," which meant his paramilitary Black Shirts would come by train from across Italy and converge on Rome unless given a role in government. The government capitulated. Once having consolidated his power, which he began in earnest in 1924, he staged his fascist Italy around a new Rome. He widened the ancient and medieval streets of the capital, demonstrating like rulers before him that power must have and define spaces to make a display of society's walkers and vehicles. In 1928 he inaugurated an expressway from Rome west to the Mediterranean.[66] Long having promoted national athleticism, in 1938 he adopted for his military the intimidating and menacing but most rigid and awkward German goose step (*Paradeschritt,* or "parade march"), which he renamed "the Roman step."[67] He put as many citizens as he could in uniform, set them marching to music, and directed them to carry on surveillance on their fellow citizens. He fostered gymnastics and pushed for sweeping urban renewal. Aware of the potential of the new film industry to command images and shape behavior, Mussolini built the large movie-making complex Cinema City in the suburbs. Keenly aware that society was a matter of *fare la bella figura* ("making a dashing appearance"), he strove to create an environment of fascist images.

The decisive round of the interwar street battles between the communist Left and fascist Right ended in January 1932 when National Socialist Adolph Hitler took control of the German government and the nation's streets in January 1933. His party won the brawl on the streets and the election at the ballot box. Without hesitating, once he took power he declared dominion over society; his police utilized roundups, purges, curfews, and rallies to take ownership of the streets and society. No one moved on them except by permission. Flags, uniforms, officer etiquette, goose-stepping parades, music, pageantry, art, propaganda, films—all were used to construct a symbolic national landscape.[68] Immense rallies, searchlights, bonfires of burning books, and torchlight parades sent the ominous message that a new German people were assembling, processing, and marching.

In 1936, the year conscription was reintroduced in Germany, the Nazis hosted the Olympics, bragging that it was to be "the best games ever." They intended to use the Olympics to proclaim that Germany was revived—and to show that Berlin had bested Vienna's grace, Paris's charm, and London's cosmopolitanism.[69] In preparation for the Olympics in Berlin, they disguised their anti-Semitism by painting over the yellow benches for Jews in the Tiergarten. They regilded the top of the Brandenburg Gates, scrubbed soot from buildings, planted new trees along Unter den Linden, and rounded up beggars and con artists. So that Berlin would indeed have the risqué urbanity of Paris, they returned to the streets seven thousand banned prostitutes, opened a number of homosexual bars, and temporarily suspended the penal code against homosexuality so that foreign *flâneurs* would not end up in the hands of the police. To add sugar to spice, "local women . . . were allowed to wear their hemlines five centimeters higher than the regime has hitherto permitted."[70] However, to make sure that pedestrians would walk Nazi streets, the Nazis also pasted swastikas all over town and printed a travel guide instructing all to see Hitler's new buildings on Wilhelmstrasse.

While making Berlin "a sublime metropolis," the Nazis were also putting the Reich on war footing.[71] The marching boot would trump the gliding, dancing shoe of the 1920s and 1930s. Preponderant, undaunted, intimidating, the marching army moved superior to all. The antithesis of the individual walker, the army expressed a regimented, disciplined, coordinated, and synchronized society with its legions of workers and leaders, pedestrians, and commuters joined in locked step. The quintessence of regimentation, the marching army constituted the antithesis of small groups going on foot, which moved by choice, at variable speeds, and with diverse destinations, and it stood in opposition to the wandering poet, the solitary explorer, the strolling of the window shopper, and the promenading elite.

No figure stood as starkly contrasted to the social regimentation of walking in the modern era as Charlie Chaplin, hero of the moviegoers. He appeared alone, humble, befuddled, mildly amused. His eccentric movements taunted an alien environment—and he occasionally kicked someone in the pants. With his quick, imprecise, mincing walk—accented by his twirling cane and precariously perched bowler hat—he found himself perpetually at odds with the army, the police, and the factory foreman as well as the lines of passing conformists and the haughty and hoity-toity promenading folks. His walk was that of the tramp; he was every little man who didn't fit the regimented world. Truly out of step in an era of dictators, marching crowds, and rushing pedestrians, Chaplin carried on a mirthful and sad contredanse that expressed everyone's insecure steps in the shadows of giant systems.

Everywhere on the streets of the West, from the beginning of the First World War until the end of the Second World War, walkers were bullied. On totalitarian streets, governments dominated. They put up their own buildings, monuments, and statues, posted rules and curfews, issued identity cards, and had ample police to check them. Spies and informers penetrated organizations, and children even informed on parents. Special police rounded up the unwanted and swept the streets clean of them. This was not an era for going about one's own business, pursuing one's pleasure and recreation, as much as one might want to do so.

Freedom remained on democratic streets for walkers. Union picket lines and strikes fought company goons and the police. Though patrolled by mounted police, political groups from the Left and Right still paraded on behalf of national and international causes. Nevertheless, there was no justified place on the streets for the legions of the vagrant and unemployed. Those on foot, especially in a crowd, still constituted a potential problem. They should be set to work. Government, on all levels, now operated under the shared prescription that society should be productive and its members, especially those without cars, should move in a common and synchronized manner.

The postwar era in the West returned commerce and freedom to the streets. But pedestrians did not unanimously claim this option. Increasingly and at accelerating rates, Americans first, followed by Europeans, chose to ride—and best of all, in cars of their own—and to live in the suburbs. The pedestrian who did remain on the streets increasingly became a stick of a person in the postwar consumer society, where walkers were made to fit allotted spaces between regimented societies and their cars.

$\overset{\textstyle\lambda}{}9\overset{\textstyle\lambda}{}$ Wheels and Cars

*The Eclipse of the
American Walker by the Motorist*

INHABITANTS of the contemporary world sit more, walk less, and do so with far less effort and far more choice than their forebears. Two of the principal causes for this changed condition, which amounted to nothing less than an irreversible revolution, were wheels and cars. Not just vital for private and public transport but also crucial for the haulage of all things, wheels accounted for why twentieth-century people walked and carried less. Mass-produced cars turned walkers into riders and created, with highways and suburbs, a whole new social order, which transformed walking and human senses of space, time, and freedom.

There were other causes of less and easier walking in the twentieth century. Medicine dramatically advanced in the last century in its treatment of feet and legs. The Napoleonic wars in Europe and the Civil War in the United States spurred on the production of prosthetic limbs.[1] Therapy improved the walking of the congenitally disabled, the injured, the diseased, and the elderly. Orthopedic operations have come a long way since Flaubert's fictional nineteenth-century doctor Charles Bovary killed off the clubfooted man he sought to cure by applying his foot-twisting and gangrene-causing box. Today's doctors supply their patients with synthetic limbs and joints. Better design and light materials of metals, plastics, and nylons have recently been employed to offer better shoes and to improve canes, crutches, braces, and other walking aids. A variety of other inventions and laws—starting with the Americans with Disabilities Act of 1990—improved surfaces, stairs, and guiderails that make for safer and easier walking.[2]

Smoother flooring, roads, and sidewalks also made for far easier and safer walking. Shoes for style rather than for service on rough and dirty roads could consequently be manufactured for the multitudes; and even white shoes for cleaner and paved streets could be made popular.[3] Thanks to level surfaces, the chance to appear in public, and the vagaries of fashion, middle-class women even took to shopping, strolling, and dancing precariously perched on top of the thinnest and lowest-cut shoe, with very high heels. With modern women going about in towns in a way the privileged of their gender were once shod for courtly balls, we have another instance of democratic society in style and manners eventually getting around to imitating royalty and nobility.[4]

Doing in the twentieth century what they never did on any scale in the past, shoe companies manufactured shoes suited for specialized activities. Having a history unto itself, the shoe industry scientifically and technologically took up not just the comfort but also the performance and well-being of the foot. Nowhere is this as manifest as in the story of the tennis shoe industry, which remained until the 1960s a secondary market.[5] Up to that point, tennis shoes, lowly *sneakers* made of canvas uppers and rubber bottoms, were kept off the main tracks of society.[6] They were confined to basketball and tennis courts and, to a lesser degree, the wet, slippery, and exclusive surfaces of yachts.[7] One historian of the shoe industry commented, "They have been around less than a century, but tennis shoes have been the subject of more technological and styling research than any shoe in history."[8]

In what at least at first glance seems a paradox, the shoe and tennis shoe industries came to care for and highlight the foot and its specialized activities in a society that has increasingly minimized walking, and has even considered not having to walk both a goal and an achievement. Movement was diminished and economized at work. The assembly line, to offer the quintessential example of the modern industrial world, brought to the workers the parts to be made into products. Warehouses and trucks, correspondingly, coordinated materials and products, diminishing walking, increasing sitting, and mechanizing lifting and carrying. Loading and unloading, at factory, post office, and warehouse, increasingly was turned over to dollies, conveyor belts, pallets, and forklifts.

Architectural designs for commercial and public buildings alike aimed at ease and efficiency of movement. This influence emerges in the design of structures ranging from museums to department stores to hospitals. In hospitals, for instance, design structure—far from perfected—must mediate among multiple forms of traffic, reconciling the needs for the performance of crucial emergency functions, sanitation, privacy, and safety, while allowing for the movement of visitors, staff, and diverse nonambulatory patients.

Developed originally for use in deep mines, elevators and escalators are two machines that have proven crucial for efficient modern building design. Both inventions curtail or eliminate climbing stairs on foot, while at the same time they shorten distances, increase speed, bear loads, and regulate traffic.[9] Elevators found multiple, widespread commercial and public uses in the second half of the nineteenth century as society at work and play had to learn to move people in mass. (They were even used on the *Titanic.*) The elevator, in combination with the use of structural steel, made possible the miracle of late-nineteenth-century architecture, the skyscraper. First appearing as scattered solitary creations on the New York skyline in the 1870s, they became by the 1880s internationally recognized works of art in Chicago, where they reached heights of 230 to 260 feet.[10] Inspired by the steel skeleton of the Eiffel Tower, Chicago architect Louis H. Sullivan and others shaped an urban landscape of canyons of concrete, steel, and glass—and blowing winds that account for the classic image of the slumped-over urban walker.[11]

Accommodating skyrocketing commerce, population, and property values, skyscrapers in the United States formed vertical and non-walking cities unto themselves. They generated a new breed of "cliff dwellers," who took pride in their status as eagles soaring over the modern city, and they prompted a fresh angle from which to conceive the city and its flowing traffic moving below.[12] From on high—looking down on turbulent Manhattan from the former World Trade Center—one could mistake oneself for a kind of celestial surveyor, with the all-powerful glance and transcendent eye of a deity, watching the traffic patterns of the antlike pedestrians down below.[13]

Although no true rival of the elevator as a people mover, the escalator—a wheeled conveyor belt of rolling steps—too proved to be effective in moving multitudes of people up and down flights of stairs in department stores, subways, train stations, and airports.[14] The rolling sidewalk, which played far less of a role in displacing walking than intended by its utopian planners, who debuted their designs at the Chicago World Exposition in 1893, has recently found increasing use in airports and elsewhere.[15]

Commercial architects found other ways to shorten foot travel and protect pedestrians from the perils of oncoming cars, bad weather, panhandling, and crime. Parking ramps and underground garages became common in the second half of the twentieth century, disrupting sidewalk traffic in order to deliver commuters to their exact location. Skyways installed during the past few decades in towns like St. Paul, Minneapolis, Houston, Cincinnati, and Milwaukee keep foot traffic between parking ramps and buildings entirely indoors, which is convenient for pedestrians seeking shopping and eating establishments, hotels, and commercial and professional activities in a single complex of interlocked corridors.

Domestic design and improvements also diminished walking in the course of the century. By the 1930s most homes had indoor running water, which ended the need to fetch water for drinking, cooking, bathing, washing, and laundry. Gas and oil furnace systems—which came after the Second World War—spared inhabitants the need to haul wood, stoke coal, and dispose of ashes. The refrigerator replaced the hauling of ice. Subscribing to the underlying tenet that the fewer steps one takes the better, today's home design integrates halls, stairs, and rooms, often seeking to do away with stairs altogether.[16] Multiplying bathrooms and closets and making bedrooms and other rooms sufficient unto themselves assures privacy and saves steps. At the same time, improved floorings provide smooth and level surfaces for safe foot travel.[17]

Contemporary design minimizes walking in other ways. Improved and increased numbers of chairs, couches, mattresses, and beds increase sitting and lounging at home, at work, and in moving vehicles. Improved air conditioning, food storage, ventilation, and lighting enhance home comfort and afford less reason to get up and go for a walk.[18] Telephone, radio, music players, and then television, computers, videos, and home entertainment systems have further transformed the home into a recreation and leisure center. There is less and less need for the streets for entertainment and sociability.

The battle between sitting and walking, which goes from the beginning of the time until now, has largely been won, thanks to mass manufacture in the nineteenth century, by regular chairs, easy chairs, tables, mattresses, desks, paper, books, computers, and, lest we forget, leisure-induced sloth.[19] Thanks to new technologies for communicating, which displace the foot and horse messenger, coupled with abundant furniture for comfortable sitting, the mass of people can stay put and keep their seat. Cell phones, faxes, photocopy machines, and e-mail make the world but a click away.[20] Open spaces, see-through glass and plastic, and intercom systems suppress the need for movement, while remote controls, thermostats, timers, and other sorts of sensors save steps as they automatically adjust heating, turn lights and radios on and off, and lock doors. Domestic technologies satisfy perennial wants and provide innovative services—and in the process do away with walking and create, as the most recent data from the United States shows, a heavier nation.[21]

Nevertheless, domestic self-sufficiency and affluence, which can produce an overweight population, didn't keep people at home. Aside from work, school, and church (to which one was likely to ride further and where one was likely to sit once there) multitudes in the twentieth century learned to play and travel as never before. Of course, not all travel and trips led to physical activity and walking. Indeed, travel and tourism forever must be differentiated between that which involves considerable and varied walking and that which is predominantly about sitting and lying about. Nevertheless, as basic needs were met at home and fresh activities and different places were learned about, choices of pleasure led people ever further afield. With fewer steps required to get more, gratification seemed, as in fairy tales, just one good trip away—and space and money did not limit will and imagination as they had through the ages. A world of necessity and limits was steadily replaced by a world of opportunity and choice.

Already by the end of the nineteenth century the Western world was caught up in a headlong race to triumph over space and other resistances to human movement and motion. Wish and fiction created a new geography, which opened to driving and foreclosed the need to walk. Already within the limits of existing technology, Jules Verne's fictional hero, barely walking, made it "around the world in eighty days," the title of his 1873 novel. (Protagonists of his earlier works had already led imaginary excursions by sitting in a machine and traveling to the center of the earth, to the bottom of the sea, and to the moon itself.[22])

As Western civilization pushed to the remotest corners of the globe, more and more explorers sat in the cockpits of machines. Sitting in an airplane in 1903, the Wright brothers flew their airplane to the height of human dreams, without the flapping of an arm. As explorers, nations, and commerce bounded across seas and continents, human wish leapfrogged reality. Imagination was unbounded from human legs. Record-breaking expeditions to both poles, though profoundly dependent on heroic walking and dog teams, also testified to a smaller world linked by transportation and communication. By the start of the century, accelerated machine-made speeds on land, on sea, and in the air made slow-footed walking an anachronism.

The conquering of space minimized walking in other ways. Indeed, if we are seeking one thing that made these new powerful and lifting machines possible and transformed humans en masse into sitting, conquering, and commanding royalty, we must turn to the wheel. Its refinement, adaptation, and propagation not only changed the landscape and human movement but also shaped them to serve the wheel. The Industrial Revolution displaced human and animal power with engines. It put wheels under objects of ever greater size and weight, pulled them by a machine when possible, and, correspondingly, made surfaces uniform and smooth for rolling. The train—the steam engine turned on its side, whose tracks defined towns and commerce, wove region and nation into a single fabric, and turned walkers into riders—was the premier wheeled engine of the nineteenth-century Industrial Revolution.

However, it was the smaller, more mobile, and mass-produced car, which appeared at the start of the twentieth century, that—as we will see in the case of the United States—marked for the masses the triumph of the wheel over the foot. It linked places far and near. It made town and country one as they had never been before. It reconfigured basic senses of motion and distance, and load. It filled in with roads the grid the train had sketched in steel. In a matter of a few decades, the car, along with its cousins, the truck and the tractor, supplanted the horse as the primary driving engine of an expanding revolution in travel, work, agriculture, and leisure. Along with introducing mechanized warfare, it left the mighty steed a recreational animal for the rich and idle. The car made doubly true what Emerson already declared to be true of the nineteenth century: "The civilized man has built a coach, but he has lost the use of his feet."[23]

Bifurcating the world into walker and rider, the car increasingly delivered people to and from the places to which they had once walked. It went a long way toward eliminating carrying and making going on foot a matter of choice and lifestyle. The car has the consequence of making the peoples across the entire world riders and drivers, at least by desire. At the same time accounting for shifts in perception, the car displaced walking as the normal pace and measure of movement. The commonest mind began to skip local boundaries in the countryside, and in the words of geographer Yi Fu Tuan, "street scenes were perceived increasingly from the interior of cars, moving staccato-fashion through regularly paced traffic lights."[24]

ROLLING ON

Carts and carriages of sundry types, along with the wheelbarrow and cannon carriage, both of which appeared in early modern history, got

Europeans in the habit of rolling things and replaced feet—animal or human—with wheels.[25] Cylinders and gears at work in mill and mine machines taught that wheels, harnessed to a power source, could speed things along. In turn, engine-driven wheels, of which the steam-propelled train is a first example, carried loads and cut through space as no walking person or pulling animal could. Indeed, the very definition of wilderness—which so occupies those who define the use of public lands—is arguably a place where wheels, the essence of industrial society, can't or shouldn't go.[26]

With ever finer internal wheels and more complex external ones, industry mass produced an array of vehicles for land, sea, and air. Myriad metal ball bearings fashioned near-frictionless rolling interiors for speeding and turning machines.[27] Casters, coasters, steel rims and spokes, and better load-carrying springs, in combination with lubrication, rubber, and then gears, levers, and pneumatic tires, form essential components of the rolling wheel's triumph over space.

Besides accounting for the great movements of industry, wheels also turn humble household objects such as "lazy Susans" and chairs. They underpin turntables and the spinning disks of computers. For the child they equal play on streets and sidewalks, on roller skates and skateboards, while their parents push, or ride, self-propelled lawn mowers across lawns. Wheels have been put under nearly everything we move. They roll large cargo containers, handcarts, cleaning carts, washing machines, ladders, scrub buckets, garbage containers of every sort, dumping hoppers, grocery and bakery carts, and, as already suggested, stairs and sidewalks. Casters and bearings having conquered the internal friction of machines allows us to put rolling wheels under the world of things. First added, according to *Famous First Facts,* to bedsteads in 1838 in New Haven, Connecticut, casters over time were added to whatever could be pushed—garment and paint racks, mobile tool cases, piano benches, baby cribs, portable bars and barbecues, whole platforms, and lightweight suitcases, which have reshaped airport walking and traffic in the last several years.[28]

Objects whose movement, whether pushing, pulling, or turning, depended on animal and human walking now are rolled and moved by engine-powered machines. Miniaturized and made of lighter materials, objects and their containers are more apt to be pushed or pulled on wheels than lifted and carried. Foot treadles and even handles disappear as buttons and automatic signaling devices trigger the movement of things. In this way, the revolution of wheels and engines has steadily transformed manual labor, consequently altering our body sizes, postures, and ways of walking. Wheels in the Western world thanks to jeeps and all-terrain vehicles, go almost everywhere.[29] Surely humanity has bet its future on rolling wheels and transformed itself into a kind of *wheeled creature.*

The turning surveyor's wheel—the perambulator—measured unbounded continents, while simultaneously another perambulator, the baby carriage, allowed mother or nanny to promenade babies along paved town streets and sidewalks. First manufactured in the 1850s for royalty and the upper classes in England, the baby carriage started its service for the nonambulatory beginnings of life in the same period as the wheelchair began to aid those who at the end of life could no longer even limp or toddle along.[30] Both stroller and wheelchair testified not only the desire to move people about but also to the existence of relatively level surfaces on which to do it.

On paved roads, which weave a nation into a single cloth, the bicycle best fits the movement and kinetics of the human leg and thus constitutes the ideal machine for efficient human self-propulsion. If we can't fly, we certainly can pedal. Invented in France in the 1790s as the *velocifère,* the bicycle (also known as the velocipede and the "swift walker" in the United States and the "hobby horse" in England) first showed up on the streets of New York in May 1819.[31] Initially it met with a reaction not unlike one that greeted skateboards in recent decades: in August 1819, the Common Council "passed a law to prevent the use of velocipedes in the public places and on the sidewalks of the city of New York."[32] Yet by the post–Civil War years, "the bone shaker," as sports enthusiasts called it, grew in popularity with its mass manufacture in the late 1870s.[33] It was amusing, a way to get out in the countryside, and a feat of balance and athleticism, but it was more than entertainment. Compared to foot and horse, it was a cheap, fast, and efficient way to cover distance.

Over the next two decades, inventors sought to adapt the bike for purposes of haulage as inventors rigged baskets and carts for carrying and delivering such divergent things as mail and animals.[34] Machine guns were mounted on the front of bicycles in the First World War. Early bicycle enthusiasts, who formed the first ranks of those advocating more and smoother roads, formed bicycle schools, societies, corps, and magazines. They held races of all sorts, including a race for women in Madison Square Garden in January 1896. Bicycling received a real boost in 1892, when B. F. Goodrich produced a hard-to-puncture cord tire. Thomas Stevens bicycled around the world between 1884 and 1887, going from San Francisco to Boston, from London to France to Serbia, Persia, India, China, Japan, and then back to San Francisco. However, if the truth be told—which Stevens did in a detailed two-volume work refreshingly dedicated to road conditions rather than to his philosophy of life and opinions of other cultures—he walked, carrying and trundling his bike, much of the way.[35] Muck and sinking surfaces were a continuous problem; steep hills and strong headwinds also proved inimical to easy rolling. Riding commonly proved impossible when he crossed mountains, deserts, and streams and often next to impossible on paths, trails, and uneven beds of railroad tracks. The same was even true at many times on available roads, whose uneven surfaces were regularly marred by potholes, crevices, and washouts and covered by rock, muck, cave-ins, and snow. Barely out of San Francisco, Stevens had to hunt down a cobbler to fit out his shoes "for hard service," as it dawned on him how much "foot riding" lay ahead.[36] To bike around the world was still equivalent to walking at least half of the way.

Overseas, the bicycle wheel sired the speedy rickshaw—a two-wheeled covered vehicle usually meant for one sitting passenger (possibly two) and pulled by a poor man. Revealing class relations across civilizations, the rickshaw puller earned his living by running and carrying at the behest of the rider, who commonly was a visitor and always someone too rich, important, and busy to walk. It is conjectured that the rickshaw was invented in 1870 in Japan, where the bicycle as a means of transportation still remains popular. It quickly grew in popularity throughout the cities of China and Southeast Asia, due to a near-perfect marriage between the Western technology of springs and bicycle-type ball-bearing wheels and a surplus of cheap labor comprised of willing backs and legs of people who earned their living competing against the more expensive horse and motorized machine.[37]

Wheeled vehicles sped twentieth- and twenty-first-century humanity along. It allowed people to sit and ride, and eventually to do so in relative comfort. Twirling, spinning, dodging, and roller-coastering vehicles filled amusement parks.[38] Scooters of every ilk, from yesterday's orange crate on discarded roller skates to today's light-wheeled silver scooter, motorcycles, motorbikes, and mopeds define movement in today's American society. The ubiquitous golf cart delivers not only golfers to greens but also bathers to beaches. It pervades parade grounds, athletic fields, and movie-studio and car lots while also finding use in lumberyards, warehouses, airports, and factories. Tanks or their mutants, half-tracks (half wheel, half track) or amphibious vehicles ("ducks"), and other all-purpose all-terrain vehicles (from the early military jeep to today's Hummer to big-wheeled three-wheel ATVs) show how wheels carry people where walking humanity once went only with considerable effort. They also show how choice and style continue to trump utility.

The automobile truly culminates the combined revolution of portable engines, complex wheels, and smooth surfaces initiated by the train. When German Nickolaus Otto built his first gas engine in 1866 and displayed it the following year at the Paris Exhibition, the horseless carriage became a possibility and the horse—which had supplied largely elite land transportation for six thousand years—could be put out to pasture.[39] The car, in a matter of a few decades, turned the walking species into the driving species. First men sat behind the wheels of cars just as they had held the reins of carriages. But then, after a few decades, women and young adolescents climbed into the seat behind the wheel. The car struck another blow against the riding aristocracy, on the one hand, and walking humanity, on the other.

More than any other machine, the car, which introduced the twentieth century, spelled the end of walking. Lewis Mumford held it responsible for "the end of the pedestrian" in this century.[40] Making every driver the ruler of space, the automobile completed the development of modern individualism and mass humanity, and its massive distribution throughout society further eroded class distinctions between walkers and sitters, walkers and riders, and walkers and drivers. [41]

The car uniquely reduced the status of the walker by making walkers throughout society more and more irrelevant. Over decades the person without a car, except perhaps in large cities, was considered somebody unable to drive one or too poor to own one. In conjunction with its wheeled cousin, the truck, it transformed the walking environment. It remade the city, gave profound impetus to urban sprawl, transformed the countryside, and dramatically expanded suburbs, which already had given birth to expanding populations, rising real estate prices, and rail travel.[42] Along with high-rise buildings, expressways, and great highways, the car emptied cities, towns, and villages of walkers, while creating whole new environments—the suburbs foremost among them—where walking was discouraged or no longer even possible.

The car widened and diminished the number of city streets and roads. It birthed and reshaped sidewalks; formed afresh and eliminated corners and intersections; gave rise to crosswalks, overpasses, and subterranean walkways; and, in the course of making auto traffic flow, eliminated blocks and whole neighborhoods.[43] In *City Life,* cultural critic Witold Rybczynski captures the automobile's role in redefining the city street:

> Modern urbanism meant abandoning the traditional street layout, wherever possible, and in the name of separating drivers and walkers, replacing sidewalks with pedestrian malls and underground or elevated walkways. Buildings no longer lined streets in a time-tested manner but stood free in plazas. Streets [which once hosted and spawned walkers' communities and cultures] were merely for transportation—the faster the traffic moved, the better. Above all, these modern improvements defined themselves by their isolation from the rest of the city, not only by the style of their architecture, which was aggressively and uncompromisingly modern, but also by their size, which was huge.[44]

Twentieth-century traffic and city planners constricted and transformed walking cities and their characteristics to accommodate automobile traffic. Governments destroyed entire neighborhoods for the sake of traffic flow. The traffic-driven city tended to homogenize walkers into alien pedestrians and passersby who, indifferent to any given neighborhood, moved in tune with the city as a whole; a bewildering array of regulating laws, signs, and signals; and an array of local and regional schedules.[45]

In the countryside cars sped where feet and hooves had long trudged and wagons bogged down and overturned. Cars made emphatic the distinctions already drawn between carriage and walker. Bifurcating humanity into walkers, on the one hand, and drivers and riders, on the other, the car distinguished "developed" societies from "undeveloped" ones. Bypassing villages and small towns by the thousands and diminishing travel by train and bus, automobiles equally transformed urban and rural societies. Joining comfort to speed, pleasure, romance, and status, the car sped past bipedal humanity—and horse, cart, and buggy too—delivering people to new lives. In conjunction with the tractor, which displaced and came to rule farmers' fields starting in the 1920s and 1930s, it set the countryside in motion as it had never been before.

The car, this great transformer, however, was far more than an invention that simply joined a seat to motor and wheels. To be the revolutionary vehicle it was, it had to start, keep going, stay on the road, stop when required, even quickly if necessary, and stay put, without injuring or terribly discomforting its driver. It needed to run on affordable fuel. Furthermore, to be popularly embraced, it had to be big enough to haul a family and cheap enough for an average family to purchase and maintain. And it had to be such that it could fit into a family and a family could shape itself to it.

Unless these conditions were met the automobile was destined to remain the curiosity that one circus hippodrome featured as "a tremendous novelty, never seen before, an ordinary road carriage driven over the common high-ways without the aid of horses or other draught animals."[46] New speeds (reaching sixty miles an hour in 1900) and spreading popularity, which even induced "Rough Rider" American President Theodore Roosevelt to take a ride in 1902, were insufficient to win the "Tin Lizzy" a nation. Instead, it took an inventor and entrepreneur who would combine inventions and technologies into the manufacture of a dependable, versatile, and relatively cheap vehicle.

Building his first car in a garage in 1896, Henry Ford emerged from many competitors passionately at work on the automobile's development and mass manufacture. He achieved this in the first decade of the twentieth century, a period during which the automobile industry output increased 3,500 percent in the United States. (There were fifty automobile manufacturers in the United States in 1898, 241 in 1908.)[47] In 1909, Detroit-based Ford made the decisive move to produce the truly affordable auto. He announced that his factory would manufacture only the model T chassis. The car he vended for $825 in 1908 he sold for only $260 in 1925.[48] Already by 1933, Ford sought to evoke with his outdoor museum of shops, at Greenfield Village, as part of the Edison Institute in Dearborn, Michigan, the world and time that he and his contemporary, Thomas Edison, had irreversibly dissolved.[49]

At the start of the twentieth century, there were only a hundred miles of paved highway in the United States. Paving had been slow in coming, despite bicycle enthusiasts and shipping advocates.[50] However, history took a quick turn once the nation climbed into the car. Already in 1913 bold proponents conceived of a paved road—the Lincoln Highway—spanning the continent from New York to San Francisco. In 1916 the Federal Aid Roads Act made its first grants to states for the construction of rural post roads. In 1925 the government established a uniform route-numbering system, and in 1930 it made its first appropriations for the Inter-American Highway, which, 90 percent complete in 1962, would link the Western hemisphere from Alaska to Chile.[51]

Automobile "firsts" augured the reconfiguration of the American landscape for driving, leaving the walker and the horse artifacts of an earlier time. Already used to deliver mail, haul cadavers, and much else, cars appeared everywhere, made into full, comfortable, and roomy sedans by Detroit's Hudson Motors in 1913. Gulf Oil offered drivers the first drive-in gas station in Pittsburgh, Pennsylvania, that same year. Also in Pittsburgh—even perhaps at the same station—the adventurous got their first automobile road map in 1914—and could plan a trip place to place, theoretically getting out of their car only to eat, sleep, and relieve themselves. A crowning achievement for staying seated in one's car was Firestone's floating balloon tire, which appeared in 1923.[52] Other amenities—from the heating and air conditioning that Packard first offered in 1939 to the radio—made for merry riding and induced the walker to get off his or her feet.

Cars and roads played leapfrog with each other. Each took up ever more room on the landscape and each pushed the walker to the side. More cars meant a demand for more and better roads, and improved roads encouraged more people's desire to drive cars. Advocates for walking were faint voices in a world that almost unequivocally equated motoring and progress. The first highway, built in 1906, was the Bronx River Parkway. Highways then appeared in the Delaware and Detroit areas in the 1920s. Expressways ran to New York's World's Fair in 1936.[53] Designed especially for trucks, the Pennsylvania Turnpike, built in the 1940s, was the first step in creating a whole national landscape of cars speeding from state to state over valleys and through mountains. Between 1935 and 1941, the German National Socialists laid down a new order of earth travel, building twenty-three hundred miles of concrete Autobahn, which was designed for speeds up to a hundred miles per hour. "By 1940," historian of roads Edward Relph writes, "the automobile had begun to weave a concrete and asphalt web across Europe and North America."[54] Walkers could only stand aside in the face of such monumental growth.

CONGESTION

Cars entered into the fray of the nation's most rapidly growing cities, introducing new levels of speed and new scales of traffic jams (already anticipated by horse and carriage in the nineteenth century) that spelled complete stoppage. As early as 1850, for example, New York's population, which had surpassed London's, experienced many of the same things their pedestrian counterparts did on the streets of London and Paris.[55] Cholera, riot, and fire all took their turn in New York, whose streets received critical appraisal, including that of Charles Dickens, who walked the city in 1842.[56] Faced by mobs and crime, New York constituted a police department of eight hundred in 1845.

Overrun by immigrants and slums in the 1850s and 1860s, the city built a necessary sewer system, paved its streets, and initiated a sanitation department in 1866.[57] Even though these improvements restored some respectability to the streets of New York, still the middle class, repelled by hordes of pedestrian traffic, withdrew itself and its business to the suburbs.[58] At the same time the walkers themselves did not escape the vicissitudes of weather, the guile of fellow humans, the waste of animals, the breakdowns of public transportation, or the bane of congestion.[59]

With the advent of motor vehicles, taxis and omnibuses, and then autos, cabs, and trucks hogged all the space they set their wheels on, battling with pedestrians, especially newly arrived gawking and illiterate country bumpkins, known as "jays"—the source of prejudice attached their name to the act and offense of jaywalking.[60] When it came to traffic, everyone and everything merited a daily cursing. Even Henry James, returning to the United States in 1904 after a twenty-four-year stay in England, took his turn. Disgusted by the change he saw and terrified by the hideous traffic, he denounced New York, his hometown, as "grossly tall and grossly ugly." Surrounded by sound, wind, dirt, pushing, and shoving, and all the time threatened by vehicles, he voiced the complaint of an idle and gazing tourist who, in his own words, "could not walk in the way of pistons and view space at his leisure."[61]

The first collision of a car and a bicycle occurred in New York in 1896. Bold New Yorker Genevra Mudge, who drove her electric car on city streets as early as 1898, skidded on ice during a race in 1899, knocking down five spectators. In the same year, New York recorded its first automobile fatality. The victim, Henry Bliss, was knocked down and run over. However, as a source of pedestrian fatalities cars were surely not worse than horses, and they saved the municipality the significant expense of removing horse manure and dead horses.[62]

The famous Broadway Squad of New York (organized in 1860) was "the first unit of police to have special functions in the field of traffic regulation," with "a special purpose to escort pedestrians across the streets and to stop traffic while so doing."[63] In 1871 the New York Police Department (NYPD) formed a mounted patrol that played a crucial role in traffic control until the 1920s, when they and horses were replaced by automobiles.[64] In 1919 the NYPD "owned just thirty-three cars." Six years later, it had "six hundred and every precinct had two or three light runabout patrol vehicles, while three- and four-man detective squads roamed the city in heavy touring cars. Police cars were not equipped with radios, though, until 1932, so walking and riding flatfoots had to call in on the once-familiar and now forgotten signal box every hour to receive assignments."[65]

Throughout the nation law and technology entered the melee to separate crowds of pedestrians and hordes of cars. Among national firsts, Connecticut regulated the speed of automobiles in 1901: twelve miles per hour on highways in the country; eight miles an hour on city highways. In 1899 Chicago instituted an automobile license board, while in 1901 New York State required automobile license plates. In 1899 the Akron, Ohio, police department equipped its finest with an electric automobile police patrol wagon.[66] In 1911 Wayne County, which included Detroit, put traffic lines on its River Road near Trenton. (Its inventor described them as a "center line safety stripe.") Mechanical help in regulating the often unruly convergence of human, animal, and machine came in Cleveland in 1914 in the form of the traffic light, replete with colors and sounds.[67]

Road markings, left-turn lanes, stop signs, and automatic traffic signals began appearing in the 1910s. In the 1920s, New York and Philadelphia started banning parking on certain streets. Congestion stifled the flow of commerce and discouraged shoppers. In 1935 Oklahoma City, soon to be followed by many other cities, introduced the parking meter. Throughout the first half of the century, the urban walking environment was defined by the introduction of concrete sidewalks, curbing and gutters, garbage cans and collection, mechanical street cleaners, and street lighting. It was further shaped by zoning and nuisance codes, not to mention the banning of cellar doors that opened onto city sidewalks and of sidewalk displays and stands that cluttered sidewalks.[68]

Traffic control—at least in the surveillant and engineering minds of a few—became a science. In 1934 Harvard offered a course in traffic engineering, which lumped walkers, one and all, into the category of "pedestrian foot traffic," a class whose definition was derived from its relationship to vehicular traffic. Pedestrian traffic, whose volume and obedience to stop-and-go signals were measured at intersections, was considered mainly with regard to how it impinged on vehicular flow.[69] Writing in 1964 with only slight hyperbole, Lewis Mumford wrote, "In America we have pushed the elimination of the pedestrian to its ultimate conclusion—the drive-in market, the drive-in movie theatre, and the drive-in bank."[70] In order to keep foot traffic flowing, certain cities in the 1950s even considered ordinances that would prohibit pedestrians from stopping on the sidewalk. As the number of cars multiplied, both pedestrian and automobile fatalities grew. Already in 1921 the ratio of motor vehicles to population reached proportions as low as 5:1 in California, Iowa, and South Dakota, 7:1 in Michigan and Wisconsin, and 13:1 in New York.[71] By 1950 the United States produced more than a million cars a year, which guaranteed more cars on the road, more miles driven and increased driver and pedestrian accident fatalities.[72]

Yet recent reductions in automobile-related mortality rates do not suggest that the car's detrimental effects on the walking environment have been mitigated. With vehicular traffic reduced to average speeds of five miles per hour during rush periods, congested downtowns provide incentives to walking, even though pedestrians find at certain points that they can barely find space to put their feet down.[73] To move at any speed, pedestrians must truly be nimble dodgers. They must avoid cars at all costs, while, as if on a crowded ice rink, weaving in and out of crowds of fellow pedestrians, quick-stepping to negotiate obstacles of every sort.

HOMES WITHOUT FOOTING

The car gave birth to pedestrian-hostile roads and intersections, high rises, and parking lots. It delivered an increasing number of Americans to the "walkingless environment" that has come to characterize so many contemporary cities, suburbs, and towns.[74] This occurred first in the 1950s in the United States, then in the 1960s and 1970s in much of Europe, and subsequently in most urban centers throughout the world.[75] In 2002, Milan—a city that increasingly seems to belong to its peripheries and its commuters, shoppers, and visitors—initiated experiments with "Ecological Sundays," which restrict driving and promote walking and cycling.[76] In the same year London, overwhelmed by traffic, required private vehicles—not cabs—to pay a fee of approximately eight dollars to enter central London. And China—with only a few cars per capita—headed in the opposite direction by taking measures to squeeze bicycles off the main streets of its principal cities in order to make way for the automobile and the economic progress it symbolizes.

The car almost everywhere devastated walking in much of urban America, although in some cities, downtown New York among them, walking continues because there is no parking and streets are so congested that walkers can outpace vehicles for blocks during rush hour. The building of expressways, the undermining of the public transport system, and the destruction of complex streetcar systems in such places as Detroit, Los Angeles, and the Twin Cities all destroyed center cities and the walking they supported. Neighborhoods of older industrial towns declined, and in their place sprawling megalopolises such as Los Angeles, Phoenix, and Atlanta sprang up.[77] Social critics have identified long lists of consequent evils, from racism to loss of community to urban life without city centers, accompanying the building of expressways and the growth of suburbs.

The car created multiple environments (parking lots, expressways, suburbs, drive-throughs, skyscrapers, etc.) that in most instances impeded walking and in some places made it impossible. A diminished number of streets per urban square mile, and a corresponding widening of streets and intersections, destroyed the sociability of the walking environment. The automobile, increasing the number of traffic lights and instructions, and quickening the pace of urban life, further transformed walkers into regulated or, in the case of New York, notoriously defiant pedestrians and made city inhabitants less tolerant of any sort of delay.[78]

While pedestrians of nations, cities, and towns move to diverse internal clocks and streetways, as shown by psychologist Robert Levine in *A Geography of Time,* cars increasingly define the metronome of contemporary urban life everywhere.[79] Global society increasingly lives, thinks, and imagines movements, transactions, and realizations according to the accelerated measure of riding in a motorized vehicle.

The speedometer, not the pedometer, defines speed, expands and diversifies destinations, and develops a range of gestures, movements, and experiences associated with traveling by car—although the immense traffic jam defines street gridlock as the absolute zero of urban movement.

The car, which left many cities without centers or residential populations, created the sprawling city (quintessentially represented by Los Angeles) and began in the second half of the twentieth century to remove people en masse to the suburbs.[80] Los Angeles had a low-density sprawl on a scale never before witnessed in an American city, with an average density of less than a half and as little as a third of that of cities like New York and Chicago. There and elsewhere air pollution steadily mounted, reaching the point where, by the 1970s, smog alerts advised people to stay indoors and children not to go out and play on playgrounds. Reliance on the automobile produced what might even be considered a car culture, which turned on an extensive network of expressways; a youth leisure culture that socialized by driving in groups from drive-in to drive-in; and an identity that joined an individual and his or her personalized vehicle to a kind of perpetual driving about. One is reminded of Jedediah Smith's remark, based on his 1826–1827 expedition to the Southwest, on Californians as inveterate riders: "The Californians are excellent horsemen. . . . They are seldom seen on foot but mount a horse to go even 200 yards."[81]

"In 1970," U.S. historian Carl Degler notes, "nearly three quarters of the suburbanites depended on their personal cars to get to work."[82] Driven by the availability of low-cost property made accessible by expressway construction, the suburbs could offer on a large scale what they had already offered on a smaller scale: a chance to escape crime, congestion, air pollution, and a changing city, which problems the increasing reliance on the car in good measure had created.[83] Suburbs offered homes with attached garages, big lawns, secluded back yards, and quiet lives. The more expensive housing developments came with big lots and wide roads that, often circling or ending in cul-de-sacs, were nearly devoid of foot traffic, not to mention crowds. The unwritten price for a dream home in the suburbs was swearing abiding allegiance to the car, renouncing the walking community, and embracing a residence without daily contact with neighbors.

In the suburbs there is often little cause to walk. Most families, as a result of industry and rising standards of living, are equipped with one or many cars. Blocks are long. They offer little or nothing to see and nowhere to go. And sidewalks, where they exist, lead literally nowhere, are eerily empty of people, and rarely furnish any social or aesthetic experience along the way. Sequestered by roads and highways, suburbanites accustom themselves to driving out of habit or necessity. They drive to church, to shop, to work, to school, to see a movie, or simply to get out and around. They are quick to equip their children with cars. Like those who live in new urban additions along commercial strips, they drive to banks, coffee shops, grocery stores, dry cleaners, and churches. With public places and private institutions located at separate and distant locations, cars alone allow a person to accomplish multiple chores on a single trip.[84]

Some would even go further and argue that walking isn't done in the contemporary suburbs because it isn't even possible. Mary Battiata writes in a recent article in the *Washington Post,*

> I can remember when—in a suburban Washington [D.C.] childhood in the '60s and '70s—walking was common, routine even. We walked to the shopping center, walked to school. . . .
>
> But somewhere between then and now, walking as an option in suburban America seems to have disappeared. The facts bear this out. Between 1980 and today, the number of children walking to school has fallen from 70 percent to less than 10 nationwide. Walking as a means of getting from here to there is 36 times more dangerous than driving.[85]

If anything permits walking and unifies the suburban world, it is the shopping mall. Fully developed only in the United States and Canada, the mall is geared primarily to the use of the car and is a consequence of suburbanization.[86] Shopping centers proliferated in the United States, Canada, and Australia after World War II as wealthy populations of car-based families situated themselves on the outskirts of towns.[87] Northgate Shopping Center was built in Seattle in 1950, Northland Center in Detroit in 1954, and Southdale in Edina on the western edge of Minneapolis in 1956.[88] The latter, located on eighty-four acres, with ample aboveground and ramp parking, is a two-story edifice, with a glass roof and multiple galleries. It includes acres of paved fields and covered decks for parking, landscaping, fountains, food courts, toilets, benches, and wide walkways that serve "mall walkers" one and all—shoppers, strollers, idle teens, the elderly, the unemployed, the bored, and others wanting and needing a walk.[89]

The world's largest mall—built by the Ghermezian Brothers, who developed the five-million-square-foot structure in West Edmonton Mall in Alberta—is the Mall of America in Bloomington, Minnesota, opened in 1992. Serving Minneapolis and St. Paul, it is situated on a seventy-eight-acre site along major east-west and north-south expressways. It has 350 stores, four major department stores, and a full-scale theme park. Because it is less than a mile from the Minneapolis–St. Paul International Airport, many of its customers are passengers between their flights.

It is no exaggeration to suggest that, increasingly, the mall already functions in North America as a new walking and talking haven for those isolated by suburban and city life. Malls have become, I might suggest, "a village for the villageless." They provide a great deal in one location. Aside from shopping, one can also eat, exercise, meet friends, stroll, and, in the larger ones, bank, receive partial or full medical care, and even ice skate or attend church. Created around a central promenade, malls, though legally considered private property, promote the casual strolling that cities and suburbs so commonly deny. They provide a degree of cherished anonymity that goes with the busiest city streets.[90] A single lap around a mall can exceed a mile, and a changing daily and seasonal schedule of events that can include antique and book fairs, talent, pet, and auto shows, and health and community information programs offer ample variety. Though in color, smells, and sights they do not equal the streets and markets of a living neighborhood, they provide the walker with a far more interesting and hospitable environment than the empty streets and deadly roads of the characteristic contemporary American city and suburb.

Dissolving localities as islands of autonomous life and meaning, the automobile transformed the rural person into a regional consumer and pleasure seeker, a national or even international traveler, and, above all else, a driver.[91] Before the advent of the car, the railroad, the telegraph, the post, newspapers, and schools had already brought the countryside to urban heel. Cars, trucks, and tractors took quit-claim deeds to rural life, work, and commerce.

Starting in the 1930s, state, county, and even some township roads were paved. The federal highway system added forty thousand miles of roads to the national transportation system starting in the 1950s. Driving determined economic, social, and recreational activities in the countryside equally for small-town and farm dweller. Cars, trucks, and farm machinery pushed humans and animals to the sides of the road.

Within a few decades of the automobile's appearance in the countryside, community leaders paved, curbed, guttered, and lit the dusty and dirty main street. Sewers, running water, fire departments, electric streetlights, street cleaning, and even occasional traffic signals were in place before the Second World War.[92] Little time lapsed before farmers, at least on Saturday nights and Sundays, put on their best clothes, scraped the manure off their boots, got in their cars, and drove off to town.

The initial resistance offered to the automobile and costly road projects soon gave way to enthusiasm for the convenience of a vehicle, which could haul farmer, kids, grain, and chickens too. Goods, people, and events in neighboring towns now became accessible. Cars, trucks, tractors, bulldozers, combines, and other farm machinery produced in a generation or two a society dependent on driving.

Schoolbuses eliminated the long walk to school, whose very memory proved one pathway for the nostalgic retracing of childhood through the dirty 1930s, when bare feet and country living still coincided for a good portion of the rural poor. Drive-in movies were planted at the edges of towns and along highways in the 1940s. Automobile salesrooms, farm machinery dealers, and construction companies multiplied at least until the 1970s.

By the second half of the twentieth century, walking had become uncommon in the countryside. The hum of the passing car became the dominant background sound. The riding agriculturist—even on the smallest tractor or motorized tiller—became the new lord of land. Field paths and animal trails grew over. Cars, pickups, tractors, combines, skid-loaders, three-wheelers, and a host of off-road vehicles further minimized farm walking. At the same time trucks and bulldozers contoured and paved roads for rural drivers.

Hitchhiking all but vanished from the countryside in the 1960s and 1970s. Even migrant workers, who spend days walking bean fields to clean them of feeds, arrive at work in their pickup trucks. Now, to escape being taken for an odd duck, the walker must let everyone know that he or she walks under doctor's orders. Or to quote South Dakota poet Leo Dangel's "How to Take a Walk,"

> This is farm country.
> The neighbors will believe
> You are crazy
> If you take a walk
> Just to think and be alone.
> So carry a shotgun
> And walk the fence line.
> Pretend you are hunting.[93]

The small-town individual who walks to work is queried whether he or she has a drivers license and even questioned whether the family can afford a second car. Except for shoppers, few walkers move back and forth on Main Street, and those who do, more than nine times out of ten, have come by car. Commerce along the new strip tailors itself to the automobile, providing drive-in banks, automatic bank tellers, restaurants, and coffee shops, along with pickups for cleaning and drive-up slots through which one banks and pays for utilities. Sometimes small towns lack even a Main Street. Often the only store that remains is the convenience store located on the nearby highway.

One also finds in many small towns, as proof of the revolutionary rule of the automobile, dilapidated malls from the 1970s, now principally occupied by public agencies.[94] These early concentrations of commerce, which undid Main Street, have in turn been displaced by commercial centers strategically posted along the highway bypass. Anchored by a large chain grocery store and a Shopko or a Wal-Mart, these new outposts are served by immense parking lots and are in the process of evolving toward becoming one-stop stores.

In opposition to the driving city, a group of city planners, called the New Urbanists, has risen up. In the tradition of John Ruskin's romantic environmentalism, the City Beautiful Movement, and the writings of Lewis Mumford and Jane Jacobs, such New Urbanist designers as Sim Van der Reyn, Peter Calthrope, Andres Duany, and Philip Langdon make walking the polar star of their hopes for an urban renaissance.[95] The guiding articles of their faith postulate a neighborhood center, a five-minute walk to work and shop, "a street pattern that acts as paths to connect community, a mixed-use downtown and [an] integration of public spaces to represent collective identity and the civic aspirations of community."[96] In *The Next American Metropolis,* Peter Calthrope described their alternative in terms of "the pedestrian who makes the essential qualities of communities meaningful." He elaborates,

> Pedestrians create the place and the time for casual encounters and the practical integration of diverse places and peoples. Without the pedestrian, a community's common ground—its parks, sidewalks, squares, and plazas—become useless obstructions to the car. Pedestrians are the lost measure of community, they set the scale for both center and edge of our neighborhoods.[97]

Collectively these New Urbanists can be judged utopian by their wish to have the foot supplant the car, to create pedestrian-friendly streets, to devise networks that directly connect local destinations, and to secure a dense and active street life.

Perhaps more than any single invention, the car has made the walker feel like a trespasser on the earth. It has delivered people to distant places and away from localities established and maintained by the walking foot. To say that contemporary humanity lives, thinks, and wishes more generally and abstractly than in the past really amounts to saying that we drive a lot and we don't walk much these days. The vehicles that fill the streets and our driveways and the inventory of specialized shoes that line the back of our closets express the limited but select use we now make of our feet.[98]

True of much of the United States and Canada, this revolution in riding has become the case in much of urban Europe and throughout not just the metropolitan centers of the world but wherever people can ride. Already in the 1970s, walker Colin Thurbon wrote in his *Journey into Cyprus* of the oddity he had become:

> In eastern Mediterranean lands nobody goes on foot unless he must. To walk out of pleasure or curiosity is unimaginable. A man walks only because he is poor. . . . In a deeply conservative land, I was an anomaly. Why should a man trudge between Limassol and Paphos when he can share a taxi for seven shillings?[99]

Like it or not, humanity has been delivered by wheels and cars to a new world of choice and opportunity in which people sit more and walk less, and when they do walk, they do so with greater comfort and more by choice than ever before. Indeed, thanks to wheels and cars, mass industrial democratic societies move on scales, at speeds, and with mobility that have produced new orders of opportunity, choice, and gratification and have reordered neighborhoods, communities, and localities. Now at question is the place of walking in human experience and fate.

Conclusion

Choose Your Steps—Reflections on the
Transformation of Walking
from Necessity to Choice

 IKE hunting, fishing, horsebackriding, swimming, and other activities that were once considered indispensable, walking in Western society, and in significant sectors of the non-Western world, has become increasingly a matter of recreation, sport, or health, an expression of style, and even a vehicle to make a political statement. In the last two centuries, walking on the whole has passed from the realm of necessity into that of choice. It has become more specialized in its forms, having differentiated itself into types of romantic country walking, urban pedestrianism, race walking, hiking, recreational walking, and even mall walking. As its principal rivals, sitting and sitting and riding, have become more accessible to and comfortable for all sectors of society, walking finds itself in competition with a multiplying number of popularized and commercialized

leisure activities and sports that appeal to a mobile, complex, and affluent society. This is especially true in North America and Western Europe, where the automobile has most penetrated and shaped society.

With private vehicles and mass transportation available, people like nineteenth-century romantic walkers and travelers now ride to the places they choose to walk. They might ride to the mall to walk for exercise, to casually shop and browse, or to walk a little, and then to sit, eat, drink, and observe others walk. In summer, today's walkers might drive miles through summer traffic jams so they eventually can stroll seaside beaches and boardwalks. Commonly, they might take their car to a nearby gym to spend half an hour on a treadmill. The boldest walkers, who must have leisure and economic means, fly across seas and continents to scale mountains. Others cross the most difficult terrain, not to discover something or even to be somewhere special, but as a test of courage and skills. Supported by specialized shoes, clothing, medicine, and even stores dedicated exclusively to walking, riding society selects when, where, and in which ways it will walk.

In the Middle Ages and Renaissance, as we saw, royalty and aristocrats, popes and bishops were the first to walk voluntarily instead of out of necessity. As they staged dances and conducted military marches, so they put their "best foot" forward in ceremonies, processions, and promenades. Anticipating the contemporary democratic consumer society, the highest levels of early modern European society dressed elaborately and walked for reasons of style in the least utilitarian, most delicate, high-heeled shoes of embroidered cloth and attached gems. They walked on smooth surfaces and in special places devoted to display. Riding in ornate carriages, they delivered themselves to put themselves and their feet on display at courtly dances, garden strolls, or suburban promenades. For them walking was no ordinary matter.

During the seventeenth and eighteenth centuries, the rising middle class followed in the aristocracy's footsteps. They walked in country and city for show and pleasure. They rode their carriages to city squares, ramparts and overlooks, nearby forests, and seasides, where they strolled and promenaded. In the course of the eighteenth century, as society took more control of its environment and governments asserted their authority over the countryside, nature, at least in the minds of those with power and money, was tamed and idealized. At least potentially, the world became selectively a projection of their ordered gardens, and the choice of walking, in contradistinction to riding society, became an effective means to distinguish and to know oneself and the world.

Starting in the late eighteenth century, mass transportation started to liberate society from the need to go on foot. At accelerating rates in the second half of the nineteenth century, transit converted local people into shoppers, pedestrians, commuters, hikers, and walking travelers. By the mid-twentieth century, with North America well in the lead, automobiles and wheels made the majority of Westerners sitters, riders, and drivers. All this occurred as governments succeeded in taking control of society, especially at its large urban centers. With governments having turned unruly street crowds into organized and law-biding citizens, other institutions defined and shaped the walking movements and interactions of mass industrial society. Wherever train and bus, car and truck penetrated, human destiny was separated from going on foot, and consequently reordered senses of space, locality, distance, movement, and body arose.

Nevertheless, going on foot continued to play an elemental role in the lives of contemporary Westerners until recent times. In remote rural Europe, as elsewhere in the world, people still relied on their legs and backs to work and survive. Although ever fewer in number, country people still traveled on foot to market, school, and church, for water, wood, and work. Even today in the most developed society soldiers, waiters, doormen, cleaning personnel, stadium hawkers, caddies, security guards, floor nurses, certain messengers and delivery persons, and types of miners walk because it is an indispensable part of their job. Yet what remains true of them stands in distinction to all those who work while sitting—to all those who no longer need to walk except for short distances or on select occasions.

Walking has lost much of its footing in the kingdom of necessity. Sitting and riding not only redefine the meaning of going on foot but also mutate age-long notions of time, speed, distance, and locality.[1] However, before we explore this phenomenon, we must show how strenuous forms of bodily movement have diminished walking as a form of athleticism and an attractive form of leisure and recreation. Nevertheless, at the same time, walking in the last hundred years has not only retained but perhaps even has gained—as superseded necessities so commonly do—an enhanced cultural significance in a riding society.

STEPPING OUT FOR RECREATION AND TRAVEL

As walking as a necessity was displaced and diminished as a consequence of sitting and riding, so elective walking developed hierarchies. In turn, walking as a kind of chosen athletic activity underwent a differentiation associated with distance, speed, skills, equipment, and costs required to perform a particular form of it.[2] To state this in other terms, as hiking eclipsed country walking so it, in turn, was superseded, at least in the popular imagination, by mountain climbing and its harrowing ascents, and the life-and-death walking associated with heroic expeditions on foot. The latter could be exemplified by the polar trekking of Robert Peary, Sir Ernest Shackleton, Ann Bancroft, and Will Steger.[3]

Developed and differentiated by class and difficulty in the nineteenth century, hiking witnessed a resurgence in the last few decades of the twentieth century. Most densely populated European towns had reactivated or established hiking trails on their outskirts. At the same time, countless resorts and parks there and in North America began to provide paths and trails for hikers. Whole industries and chain stores have responded by devoting themselves to the manufacture and sale of specialized equipment, apparel, and books—even adjustable light walking sticks, with variable tips for different terrains, which can be collapsed and carried on a belt loop. One now finds microregional hiking trails throughout Europe, Asia, Latin America, and North America, where certain regions are joined by immense trails like the Appalachian Trail, which, supported by a fourteen-state organization, covers more than two thousand miles, from Mount Katahdin in Maine and to Mount Oglethorpe in Georgia.[4]

Hiking, however, as a select recreational form of walking remains underappreciated simply because it is not easily differentiated from back-packing (which can mean carrying packs of military sizes of sixty and even eighty pounds), camping (which means sleeping under stars), and hunting. It can also go with some climbing, orienteering, skiing, and snowshoeing. Even when carried out under the sanction of prestigious clubs and with the promise of inspiring vistas, hiking as a recreation does not escape association with the ordeal and boredom of long forced marches and the inconvenience of harassing insects, fickle weather, common blisters and chafing, the use of improvised toilets, and other pains and inconveniences.

Hiking invariably is shadowed by mountain climbing. With prestige derived from higher risk, more exotic travel, greater cost, and international flavor, mountain climbing maintains its claim as the supreme test of human foot and spirit. Nevertheless, even mountain climbing has begun its descent to vulgar ground due to its popularity, ergo vulgarization, as a result of a society long on leisure and correspondingly short on thrills, with a surplus of money, cheap transportation systems, and abundant and multiple communication and rescue systems. With everything becoming a commodity, including the experience of risking falling off a mountain and breaking one's neck, in the last twenty years mountain climbers have literally populated select peaks. Indeed, the very summit of Mt. Everest is increasingly crowded with climbers, guides, native bearers, used oxygen canisters, and frozen bodies.[5] At lower levels, mountain-climbing schools have become an industry and popular pastime, while rock climbing, appealing to a more youthful crowd, is practiced wherever a challenging set of toe- and handholds can be found—be it a sculpted desert boulder, a rocky riverside cliff, or yet an artificial mountain erected, for instance, in the glass front of a three-story cooperative outdoor equipment store along Expressway 94, on the south side of the Twin Cities.

Race walking, which involves a great test of the walker, never made into the multichambered mansion of contemporary sport. In fact, it never truly escaped the traditional perimeters of its eccentric university practitioners who at Oxford and Cambridge systematized their regular five-plus-mile walks as "grinds" and "stretches." Over the long haul their "speed footing" (race walking) never quite formed itself into a sporting event equal to such sports as rowing, cricket, and riding.[6] And even the most legendary "feats of feet" of these academic pacers never reached the heights of mountain climbing or beguiled spectators as did more quick and fanciful footwork involving running, chasing, kicking, catching, and hitting a ball, which caught the popular fancy. Even the safest but most "finicky of all games," golf, outstaged race walking in its ascent to popularity. This "good walk spoiled" (to use Mark Twain's popular definition of golf), which disseminated to the English-speaking world from Scottish seaside clubs in the second half of the century, seemed to country club enthusiasts the most intriguing walk of all.[7]

The heyday of race walking as a sport was the mid- and late-nineteenth century, a brief period. It occurred when it had less competition and when people, who did more cross-city and cross-country walking, were better equipped to appreciate it, and its records for speed and covering long distances had not yet been diminished by the human-propelled machine, the bike.[8] One champion walker who did his best to popularize the sport was Sir Leslie Stephen, mentioned earlier, who staged many attention-getting races, some even against university runners, while each term he established afresh a walking path from his residence in Ely to Cambridge University. Edward Payson Weston—reputedly "the greatest pedestrian that ever lived"—astonished America from the 1860s until the 1910s with his extraordinary walks.[9] At age sixty-seven he walked, as he had once before, from Philadelphia to New York in less than twenty-four hours; at sixty-nine years old, he duplicated another walk, striding all the way from Portland to Chicago.[10]

By the end of the nineteenth century, many sports and pastimes surpassed walking. With an accent on speed and agility, track, rowing, and ice skating got their share of limelight, while bicycling—as both a sport and a cheap and efficient mode of travel—joined foot and wheel in races of speed, distance, terrain, and all three. Prefiguring auto racing, the speeding wheeling of bicycling races, with its ordeals and crashes, left walking in the dust. Organized into amateur group competitions in Europe and North America starting in the 1870s, bicycling gave rise to varied types of races by the turn of the century, most notably the grueling Tour de France in 1903. It also took a prominent place in the restored Olympics in 1896, which expended the surplus energy of society's elite.[11]

The heroics of nineteenth-century walkers (who may well have jogged as much as they walked) did not win them immediate entrance into the glorious arena of Olympic sporting competition, which mirrored the era's mounting athleticism and nationalism. Its direct foot competitor, track and field events, offered more varied, faster, and more intricate motion, and, aside from the marathon itself, had the distinct advantage that they could be staged in a set place at a given time.[12] Even though race walking was eventually incorporated into the 1906 Olympics, it remained far behind most other sports in popularity. The notion of walking great distances, without crashes and ordeals, didn't excite; the ungainly scurrying steps of the race walker's exaggerated heel and toe action and peculiar rotating hip motion infatuated few. And whatever best chance it had of winning the gold with spectators was tarnished by an ongoing and intractable dispute over applying its all-important rule, which distinguishes walking and running, that one foot "must always be in contact with the ground."[13]

Even though in the course of the twentieth century, individual walkers produced record-book accomplishments by traveling forward or backwards for miles, days, weeks, months, or even years on end, their feats of bipedalism had a circus and old-fashioned quality about them.[14] From a jaundiced point of view a champion walker could appear to achieve only what the hungry, poorest person and the lowliest soldier did to survive. Nevertheless, certain exceptional acts of pedestrianism did win fleeting attention. For instance, in 1960 two transcontinental walks from California to New York—one by a pair of British soldiers and a second by a middle-aged woman nutritionist—caught media attention, which neither group verbally exploited.[15] One of the soldiers declared at the conclusion of the trip, "If you haven't got a good pair of feet, you haven't got a thing." Having persevered through snowdrifts and having even been hit by a car, the nutritionist attributed her success to her vegetarianism.[16]

Recent extraordinary walks included Minnesotan David Kunst. Accompanied at the beginning by his younger brother John (who was later shot to death by bandits in Afghanistan), Kunst carried out a four-year epic walk around the world from 1970 to 1974. Traversing 14,450 miles on foot, David, traveling with a dog, a wagon, and a mule (actually four mules) wore out almost two dozen pairs of shoes in his record-breaking circumambulation.[17]

There were other notable walks like Tomas Carlos Pereira's ten-year journey on foot around five continents and Steven Newman's four-year traversing of twenty countries and five continents.[18] Yet such phenomenal acts did not gain either distance walking or speed walking the popularity of an established sport. Spectators turned their appreciation to faster, more dramatic, and less time-consuming sports, while those who sought participation and use of their own feet and legs could choose from a long list including golf, track events, soccer, tennis, skating, or even mountain climbing. Not winning recognition as a sport or recreation, speed and endurance walking had to find its audience in the utilitarian demands of the military or the health establishment. England, Sweden, and the Netherlands made walking an established test of fitness.[19] American President Kennedy sought to elevate walking to the center of American notions of fitness when he challenged contemporary Marines to walk fifty miles in twenty hours as their 1908 counterparts did. Starting in the 1990s South Koreans, with their war commemorative march in Wonju (composed of hiking routes from ten to fifty kilometers), sought to merge motifs of world peace and health in an international walking festival.[20]

Although swept to the side of the road by mass transportation, walking increasingly is chosen as an alternative within driving and riding society. In forms of hiking and mountain climbing, walking becomes a measure of physical endurance and spiritual strength. It also is seen as the sole means to enter into direct contact with the back-country and wilderness, whose freedom from the sounds, noises, wheels, and motors of riding society elevated its status as unique and exclusive in pervasive mass, industrial society. In turn, long walks and hiking constitute the attraction of certain forms of tourism to certain historic cities, natural sites, or small towns—especially those located on a hill or seaside. Bird watching, which has emerged as one of North America's favorite pastimes, has the support of countless organizations, and is practiced by followers with higher and more discretionary income and a greater willingness to travel more, also supports walking, even though it can appeal to the sedentary and stay-at-home.

Walking also has developed a singular importance in contemporary medical diagnosis. At a moderate pace, thirty to forty minutes of walking is recommended by American doctors as a minimal physical need and a common prescription for obesity, heart conditions, and other medical problems. Walking is understood as the principal antidote against being fat in the United States, where two-thirds of the populations is considered overweight.[21] And, though significantly displaced by riding society and of diminished importance among sporting activities, walking takes on enhanced symbolic significance in a sitting and driving society in which even its dogs grow fat. And this accounts for its place in contemporary political and moral expression.

WALKING FOR POLITICAL EFFECT

Though walking has been displaced and diminished in the twentieth century, it has not at all lost its political significance. Even though in the nineteenth and twentieth centuries society's parading and marching were increasingly organized and regimented, they did not entirely lose the spontaneous and protesting quality that characterized the crowds of early modern history. Street demonstrations continued in recent decades—as witnessed by recent protests against Israeli occupation of the West Bank, the United States' war against Iraq, and recent summits by the G8 (the group of eight major industrial democracies) on world economic integration. Nevertheless, marching groups in Western society no longer on the whole resemble the threatening, spontaneous, and chameleon mobs of the previous centuries. With significant exceptions for soccer games, staged police-student conflicts such as they have in Japan, and frequent riots arising out of interactions of police and demonstrators, protesting crowds move in an orderly fashion. They do not express their causes with dance, riot, looting, or street festivals but in an articulate, sanitary, peaceful, and even discreet way, with placards, speakers, schedules, and their own parade masters.

Contemporary political footwork subordinates walking to talking. Protest marches are ideologically laden and shaped into symbolic journeys. They aim, almost as a lawyer's brief does, at making a case and influencing public judgment. Even though individual parades and marches can be colorful and taunting, the vast majority is not spontaneous, of lengthy duration, or free of police supervision. Planned in advance, they aim at being "a decisive step" on the way to forming a coalition and changing a government policy. While individual participation can be emotional, ceremonial, and even a rite of passage, today's walking protests make the streets resound with tried ideas and worn slogans.

Walking by itself has symbolic connotations in a society that rides. It stands for—or is construed to represent—the people's historic way. Taking to one's feet adds solemnity, humility, and an air of sacrifice to one's cause. In some roughly equivalent way, earnestness increases as the distance of the march magnifies and the likelihood of confrontation with authority increases. Because of these characteristics, walking understandably has come to form a principal tool of nonviolent reformers in the spirit of Mohandas Gandhi. Gandhi molded the confrontational walk into the arsenal of nonviolent resistance with his famous 1930 two-hundred-mile journey to the sea (where he would make salt) to campaign against the British monopoly of and tax on salt. In the 1950s and 1960s, the American civil rights leader (and admirer of Gandhi) Martin Luther King, Jr., incorporated pickets and marches, along with sit-ins, into his protests against segregation. The most notable of these was probably the five-day, fifty-four-mile march that King and three thousand others made in March 1965 from Selma to Montgomery, Alabama, leading in August of that year to the passage of the Voting Rights Act.[22] King was assassinated in April 1968, on the eve of planning the "Poor People's March" to Washington.

The 1960s and 1970s spawned a plethora of political marches on foot, as well as sit-ins and sit-downs. They took multiple forms, from solemn candle-carrying, hymn-chanting processions to disorganized, carnival-like strolls to defiant and militant demonstrations, most of which at the start—at least originally—protested segregation in the South and then the United States involvement in the Vietnam War. Draft boards were picketed, as were military installations, war munitions plants, the homes of well-known war supporters, the White House, and even shopping malls, where the right to picket raised complex legal questions about determining what is public and what is private space.

A major rally and walk on behalf of peace occurred in mid–October 1967. Under the sponsorship of the National Mobilization Committee to End the War in Vietnam, a rally composed seventy thousand demonstrators was assembled on October 21 at the Lincoln Memorial. It was addressed by famous speakers, spurred on by draft protests, and joined by the Peace Torch Marathon. A torch, which was lighted on August 6 in Hiroshima and then flown to San Francisco, was carried on foot to Washington. The rally, which was fifty thousand strong, crossed the Memorial Bridge and concluded at its planned target, the Pentagon, where many were forcefully evicted and arrested.[23] (The whole weekend of protest in Washington produced 681 arrests. This demonstration was paralleled in six European nations, Israel, Japan, and Australia, which all witnessed marches against the U.S. presence in Vietnam.)

Political street battles hit a peak in both the United States and Europe in 1968. In May of that year French students, in the revolutionary tradition of 1848, tore out paving stones and heaved them at police and succeeded in leading a general strike that lasted several weeks and brought down the government of Charles de Gaulle. In August Czechoslovakians on foot sought, though unsuccessfully, to nonviolently defy Soviet tanks on the streets of Prague. They went so far as to plant flowers in the barrels of tanks and in the hands of their conquerors. And late in August American antiwar protesters, supporters of alternative Democratic presidential candidate Eugene McCarthy, and assorted radical groups battled police for control of the streets of Chicago against the backdrop of a sharply contested Democratic National Convention.

In the wake of 1968, the majority of protests refocused on the university and multiplied. Across America and Western Europe, students, who still walk more than most groups in society, began to parade and sit in for changes in university policy. Aside from continuing to make a stand on behalf of racial, social, and international justice, protesters took to the streets for what up to then had been closet matters of gender and homosexual rights. Meanwhile, in the 1970s, environmental groups took their complaints to rural main streets and even remote logging trails, calling for the cleanup of polluted sites and defending endangered animal species against lumbering.

Political demonstrations did not belong to the province of the Left alone. In the 1970s citizens in various locales—Warren, Michigan, being one—paraded against court-ordered busing, which sought to end racial division in education. Nazis filed through the largely Jewish Chicago suburb of Skokie, proving that all ideas and opinions have access to the streets in an open society. And prolife forces across the nation mounted rallies and vigils at—and, later, on account of a Supreme Court ruling, across the street from—abortion clinics.

Street demonstrations express both a direct and a tacit relationship between walking and the rights of free speech and assembly. (How else do we in a democratic society get nose to nose in order to express our passionately felt opinions except on foot?) In this age of riding, walking protests have a heightened function in symbolic discourse, especially when they don't observe the rules of traffic or follow routes prescribed by authority.[24] They win the attention of those who sit and rule, including the police, who often must abandon their cruisers and go on foot, or even horseback, for the sake of crowd control.

Walking is now utilized for people to take sides with locality against the outside world. Just as English villagers and country people continued in centuries past to tread traditional pathways to retain access to the commons (traditional open community lands) and to battle against spreading enclosure, so, in this tradition, do contemporary English country walkers intentionally cross private lands to maintain a right of way. In Europe and America walks are staged against the building of roads, the establishing of waste sites, and other encroachments on natural places, traditional sites, and communities.[25] In September 2000, the walkers of the "Walking the Land for Our Ancient Rights Peace Walk" arrived in Sydney after traveling "for 85 days over 3,000 kilometers from Lake Eyre in the north of South Africa."[26] Pitting foot against the urban order, the machine, and the corporation, walking speaks on behalf of the vanishing rural order: the autonomous locale, the small town, and the peasant.

Being on foot proves to be a many-tongued rhetoric. Barefoot walking, to take an eccentric example, professes among many things a quest for a more natural life free of the metals and glass, and the rush and crush of people of industrial urban society.[27] On the other hand, of a more serious nature, protests that end in direct confrontation with authorities prove a direct way to "put one's body on the line."

Long, pacific walks serve myriad causes. In fourteen months, concluding in February 2000, Dorris Haddock of Dublin, New Hampshire, an eighty-nine-year-old great-grandmother who became nicknamed Grandma D, made a thirty-two-hundred-mile trek on foot from Los Angeles to Washington, D.C., at the pace of ten miles a day, to reform campaign finance.[28] In support of a grab bag of causes, including protecting the earth and native peoples, and a range of personal reasons ranging from an unstable childhood to hatred of her father and jealousy about male bonding, Ffyona Campbell, British woman walker extraordinaire, paced off entire continents on foot. In the late 1980s and early 1990s, she racked up twenty thousand miles in all, wrote several popular books, and established the Guinness record for distance walked.[29]

Reflecting the overall pacific character of contemporary marches and protests and the ability to use walking to display moral earnestness during the last few decades, an incalculable number of American civic groups, with corporate support, have organized "walkathons."[30] The March of Dimes alone holds eleven hundred walkathons a year, accounting for over one hundred million dollars of its annual budget. There were twenty-five charity walks held in New York City's Central Park in 2003 alone.[31] Serving many causes—to fight hunger, diabetes, and AIDS, or to support an athletic team or some other social good—the walkathon collects money through grassroots participation. Each walker goes out into the community to gather as many pledges of money as he or she can for each mile to be traversed. The walkathon, which has bred the dog walkathon, runs, and even the long-distance bike-a-thon, usually covers five or six miles or less, and occurs on smooth and safe roads and sidewalks. Treating walking as an act of significance, which it is in a sitting society, walkathons are frequently dedicated to victims who cannot walk themselves and seek to express a community commitment to cure a disease or solve a problem.

Walkathons, marches, parades, and pickets fit the recent Western transformation of going on foot from a nearly universal activity into a chosen, segmented, and planned act of walking. Walking has been tailored to landscapes and tastes. Walk as you choose! Let everyone make his or her own walk! Let there be—if we carry these contemporary prescriptions to the nth degree—a Monty Python "Ministry of Silly Walks," where one copyrights his or her own walk, if it be deemed unique. In my recent interview with Belgium's most famous walker, Julien van Remoortere, he repeatedly spoke of "making a walk" rather than "taking a walk," as he explained how he assembled information about hundreds of walks—all or most all of which he had taken—in some forty books.[32] Van Remoortere, often with his wife, scouted out and wrote down descriptions of walks in the Ardennes, the forests of Antwerp, and across Belgium, designing them with an eye for interesting trails leading to natural vistas and historical sites. His phrase "to make a walk" jarred my ear. But as I eventually recognized, his use of language and his meaning felicitously coincided. He was simply doing what walkers, walking clubs, tour guides, and writers of travel books have collectively been doing on an ever larger scale for nearly two centuries: he was calling attention to the fact that, in the modern world, in city and countryside, walks are made up to fit the coordinates of scenery, time, cost, and the convenience of driving to and from the walking site.

The March 3, 2002, *Minneapolis Star Tribune* directs its readers to the Web site of "The Wayfarers," with classic, adventure, and gourmet walks in Europe, Australia, New Zealand, and the United States, as well as to the sites "European Walking Tours," "Country Walks," "Backroads," "Cross-Country International," and "The Earth Is Yours Walking." Large cities, old trails of pilgrims and travelers, and traditional regions identified with hiking, like the Alps, Appalachians, and Canadian Rockies, all support walks. The national and international Volksmarch offers a great range of noncompetitive hikes, while Elder Hostel offers its clientele walks and hikes of varying complexity in North America and overseas. One tourism company, Maupin Treks, dedicated its 2000 brochure to walks in places as diverse as Colorado, Ireland, Costa Rica, Peru, Australia, and Botswana. One reads regularly in the travel section of the newspaper of exotic trips: in Tibet one's thirty-three-mile circumambulation of a mountain from monastery to monastery amounts to "a sacred circuit" while, more hedonistically, in rural northern Japan "a frugal traveler hikes from tub to tub."[33] Meanwhile, a magazine called *Walking* promotes—in the words of its subtitle—"smart health and fitness," along with the implicit promise of enduring youth and sexual vitality, while selling foods, clothes, vacations, and, revealingly, both hammocks and treadmills.

OFF THEIR FEET

That walking, at least in certain forms, has become a commodity expresses the fact that it is no longer a common and necessary condition. It is a testimony that walking, along with standing, squatting, crouching, leaning, crawling, climbing, carrying, pushing, and pulling, has been circumscribed and even displaced in the West and in urban centers across the world. Thanks to improved technology, smooth and abundant roads, and the development of transportation and communications, humanity less and less needs to exert itself by going on foot. Freed of many of the most constrictive limits of and demanding terrains of space, humanity, with a resulting surplus of energy and time, journeys and imagines travel in new ways.[34]

Now that we have seen how walking has been displaced by revolutions in transportation, communication, and haulage, it only remains to speculate about the future of walking in human experience. This speculation, which concludes an overview of four and a half million years or so of walking, is premised on the notion that our civilization has diminished the dependence on foot travel that once affixed humanity to the landscape.

Fundamentals of human experience have been progressively metamorphosed in our times. Space has been diminished in its power to require human effort and drain human energy. Dependence on and autonomy of place have disappeared. Although countless places become worthy of visiting—according to their boosters, they merit at least a half-day walking tour—most localities are emptied of particular significance and selectively skipped over by even their own riding and racing inhabitants. Reduced to being mere geographical points on a map and without inhabitants who have local experience, knowledge, and passions of home, the great majority of places now exist as revolving doors, under outside control and manipulation. Places we now deem worthy of attention we import into our living room or workplace. We select and miniaturize the world—past and present—free of the ordeal of travel. With books, telephones, movies, television, videos, faxes, and computers we jump space. We have long since taken to heart the phrase popularized in the 1960s Yellow Pages ad campaign, "Let your fingers do the walking."

When we do travel, we travel as humanity never did before. We travel selectively, and largely safely. We now ride comfortably—not on the hard rocking back of an animal, or a swaying litter or bumping cart. Once one becomes accustomed to riding in comfort, one never easily returns to walking. In fact only war and natural disaster return those who have ridden to their feet.[35]

The assumption that riding is a valid substitute for walking pervades the contemporary world. It shows up in serious and frivolous matters. Ruling on the side of a disabled golfer who wished to compete in professional golf tournaments riding in a cart, the U.S. Supreme Court in 2001 rejected the Professional Golf Association's contention that walking is an integral part of golf competition.[36] In the wake of September 11, 2001, the commander in chief, George Bush, Jr., summoned Americans to a war against terrorism not with "Forward March!" but with "Let's Roll!"—unwittingly acknowledging that the nation and the army move more on wheels than on feet. And even when the army does march—which the 101st Airborne did for more than a hundred miles on its invasion of Iraq—it has the support of helicopters, all-terrain vehicles, and civil engineers for crossing all obstacles, as well as the use of world-communications and satellite-positioning systems for identifying location and destination.

The momentum toward riding and the reflex to make a world with less walking continues on all fronts. Design not just of wheeled vehicles but also of homes, buildings, and public space will accent speed, lightness, and accessibility. Automobile ownership will continue to expand throughout the population. More and more people will be offered carts and vehicles for their convenience in commercial and public areas. Work on a practical portable motorized riding vehicle goes on, as does the overall push in the direction of making a world of smoother surfaces and fewer obstacles. Escalators and elevators will be yet more bountiful. Airports and commercial buildings will utilize more and more moving walks and rolling stairways as they expand in size. At the same time, drive-in stores of every variety and in-store and home delivery will increase as shoppers, who may still mall walk and shop for fun, wish to walk shorter distances and spend less time shopping for matters of ordinary consumption. Even in parks and wilderness areas there will be ever greater pressures to provide vehicular excess in one form or another.

Even though the distant future has no covenant with universal riding, and the inherent consequences of emerging worldwide mass transit or automobile ownership (such as gridlock, pollution, fuel costs, etc.) are incalculable, the momentum to supplant and dispense with walking will continue to be a force. (The automobile already exercises its profound transforming powers in Latin America and even urban and official China.)[37] Assuming that sitting and riding or bringing the world to one's feet are good, the drive to displace walking will not relent for the simplest reason: long after supporters of walking have persuasively made solid cases for walking for reasons of health and community, going on foot will continue to be experienced as a waste of time, an inconvenience, and an impediment to opportunity and experience. Walking, especially in an unprecedented age of comfortable sitting, riding, and travel, is experienced as an act of exertion. To walk one must get up. One loses time doing it and something could happen along the way. People are always disposed to take a lift or catch a ride, and to ask the frequent local walker whether he or she has a drivers license. Rationalizations for not walking, such as that one can always walk later, suggest ways in which walking is eclipsed even in a society increasingly, at least by words, dedicated to physical activity.

Other material factors point toward the displacement of walking. The disjunction between residence and walking community will in all likelihood grow. Experience from the past several decades already argues that even in cities, towns, and suburbs where sidewalks are abundant, walking will not flourish. Sidewalks adjacent to streets with wider lanes and intersections, designed for the flow of automobile traffic, do not foster pedestrians. Furthermore, there is no appeal to sidewalks that lead nowhere and promise nothing or no one to see.

Beyond that, even where downtown malls or whole walking communities are set up they will continue to be fit into the dominant material and cultural grid of the automobile and a riding society. In effect, if society must expand space, time, locality, and place in order to increase walking, its prospects are not good.

However, contrasting this line of analysis, at least in part, there are limits to how far humans can go in their conquest of nature and society. On behalf of the future of walking, it can be said, only so much of the world can be put on wheels and only so many surfaces can be made straight and level. Only so much of reality can be electronically miniaturized and imported and only so many places can be integrated into unifying systems. As space ultimately cannot be collapsed into nothingness, time ultimately cannot be made instantaneous. For these reasons, walking will always keep its foot, or at least a toe, in the door of society and human experience.

Additionally, supporting walking's place in human experience, there will continue to be people who value it as a singularly unmediated and intimate form of travel, one that lets us see and taste directly. People will also travel to find work, to court a mate, to be with their own kind, and to trace the footprints of their own childhood. Boredom, too, or the simple desire to do something different, will invariably set people in bipedal motion. Humanity will remain a disconsolate creature. Men and women will walk to maintain their health and to distract themselves. Walking, which will not replace riding, speed, and other bodily contests for pleasure, will nonetheless offer its distinct pleasures for those who wish to observe birds, catch butterflies, collect fossils, or gather sea shells. And beyond this, the natural place of walking will still offer experiences and ecstasies that neither sitting nor running nor riding can provide. Indeed, the more we sit, recline, and ride, the more certain it is that individuals and groups will want to walk if only for the sake of having a walking experience.

As we have seen since the eighteenth-century romantics and American master saunterer Thoreau, walking will be utilized as a means and an ideal with which to criticize riding society. It will serve individual critics of contemporary mass and industrial society, such as contemporary ecological activists like Edward Abbey, who wrote,

You can't see *anything* from a car; you have got to get out of the god-damned contraption and walk, better yet crawl, on hands and knees over the sandstone and through the thorn bush and cactus. When traces of blood begin to mark your trail you'll see something, maybe.[38]

Collective protest, as the recent street demonstrations against war with Iraq show, will invariably turn to the streets on foot to state their cause. Pickets and marches will continue to find mingling and walking on the street crucial to displaying the determination of those who follow a cause. At the same time, city and town planners, as we saw in the case of the New Urbanists, along with commercial building designers, will look to walking as an alternate measure to driving and a necessary ingredient of human-scale communities.

Walking, the key to promenading on the old boardwalks, has recently been key in building theme parks. Walks down memory lane not only evoke comforting nostalgia in people and make individuals and families more at home in a place but also entice them to stay longer and buy more. Such walks can even induce people to buy homes in places organized around the old way. Near Orlando, Florida, in the shadows of Walt Disney World, Sea World, and Cypress Gardens, "Board Walk and Baseball" invites all, on twenty-foot-wide walkways (with timber imported from Australia) to enter baseball and the Coney Island of old.[39] In what was once an impenetrable cypress swamp on the edge of its property, Disney took a plank from its own boardwalk and in the year 2000 engineered a town (projected to have twenty thousand inhabitants) around "walkable streets and pleasing public squares." The town, Celebration, represents the Disney Company's ambitious answer to the perceived lack of community in American life.[40]

Walking has continued to be a focus in urban restoration. Increasingly it is understood that the walker makes and becomes the city he or she walks. It is conceded that walking plays an indispensable role in restoring neighborhoods, luring tourists and shoppers, designing beautiful streets, and adding vitality to an entire city.[41] It is also understood that walking cannot be politically willed or conjured by planning. Whatever you, a town, or commerce does—build sidewalks, block off streets, or increase shops—walkers do not inevitably come and a walking environment is not necessarily achieved. Nevertheless, the overall public reluctance and even resistance to the act of walking does not suppress the growing call to return to walking, which, similar to the century-long drive to save nature by protesting wilderness areas, forms an indispensable rhetoric and angle of analysis on the city lost and the city to be regained.

In January 2002, Minneapolis's new mayor, R. T. Rybak, used his inaugural address to summon citizens to walk the city they love. And like his mayoral counterpart in St. Paul, also freshly installed, Randy Kelly, Rybak has gone on to stress that walking is vital to transportation and health, and constitutes a good lifestyle choice.[42] The *Minneapolis Star Tribune* used an editorial to transform Rybak's inaugural call to walk the city into an assessment of Minneapolis's contemporary condition. Great cities like Stockholm, Montreal, Boston, and Chicago are walking cities, the editorial premised its comments. "Places that inspire true affection in residents and visitors have one thing in common: the probability of sore feet."[43] The editorial proceeded to point out that as much as one's spirit might soar walking the outer perimeter of the city's many lakes, in other sections of town one might for safety lock one's car doors and hit the gas pedal. Litter, filth, poverty, and despair are all to be read in the city's streets, and its recently renovated downtown areas, which do not permit easy driving, are without trees, "barren and antiseptic"—anything but an invitation to stroll on foot. In sum, the editorial reiterated for Minneapolis what Jane Jacobs in effect said forty years earlier for the nation in *The Death and Life of Great American Cities* (1961): an unwalked city is a dead city; arguably it is no city at all.[44] Surely in Minneapolis, as in the case of St. Paul and countless other American and European cities, civic leadership, urban planning, and public and private money are not in themselves enough to put a civilization and its inhabitants back on their feet again.

END OF THE TRAIL

Feet, it should not be forgotten, are old friends—perhaps our truest and best friends. They coordinate wonderfully with our arms, torso, and eyes. They provide precise and adjustable locomotion. Legs and feet evolved perfectly over millions of years to serve us on any terrain. They bear our loads and us on the longest marches. They chase down the fleeing toddler, cross a stream on a log, or climb the soft, crumbly surface of a hill. They slow down easily, accelerate, reverse directions, and turn on a dime, making precision marching or ballroom dancing possible. They respond without hesitation to the mercurial demands of eye and hand.

Going on foot provides the child with his or her first contacts with the earth. It gives the child elemental senses of up and down, straight and curved, short and long, fast and slow, standing and falling, hard and soft. At the same time, parents watch their children's first steps to discover whom they have brought into the world. They read the child's walk to discern health, grace, athleticism, character, and attitude.[45] Aside from parents, the Pentagon as part of its antiterrorist campaign too seeks to scrutinize individuals' walks with a radar-based device, operating on the theory that a person's walk is as unique as his or her signature.[46]

With ease perfected since our most distant ancestor walked erectly, we pace off the world around us. Walking provides a platform and engine for our locomotion. It is our first way to move across, to survey, and to take possession of the earth. A stepping foot connotes ownership of the land it treads. A pawing foot expresses reluctance and discomfort, while a kicking foot serves defense and attack.

The foot remains indispensable for taking complex and delicate steps, carrying out "fancy footwork." Nothing equals it for working on high steel, moving in a tight mining shaft, getting in and out of the woods, moving over boulders or along a tree-lined shore, climbing in and out of tipsy boats, or pushing a bike along the shoulder of the road when a tire goes flat. Only on foot can one work one's way through shifting crowds, find a spot on a crowded beach, climb the stairs of a lofty medieval cathedral, or go door to door on a get-out-the-vote campaign. Going on foot literally proves that one can "walk the walk"—live up to one's words. Mountain, forest, and desert peoples still must walk paths and trails—and many villagers in the world continue to travel on foot to get water, wood, and food, to attend school, to reach a store, to make a telephone call, or to get their mail.[47]

Millions of people still make remarkable journeys afoot to escape famine, seek medical care, or find their way to a bus or train that promises delivery to a better world, one in which there is less walking and more sitting.

Feet still dazzlingly display human skills, strength, and beauty. The near universal popularity of soccer (in both the developed and under-developed world) suggests how foot speed and foot play mesmerize the multitudes. Dance steps still captivate the eye and join the body to catchy tunes and even elemental rhythms. And walking, with its myr-iad forms, from pit-a-pat baby steps to casual saunters to striding marches to moon walking, still forms a polyphonic voice of human movement.

Walking establishes intimate contact with place. It attaches us to a landscape—its trees, rocks, hills, and riverbanks.[48] It makes us in good measure the streets and paths we walk. It puts us in contact with local communities.[49] Walking coagulates time, expands distance, and makes places dense and prickly with details and complexities. It expands and defends localities against the reductionism and systematization of roads, commerce, government, and mass culture. It makes the case for individual localities in an era of rampant globalism.[50]

Walking does things for the individual walker as well. Beyond fos-tering health, walking allows the feet to lead the mind and heart; it gives us back our body and senses. With a fixed rhythm and established breathing, it releases the walker from his or her normally interrupted, if not conflict-filled, consciousness and provides an altered state of mind for prayer, reflection, or simply talking to oneself. While walk-ing fulfills the wish to put one's foot solidly on the ground, its move-ment, which, similar to that of skating, rowing, and running, when it matches our breathing brings an invigorating experience of rhythm, flow, power, and freedom. Arguably, walking in circles can return us to deeper layers of the self.

Surely, it puts we modern people living in an age of speed in imag-inative communion with slower times and forgotten places, and it cre-ates fixed ties to an environment. It allows walkers with historical imagination vicariously to join Roman legionnaires on their cam-paigns and pilgrims on their search; to join Napoleon's defeated troops on their winter retreat from burning Moscow; to accompany Humboldt in exploring the Americas; to circumambulate the wood around Walden Pond with Thoreau; or to travel cross-country with Muir. Afoot we commune with those who walked before us and deepen the path for those who will come after.

Walking provides, at least for some, the most simple and straightforward way to the self and the world. It puts us back in touch with our faithful old friends—our feet, which truly do deserve a daily walk and a nightly rub. Feet also represent the pejorative of being down and below, explaining why anti-American Iraqis taunted, "Bush down shoes!" and "America down shoes!"—implying that both are dirt and only good for being trampled on.[51]

Whatever walking's future in human history, it remains—as we are continuously reminded by the peoples of parts of the underdeveloped world—a primary measure of life. No matter how far we penetrate the infinite greatness and the equally infinite smallness of things, so we return in mind, in almost springlike fashion, to walking to sense our place and motion in space. However fast and far we travel, we return to walking—a biological acquisition of millions of years—to understand our own natural speed and movement. Leg and foot pace off our place in life and continue to constitute an underlying compass of our bodies in space and time. Although we now measure and parcel the planet via satellites, our most elemental senses of our standing in this world still derive from being on foot.

To walk in a sitting and riding society is always, at least potentially, the beginning of a renaissance. Going on foot returns us, at least those of us who did significant walking as children, to our first self. It delivers us to the simpler movement of ambling and flowing, which may fit and serve the movements of our mind and spirits better than sitting and riding.[52] Indeed, the more we supplant walking with riding, the more we may feel compelled to go on foot to heal and to amuse ourselves. Walking, after all, is perhaps our best way to be face to face and arm and arm with others, our neighbors, and the earth. We will continue to look to it in one of its many forms—hiking, beach walking, window shopping, or even, most recently, labyrinth walking—for therapy and self-illumination.[53]

Given all these advantages of going on foot, walking ultimately constitutes an impassable border, which a riding and sitting civilization cannot transcend. No matter how much contemporary civilization advances and the rest of the world follows in its steps, walking remains at the heart of human life and movement. Indeed, walking cannot be disposed of, unless bipedal humanity itself is to be done away with.

Notes

NOTES TO INTRODUCTION

1. Honoré de Balzac, *Théorie de la démarche* (Paris: Pandora, 1978), x.

2. I found the following works especially useful for elaborating a history of walking. Historian Gudrun König's, *Eine Kulturgeschichte des Spazierganges: Spuren einer bürgerlichen Praktik, 1780–1850* (Vienna: Böhlau, 1996) depicts the spread and transformation of walking in Germany during the years from 1780 to 1850. Mark Girouard's *Life in the English Country House* (New York: Penguin Books, 1980) and his *Cities and People* (New Haven, CT: Yale University Press, 1985) sketches the material context of promenading and city walking in early modern European history. Historians Jan Bremmer and Herman Roodenburg's *Cultural History of Gesture* (Ithaca, NY: Cornell University Press, 1991) and Marcel Mauss's "Les Techniques du Corps," *Medical Psychology and Social Science and Medicine* 13 (1979), 97–123, make it clear that walking belongs to the order of manners and gestures. In disagreement, literary critics Anne D. Wallace, in *Walking, Literature, and English Culture: The Origins and Uses of the Peripatetic in the Nineteenth Century* (Oxford: Clarendon Press, 1993) and Robin Jarvis, in *Romantic Writing and Pedestrian Travel* (New York: St. Martin's Press, 1997) confront the issues of when, who, and what transformed walking from an or-dinary act into a cultural critique of the era. Appearing after I had outlined my work on walking and at the same time as my first experiment in cultural history, *Dust: A History of the Small and Invisible* (Berkeley: University of California Press, 2000), writer Rebecca Solnit's *Wanderlust: A History of Walking* (New York: Viking, 2000) proved useful. It was an intelligent attempt to fashion a history of walking principally in service of a fashionable critique of contemporary society.

3. Michael J. Sniffen, "Telling by the Way They Walk," *Hartford Courant*, May 21, 2003.

4. For a short history of gesture, see Keith Thomas's "Introduction," in Bremmer and Roodenburg, eds., *A Cultural History of Gesture*, 1–14, and "Les Techniques du Corps." 5. For a recent study of a life without walking, see *When Walking Fails: Mobility Problems of Adults with Chronic Conditions* (Berkeley: University of California Press, 2003).

6. Therapists know that walking requires an awareness of the body. And it is precisely this "proprioception" that has been lost in the hurried step of the Parkinson patient; the slapping-step of the neurologically damaged syphilitic walker; the pawing of the circulatory-defective diabetic; and the tentative stepping of woozy patients suffering from meningitis and other brain and ear infections. With balance being the all-crucial matter, they grasp how drugs, alcohol,

and infections of the brain and inner ear produce a vertigo that destabilizes the walker. At the same time, they perceive why walkers forever distort their walk to avoid pain while maintaining balance. Walking mechanics also explain why the difference in hip structures between men and women results in variation of gait. They account for the way pregnancy, like obesity, accounts for waddling. Defects in walking can be congenital or the result of an underlying disease, long-standing abuse, or recent injuries. Morton's toe, infections, tendinitis, sprains, dislocations, fractures, arthritis, gout, plantar fasciitis (strain tissue on the foot's bottom), warts, bruises, calluses, bunions, corns, ulcers, and ingrown toenails form only part of a doleful list of maladies that account for why mankind has hobbled and wobbled its way across the ages.

7. Web page of American Academy of Orthopaedic Surgeons, http://www.aaos.org, accessed January 2, 2001. Also see "Your Feet Don't Have to Hurt," http://www.foot.com/google .html. Also see "Fun Foot Facts," *Independent* (Marshall, MN), April 19, 2003, 6.

8. Phrase is from Plato, in Diogenese Laertes, *Vitae Philosophorum,* ed. Miroslav Marcovich, vol. 1, books 1–10 (Stuttgart: B. G. Teubeneri, 1999), 399.

9. For verbs for "to walk" in twenty languages, see "To Walk," http://guardian.curtin.edu.au/ cga/art/literature.html. For a short discussion of "English Verbs in Directed Motion Sentences," see http://elies.rediris.es/elies11/cap61.htm.

10. Joseph Shipley, *Dictionary of Word Origins* (Paterson, NJ: Littlefield, Adams, 1961), 384.

11. In his *Dictionary of Word Origins* (New York: Arcade Publishing, 1990), John Ayto additionally suggests that *saunter* derives from the fifteenth-century term *saunterell,* meaning "pretend saint, sanctimonious person," 458. In his classic essay "Walking," Thoreau suggests in jest that *saunter* derived from the pilgrims who went to the *sainte terre* (holy land), Henry David Thoreau, *The Natural History Essays* (Salt Lake City, UT: Peregrine Smith Books, 1980), 93.

12. Lesley Brown, ed., *The New Shorter Oxford Dictionary,* 2 vols. (Oxford: Clarendon Press, 1993), 2:2163–64.

13. *Shorter Oxford Dictionary,* 2:3025.

14. Ibid., 1:1234.

15. Terms were borrowed from Gertrude Jobes, *Folklore and Symbols* (New York: Scarecrow Press, 1961), 1663.

16. Reflexology finds the condition of the whole person in the soles of the feet, http://www.vaxxine.com/eves/feet.htm.

17. The foot also names things like footbridge,

footbath, footrest, footsore, footrace, or footloose and establishes such analogies as sitting at someone's feet, washing another's feet, dragging one's feet, or standing on one's own two feet.

18. For a discussion of gesture as voicing the soul of a person, see Bremmer and Roodenburg, eds., *A Cultural History of Gesture,* 8.

19. Joseph Conrad, *Chance* (Garden City, NY: Doubleday, 1923).

20. Heinrich Heine, *Journey to Italy* (New York: Marsilic Publishers, 1998), 271.

21. Nomura Masichi, "Redmodelling the Japanese Body," *Culture Embodied,* ed. Michael Moerman and Msaichi Nomura (Osaka, Japan: National Museum of Ethnography, 1990) 263–64.

22. There is some evidence that in the past the Mongols, Turks, and other Asian peoples also walked in the *namba* way. For the sake of a level ride for mounted archers, Japanese horses—similar to Western harness horses—were trained to run the *namba* way.

23. In contrast to the Westerners who walk on their heels, "Japanese are more likely to step flatly or forward on their toes. Other styles include sliding their feet, keeping their arms by their sides or stepping high," Nicholas Kristof, "Namba Anyone? Some Scholars Say Japanese Once Taught Distinctive Walk," *Minneapolis Star Tribune,* April 25, 1999, A21, 24

24. Jan Bremmer, "Walking, Standing, and Sitting in Ancient Greek Culture," in Bremmer and Roodenburg, eds., *A Cultural History of Gesture,* 15–35.

25. Bremmer, "Walking," 21.

26. For a useful article on forms and perceptions of walking and carrying, see André Haudricourt, "Relations entre gestes habituels, forme des vêtements et manière de porter les charges," *Revue de Geographie humaine et d'ethnologie,* no. 3 (Juillet–Septembre, 1948), 58–67.

27. M. I. Finley, ed., *The Greek Historians* (New York: Viking Press, 1959), 68.

28. Modern vests and suspenders, which today serve as decorative clothing apparel, may have had their origin in helping people carry heavy objects on their shoulders and back, as suggested by contemporary military gear, http://www. blackhawkindustries.com.

29. Sir Peter Hall, *Cities in Civilization* (New York: Pantheon, 1998), 564.

30. Martin Heidegger, *Poetry, Language, Thought* (New York: Harper & Row, 1971), 33–35.

31. Interview with local shoemaker, Scott Vick, approximately in fall of 2001, in his store in Marshall, Minnesota.

32. The limp of Roman Emperor Claudius afforded Italians with names and their language with the verb and adjective *claudicare* and *claudicante*. "Foljame" in French means "silly or crazy legs," Patrick Hanks and Flavia Hodges, *A Dictionary of Surnames* (Oxford: Oxford University Press, 1988), 188, 516.

33. For *Prokuv*, see Henry Liddell and Robert Scott, comps., *A Greek-English Lexicon* (Oxford: Clarendon Press, 1968), 1518.

34. *Shorter Oxford Dictionary*, 2:995. Italians labeled a *pedone* a person who travels a lot, is a sentry, moves slowly, or simply has an exceptionally large foot. The English called one family "Stride," suggesting someone with long legs and a purposeful gait.

35. Lewis Maybury, *Millenium: Tribal Wisdom of the Modern World* (New York: Viking, 1992), 37–38. Also useful on the superior position of sitting to walking is Galen Cranz, *The Chair: Rethinking Culture, Body, and Design* (New York: Norton, 1998), esp. 23–40.

36. To go barefoot can suggest respect, signal mourning, or show repentance as in the case of Henry IV, who stood barefoot in the snow at the pope's dwelling in Canossa awaiting Pope Gregory VII's forgiveness and his acknowledgment of Henry's legitimacy to rule his kingdom. Moses put off his shoes to approach the burning bush, Jobes, *Folklore and Symbols*, 558. In imitation of Christ at the Last Supper and practicing an established Jewish tradition, participants at Holy Thursday mass wash each other's feet. The bare foot also sexually entices, Richard Onians, *The Origins of European Thought: About the Body, the Mind, the Soul, the World, Time, and Fate* (Cambridge: Cambridge University Press, 1988), 531.

37. J. E. Cirlot, *A Dictionary of Symbols*, 2nd ed. (New York: Philosophical Library, 1971), 111. A single shoe, as books of folklore suggest, can symbolize female genitals, prosperity, protection, servitude, submission, or many more things. Shoes dragged from the back of honeymoon cars express a wish for fertility, while the wearing of another's shoes can suggest a transfer of power, Jobes, *Folklore and Symbols*, 1440–41.

38. The Chinese placed the strongest taboo against a man seeing a woman's bare feet. Even husbands dared not sneak a look. Onians, *The Origins of European Thought*, 524–25.

39. To show a man one's foot amounted to surrendering one's virginity, *la dernière faveur*. Spanish carriages were designed prudently to lower a screen when they stopped, so the feet and shoes of the descending women would not be seen. Lengthy skirts of the good ladies reached the ground at all times to protect them from sight, Onians, *The Origins of European Thought*, 529.

40. Marcel Granet, *Chinese Civilization* (New York: Meridian Books, 1958), 371.

41. John Fairbanks, who supplied the quotation, added in his autobiography, "Aside from the Manchu, nomadic people, low-class boat women, and others, the great majority of Chinese women were hobbled for a thousand years. Until very recent times, young girls had their feet bound at the age of seven, endured years of pain until at thirteen the toes were turned under so that one could see them on the inner and under side of the foot," *Chinabound: A Fifty-Year Memoir* (New York: Harper & Row, 1982), 54–55.

42. Pierre Jakez Hélias, *Le Cheval d'Orgueil* (Paris: Plon, 1975), 565–67. Hélias also went on to write, "The young peasants no longer walk like their fathers. . . . They wear different shoes; the roads are tarred; and there are not so many slopes. Nor is their bearing like that of the old peasant. That is because they use different tools. They move faster." Cited in Eugen Weber, *France, Fin du Siècle* (Cambridge, MA: Harvard University Press, 1986), 82.

43. Cited in Anne Fadiman, *The Spirit Catches You and You Fall Down: A Hmong Child, Her American Doctor, and the Collison of Two Cultures* (New York: Farrar, Straus, Giroux, 1997), 120.

44. Cited in Jack Nisbet, *Sources of the River: Tracking David Thompson across Western North America* (Seattle: Sasquatch Books, 1994), 25. For similar opinions on how the Indian walk put the white person's walk to shame, see Clark Wissler, *Indians of the United States*, rev. ed. (New York: Anchor Books, 1989), 298–99.

45. Jack Larkin, *The Reshaping of Everyday Life, 1790–1840* (New York: Harper & Row, 1988), 149–51.

46. Larry McMurty, *Walter Benjamin at the Dairy Queen* (New York: Simon & Schuster, 1999), 67.

47. Mauss, "Les Techniques du Corps." For additional notes on French body talk, see Laurence Wylie, *Beau Gestes* (Cambridge, MA: Undergraduate Press, 1977).

NOTES TO CHAPTER I

1. Marvin Harris, *Cultural Anthropology*, 2nd ed. (New York: Harper & Row, 1987), 29.

2. For a survey of recent literature on human origins, which has added four new species of hominids since 1994, see Michael Lemonick and Andrea Dorfman, "Despite the Protests of Creationists," *Time*, October 23, 1999, 51–58. Also, for a recent view of human origins, see Clive Gamble, *Timewalkers: The Prehistory of Global*

Colonization (Cambridge, MA: Harvard University Press, 1994), esp. 1–95. A popular account showing that temporal proximity does not assure physical likeness to Homo sapiens is Lee Berger, "The Dawn of Human: Redrawing Our Family Tree?" *National Geographic*, August, 1998, 91–98.

3. John Noble Wilford, "The Transforming Leap, from Four Legs to Two," *New York Times*, September 5, 1995, B5.

4. For a recent popular survey of the debate on why, where, and when human ancestors took to their feet, which arguably could be six million years ago, see Michael Lemonick and Andrea Dorfman's lead essay, "One Giant Step for Mankind," *Time*, July 23, 2001, 54–61. Also, for the most recent speculations on human evolution, with reference to the formation of the human body, bipedalism, and first migrations, see Craig Stanford, *Upright: The Evolutionary Key to Becoming Human* (Boston: Houghton Mifflin, 2003) and "New Look at Human Evolution," special edition of *Scientific American*, August 25, 2003.

5. C. Owen Lovejoy, "Evolution of Human Walking," *Scientific American*, November 1988, 118–25, and John Noble Wilford, "The Transforming Leap," B5, B8.

6. William Leonard, "Food for Thought: Dietary Change Was a Driving Force in Human Evolution," *Scientific American*, August 25, 2003, esp. 65–67.

7. Jay Ingram, *The Science of Everyday Life* (Toronto: Penguin Books, 1990), 91.

8. Ibid., 97–98.

9. Patricia Ann Kramer seeks to calculate the cost in speed and energy of carrying children in "The Costs of Human Locomotion: Maternal Investment in Child Transport," *American Journal of Physical Anthropology* 107 (1998), 71–85.

10. Carl Hall contends that early hominids had to walk on two legs before they could laugh, "Stand-Up Comedy," *San Francisco Chronicle*, January 10, 2000. Also, noted in "Walk before You Talk," *Science*, June 29, 2001, 2429.

11. Richard E. Leaky and Roger Lewin, *Origins* (New York: Dutton, 1977), 72–77. For a recent discussion of early humans' use of fire, see Stephen Pyne, *Vestal Fire: An Environmental History, Told through Fire, of Europe, and Europe's Encounter with the World* (Seattle: University of Washington Press, 1997), 25–32.

12. Frank Wilson, *The Hand: How Its Use Shapes the Brain, Language, and Human Culture* (New York: Pantheon Books, 1998), 58–59.

13. To tease yet another meaning out of bipedalism, walking on two feet lifted the human nose off the ground. It distanced the brain of the walker from immediate contact with the olfactory mazes of the earth and one's own kind, and it made the surveying eye, the most abstract of the senses, the primary judge. Reckoning the environment close up and afar, reliance on the eye added to the polarity of experience and metaphor between the abstract and concrete, a division already established by earthly foot and quick and reaching hand.

14. Lemonick and Dorfman, "Despite the Protests of Creationists," 57. For a critical review of the concept and evidence for Homo erectus, see W. W. Howells, "Homo Erectus: Who, When, and Where: A Survey," *Yearbook of Physical Anthropology* 23 (1980), 1–23, and "Homo Erectus," *Biology and Culture in Modern Perspective* (San Francisco: Freeman, 1972), 37–44. For a discovery of Homo erectus's persistence in Java until fifty thousand years ago, see Carl C. Swisher III, Garniss H. Curtis, and Roger Lewin, *Java Man: How Two Geologists' Dramatic Discoveries Changed Our Understanding of the Evolutionary Path to Modern Humans* (New York: Scribner, 2001).

15. Clive Gamble, *Timewalkers* (Cambridge, MA: Harvard University Press, 1994), 9, 47.

16. Konrad Spindler, cited in Gary Farr, "Ötzi: The Man in the Ice," April 20, 2002, http://www.becomehealthynow.com/ebookprint.php?id=617. Also, for a fuller description of the man and especially his clothes, see Konrad Spindler, *The Man in Ice* (New York: Harmony Books, 1994), 132–47.

17. R. A. Gould, "Subsistence Behavior among the Western Desert Aborigines of Australia," *Oceania* 39 (4): 254–74, cited in Robert Tonkinson, *The Mardudjara Aborigines* (New York: Holt, Rinehart and Winston, 1978), 29.

18. Tonkinson, *The Mardudjara Aborigines*, 34–35.

19. Ibid., 30.

20. Ibid., 70.

21. At some point, the old of the tribe declare themselves unequal to the arduous journey ahead. They ask to be left behind, and if no alternatives exist and the lives of others are endangered by the band's lessened mobility, their wish may be granted, Tonkinson, *The Mardudjara Aborigines*, 83.

22. E. Adamson Hoebel, *Man in the Primitive World* (New York: McGraw-Hill, 1949), 113.

23. Peter Farb, *Man's Rise to Civilisation* (London: Paladin, 1969), 197.

24. Lewis Mumford, *The City in History: Its Origins, Its Transformations, and Its Prospects* (New York: Harcourt, Brace, and World, 1961), 5.

25. For Indian use of dogs to carry and pull the travois, see Hebert Lowie, *Indians of the Plains*

(Garden City, NY: Natural History Press, 1954), 39–44.

26. In Africa pastoralism, according to Hoebel, "covers the whole Sahara, where it centers on the camel and horse. . . . In northern Sudan and most of East Africa it combines with hoe culture, and in the extreme south the Hottentots and Hereros live on their cattle. The great Asiatic steppes, from the east shores of the Caspian to the boundaries of China, from the Himalayas to the Arctic wastes, support such eminently pastoral peoples as the Finn, Kazak, Tatar, Altai, Kalmuck, and Mongols, and the reindeer-riding Ostyak, Tungus, Yakut, Yukaghir, Chukchi, Koryak, and others," *Man in the Primitive World,* 113.

27. Royal Hassrick, *The Sioux: Life and Customs of a Warrior Society* (Norman: University of Oklahoma Press, 1964), 171.

28. For a suggestive work on the roles of barter and exchange in early peoples' lives, see Melville Herskovits, *Economic Anthropology: The Economic Life of Primitive Peoples* (New York: Norton, 1952).

29. T. K. Derry and Trevor I. Williams, *A Short History of Technology: From the Earliest Times to A.D. 1900* (New York: Dover Publications, 1960), 163.

30. Isaiah 40:3–4.

31. *The Interpreter's Dictionary of the Bible,* ed. George Buttnick (New York: Abingdon Press, 1962), 213. Assyrian and Syrian footwear can be observed in sculpture at the British Museum.

32. Adolf Erman, *Life in Ancient Egypt* (New York: Dover, 1971), 448, 490.

33. Georges Contenau, *Everyday Life in Babylon and Assyria* (New York: Norton, 1966), 62–63.

34. Ibid., 63–64.

35. Ibid., 82.

36. *The March Up Country,* a translation of Xenophon's *Anabasis,* trans. W. H. D. Rouse (New York: Mentor Books, n.d.), 81–82.

37. Peter Green, *Alexander of Macedon, 356–323 B.C.: A Historical Biography* (Berkeley: University of California Press, 1991), 157–60. Philip reformed the army infantry into "foot companions," composed of phalangites (soldiers of the phalanx), who were armed with spears and had heavily armored front ranks. The "foot companions" were supplemented by the more lightly armored hypaspists—the shield bearers, and yet other companies of peltasts, named for their light-weight wicker shields. Additional units of lightly armed soldiers, archers, and slingers joined core elite hoplite units and select armed cavalry, which may have sprung up as the king's guard. Lesley Adkins and Roy Adkins, *Handbook to Life in Ancient Greece* (New York: Oxford Uni-

versity Press, 1998), 91–95. Yet, it was on flat and open land that king and general could deploy their armies and soldiers and test their legs and courage. The army often assembled under a barrage of incoming arrows and stones, after days and months of walking had brought them to what would be less than an hour's, perhaps only a few minutes' test. Spurred on by the Macedonian scream—*Alalalalai*—with separate units perhaps accompanied by song, flute, horn, or drum, they charged forward, hurtling themselves as a single running mass against an opposing army. Speed added thrust and piercing power to their spears. If not routed by the mere sight of the terrible phalanx, opponents usually quailed at the intense shock of colliding armies—the mashing of bodies, spears, and swords, which could be followed by dagger thrusting, beard pulling, and trampling. The victors pursued their fleeing opponents as far as they and their cavalry could. Then they returned, passing among the dead and wounded, identifying, aiding, and dispatching as emotions and orders commanded. For an engaging introduction to the actual face of Greek warfare, see Victor Davis Hanson, *The Western Way: Infantry Battle in Classical Greece* (Berkeley: University of California Press, 1989).

38. Sarah Pomeroy, Stanley Burstein, et al., *Ancient Greece: A Political, Social, and Cultural History* (New York: Oxford University Press, 1999), 423.

39. Green, *Alexander,* 435.

40. Ibid., 435.

41. Michael Grant, *The Ancient Mediterranean* (New York: Penguin, 1988), 48–50.

42. J. W. Gregory, *The Story of the Road: From the Beginning Down to A.D. 1931* (London: Alexander, Maclehose, 1931) and R. J. Forbes, *Notes on the History of Ancient Roads and Their Construction* (Chicago: Argonaut, 1967).

43. For road gods, see *Larousse Dictionary of Mythology* (New York: Prometheus, 1968), 38, 416.

44. For Chinese roads and canals, see Irene Franck and David Brownstone, "The Ambassador's Road and the Burma Road," *To the Ends of the Earth: The Great Travel and Trade Routes of Human History* (New York: Facts on File Publications, 1984), 1–16.

45. For the changing composition of the Roman army, see Lesley Adkins and Roy A. Adkins, *Handbook to Life in Ancient Rome* (New York: Oxford University Press, 1994), 173; for its logistics, see Adrian Keith Goldsworthy, *The Roman Army at War, 100 B.C.–A.D. 200* (Oxford: Oxford University Press, 1998), esp. 287–96. For the army's sandals, their heavy boots, and the hobnails that gave them long life, see www.larp.com/legioxx/caligae.html.

46. For the army's innovative marching camp, see Goldsworthy, *The Roman Army,* 111–13, 143–45.

47. G.R.Watson, *The Roman Soldier* (Ithaca, NY: Cornell University Press, 1969), 54–55; also see Adkins and Adkins, *Handbook to Life in Ancient Rome,* 90, and Vegetius, *The Epitome of Military Science* (Liverpool: Liverpool University Press, 1993), 10.

48. Flauvius Vegetius Renatus, *The Military Institutions of Rome* (Harrisburg, PA: Stackpole Books, 1960), 30–31.

49. Vegetius, *The Epitome of Military Science,* 10.

50. William McNeill, *Keeping Time Together: Dance and Drill in Human History* (Cambridge, MA: Harvard University Press, 1995), 4. Aside from its power to lend cohesion, "marching in cadence," McNeill quotes Maurice de Saxe, eighteenth-century marshall of France, "is the whole secret, and it's the military step of the Roman. . . . Everyone has seen people dancing all night. But take a man and make him dance for a quarter of an hour without music and see if he can bear it. . . . Movement to music is natural and automatic," McNeill, *Keeping Time Together,* 9. There is no evidence, however, that Romans ever used drums for marching, at least from the Republic through the first three centuries. They did have horns, which may have been used for battlefield signaling rather than marching, e-mail correspondence received from Matthew Amt/Quintus, Commander Legion XX, May 17, 2000.

51. John Keegan, *A History of Warfare* (New York: Vintage Books, 1993), 303.

52. For Appian Way, see Franck and Brownstone, *To the Ends of the Earth,* 33–48.

53. Jérôme Carcopino, *Daily Life in Ancient Rome* (New Haven, CT: Yale University Press, 1940), 10–21. In a more argumentative approach, Lewis Mumford argued that Rome evolved from "Megalopolis into Necropolis," Mumford, *The City in History: Its Origins,* 205–42.

54. Alexander McKay, *Houses, Villas, and Palaces in the Roman World* (Baltimore, MD: Johns Hopkins University Press, 1998), 167.

55. Roman property was manipulated by unscrupulous landlords, including one, Crassus, who literally bought burning property at a discount, put out the fire with his slaves, and then quickly threw up new rental dwellings in their place, Carcopino, *Daily Life in Ancient Rome,* 28–32.

56. Registering the esteem of sitting and owning a chair, the large chair became *cathedra* (the mighty seat), occupied in successive ages by the illustrious: pope, bishop, king, and eventually learned professor of a subject. "Ordinarily," Carcopino commented, "the Romans were content with benches (*scamna*) or stools (*subsellia*) or *sellae,* without arms or back, which they carried about with them out of doors" to take the load off their feet, Carcopino, *Daily Life in Ancient Rome,* 36, 34–39.

57. Roads and streets shaped Roman life. With names rural in origin, there was the *actus* (local road or track for animals or vehicles, originating from *agere,* meaning "to drive cattle"); *angiportus,* a narrow street or alley; *callis* for seasonal transhumance; *clivus,* street on a slope; *crepido,* pavement; *iter,* route or right of way for travelers on foot, horseback, or in litters; *limes,* boundary path or track; *puverium,* thoroughfare; *platea,* street; *semita,* narrow path; *strata,* an embanked road that came to rival *via; via,* road for vehicles; *rupta,* a substitute for *via* in certain districts, meaning the beaten track and the source of the French *route; trames,* footpath; and *vicus,* word for city street or lane, Adkins and Adkins, *Handbook to Life in Ancient Rome,* 173; also, on Roman roads, see Raymond Chevallier, *Roman Roads* (Berkeley: University of California Press, 1976), 16–17, and Betrand Lançon, *Rome in Late Antiquity: Everyday Life and Urban Change, A.D. 312–609* (New York: Routledge, 2001).

58. Carcopino, *Daily Life in Ancient Rome,* 46–48, 50.

59. Lionel Casson, *Everyday Life in Ancient Rome,* rev. ed. (Baltimore, MD: Johns Hopkins University Press, 1998), 53.

60. Also, Romans saw the mountain as a central place, the microcosm of the macrocosm, where a person could feel a true connection with all things, J. Donald Hughes, "The View from Etna: A Search for Ancient Landscape Appreciation," *The Trumpeter: The Journal of Ecosophy* 1, no. 1 (Fall 1983), 7–13.

61. P.V. Baldson, *Life and Leisure in Ancient Rome* (New York: McGraw Hill, 1969), 224.

62. Lionel Casson, *Travel in the Ancient World* (Baltimore, MD: Johns Hopkins University Press, 1994), 147.

63. Chevallier, *Roman Roads,* 20–26, 179–81.

64. For road travel for the Romans, see Casson, *Everyday Life in Rome,* 109–24.

65. The walking stick, the staff, off the road and in the hands of authority, has symbolic usage. As stylized scepter, it was the symbol of the king; as processional crosier, emblem for bishop; as crook, common sign of shepherd. *Staff* also came to indicate a group of humans offering essential services to army and institutions. Yet such symbolic power only suggests how indispensable the walking stick remained through most of history. On the road it is indeed the walker's most trusty companion. For suggestive uses of the word *staff*, see *The New Shorter Oxford Dictionary*, 2 vols. (Oxford: Clarendon Press, 1993), 2:3019–20. Even Christ recognized his apostles' need for a walking staff. He charges the apostles to go forth into the world taking nothing for their journey—"no scrip [bag], no bread, no money in their purse"—"*save a staff*" (Mark 6:8). The staff—the weapon with which Cain killed Abel—found many purposes for the country walker. It supported the injured or defective limb and proved a useful, even an awesome, cudgel against man and beast. Additionally, it stabilized its holder, allowed the vaulting of ravines, probed the depths of water, and pushed back grass and thicket, while doubling as a pry bar, measuring stick, fishing rod, and tent pole. Carved and decorated, it often singularly carried individual and group identity (the tribe is assembled where the staff is planted). For one example of decorated walking sticks, see Claude Savary, "Une canne sculpté de l'Afrique del ouest," *Musée de Gènève*, no. 319 (July–August 1992), 14–22.

66. Casson, *Travel in the Ancient World*, 177–78, 180.

67. For Roman preference for sea travel, see Casson, *Everyday Life in Ancient Rome*, 109–13.

68. Also, collapsing space and time, tom-toms and visual signals relayed messages over short distances. Official relay horsemen and organized runners, working between uniformly located stations, provided relatively rapid communications over long distances, Chevallier, *Roman Roads*, 181–95.

69. Chevallier, *Roman Roads*, 205.

NOTES TO CHAPTER 2

1. Michael Prestwich, *Armies and Warfare in the Middle Ages: The English Experience* (New Haven, CT: Yale University Press, 1996), 115–45. Also, see "War," H. R. Loyn, ed., *The Middle Ages: A Concise Encyclopaedia* (London: Thames & Hudson, 1989), 135.

2. For processions, see *New Catholic Encyclopedia*, vol. 11 (New York: McGraw Hill, 1967), 819–21.

3. For childhood in a medieval town, see Barbara Hanawalt, *Growing up in Medieval London: The Experience of Childhood in History* (New York: Oxford University Press, 1993).

4. Cited in Compton Reeves, *Pleasures and Pas-*

times *in Medieval England* (Oxford: Oxford University Press, 1998), 73.

5. For medieval dress, see James Laver, *Costume and Fashion: A Concise History* (New York: Thames and Hudson, 1995), 50–73.

6. Pierre Riché, *Daily Life in the World of Charlemagne* (Philadelphia: University of Pennsylvania Press, 1978), 161.

7. Sarah Gibson and Alicia Faxon, "Journey/Flight," *Encyclopedia of Comparative Iconography*, ed. Helene Roberts, vol. 1 (Chicago: Fotzroy Dearborn Publishers, 1998), 435–48.

8. Luke 3:4.

9. Matthew 4:23. For the land that Jesus traveled, see "Palestine during the Ministry of Jesus," George Wright and Floyd Filson, eds., *The Westminster Historical Atlas to the Bible* (Philadelphia: Westminster Press, 1956.)

10. Luke 9:58.

11. Mark 6:7–8.

12. Luke 9:3.

13. Christine Boecki, "Path/Road/Crossroads," *Encyclopedia of Comparative Iconography*, ed. Helene Roberts, vol. 1 (Chicago: Fotzroy Dearborn Publishers, 1998), 687–88.

14. Europeans reported sightings of the Wandering Jew as late as the nineteenth century. He became a staple figure of both oral and literary tradition, "Wandering Jew," *Larousse Dictionary of World Folklore* (New York: Larousse, 1996), 449.

15. See note 64 in chapter 1.

16. Jean Chevalier and Alain Gheerbrant, *A Dictionary of Symbols* (London: Blackwell, 1984), 257–61.

17. Cited in Richè, *Daily Life in the World of Charlemagne*, 1978), 6.

18. For the travel of king and court, see Marjorie Rowling, *Everyday Life of Medieval Travelers* (New York: Putnam's, 1971), 47–64.

19. Richè, *Daily Life*, 14–16.

20. J. J. Jusserand, *English Wayfaring Life in the Middle Ages* (New York: Putnam's, 1925), 104.

21. Jeffrey Singman, *Daily Life in Medieval Europe* (Westport, CT: Greenwood Press, 1999), 215.

22. Jacques Le Goff, *Medieval Civilization, 1400–1500* (Oxford: Blackwell, 1990), 25. For a short but useful survey of the decline of Roman roads, see *Ways of the World: A History of the World's Roads and of the Vehicles That Used Them* (New Brunswick, NJ: Rutgers University Press, 1992), 57–63.

23. Le Goff, *Medieval Civilization*, 136.

24. Richè, *Daily Life*, 20–21. For bridges, Rowling, *Everyday Life*, 15–17.

25. Le Goff, *Medieval Civilization*, 216.

26. Ibid., 215.

27. Jean Gimpel, *The Cathedral Builders* (New

York: Harper & Row, 1980), 95–98, passim. Also see Frances Gies and Joseph Gies, *Cathedral, Forge, and Waterwheel: Technology and Invention in the Middle Ages* (New York: Harper & Row, 1994), 192–200.

28. Cited ibid., 215.

29. Andrew McCall, *The Medieval Underworld* (New York: Barnes & Noble, 1993), 148. Useful for an overview is Henri Pirenne, *Economic and Social History of Medieval Europe* (New York: Harcourt, Brace, and Company, 1937), esp. 1–56.

30. Estimate of peasantry by Frances Gies and Joseph Gies, *Life in a Medieval Village* (New York: HarperCollins, 1990), 1.

31. Werner Rosener, *Peasants in the Middle Ages* (Chicago: University of Illinois Press, 1992), 12, 16, 20, 27, 52–53, 163, passim. For images of the peasantry, see Margaret Sullivan, "Peasantry," *Encyclopedia of Comparative Iconography,* 707–15.

32. Cited in Bridget Henisch, "Farm Work in the Medieval Calendar Tradition," *Agriculture in the Middle Ages: Technology, Practice, and Representation,* ed. Del Sweeny (Philadelphia: University of Pennslyvania Press, 1995), 316.

33. For a general consideration, see "Pilgrimage," *Medieval Folklore: An Encyclopedia of Beliefs, Customs, Tales, Music and Art,* vol. 2 (Santa Barbara, CA: ABC-CLIO, 2000), 647–49; for pilgrims as sources of early travel literatures, see Elizabeth Macdaniel, "Travel Literature," ibid., 988–99; for two general books, see John Wilkinson, *Jerusalem Pilgrimage, 1099–1185* (London: Hakluyt Society, 1988) and Jonathan Sumption, *Pilgrimage: An Image of Mediaeval Religion* (Towota, NJ: Rowman & Littlefield, 1975).

34. Patrick Geary, *Living with the Dead in the Middle Ages* (Ithaca, NY: Cornell University Press, 1994), 166.

35. Riché, *Daily Life,* 285.

36. Jean-Louis Goglin, *Les Misérables dans l'Occident médiéval* (Paris: Éditions du Seuil, 1976), 196–97.

37. Geary, *Living with the Dead,* 164.

38. Jacques Le Goff, *Medieval Civilization,* 135.

39. For the expansion of Europe, see Robert Bartlett, ed., *The Making of Europe: Conquest, Colonization, and Cultural Change, 950–1350* (Princeton, NJ: Princeton University Press, 1993).

40. Goglin, *Les Misérables,* 160.

41. Ibid., 60–61.

42. For the transformation of pilgrims' goals and local and universal saints, see Geary, *Living with the Dead,* 174–76.

43. Marjorie Rowling, *Life in Medieval Times* (New York: Perigee, 1973), 50.

44. Sumption, *Pilgrimage,* 289–302.

45. Ibid., 299–302.

46. Ibid.

47. Ibid., 168–71.

48. Ibid., 171–72.

49. Henry Reuss and Margaret Reuss, *Southern France: A History Buff's Guide* (Cambridge, MA: Harvard Common Press, 1991), 61.

50. Herod, legend says, beheaded St. James on his return to Jerusalem after his mission to Spain. The dead saint lured Charlemagne to his grave and there won Europe's emperor's commitment to deliver him and his church from the Saracens. Obedient to the Charlemagne's vow to St. James, Charlemagne's mounted warriors, among the ranks of which the mighty Roland numbered first, fought to death. Charlemagne, in turn, faithful to them, brought their remains back to churches along the Compostella trail. *Les chansons de geste*—of the eleventh century—transformed their fates into heroic tales, Reuss and Reuss, *Southern France,* 70.

51. For a useful map of pilgrims' routes to Compostella, see map 13.1, Gloria Fiero, *The Humanistic Tradition* (New York: McGraw Hill, 1998). For an introduction to the pilgrimage to Compostella, see Vera and Hellmut Hell, *The Great Pilgrimage of the Middle Ages* (London: Barrie & Rockcliff, 1966).

52. Morris Bishop, *The Middle Ages* (Boston: Houghton Mifflin, 1968), 149.

53. Reuss and Reuss, *Southern France,* 70–71.

54. Ibid., 70.

55. Sumption, *Pilgrimage,* 177.

56. The legend of the miracle of St. James is cited in Jacques Le Goff, *Medieval Civilization,* 230.

57. For examples of German norms regulating treatment of strangers by villagers and inns, see G. F. Coulton, *Medieval Village, Manor, and Monastery* (New York: Harper & Brothers, 1960), 277. Also, see Tara Neelakantappa, "Inns and Taverns," *Medieval Folklore: An Encyclopedia of Myths, Legends, Beliefs, Customs,* ed. Carl Lindahl, vol. 1 (Santa Barbara, CA: ABC-CLIO, 2000), 512–15.

58. Sumption, *Pilgrimage,* 182.

59. The Knights Templar reaped a sizable fortune through its plunder of the Holy Land, which allowed them to become for awhile the bankers of Europe until they ran afoul of France's Philip IV and were officially suppressed by Pope Clement V in 1312.

60. McCall, *Medieval Underworld,* 91–97.

61. C. J. Ribton-Turner, *A History of Vagrants and Vagrancy and Beggars and Begging* (Montclair, NJ: Patterson Smith, 1972), 40.

62. Jacques Le Goff, "Introduction," *The Medieval World,* ed. Jacques Le Goff (London: Collins & Brown, 1990), 6–7.

63. *The Rule of St. Benedict, Sources of the Medieval History.* Vol. 1, *The Middle Ages,* ed. Brian Tierney (New York: Knopf, 1983), 73.

64. Peter Damiani, James Ross, and Mary McLaughlin, eds., *The Portable Viking Reader* (New York: Penguin Books, 1955), 50–52.

65. Unable to preach without episcopal approval, Peter Valdes' followers, the Waldensians, were expelled from Lyon and in 1184 were named as heretics. Against the background of the church's struggle against the Cathar heresy in southern France, the Waldensian determination "to teach the scriptures in the vernacular alarmed the authorities." Condemnation did not stop the spread of the new message, which found adherents in Lombardy, Spain, Germany, and Austria, and later Bohemia, Poland, and Hungary, Loyn, ed., *The Middle Ages,* 331–32.

66. Loyn, ed., *The Middle Ages,* 113–14, and Thomas Franklin O'Meara, *Thomas Aquinas, Theologian* (Notre Dame, IN: Notre Dame University Press, 1997), 34.

67. Jacques Le Goff, *Les intellectuels au Moyen Âge* (Paris: Éditions du Seuil, 1985), 29.

68. Cited in Rowling, *Everyday Life of Medieval Travelers,* 104.

69. A famous Giotto fresco in the upper church of Assisi depicts the bishop covering the nude St. Francis, who has stripped naked and flung his clothes at his father.

70. Matthew 19:21–24.

71. Julien Green, *God's Fool* (New York: Harper & Row, 1987), 104.

72. For the fourteenth-century dancing mania, see Marjorie Rowling, *Everyday Life of Medieval Travelers,* 120–21.

73. Ibid. For a recent examination of the dance mania, which reaches from the eleventh to the seventeenth century, see Robert Bartholomew, "Rethinking the Dancing Mania," *Skeptical Inquirer,* July/August 2000, 42–47.

74. For a recent general guide to the Crusades, see Jonathan Riley-Smith, ed., *The Oxford Illustrated History of the Crusades* (Oxford: Oxford University Press, 1995).

75. Crusade goals were shifting and temporal—to save Sicily or Spain from Islam, to wipe out the Cathars in southern France, to spare Eastern Europe from paganism or orthodoxy, or, most gloriously of all, to take the Holy Land from the infidel. Crusaders themselves varied. They included fervent believers, glory-seeking second sons who had just enough for armor and groom, and even that most curious Holy Roman Emperor of Sicily, Frederick II, who, much to the pope's anger, fulfilled his crusading vow in 1228 by conducting a goodwill and informational tour of the infidel-controlled Holy Land, Morris Bishop, *The Middle Ages* (Boston: Houghton Mifflin, 1987), 105.

76. Jusserand, *English Wayfaring Life,* 91.

77. Macdaniel, "Travel Literature," 987–92.

78. The arrival of the Huns in the fifth century AD marked the appearance of the alien mounted warrior. According to military historian John Keegan, the Huns were "a truly new sort of people, previously unknown to the world." Creators of a type of equine *Blitzkrieg,* the Huns introduced horses into warfare, thus ushering new dimensions of heightened speed and increased distance into contemporary warfare. Only the need for extensive pastureland, caused by each warrior having five horses, and the temptation to loot and pillage restrained the Huns in their march across Eurasia, *A History of Warfare* (New York: Random House, 1993), 188–89.

79. Constance Brittain Bouchard, *"Strong of Body, Brave and Noble": Chivalry and Society in Medieval France* (Ithaca, NY: Cornell University Press, 1998), 10–11.

80. Riley-Smith, *History of the Crusades,* 21.

81. Bishop, *The Middle Ages,* 95.

82. Keegan, *A History of Warfare,* 208.

83. George Duby, *Rural Economy and Country Life in the Medieval West* (Philadelphia: University of Pennsylvania Press, 1998), 91. For additional consideration of the spread of the horse on Europe's better lands, the role of the monarch in supporting stud farms and developing a cavalry, and the limiting factor of inability to grow oats in Mediterranean regions of Europe, see Duby, *Rural Economy,* 110–11; Prestwich, *Armies and Warfare,* 31–36; Matthew Bennett, "The Medieval Warhorse Reconsidered," *Medieval Knighthood, V: Papers from the Sixth Strawberry Hill Conference,* ed. Stephen Church and Ruth Harvey (Woodbridge, England, 1995), 19–40, and F. M. L. Thompson, ed., *Horses in European Economic History* (Reading: British Agricultural Historical Society, 1983), esp. R. H. C. Davis's essay, "The Medieval Warhorse," 4–20.

84. Prestwich, *Armies and Warfare,* 222.

85. For a brief discussion of nobility and knighthood, see Bouchard, *"Strong of Body, Brave, and Noble,"* 110–11, and Prestwich, *Armies and Warfare,* 222–24. Also, see Sidney Painter's classic *French Chivalry* (Ithaca, NY: Cornell University Press, 1964).

86. Bouchard, *"Strong of Body, Brave, and Noble,"* 15.

87. At the same time, the horse eclipsed the ox and donkey even though the ox and donkey played a considerable role throughout Europe, not just the Mediterranean region, until the thirteenth century, Le Goff, *Medieval Civilization,* 213–14.

88. Jusserand, *English Wayfaring Life,* 84.

89. Lisa Cooper, "Tournament," *Medieval Folklore,* 985.

90. Franco Cardini, "The Warrior and the Knight," *The Medieval World,* ed. Le Goff, 107–8.

91. Richard Barber, *The Penguin Guide to Medieval Europe* (New York: Penguin Books, 1984), 274.

92. Peter Reitbergen, *Europe: A Cultural History* (London: Routledge, 1998), 172–73.

93. Jusserand, *English Wayfaring Life,* 29.

94. For a history of the English foot in contrast to the Rhineland foot and the Marseilles pan, see Edward Nicholson, *Men and Measures: A History of Weights and Measures* (London: Smith, Elder, 1912), 48–59. Helping define the Renaissance theory of human proportions, fifteenth-century thinker and artist Alberti further refined Vitruvius's notion that "the foot is equal to one sixth of the total length of the body," Erwin Panofsky, *Meaning in the Visual Arts* (Garden City, NY: Doubleday Anchor, 1955), 95.

95. Henri Pirenne, *Medieval Cities: Their Origins and Revival of Trade* (Garden City, NY: Doubleday Anchor, 1925), 153, and Howard Adelson, *Medieval Commerce* (Princeton, NJ: Van Nostrand, 1962), 68.

96. Sir Peter Hall, *Cities in Civilization* (New York: Pantheon Books, 1998), 78–80, and Lewis Mumford, *The City in History* (New York: Harcourt, Brace, 1961), 312–14.

97. Europe's largest cities drew population from society at large rather the surrounding countryside. Sylvia Troop suggests this to be true in the case of London, *The Merchant Class of Medieval London* (Ann Arbor: University of Michigan Press, 1962), 207–8.

98. Bishop, *The Middle Ages,* 186.

99. Ibid.

100. Ibid., 186–87.

101. For a useful introduction to premodern travel and contact between East and West, see Jerry Bentley, *Old World Encounters: Cross-Cultural Contacts and Exchanges in Pre-Modern Times* (New York: Oxford University Press, 1993), esp. maps 30, 34, 112, 116, and 166.

102. Sir Henry Yule, cited in Eileen Power, *Medieval People* (Garden City, NY: Doubleday, 1924), 67. For a recent work on the diverse people who traveled and serviced the travelers of the Silk Road, see Susan Whitfield, *Life along the Silk Road* (Berkeley: University of California Press, 1999), esp., for horses and horsemen, 76–94.

103. According to Marco Polo, the Khan "kept up a stud of about ten thousand horses," which

were shown such great reverence that only the descendents of Chingis-Khan could drink their mares' milk and no one could "place himself before them or impede their movement," *The Travels of Marco Polo* (New York: Dell Publishing, 1961), 141.

104. See Ribton-Turner, *Vagrants and Vagrancy,* 1–34.

105. Le Goff, *Medieval Civilization,* 134.

106. Ribton-Turner, *Vagrants and Vagrancy,* 55.

107. Depicted by medieval iconography, "Nudity signifies utter poverty. Emaciation connotes hunger. Sores, deformities, and crutches represent physical handicaps; and the dog suggests the absence of human companionship." This iconography squares with chroniclers, preachers, hagiographers, and others who collectively depicted the pauper as "either naked or clad in rags, or a wretch clad of a hide. He is as hairy as a man of the forest. . . . [He] always goes barefoot even though he is frequently on the move, either alone or in a group. But he never wanders far from the gate of the city, monastery, or castle that is the center of his existence," Michel Mollat, *The Poor in the Middle Ages* (New Haven, CT: Yale University Press, 1986), 64–65.

108. Ribton-Turner, *Vagrants and Vagrancy,* 45.

109. For guides to the medieval underclass, see Goglin, *Les Misérables,* Mollat, *The Poor,* and McCall, *The Medieval Underworld.*

110. Ribton-Turner, *Vagrants and Vagrancy,* 58.

111. Ibid., 60–62.

112. Attempting to establish a distinction between true and false beggars—who obviously couldn't own a horse—one thirteenth-century Parisian clerical writer argued that begging should be permitted for one or all the following reasons: ignorance of all trades, sickness, old age, dotage, delicate upbringing undermining a capacity to work, inability to find work, inadequate wages to buy bread, or the desire "to undertake some knightly deed," McCall, *Medieval Underworld,* 147.

113. For an overview of the social conflict and the contested streets of the medieval city, see Mark Girouard, *Cities and People* (New Haven, CT: Yale University Press, 1985), 15–40. For a useful introduction to the crowds and conditions of London, see Charles Pendrill, *London Life in the Fourteenth Century* (Port Washington, NY: Kennikat Press, 1971), 7–66.

114. Le Goff, *The Medieval World,* 25–26, Le Goff, *Medieval Civilization,* 322.

115. McCall, *The Medieval Underworld,* 147.

116. Incident and law cited in John Ricker and John Saywell, *Medieval Europe: The Birth of a New Civilization* (Toronto: Clarke, Irwin, 1973), 39.

117. Girouard, *Cities and People,* 73.

118. Water supply constituted a first and fundamental preoccupation for authority as increased congestion and commercial activity intensified contamination. ("At Bruges the custodian of the Water House took an oath to be diligent and faithful, to guard everything pertaining to the water," George Rosen, *A History of Public Health,* rev. ed. (Baltimore, MD: Johns Hopkins University Press, 1958), 32. Many towns controlled building and, fearing fire, regulated chimneys and roofs.

119. Girouard, *Cities and People,* 55.

120. Ibid., 64–65.

121. Ibid.

122. Ribton-Turner, *Vagrants and Vagrancy,* 51–52.

123. Simon Schama, *The Embarrassment of Riches* (Berkeley: University of California Press, 1988), 582–83. Also, for the issue of commitment, see Pieter Spierenburg, "The Sociogenesis of Confinement and Its Development in Early Modern Europe," *The Emergence of Carceral Institutions: Prisons, Galleys, and Lunatic Asylums, 1550–1900,* ed. Spierenburg, et al. (Rotterdam: Centrum voor Maatschappij Geschiednis, Erasmus Universiteit, 1984), 9–77.

124. Le Goff shares this opinion in the introduction to his edited volume, *Medieval World,* 19.

NOTES TO CHAPTER 3

1. For an estimate of world population, see Fernand Braudel, *Civilization and Capitalism, Fifteenth–Eighteenth Century.* Vol. 1, *The Structure of Everyday Life: The Limits of the Possible* (New York: Harper & Row, 1979), 31–51.

2. For Fernand Braudel's calculations, see *The Mediterranean World,* vol. 1 (New York: Harper & Row, 1975), 394–98, 402–18.

3. Ibid., 448.

4. Ibid., 756–60, et passim.

5. Ibid., 415–18.

6. Braudel, *The Structure of Everyday Life,* 429.

7. Braudel, *The Mediterranean,* 402.

8. Samuel Johnson, *Journey to the Western Islands,* and James Boswell, *The Journal of a Tour of the Hebrides with Samuel Johnson* (Boston: Houghton Mifflin, 1965), 20, 21.

9. John Crofts, "The Roads," *Everyman in Europe: Essays in Social History,* vol. 1, 2nd ed. (Englewood Cliffs, NJ: Prentice-Hall, 1981), 185.

10. Crofts, "Roads," 187.

11. For an introduction to Catholic gestures, see "Liturgical Gestures" and "Liturgy, Structural El-ements," *New Catholic Encyclopedia,* vol. 8 (New York: McGraw-Hill, 1967), 894–95, 941.

12. For an introduction to the history of carriages, see M. G. Lay, *Ways of the World: A History of the World's Roads and of the Vehicles That Used Them* (New Brunswick, NJ: Rutgers University Press, 1992), 121–26. Also, useful for overview, "Carriage," *Encyclopaedia Britannica,* vol. 4 (Chicago: Encyclopaedia Britannica, 1970), 961–64.

13. For manners and their dissemination process from the court to society, see Norbert Elias, *The Civilizing Process* (New York: Pantheon Books, 1978–1983), 19–20, 27.

14. Peter Rietbergen, *Europe: A Cultural History* (London: Routledge, 1998), 268.

15. A. G. Dickens, ed., *The Courts of Europe, Patronage and Royalty, 1400–1800* (New York: McGraw-Hill, 1977), 7.

16. Ibid., 268.

17. Rietbergen, *Europe,* 269.

18. Wendy Hilton, "Minuet," *International Encyclopedia of Dance,* vol. 4 (New York: Oxford University Press, 1998), 431.

19. Ibid., 269.

20. For processions and the use of open space in France, see Thomas Munck, *The Enlightenment: A Comparative Social History, 1721–1794* (New York: Oxford University Press, 2000), 35–45.

21. The greatest of the horse displays was *Il Mondo Festiggiante,* performed in 1661 in the Boboli Gardens in Florence on the occasion of the marriage of Cosimo III to Marguerite-Louise d'Orléans. Ruth Sander, "Horse Ballet," *International Encyclopedia of Dance,* vol. 3 (New York: Oxford University Press, 1998), 381–83. Also see, for the history of the horse, Sylvia Loch, *The Royal Horse of Europe: The Story of the Andalusian and Lusitano* (London: J. A. Allen, 1986). Vienna's drilled Lipizzan horses date back to the time of Emperor Maximillian II, who introduced the breeding of Spanish horses in 1562.

22. William McNeill, *Keeping Together in Time: Dance and Drill in Human History* (Cambridge, MA: Harvard University Press, 1995).

23. Michael Roberts, *The Military Revolution, 1560–1660* (Belfast: Marjory Boyd, 1956), 10–11.

24. The goose step, the *Parademarsch* of the Prussian army, was brought to Germany by the troops of the military-minded Karl von Hessen-Hassel in 1730. One of his regiments learned in Italy and Sicily to march in step in the service of the Holy Roman Emperor, U.S. Army Military History Institute, Carlisle Barracks, Carlisle, PA, Ref. Branch, folder, "Marching," js 1972. The surprising notion that enlisted men could march with the same step caught on with and was

popularized by Frederick the Great. In order to train the colonists in their War of Independence, Prussian officer Baron von Steuben wrote for commander George Washington his *Regulations for the Order and Discipline of the Troops of the United States,* which became the foundation of the new nation's military training. At Valley Forge, von Steuben built a model drill company of 120 select men. His *Regulations,* "commonly known as the army's 'blue book,'" was considered only slightly less authoritative than the Bible," Baron von Steuben's Revolutionary War Drill Manual, facsimile reprint of 1794 edition (New York: Dover Publications, 1985), n.p. It was altered over history, U.S. Army, "Drill and Ceremonies," FM (Field Manual) 22-5 (Headquarters, Department of the Army, December 1986), esp. iii–iv. The influence of Von Steuben's drilling remains, however, with training through marches, "Physical Fitness and Training," FM (Field Manual) 21-20 (ibid., September 1992).

25. This description of the goose step is borrowed in part from Norman Davies, *Europe, a History* (New York: Harper Perennial, 1998), 612.

26. McNeill, *Keeping Together,* 133.

27. For what has become a classic on the development of manners and gestures, see Nobert Elias, *The Civilizing Process,* comprising three volumes, *The History of Manners* (New York: Pantheon Books, 1978), *Power and Civility* (1982), and *The Court and Society* (1983).

28. Alicia M. Annas, "The Elegant Art of Movement," *An Elegant Art: Fashion and Fantasy in the Eighteenth Century* (Los Angeles: Los Angeles County Museum of Art, 1983), 47. Elsewhere, she notes the way in which corseted women led with their bosoms and were most tested by managing their skirts, while men accompanying women, projecting curved and thus developed calves, strove to go neither too fast nor too slow, while seeking above all else not to trample a woman's luxurious skirt, 45.

29. For suggestive ideas on the history of sitting and chairs in modern history, see Galen Cranz, *The Chair: Rethinking Culture, Body, and Design* (New York: Norton, 1998), 41–43, and Witold Rybczynski, *Home: A Short History of an Idea* (New York: Viking, 1986), 81–83, 93, passim.

30. Annas, "The Elegant Art of Movement," 48.

31. Yves Gulicher, "France: Recreational Dance," *International Encyclopedia of Dance,* vol. 3 (New York: Oxford University Press, 1998), 62–65, and Wendy Hilton, "Minuet," 431–33. For notes on the waltz and the minuet, see Jacques Barzun, *From Dawn to Decadence, 1500 to the Present: Five Hundred Years of Western Cultural Life*

(New York: HarperCollins, 2000), 188–89. The nobility and bourgeoisie did embrace the waltz at the end of the eighteenth century, Peter Burke, *Popular Culture in Early Modern Europe* (New York: Harper & Row, 1978), 118.

32. Gulicher, "France: Recreational Dance," 63.

33. Ibid.

34. For a discussion of the new cemeteries of the eighteenth century, see John McManners, *The Enlightenment: Changing Attitudes to Death among Christians and Unbelievers in Eighteenth-Century France* (Oxford: Oxford University Press, 1985), 303–67.

35. Mark Girouard, *Life in the English Country House* (New York: Penguin Books, 1980), 217. Aside from being sites for concerts, fireworks displays, and other attractions, the most opulent gardens contained plants and animals brought from around the world.

36. Ibid., 210.

37. Derek Plint Clifford, "Garden and Landscape Design," vol. 19, *The New Encyclopaedia Britannica* (Chicago: Encyclopaedia Britannica, 1997), 662–67.

38. Ibid., 665.

39. In *The Wildest Place on Earth: Italian Gardens and the Invention of Wilderness* (Washington, DC: Counterpoint, 2001), John Hanson Mitchell argues that nineteenth-century American thinkers formed their conception of wilderness in opposition to the Italian garden, 20–22, 90–103.

40. Girouard, *Life in the English Country House,* 217.

41. F. Roy Willis, *Western Civilization: An Urban Perspective,* vol. 2 (New York: Heath, 1973), 483.

42. Willis, *Western Civilization,* 483.

43. Lewis Mumford, *The Culture of Cities* (New York: Harcourt Brace Jovanovich, 1970), esp. 73–142.

44. Ibid., 95.

45. This contrast was taken from John Wain, *Samuel Johnson* (New York: Viking Press, 1974), 79.

46. There were many types of carriages, L. P. S., "Carriages," *Encyclopaedia Britannica,* vol. 4 (Chicago: Encyclopaedia Britannica, 1970), 961–64. They distinguished their owners. There were carriages for kings and queens, like the golden carriage of Willhelm of Holland, which was used until 1898. They also distinguished their user's post, as did the ornate coach of London's Lord Mayor. Contemporary museums in London, Palermo, Madrid, Moscow, and Vienna make it amply clear that carriages and sedan chairs simultaneously the most efficient and the most luxurious way to go about. In the Wagenburg at Schönbrunn in Vienna, there are sixty state coaches, sledges, and sedan chairs, including the decorated Imperial Coach, used for coronations and weddings, and the Funerary Coach.

47. Mumford, *The Culture of Cities,* 97.

48. Ibid., 97–98.

49. Ibid., 99, 102.

50. For a useful overview of its formulation in France, see Maurice Magendie, *La politesse mondaine et les théories de l' honnêteté en France au XVIIe siècle, de 1600 à 1660,* 2 vols. (Genève: Slatkine, 1970).

51. Dorene Yarwood, "Dress and Adornment" *The New Encyclopaedia Britannica,* vol. 17 (Chicago: Encyclopaedia Britannica, 1997), 489–93.

52. For a useful guide to shoes, boots, clogs, cloaks, and other material that defined world walking, see Doreen Yarwood's amply illustrated *Encyclopaedia of World Costume* (London: B. T. Batsford, 1978).

53. For pattens, chopines, and Venetian *zoccolo,* which reached two feet in height, see Doreen Yarwood, *Costume of the Western World: Pictorial Guide and Glossary* (New York: St. Martins, 1980), 91–92, 187–88. For the demands of fashion and heels so high their wearers had to use canes and walk rigidly, see Alfred Franklin, *La civilité, L'étiquette, la mode, le bon ton, du xiiie au xixe siècle,* vol. 2 (Paris: Émile-Paul, 1908). Clogs were commonly worn by peasants. They were known as *ciompi* in Florence and identified the craft of their wearers with those who worked in wash houses, Christopher Hibbert, *The Rise and the Fall of the House of Medici* (New York: Penguin Books, 1979), 76. For a fine short overview of shoes across the world and throughout the ages, see the website of Toronto's Bata Shoe Museum, at http://www.batashoemuseum.ca/.

54. Cited in Daniel Pool, *What Jane Austen Ate and Charles Dickens Knew: From Fox Hunting to Whist—the Facts of Daily Life in Nineteenth-Century England* (New York: Simon & Schuster, 1993), 350.

55. For seventeenth- and eighteenth-century shoes, see Bata Museum electronic site (note 53 above).

56. For history of the boot, see Yarwood, *World Costume,* 42–46.

57. See chapter 2, p. 000, and chapter 1, esp. footnote 65.

58. "Cane, Walking Stick," *The Columbia Encyclopedia,* 6th ed., 2001, online http://www.Bartleby.com.

59. For a short note on the cane's history, see "Cane," *Columbia Desk Encyclopedia,* 3rd ed. (New York: Columbia University Press, 1963), 333.

60. For a useful short history of walking sticks and canes, see Catherine Dike, *Walking Sticks* (Buckinghamshire: Shire Publications, 1990).

61. For a general history of the umbrella, from origin to modern history, see T. S. Crawford, *A History of the Umbrella* (New York: Taplinger Publishing, 1970).

62. "Umbrella," *The New Encyclopaedia Britannica,* vol. 12 (Chicago: Encyclopaedia Britannica, 1997), 122. The umbrella, so distinctly British, established its separate identity from the lighter, more gracious and colorful parasol at the start of the century and has a rich and diverse history thereafter, see Crawford, *A History of the Umbrella,* 133–51, 179–200.

63 The umbrella entered social discourse on other levels. It became a complex apparatus for displaying manners, or their absence, as one entered and exited foyers and met and accompanied others along the street. In twentieth-century film, Gene Kelly, in his famous dashing, tapping, and jumping dance routine in "Singing in the Rain," transformed the umbrella into a wonderful stage prop.

64. For an early expression of English manners, see *Rules of Civility; or, Certain Ways of Deportment Observed amongst All Persons of Quality upon Several Occasions* (London: R. Chiswell, 1685). This book provides particular instruction in how to approach, address, pass, and walk with a superior in and outside of the court.

65. Joan Wildeblood, *The Polite World: A Guide to English Manners and Deportment from the Thirteenth to the Nineteenth Century* (London: Oxford University Press, 1965), 37.

66. For nineteenth-century dissemination of manners, see Michael Curtin, *Propriety and Position: A Study of Victorian Manners* (New York: Garland Publishing, 1987); for suggestive primary sources, see Hamilton Moore, *The Young Gentleman and Lady's Monitor and English Teacher's Assistant* (Hudson, NY: Ashbel, Stoddard, 1809), and *Thomas Hill's Manual. Never Give a Lady a Restive Horse: A Nineteenth-Century Handbook of Etiquette,* a reprint of *Hill's Manual of Social & Business Forms* and *Hill's Album of Biography and Art* (Cleveland: World Publishing Company, 1969). To examine the two faces of the diffusion of manners and style, see James Laver, *Dandies* (London: Weidenfeld & Nicolson, 1968) and Bernard Shaw's *Pygmalion* (1913). For one book on etiquette of countless many, see Millicent Fenwick's *Vogue's Book of Etiquette: A Complete Guide to Traditional Forms and Modern Usage* (New York: Simon & Schuster, 1948).

67. Aside from Wildeblood, *The Polite World,* also see John Mason, *Gentlefolk in the Making:*

Studies in the History of English Courtesy Literature and Related Topics from 1531 to 1774 (New York: Octagon Books, 1971) and Maurice J. Quinlan, *Victorian Prelude: A History of Manners, 1700–1830* (Hamden, CT: Archon Books, 1965).

68. Wildeblood, *The Polite World,* 9.

69. Ibid., 151.

70. Cited in David McCullough, *John Adams* (New York: Simon & Schuster, 2001), 259.

71. Samuel Pepys describes how Lady Batten lost one of her galoshes in the mud, *The Diary of Samuel Pepys: Selections,* ed. O. F. Morshead (New York: Harper & Row, 1960), 282.

72. McCullough, *John Adams,* 303, 328.

73. Wildeblood, *The Polite World,* 152.

74. Cited in Wildeblood, *The Polite World,* 192, 213.

75. Cited in Ruth Kelso, *The Doctrine of the English Gentleman in the Sixteenth Century* (Gloucester, MA: Peter Smith, 1964), 160.

76. Wildeblood, *The Polite World,* 214.

77. Peter Rietbergen, *Europe: A Cultural History* (London: Routledge, 1998), 263–75. Also see Christopher Hibbert, *The Grand Tour* (New York: Putnam's, 1969) and Jeremy Black, *The British Abroad: The Grand Tour in the Eighteenth Century* (Phoenix Mill, England: Sutton Publishing, 2003).

78. Mark Girouard, *Life in the English Country House,* 190. Pepys, who seemed to love movement itself, continually rushed about. "At any moment he was ready to plunge on the miry and unmetalled roads to Cambridge; on to Huntington the next day and back to London on the third, exclaiming next morning that he never felt better in his life," cited in Lawrence Herson, *The Politics of Ideas: Political Theory and American Public Policy* (Prospects Heights, IL: Waveland Press, 1984), 69.

79. Marjorie Morgan, *Manners, Morals and Class in England, 1774–1858* (New York: St. Martin's Press, 1994), 44–45.

80. Morgan, *Manners, Morals and Class in England,* 44.

81. Cited ibid., 45. English villagers and country folk did not exhibit the variety of language and dress of their continental counterparts, according to Paul Langford, *Englishness Identified: Manners and Character, 1650–1850* (Oxford: Oxford University Press, 2000), 15.

82. Cited ibid., 37.

83. Ibid.

84. Ibid.

85. For an overview of travel in early modern Europe, see Rietenberg, *Europe,* 259–83.

86. For general overview of transport and communication, from the seventeenth to the first decades of the nineteenth century, see Eugen Weber, *A Modern History: Men, Cultures, and Societies from the Renaissance to the Present* (New York: Norton, 1971), 447–50; for France, the most developed country in Europe, see Daniel Roche, *France in the Enlightenment* (Cambridge, MA: Harvard University Press, 1998), 41.

87. Weber, *A Modern History,* 448. Also, estimates of improved transportation are found in Rosamond Bayne-Powell, *Travellers in Eighteenth-Century England* (New York: Benjamin Blom, 1972), 8–25, and in Roche, *France in the Enlightenment,* 55.

88. For the favorable travel conditions that gave rise to the first modern business contract, see Thomas Haskell, "Capitalism and the Origins of Humanitarian Sensibility," *American Historical Review* 90, nos. 2 & 3 (April 1985 and June 1985), 339–61 and 547–66.

89. Weber, *A Modern History,* 448.

90. Braudel, *The Structure of Everyday Life,* 415–30.

91. Victoria Glendinning, *Jonathan Swift: A Portrait* (New York: Henry Holt, 1998), 47–48.

92. Cited in Lay, *Ways of the World,* 66. For a short history of English roads, Christopher Savage, "Road," *Chambers Encyclopedia,* vol. 11 (Oxford: Pergamon Press, 1967), 705–12.

93. Cited in Lay, *Ways of the World,* 107.

94. For the development of French roads in the eighteenth century, see Lay, *Ways of the World,* 112–14; also see Braudel, *The Structure of Everyday Life,* 424–25.

95. Pierre Goubert described a journey in eighteenth-century France in his *Ancien Régime: French Society, 1600–1750* (New York: Harper & Row, 1969), 58.

96. Roche, *France in the Enlightenment,* 41.

97. John Lough, *France Observed in the Seventeenth Century by British Travellers* (Boston: Oriels Press, 1984), 26–27.

98. Goubert, *The Ancien Régime,* 59.

99. Ibid., 59–60. For an introduction to the development of artillery in early modern history and the role of horse and wheels in providing it with mobility, see Aaron Bradshaw Jr., "Artillery," *The Encyclopedia Americana* (New York: Americana, 1949), 363–65.

100. Maurice Vaussard, *Daily Life in Eighteenth-Century Italy* (New York: Macmillan, 1963), 50.

101. Ibid., 51.

102. Ibid., 52.

103. In an early index of types of vagabonds, in 1627, Giancinto Nobili, a Dominican monk of Viterbo, published under papal sanction a work entitled *Il Vagabondo overo sferza de Bianti e Vagabondi,* which distinguished among false pilgrims, monks, priests, tremblers, prophets, phonies, and pretenders—thirty-four types of charlatans in all, cited in C. J. Ribton-Turner, *A History of Vagrants and Vagrancy and Beggars and Begging* (Montclair, NJ: Patterson Smith, 1972), 557–60, 593.

104. *Letters from the Right Honourable Lady Mary Wortley Montgau, 1709 to 1762* (London: J. M. Dent, 1906), 80.

105. He instructed those who were to ride in Russian carriages to retain carriages with high ceilings to escape terrible bumps to the head and to be prepared for rough riding, for even the best-padded seats broke bottles stored below the springs. He also cautioned against the reckless stage driver and advised travelers to force such drivers to slow their precipitous downhill descents into river valleys, where vehicles commonly overturned. He also warned that a day of bumping and banging will produce terrible headaches and nausea that will make even the worst of thief-filled inns seem an oasis, Marquis de Custine, *Empire of the Czar: A Journey through Eternal Russia* (New York: Doubleday, 1989).

106. Custine, *Empire of the Czar,* 45.

NOTES TO CHAPTER 4

1. Cultural historian Gudrun König traces the transformation of walking in middle-class Germany during the years from 1780 to 1850, *Eine Kulturgeschichte des Spazierganges: Spuren einer bürgerlichen Praktik, 1780–1850* (Vienna: Böhlau, 1996).

2. Ibid., 21.

3. Ibid., 29–30. König notes there that Goethe had once anticipatorily joined the words with his neologism *Spazierwanderung.*

4. Ibid., 13.

5. Simon Schama, *Fate of the Empire, 1776–2000,* vol. 3 of *History of Britain* (New York: Hyperion, 2002), 12.

6. Ibid., 16.

7. Ibid., 6.

8. Ibid., 10. While the mere following of traditional footpaths could not in itself reverse the effects of enclosure, it consecrated an earlier landscape and suggested an alternative mode of ordering and utilizing the land, Anne D. Wallace, *Walking, Literature, and English Culture: The Origins and Uses of the Peripatetic in the Nineteenth Century* (Oxford: Clarendon Press, 1993), 11.

9. Ibid., 8–9.

10. Ibid., 10, 18. Wallace, specifically, conceives the peripatetic as a response to the aesthetic problems generated by the transport revolution

and enclosure. She argues that the improved speed and reduced cost of travel between 1750 and 1850 transformed the place of walking in society, ibid., 62–64. As Robin Jarvis shows in *Romantic Writing and Pedestrian Travel* (New York: St. Martin's Press, 1997), 20, her argument depends on predating the transport revolution, which really didn't start to take from until 1830, as articulated by Philip Bagwell, *Transport Revolution* (New York: Barnes & Noble, 1974), esp. 35–60.

11. Jarvis, *Romantic Writing,* 7.

12. Ibid., 8.; also see Schama, *History of Britain,* 16.

13. Ibid., 17.

14. C. P. Moritz's *Travels through Several Parts of England* is found in John Pinkerton, ed., *Voyages and Travels in all Parts of the World,* vol. 2 (Philadelphia: Kimber and Conrad, 1810), 489–573.

15. Jarvis, *Romantic Writing,* 9–10, and Morris Marples, *Shanks's Pony: A Study of Walking* (London: Dent, 1959), 134.

16. Cited ibid., 12.

17. "John Towner calculates . . . that between the mid-sixteenth century and the 1830s the average age of the Tourist rose from 23 to 42, while the average duration of the Tour declined from 40 months to only 4 months," Jarvis, *Romantic Writing,* 12.

18. Ibid., 13.

19. As late as the 1820s, Jarvis argues, roads and stagecoaches did not penetrate much of England or Europe. He concurs with transportation historian Philip Bagwell that the cost of riding, which vastly exceeded workers' irregular and low wages, remained a luxury. Furthermore, the fastest pedestrians could outpace a typical carriage. (Traveling four miles an hour and more than twenty-five miles a day, a long-legged "heel-and-toer" overtook all but the fastest carriages, except on freshly macadamized roads on which carriages reached speeds up to ten miles per hour.) Ibid., 20. French historian Fernand Braudel concurs that the development of road systems only came with the first upsurge of the Industrial Revolution in the feverish decade of the 1830s, while noting that in many rural areas in both Europe and North America roads are latecomers, following the tracks of the railroad system, Fernand Braudel, *The Structure of Everyday Life: The Limits of the Possible,* vol. 1 of *Civilization and Capitalism, Fifteenth–Eighteenth Century* (New York: Harper & Row, 1979), 428.

20. That romantics in some measure made up the people they praised is an argument made by Eric Hobsbawm in his *The Invention of Tradition* (Cambridge: Cambridge University Press, 1983).

21. Maurice Cranston, *The Noble Savage: Jean-Jacques Rousseau, 1754–1762*, vol. 3 of *Jean-Jacques Rousseau* (Chicago: University of Chicago Press, 1991), xiii.

22. Will Durant and Ariel Durant, *Rousseau and Revolution*, vol. 10 of *The Story of Civilization* (New York: Simon & Schuster, 1967), 11.

23. Rousseau, *The Confessions* (Baltimore: Penguin Books, 1953), 382.

24. Maurice Cranston, *The Early Life and Work of Jean-Jacques Rousseau, 1712–54*, vol. 2 of *Jean-Jacques Rousseau* (Chicago: University of Chicago Press, 1992), 227–29.

25. Durant and Durant, *Rousseau and Revolution*, 11.

26. For an eighteenth-century *compagnon* life, see Jacques-Louis Ménétra, *Journals of My Life* (New York: Columbia University Press, 1986), esp. Daniel Roche's introduction, 1–13, and for its triumphs and ordeals, 30–80 and passim. For an additional accounting of the travels, pains, and pleasures of a nineteenth-century *compagnon*, read Agricol Perdiguer, *Mémoires d'un compagnon*, new ed. (Paris: Editions Denoël, 1943). Perdiguer recounts traveling with friends, their fights along the road, cavalcades they joined, and the cities they paced in the evening for pleasure, and much more.

27. Cranston, *The Noble Savage*, xiii.

28. Rousseau discovered friendship, intimacy, and love by strolling in the countryside and promenading in the hidden quarters of gardens. Rousseau's *Confessions* abundantly testifies to how commonplace outdoor flirting was. In *The Confessions* he recollects his joy botanizing and fruit picking with "Mamma," Madame Warren, who "although somewhat round and fat," he writes, "was not a bad walker," and he remembers long solitary walks with Madame de Larnage, ibid., 241.

29. A fragment of his *Confession* reads, "I was so tired of reception rooms, fountains, shrubberies, and flower-beds, and those tiresome people who make a show of them; I was so weary of pamphlets, clavichords, wool-sorting, and making knots, of stupid witticisms and tedious affectations," ibid., 384.

30. Ibid., 374.

31. For a discussion of Rousseau as "The Moralist," see Cranston, *Jean-Jacques Rousseau*, 230–70.

32. Ibid., 155.

33. Rousseau, *The Confessions*, 591.

34. Ibid., 374–76. For a discussion of Rousseau's relationship to his wife, see Cranston, *Jean-Jacques Rousseau*, 198–200, passim.

35. Ibid., 376.

36. Ibid.

37. For the botanizing of itinerant Rousseau, see Georges May, *Rousseau par lui même* (Paris: Éditions du Seuil, 1961), esp. 5–32, 113–14.

38. Jean-Jacques Rousseau, *The Reveries of the Solitary Walker* (New York: Harper & Row, 1979), 103. In 1772, taking long notes on his walks and collecting plants as he went, he composed his *Elementary Letters on Botany* for a friend's daughter.

39. Joseph Amato, *Ethics, Living or Dead?* (Tuscaloosa, AL: Portals Press, 1982), 17–18.

40. Cited ibid., 18.

41. Cited ibid., 19.

42. For Georges Van den Abbeele, Rousseau democratized travel by allowing the walker to lay claim to the great thoughts experienced along the way. Certainly, the Romantics appropriated the idea of reflective itinerancy and passed it on to subsequent generation of bourgeois adventurers in sentimentality such as Stendhal (whose 1838 *Mémoires d'un touriste* first gave legitimacy to the word in French), *Travel as Metaphor: From Montaigne to Rousseau* (Minneapolis: University of Minnesota Press, 1992), 130.

43. Goethe described his trip in his *Italian Journey (1786–1788)*; the edition used here was translated by W. H. Auden and Elizabeth Mayer (New York: Penguin Books, 1970).

44. Cited in Wallace, *Walking*, 53.

45. This assessment of Goethe as scientist is drawn from Jacques Barzun, *From Dawn to Decadence, 1500 to the Present* (New York: HarperCollins, 2000), 501.

46. Michelin, *Sicily* (Waterford, Great Britain: Michelin, 1998), 69.

47. Goethe, *Italian Journey*, 269. Riedesel casts his book as a letter to his teacher, renowned archeologist and art historian Johann Joachim Winckelmann (1717–1768), whose own *Geschichte der Kunst des Altertums* (history of art in antiquity) laid the foundation for modern scientific archeology and pointed German scholars south. For Riedesel see Hélène Tuzet, *Viaggiatori in Sicilia nel XVIII secolo*, 2nd ed. (Palermo: Sellerio Editore, 1995), 37–40.

48. Cited in Michelin, *Sicily*, 69.

49. Goethe, *Italian Journey*, 232.

50. Ibid., 235.

51. Ibid., 285.

52. For Goethe's return from Sicily, see his *Italian Journey*, 284–85.

53. Cited in Michelin, *Sicily*, 68.

54. On this "revolution in gardens," see Rebecca Solnit, *Wanderlust: A History of Walking* (New York: Viking, 2000), 87.

55. Lynn Gamwell, *Exploring the Invisible: Art, Science, and the Spiritual* (Princeton, NJ: Princeton University Press, 2002), 33–45.

56. Erick Hobsbawm, *The Invention of Tradition* (Cambridge: Cambridge University Press, 1983).
57. In his influential work of popular science, *Cosmos* (1845–62), Humboldt asserted that from the time of the Greeks landscape painters fused the landscape as seen and as idealized. And he pointed out that starting with early modern art "the relations between the inner tones of feelings and the delineation of external nature became more intimate," Alexander von Humboldt, *Cosmos: A Sketch of the Physical Description of the Universe,* vol. 2 (Baltimore, MD: Johns Hopkins University Press, 1997), 86–89.
58. Over the course of subsequent decades, in *Voyage de Humboldt et Bonpland* (23 vols., 1805–1834), Humboldt, situated at the center of the scientific world in Paris, sorted, analyzed, and published the findings of his and his colleague A. J. A. Bonpland's epochal expedition. Humboldt offered a lengthy narrative of their journey in his *Aspects of Nature in Different Lands and Different Climates,* vol. 2 (London: Longman, 1849), 3–4. There he established the use of isotherms and studied tropical storms, increased magnetic activity towards the poles, and the relationship between geography and plant distribution, according to *The Columbia Desk Encyclopedia,* 3rd ed. (New York: Columbia University Press, 1963), 984.
59. Description of Humboldt's work from Malcolm Nicolson, "Historical Introduction," Alexander von Humboldt, *Personal Narrative* (New York: Penguin Books, 1995), x.
60. Barzun, *From Dawn to Decadence,* 501.
61. Humboldt, *Aspects of Nature,* 3–4.
62. For a recent assessment of Humboldt's influence, see "Alexander von Humboldt's Natural Legacy and Its Relevance for Today," *Northeastern Naturalist* 8, special issue, no. 1 (2001). Of particular interest in this issue of *Northeastern Naturalist* is Laura Dassow Walls, "'Hero of Knowledge, Be Our Tribute Thine': Alexander von Humboldt in Victorian America," 121–34. There Walls tracks the immense but now largely forgotten influence of Humboldt on nineteenth-century American culture, offering as one proof a list of "Humboldt Place Names" in the United States, 122.
63. Wall also points out that the founder of American environmental thought, George Perkins Marsh—author of *Man and Nature; or, Physical Geography as Modified by Human Action* (1864)—took himself to be a follower of Humboldt and Guyot, "Alexander von Humboldt," 129.
64. For a useful study of Muir and his trip, see Steven Holmes, *The Young John Muir: An Environmental Biography* (Madison: University of Wisconsin Press, 1999), esp. 161–88. The journal Muir kept on his trip was published as *A Thousand-Mile Walk to the Gulf* (Boston: Houghton Mifflin, 1916).
65. In *Mountain Gloom and Mountain Glory,* Marjorie Nicolson explores the transformation of western attitudes towards mountains, which helps account for walkers', hikers', and climbers' ascent into them (New York: Norton, 1959). For an anthology of uses and views of mountains, see A. C. Spectorsky, ed., *The Book of the Mountains* (New York: Appleton-Century-Croft, 1955).
66. For art's transformation of the landscape, see William Vaughan, *Romantic Art* (New York: Oxford University Press, 1978), esp., for the sublime and the picturesque, 32–44; also, see Malcolm Andrews, *The Search for the Picturesque: Landscape Aesthetics and Tourism in Britain, 1760–1800* (Aldershot, England: Scolar Press, 1989).
67. Dan Flores, *The Natural West: Environmental History in the Great Plains and the Rocky Mountains* (Norman: University of Oklahoma Press, 2001), 117.
68. Ibid.
69. Ibid., 157. For an introduction to British mountain climbing, see R. L. G. Irving, *A History of British Mountaineering* (London: B. T. Batsford, 1955); for an anthology, see Michael Ward, ed., *The Mountaineer's Companion* (London: Eyre and Spottiswood, 1966); for a classic, see Edmund Hillary, *High Adventure* (London: Hodder & Stoughton, 1955).
70. Peter Donnelley, "Mountain Climbing," *Encyclopedia of World Sport from Ancient Times to the Present* (Oxford: Oxford University Press, 1999), 262–64.
71. For the story of Mt. Everest, see Solnit, *Wanderlust,* 138–41.
72. Jonas Frykman and Orvar Löfgren, *Culture Builders: A Historical Anthropology of Middle-Class Life* (New Brunswick, NJ: Rutgers University Press, 1987), 52.
73. Alain Corbin, *The Lure of the Sea: The Discovery of the Seaside in the Western World, 1750–1840* (Berkeley: University of California Press, 1994), 53. Corbin attributes three factors to the reevaluation of the sea: "the idyllic vision of the prophets of natural theology; the exaltation of the fruitful shores of Holland . . . ; and the fashion for the classical voyage around the luminous shores of the Bay of Naples."
74. Paul Johnson, *The Birth of the Modern, World Society, 1815–1830* (New York: Harper Perennial, 1991), 754.
75. Ibid., 162, 164. Mark Girouard, *Cities and People* (New Haven, CT: Yale University Press, 1985), 198.

76. Frykmann and Lögren, *Culture Builders,* 51.

77. Orvar Löfgren, *On Holiday: A History of Vacationing* (Berkeley: University of California Press, 1999), 161.

78. Cited in Löfgren, *On Holiday,* 50.

79. Ibid., 50–51.

80. Cited ibid., 50.

81. For useful introductions to tourism, see M. De Lucia, *Viaggi in Europa: Vie di communicazione e turismo nello svi luppoeconomico europeo* (Naples: Edizione Scientifiche Italiane, 2002) and Rudy Koshar, "'What ought to be seen': Tourists' Guidebooks and National Identities in Modern Germany and Modern Europe," *Journal of Contemporary History* 33, no. 3 (July 1998), 323–40.

82. This distinction is made in introduction to Shoumantoff's *In Southern Light* in Ron Strickland, ed., *Shank's Mare: A Compendium of Remarkable Walks* (New York: Paragon House, 1988), 57.

83. Paul Fussell, *Abroad: British Literary Traveling between the Wars* (Oxford: Oxford University Press, 1980), 38, emphasis his.

84. Ibid., 39, emphasis his.

85. Marples, *Shanks's Pony,* 133.

86. With a new residence and a wife in London, Sir Leslie Stephens filled his free time with solitary speed walking around town, while his recreational weekend walking was social and formed the nucleus of a weekend club known as the "Sunday Tramps." Marples, *Shanks's Pony,* 135.

87. Ibid., 113.

88. For an example of the conjunction of art and science and their transformation, see Madelaine Pinault, *The Painter as Naturalist from Dürer to Redouté* (Paris: Flammarion, 1991) and Gamwell, *Exploring the Invisible,* 13–45. Keith Thomas, *Man and the Natural World: Changing Attitudes in England, 1500–1800* (Oxford: Oxford University, Press, 1983). Also, see Harriet Ritvo, *The Animal Estate: The English and Other Creatures in the Victorian Age* (Cambridge, MA: Harvard University Press, 1987), esp. 1–42.

89. An introduction to the walking a geologist does, even under the sea, is found in Alexander Winchell, *Walks and Talks in the Geological Field* (New York: Chautauqua Press, 1886), esp. 9–12, 56–61.

90. Cited in Edward O. Wilson, *Naturalist* (Washington, DC: Island Press, 1994), 28–29.

91. Jeffrey Robinson, *The Walk: Notes on a Romantic Image* (Norman: University of Oklahoma Press, 1989), 17. The origins of the word *pedestrian* are offered in Jarvis, *Romantic Writing,* 1.

92. For a short introduction to the history, literature, and poetry of pathways, see Kim Taplin, *The English Path* (Ipswich: Boydell Press, 1979).

93. For a study ahead of its time on how ancient trails, beacon hills, mounds, and pagan sites fell in straight lines, see Alfred Watkins, *The Old Straight Track: Its Mounds, Beacons, Moats, Sites and Mark Stones* (New York: Ballantine Books, 1973).

94. For an example, the tradition of romantic foot travel in rural Scotland, no longer ever far from the intrusion of automobiles, tourist hotels, and shops, see D. C. Cuthbertson, *Highlands, Highways, and Heroes* (Edinburgh: Robert Grant & Son, 1931). For even Cuthbertson's recognition of the encroachment of the new upon the old, see 115, 121, 152, and 256.

95. For a survey and bibliography of walking writers, see Roger Gilbert, *Walks in the World: Representation and Experience in Modern American Poetry* (Princeton, NJ: Princeton University Press, 1991).

96. Paul Valéry, cited in Gilbert, *Walks in the World,* 19.

NOTES TO CHAPTER 5

1. For a description of early Massachusetts, see Samuel Eliot Morison, *The Maritime History of Massachusetts, 1783–1860* (Boston: Houghton Mifflin, 1961), 8–18.

2. Edward Savage, *Nineteenth-Century Boston Police Records and Recollections for 240 Years* (Boston: Dale, 1873), 15.

3. Ibid., 29–30.

4. Emerson's quotation is found in editors of *Walking Magazine, The Quotable Walker* (New York: R. D. Walking, 2000), 100.

5. The most comprehensive piece I found on the horse and America was an unpublished essay by amateur historian Gordon Hull, "The Horse's Role in Developing This Land." Focused on agriculture, it grasped the importance of the horse as an engine of work and haulage.

6. Dan Flores, *Horizontal Yellow: Nature and History in the New Southwest* (Albuquerque: University of New Mexico Press, 1999), 82.

7. Edward Saveth, "The Walking Purchase," *The Encyclopedia Americana,* vol. 28 (Danbury, CT: Grolier, 1999), 289. Also "Walking Purchase," *The Encyclopedia Britannica,* vol. 12 (Chicago: Encyclopaedia Britannica, 1997), 465.

8. Saveth, "The Walking Purchase," 289.

9. For the mounted warrior's dominance of the Plains, see C. Eliott West, *The Contested Plains: Indians, Gold Seekers, and the Rush to Colorado* (Lawrence: University Press of Kansas, 1998), esp. 49–53.

10. Hal Borand, ed., *The Gentle Art of Walking* (New York: Arno Press/Random House, 1971), vii.

11. Ibid.

12. Cited in Reader's Digest, *Great Adventures That Changed Our World: The World's Great Explorers, Their Triumphs and Tragedies* (Pleasantville, NY: Reader's Digest Association, 1978), 129.

13. David Dary, *The Santa Fe Trail: Its History, Legends, and Lore* (New York: Knopf, 2000), 18.

14. Parkman and La Salle are cited in *Great Adventures That Changed Our World*, 166. For a full accounting of La Salle's epic travels, see Francis Parkman, *La Salle and the Discovery of the Great West* (New York: Modern Library, 1999).

15. Marion Cross, trans., *Father Louis Hennepin's Description of Louisiana: Newly Discovered to the Southwest of New France by Order of the King* (St. Paul: University of Minnesota Press, 1938), 105. Also see Parkman, *La Salle*, 160–61.

16. Val Hart, *The Story of American Roads* (New York: William Sloane Associates, 1950), 41.

17. Ibid., 59.

18. Ibid., 63.

19. Richardson Wright, *Hawkers and Walkers in Early America: Strolling Peddlers, Preachers, Lawyers, Doctors, Players, and Others, from the Beginning to the Civil War* (Philadelphia: J. B. Lippincott, 1927), 27.

20. Robert L. Kincaid, *The Wilderness Road* (Harrogate, TN: Lincoln Memorial University Press, 1955), n.p. The road was eventually abandoned in light of government improvements to the National Road through the Cumberland Gap, which itself started as a path made famous by the young Washington and General Bradock in revolutionary times.

21. Hart, *American Roads*, 29.

22. Ibid., 37.

23. For the expedition, see the convenient edition of Meriwether Lewis and William Clark's complete journals, Elliot Coues, ed., *The History of the Lewis and Clark Expedition*, 3 vols. (New York: Dover Publications, 1893). A recent popular rendering of the expedition is Stephen Ambrose, *Undaunted Courage* (New York: Simon & Schuster, 1996).

24. D. W. Meinig, *The Shaping of America*. Vol. 2, *Continental America, 1800–1867* (New Haven, CT: Yale University Press, 1993), 66–67.

25. Cited in Ambrose, *Undaunted Courage*, 252.

26. Ibid., 253.

27. A useful collection is John Francis McDermott, ed., *Travelers on the Western Frontier* (Urbana: University of Illinois Press, 1970).

28. Garrison Keillor, "Writers Almanac," Minnesota Public Radio, September 26, 2001.

29. Paul Johnson, *The Birth of the Modern* (New York: Harper Perennial, 1991), 278.

30. Ibid.

31. *The Columbia Desk Encyclopedia*, 3rd ed. (New York: Columbia University Press, 1963), 1978.

32. For a single illustrative life of a frontier fur trapper, see Osborn Russell, *Journal of a Trapper: A Hunter's Rambles among the Wild Regions of the Rocky Mountains, 1834–1843* (New York: MSF Books, 1997); also see Robert Glass Cleland, *This Reckless Breed of Men: The Trappers and Fur Traders of the Southwest* (New York: Knopf, 1963).

33. Elliot West, "Empire of Grass," *Wyoming Wildlife*, Dec. 2000, 10.

34. Francis Parkman, who started his trip on the trail in 1846 to improve his health and observe the Indians, left an account of his journey in his classic, *The California and Oregon Trail* (1849), republished in subsequent editions as simply *The Oregon Trail*.

35. Seymour Dunbar, *A History of Travel in America*, vol. 4 (Indianapolis: Bobbs-Merrill, 1915), 1298.

36. For a classic account of the journey along the trail, see Francis Parkman, *The Oregon Trail* (New York: Airmont Publishing, 1964).

37. Ibid., 57.

38. James E. Sherow, "Working of the Geodialectic: High Plains Indians and Their Horses in the Region of the Arkansas River Valley, 1880–1870," *Environmental History Review* 16, no. 2 (1992), 69.

39. For an early depiction of roads, see "Colonial Roads and Wheeled Vehicles," *William and Mary College Quarterly Historical Magazine* 8, no. 1 (July 1899), 37–43.

40. Seymour Dunbar, *A History of Travel in America*, vol. 2 (Indianapolis: Bobbs-Merrill, 1915), 660–61.

41. Hart, *American Roads*, 52–56.

42. Roderick Nash, *Wilderness and the American Mind*, 4th ed. (New Haven, CT: Yale University Press, 2001), 55–57.

43. Ibid., 56.

44. Ibid.

45. The title of the book he wrote describing his travels—*A Pedestrious Tour of Four Thousand Miles through the Western States and Territories during the Winter and Spring of 1818* (Concord, NH, 1819)—raises questions about the true extent of his travels. Even if he traveled uninterruptedly from January 1 to May 30, five months in all, averaging twenty miles a day—an incredible feat in itself—he would have covered only three thousand miles.

46. Ibid., 56.

47. For impressions of New York streets about 1840, see John Tallis, *London Street Views, 1838–1840* (London: Nattali & Maurice, 1969), 19.

48. Ralph Waldo Emerson, "Thoreau," Henry David Thoreau, *Walden and Civil Disobedience* (New York: Norton, 1966), 279.

49. Henry David Thoreau, *Maine Woods* (New York: Library of America, 1985), 660.

50. Van Wyck Brooks, "Thoreau," *Walden and Civil Disobedience,* 293.

51. Robert Richardson, *Thoreau: A Life of the Mind* (Berkeley: University of California Press, 1986), 5.

52. Brooks, "Thoreau," 293.

53. Richardson, *Thoreau,* 135.

54. For Thoreau's continuous and diverse observations, see his *Journals,* in one of a variety of editions. Of particular use is the two-volume Dover edition, which gathers the fourteen volumes from 1837 to 1861: Bradford Torrey and Francis H. Allen, eds., *The Journals of Henry D. Thoreau* (New York: Dover Publications, 1962). Also see *Writings of Henry D. Thoreau: Journal,* ed. Elizabeth Hall Witherell, 5 vols. (Princeton, NJ: Princeton University Press, 1999). For Thoreau's neighbors and their interaction with the environment, see *Men of Concord* (New York: Bonanza Books, 1936).

55. A useful essay on how integral Thoreau's walking was to his thinking, which I discovered after I had written this chapter, is Kent C. Ryden, *Mapping the Invisible Landscape: Folklore, Writing, and Sense of Place* (Iowa City: University of Iowa Press, 1993), 222–23.

56. For a discussion of walking in the case of Thoreau and other modern poets, see Roger Gilbert, *Walks in the World: Representations and Experience in Modern American Poetry* (Princeton, NJ: Princeton University Press, 1991), esp. 45–48.

57. For a useful introduction to Emerson and his relationship to Thoreau, see Robert Richardson, *Emerson: The Mind on Fire* (Berkeley: University of California Press, 1995); for a recent biography of Emerson, see Laura Dassow Walls, *Emerson's Life in Science: The Culture of Truth* (Ithaca, NY: Cornell University Press, 2003); for a useful collection of Emerson's writings, see *Ralph Waldo Emerson, Essays and Lectures* (New York: Library of America, 1983), 461–64, passim.

58. Leo Marx, "The Struggle over Thoreau," *New York Review of Books,* June 24, 1999, 60.

59. For this definition and the Emerson quotation, see Patricia McDonnell, "El Dorado: Marsden Hartley in Imperial Berlin," *Dictated by Life* (Madison: University of Wisconsin Press, 1995), 17–18. More technically, transcendentalism could be understood as a derivative form of German idealism that promised the unification of mind and truth, which the loss of Plato, Aris-

totle, and Christianity had cost them and the analytic epistemologies of John Locke and Immanuel Kant seemed to forbid them.

60. For an introduction to Thoreau on science, see Laura Dassow Walls, ed., *Material Faith: Thoreau on Science* (Boston: Houghton Mifflin, 1999) and her *Seeing New Worlds: Henry David Thoreau and Nineteenth-Century Natural Science* (Madison: University of Wisconsin Press, 1995).

61. For Emerson's botanical interests, see Richardson, *Emerson,* 101, 433, passim; for the emerging English interest in gardens, trees, flowers, and botany, and for how foreign naturalists treated England as their mecca, see Keith Thomas, *Man and the Natural World* (New York: Pantheon Books, 1983), 212–42, 284–85.

62. Lewis Perry, *Boats against the Current: American Culture between Revolution and Modernity, 1820–1860* (New York: Oxford University Press, 1993), 200.

63. Ibid.

64. Ibid., 207.

65. Leo Marx, *Machines in the Garden: Technology and the Pastoral Ideal in America* (New York: Oxford University Press, 1964), 242–43.

66. James McKusick, "From Coleridge to John Muir: The Romantic Origins of Environmentalism," *Wordsworth Circle* 26 (1995), 36–40.

67. For an earlier discussion of Muir, see chapter 4, 117. Richardson, *Emerson,* 514–15. The fact that the aging Emerson, whom he revered, declined his invitation to sleep out under the stars is made proof by overzealous ecologists that Emerson's transcendental aspiration was not matched by a terrestrial commitment.

68. Richardson, *Thoreau,* 138–39, and Marx, *Machine in the Garden,* 242–65.

69. For a treatment of how the American landscape came to be depicted in the first half of the nineteenth century as sublime, see Andrew Wilton and Tim Barringer, *American Sublime: Landscape Painting in the United States, 1820–1880* (Princeton, NJ: Princeton University Press, 2002).

70. Henry David Thoreau, *Cape Cod* (New York: Literary Classics of America, 1985), 851.

71. Richardson, *Thoreau,* 202.

72. On his first and third trips, taken in 1849 and 1855, respectively, he was accompanied by friend and fellow walker, poet William Ellery Channing. He made the second trip in 1850 alone.

73. Leo Marx agrees that Thoreau, like Jefferson, did not wish to choose between society and wilderness, *Machines in the Garden,* 246.

74. Henry David Thoreau, *The Maine Woods* (New York: Literary Classics of America, 1985), 624.

75. Leo Marx, "The Full Thoreau," *New York Review of Books,* July 15, 1999, 43.

76. Thoreau, *The Maine Woods,* 654–55.

77. Ibid., 644–45.

78. Ibid., 645.

79. Henry David Thoreau, "Walking," *The Natural History Essays* (Salt Lake City, UT: Peregrine Smith Books, 1980), 93.

80. Ibid., 94.

81. Ibid., 108–9, 111, 116.

82. Cited in Marx, "The Struggle over Thoreau," 61; also see Marx's subsequent article, "The Full Thoreau," 44–47.

83. For Thoreau's trip to Minnesota, read John Flanagan, *Minnesota's Literary Visitors* (n.p.: Pogo Press, 1993), 77–90, and Henry David Thoreau, "Redwood Falls," *Southwest Minnesota: The Land and the People,* ed. David Pichaske and Joseph Amato (Marshall, MN: Crossings Press, 2000), 49–52.

84. Preface, Thoreau cited in Flanagan, *Literary Visitors,* 82.

85. A useful account of the Sioux Uprising of 1862 is Duane Schultz, *Over the Earth I Come: The Great Sioux Uprising of 1862* (New York: St. Martin's Press, 1992), 259–84.

NOTES TO CHAPTER 6

1. Paul Johnson, *The Birth of the Modern: World Society, 1815–1830* (New York: Harper Perennial, 1991), 702.

2. Mack Smith, *Mazzini* (New Haven, CT: Yale University Press, 1994), 21. Republican Mazzini would have found no ideological advantage in explaining how he economized. He did it by not taking cabs rather than by restraining such practices as drinking wine and beer, smoking cigars, eating out, and employing a maid who bought him breakfast in bed and a boy who cleaned the shoes that he, like everyone else, soiled on his trips across London.

3. Johnson, *The Birth of the Modern,* 703.

4. Ibid., 703.

5. Cited in Daniel Halévy, *La vie de Proudhon, 1809–1847* (Paris: Editions Stock, 1948), 185.

6. Eugen Weber's foreword to Française Gaspar's *Little Town in France* (Cambridge, MA: Harvard University Press, 1995), vii.

7. Eve Curie, *Madame Curie: A Biography* (Garden City, NY: Doubleday, Doral, 1937), 138.

8. Ibid., 139.

9. This note on the death of Paul Curie was furnished by European and French cultural historian Eugen Weber, November 2002.

10. Jonathan Rose, *The Intellectual Life of the British Working Classes* (New Haven, CT: Yale University Press, 2001), esp. 342.

11. *London: Eyewitness Travel Guides* (London: Dorling Kindersley, 2001), 56.

12. Editors of the *Walking Magazine, The Quotable Walker* (New York: Lyons Press, 2000), 216,

13. Rose, *The Intellectual Life,* 342.

14. Ibid., 342. Though it is anachronistic, he offers the following vivid example of how locality defined the horizons of working-class consciousness:

> In search of work, John Clare [at the start of the nineteenth century] once walked just twenty-one miles to Grantham, "and I thought to be sure I was out of the world." Proceeding to Newark-on-Trent "I felt quite lost.... I had never been from home before scarcely farther than out of sight of the steeple I became so ignorant in this far land I could not tell from what quarter the wind blew from and I was even foolish enough to think the sun's course was altered and that it rose in the west and set in the east."

15. Robert Roberts, *The Classic Slum: Salford Life in the First Quarter of the Century* (London: Penguin, 1971), 48–49.

16. William Woodruff, *The Road to Nab End: A Lancashire Childhood* (Chicago: New Amsterdam Books, 2000), 9–11. It became impolite to make a loud sound on Sunday in one's clogs, even though they were the only footwear artisans had to wear, Roberts, *Classic Slum,* 38.

17. Two semi-autobiographical memoirs of the end of the foot-based and insulated rural world are Emile Guillaumin, *Life of a Simple Man* (Hanover, NH: University Press of New England, 1983), and Pierre Jakez Hélias, *The Horse of Pride* (New Haven, CT: Yale University Press, 1978). A recent book that treats Dutch village life as a casualty of the car is Geert Mak, *Jorwerd: The Death of the Village in Late-Twentieth-Century Europe* (London: Harvill Press, 2000).

18. Cited in Paul Langford, *Englishness Identified: Manners and Character, 1650–1850* (Oxford: Oxford University Press, 2000), 36, 37.

19. Cited ibid., 37.

20. Ibid.

21. Ibid., 38.

22. Ibid.

23. Cited ibid., 39.

24. Ibid., 38. London's famed flagstones, the envy of Parisians, dated, Langford notes, from the paving commissions of the 1760s.

25. Cited in ibid., 38. Linking shopping and

promenading, the word *mall* is derived, according to *The New Shorter Oxford Dictionary*, from The Mall, a walk bordered by trees in St. James's Park, London. In turn, joining at its origin pedestrian play and walking, *mall* referred to an alley for a game (Oxford: Oxford University Press, 1994), 1677.

26. Mark Girouard, *Cities and People* (New Haven, CT: Yale University Press, 1985), 191.

27. Ibid., 199–200.

28. Ibid., 191–92.

29. Walter Besant, "London Streets," *London in the Eighteenth Century* (New York: Macmillan, 1903), 88–136.

30. Théophile Gautier, *Études philosophiques: Paris et les Parisiens au XIXe siècle* (Paris, 1856), 26.

31. Besant, "London Streets," 128.

32. Johnson, *The Birth of the Modern*, 280.

33. Rosamond Bayne-Powell, *Eighteenth-Century London Life* (New York: Dutton, 1938), 117.

34. Liza Picard, *Dr. Johnson's London, 1740–1770* (London: Phoenix Press, 2000), 102.

35. Besant, "London Streets," 340.

36. Alison Adburgham, *Shops and Shopping, 1800–1914* (London: Allen & Unwin, 1964), 32; for the history of shoemaking crafts and political action, see Paul Glennie-Smith, "Shoes," *Encyclopedia Britannica*, vol. 20 (Chicago: Encyclopedia Britannica, 1970), 435–38, Eric Hobsbawm and John Scott, "Political Shoemakers," *Workers' Worlds of Labor* (New York: Pantheon Books, 1984), 103–30.

37. Picard, *Dr. Johnson's London,* 31, 75–76, and Besant, "London Streets," 270–71.

38. Picard, *Dr. Johnson's London,* 129–30, and Besant, "London Streets," 350–51, passim.

39. For illustrations of eighteenth- and nineteenth-century pedestrianism, see Hugh Phillips, *Mid-Georgian London: A Topographical and Social Survey of Central and Western London about 1750* (London: Collins, 1964), 33–35, 4–41, 51–52, 70, 81, 86, passim.

40. Francis Sheppard, *London: A History* (Oxford: Oxford University Press, 1998), 215.

41. In *The Making of the English Landscape*, W. G. Hoskins described the scale of the work of canal and railroad: "Nothing like their earthworks had been seen since the earlier Iron Age of pre-Roman times" (London: Penguin Books, 1955), 256–57. For an overview of the transport revolution in England, see Philip Bagwell, *The Transport Revolution from 1770* (New York: Barnes & Noble, 1974).

42. Lewis Mumford, *The Culture of Cities* (New York: Harcourt Brace Janovich, 1970), 227. For another vision of the industrial city, see Friedrich Engels, *The Conditions of the Working Class in England* [1845] (New York: Penguin Books, 1987).

43. Ibid., 227.

44. M. G. Lay, *Ways of the World: A History of the World's Roads and of the Vehicles That Used Them* (New Brunswick, NJ: Rutgers University Press, 1992), 303.

45. Ibid., 303. For an interesting essay on the changing faces of walking London, see Betsy Blackmar, "Rewalking the 'Walking City': Housing and Property Relations in New York City, 1780–1840," *Material Life in America, 1600–1860*, ed. Robert Blair St. George (Boston: Northeastern University Press, 1988), 371–84.

46. According to Robert Fishman, the suburb—an eighteenth-century London creation—did not simply evolve from the outlying districts. "[It] required a total transformation of urban values: not only a reversal in the meaning of core and periphery, but a separation of work and family life and the creation of new forms of urban space that would be both class-segregated and wholly residential," *Bourgeois Utopia: The Rise and Fall of Suburbia* (New York: Basic Books, 1987), 8.

47. For suggestive numbers on the decline of historic centers in the eighteenth and nineteenth centuries, see Lay, *Ways of the World*, 302–3.

48. Peter Ackroyd, "Silence Is Golden," in his *London: The Biography* (London: Vintage, 2001), 81–85.

49. Ralph Turvey, "Street Mud, Dust and Noise," *London Journal* 21, no. 2 (1996), 136.

50. Along with canes (British "walking sticks"), umbrellas occasioned a new business in the 1830s. It still survives on New Oxford Street, John Richardson, *The Annals of London: A Year-by-Year Record of a Thousand Years of History* (Berkeley: University of California Press, 2000), 255. Also see T. S. Crawford, *A History of the Umbrella* (New York: Taplinger, 1970), 179–200.

51. Charles Dickens, *Bleak House* (Garden City, NY: Literary Guild of America, 1953), 1.

52. In chapter 47 of *London*, "A Foggy Day," Ackroyd examines the place of fog in the city's history, 431–38.

53. Ackroyd, *London,* 433.

54. Cited in Richardson, *Annals of London,* 240.

55. "In 1873," Ackroyd writes in *London,* "there were seven hundred 'extra' deaths, nineteen of them the result of pedestrians walking into the Thames, the docks, or [the remaining] canals," 432. He explains, "The fog sometimes came and went rapidly, their smoke and gloom blown across the streets of the cities by the prevailing winds, but often they lingered for days with sun briefly seen through the yellow mist. The worst decade for fogs was the 1880s; the worst month was always November," 432. He goes on,

"Against London's fog sounds barely penetrated; its new gas light faintly radiated. In its banks crime burrowed and fomented," 433. Fog veiled Sherlock Holmes's cases, and in it Jack the Ripper stalked, 433–35. In the middle decades of the twentieth century—showing that everything, even fog, has a history—fog was transmogrified into asphyxiating and lethal smog.

56. For London's street people, see Ackroyd, *London,* 504–5, passim. For a discussion of this pervasive fear of dying in a charitable home for the poor, see Ruth Richardson, *Death, Dissection, and the Destitute* (New York: Penguin, 1988), 104, 277–79, passim.

57. Ackroyd, *London,* 76; also see Ralph Turvey, "Street Mud, Dust and Noise," 137–40. To the same end, the city put booties on horses' hooves. The eventual silencing of the horses' hooves led a nostalgic Cockney lady to remark, "I shall miss the 'orses' feet at night, somethin' shockin', they *were sech comp'ny like.*" Ackroyd, *London,* 76.

58. Ibid., 166–67.

59. This information derived from a display sign "Street Life" in the Museum of London, December 2001.

60. For the nature of the London crowds, see chapter 43, "Mobocracy," Ackroyd, *London,* 389–99. In his historical novel, *A Conspiracy of Paper* (New York: Abacus, 2000), David List comments on the spontaneity of the crowd, see esp. 269–70.

61. In *A Conspiracy of Paper,* David List enumerated the skills a London night walker needed for survival, before the town was truly illuminated at the end of the nineteenth century, see esp. 161–62, also 332–33.

62. Michael Ball and David Sunderland, *An Economic History of London, 1800–1914* (London: Routledge, 2001), 228.

63. Ibid., 229.

64. These adapted figures, with accompanying charts and explanation, were taken from appendixes 1 and 2, Sheppard, *London,* 365, 366.

65. Theo Barker, *Moving Millions: A Pictorial History of London Transport* (London: London Transport Museum, 1990), xx. The title of this section is adopted from Barker's text, which itself is dependent on T. C. Barker and Michael Robbins, *History of London Transport,* 2 vols. (London: Allen & Unwin, 1975).

66. Sheppard, *London,* 272.

67. John Yorath and the London Transport Museum Education Service, "The First Underground and the Metropolitan Railway" (London: London Transport Museum, n.d.), 2; and "The First Underground," Information Sheet 2" (London: London Transport Museum, 1994), 2.

68. "The Tube Story," Information Sheet 4 (London: London Transport Museum, 1994), 1. For a brief survey of other subway systems, see Edward Allen Course, "Subway (Underground Railway)," *Encyclopaedia Britannica,* vol. 21 (Chicago: Encyclopedia Britannica, 1970), 347–49.

69. Yorath, "Underground and the Metropolitan Railway," 3.

70. Roy Porter, *London: A Social History* (Cambridge, MA: Harvard University Press, 1994), 227.

71. Sheppard, *London,* 270.

72. In 1890 there were five "million cities," London, Paris, Berlin, Vienna, and Moscow; in 1940 there were fourteen in Europe and eleven in the United States, Porter, *London,* 306. Mumford, *The Culture of Cities,* 225.

73. "The Growth of London," Information Sheet 8 (London: London Transport Museum, 1994), 1.

74. "The Birth of the Public Transport," Information Sheet 1 (London: London Transport Museum, 1994), 4. For a survey of the rise of urban mass transport in Europe, see John P. McKay, *Trams and Trolleys* (Princeton, NJ: Princeton University Press, 1976); for a survey of America transport, see John H. White, *Horsecars, Cable Cars and Omnibuses* (New York: Dover Publications, 1974).

75. Porter, *London,* 227.

76. For a fine collection of essays, supplemented by many telling photographs, see George R. Sims, *Living London: Its Work and Its Play, Its Humour and Its Pathos, Its Sights and Scenes,* 2 vols. (London: Cassell and Company, 1903).

77. Barker, *Moving Millions,* 52.

78. Ibid., 3. Also see for short introductions to London and world urban transport, Sheppard, *London,* 264–73, and Lay, *Ways of the World,* 305–8.

79. Barker, *Moving Millions,* 71.

80. In the first half of the century, private corporations spanned the Thames with three bridges. Steamboats, which began to ply the Thames in 1815, had small profits and comparatively few passengers. Many streets were macadamized. The city widened Holborn and Fleet Streets, destroying the latter's market. Turnpike companies opened several new roads into town in the north. In 1829, George Shillibeer introduced the Parisian omnibus to London, which by the 1840s successfully displaced its competition, the short-distance stagecoach in the outskirts. Eventually carrying tens of millions of passengers annually, it became endearingly popular with the clerks, shopkeepers, and civil servants. Nevertheless, the omnibus did not quite live up to its name. Its fares were prohibitive to the working classes, according to Stephen Inwood, *A History of London* (New York: Macmillan, 2000), 546–47. Up to midcentury, the story of the train's success in London, which started in 1836, also was limited. Although the train did not penetrate the inner city, it vanquished the stagecoach on long runs as the omnibus had won out on short runs. Its principal stations—Euston (1837), Paddington (1838), and King's Cross (1852)—handled longer-distance traffic. Only London Bridge and Fenchurch delivered heavy short-distance traffic, Inwood, *London,* 547. Although by 1854 trains annually carried multiple millions of passengers to the city's perimeter, daily they delivered to their jobs only a few thousand workers, who would have had to sacrifice, it is estimated, as much as a sixth of their day's wages to ride either it or the omnibus daily, Barker, *Moving Millions,* 23. "In 1854," Inwood wrote, "fewer than 10,000 commuters arrived in the city by train, around 15,000 by steamboat, and at most 15,000 by omnibus, about 200,000 came on foot," Inwood, *London,* 556. In sum, by midcentury, 1850 transit and city planning had not turned congestion into flowing traffic. To the contrary, congestion—depicted at its extremes by Gustave Doré in "A City Thoroughfare" and "Ludgate Hill"—had only been compounded. Each new train station and dock required more horses, carts, drays, and deliverymen. The omnibus system did its share in slowing traffic in London's sclerotic arteries by putting approximately thirteen hundred lumbering vehicles on the road. The vehicles required thirteen thousand horses. Similarly, two- and four-wheeled cabs increased in number from twenty-five hundred in 1845 to sixty-eight hundred in 1863 to eleven thousand in 1888. This added to the invasion of London by horses, Inwood, *London* 548. Pedestrians, as photographs and early movies show, scurried perilously between walking horses and the carts, carriages, buses, and trams they pulled. London truly was a city of dangers and strangers.

81. "The word *slum,* first used in the 1820s, has its origins in the old provincial world *slump* meaning 'wet mire,'" which describes "the dreadful state of [contemporary] streets and courtyards on these undrained sites," Hoskins, *English Landscape,* 225.

82. Sheppard, *London,* 271. Slum clearance in the city and wetland drainage in the countryside can be understood as parallel activities having their source in the same contemporary drive to transform the human landscape.

83. Charles Dickens, *Dombey and Son* (1848), cited in Lynda Nead, *Victorian Babylon: People,* *Streets and Images in Nineteenth-Century London* (New Haven, CT: Yale University Press, 2000), 34–35.

84. Sheppard, *London,* 271.

85. Cited in Inwood, *London,* 504.

86. Sheppard offered these statistics from 1906, *London,* 272.

87. For the quotation and a discussion of the new era of illumination, see Joseph A. Amato, *Dust* (Berkeley: University of California Press, 2000), 84–87, and Wolfgang Schivelbusch, *Disenchanted Night: The Industrialization of Light* (Berkeley: University of California Press, 1998), 178. For the electrification of the United States and the profound transformation it wrought on nightlife at the end of the nineteenth century, see David Nasaw, "It Begins with the Lights: Electrification and the Rise of Public Entertainment," *On the Edge of Your Seat,* ed. Patricia McDonnell (New Haven, CT: Yale University Press, 2002), 45–60.

88. For the history of spreading wealth and well-being, see John Burnett, *Plenty and Want: A Social History of Diet in England from 1815 to the Present* (London: Harmondsworth, 1966); for the United States, see Edgar Martin, *The Standard of Living in 1860* (Chicago: University of Chicago Press, 1942). For contemporary shoppers, see Dorothy Davis, *A History of Shopping* (London: Routledge & Kegan Paul, 1966) and Alison Adburgham, *Shops and Shopping, 1800–1914* (London: Allen and Unwin, 1964).

89. Richardson, *Annals of London,* 244.

90. Inwood, *A History of London,* 651; also see whole section on "Department Stores," 651–54.

91. Ibid., 652–53, Davis, *A History of Shopping,* 278.

92. Inwood, *A History of London,* 653.

93. Ibid., 654.

94. For Paxton's proposal and an introduction to London city planning, see the introduction and part 1, "Mapping Movement," Nead, *Victorian Babylon,* 1–12, 27–28, 13–82.

95. For the distinction between two cities, one formed by an abstract view from on high and the other derived from a concrete encounter on foot, see Michel de Certeau, "Walking in the City," *The Cultural Studies Reader,* ed. Simon During (London: Routledge, 1993), 151–60.

96. Galleries and arcades become synonyms in the nineteenth century for describing new structures that house a collection of shops that predate the department store much as small neighborhood malls of the middle of the twentieth century predate the megamalls of the closing decades of the century.

97. Part of this description comes from Leon

Brody, review of the recent publication of Walter Benjamin's *Arcades Project* (Cambridge, MA: Belknap, 1999), in the *Library Journal,* January 2000, 118.

98. Mark Kingwell, "Arcadian Adventures: Walter Benjamin, the Connoisseur of Everyday Life," review of *The Arcades Project* (see n. 97), *Harper's Magazine,* March 2000, 72.

99. Ideas in this paragraph were derived from Howard Eiland and Kevin McLaughlin, "Translators' Foreword" to Benjamin, *Arcades Project,* 10.

100. Girouard, *Cities and People,* 210.

101. On St. Petersburg's streets, Dostoevsky's *Underground Man,* jostled as urban pedestrians commonly were, took it as an intolerable insult when a military officer set him aside as if he were a nothing. On the same streets, the fate of Raskolnikov, the protagonist of *Crime and Punishment,* played out. A dream of the brutal slaughter of a horse forewarned him of the evil inherent in his planned murder of a pawnbroker. After the murder Raskolnikov encountered the young streetwalker, Sonia, who supports her family, even her alcoholic father, who eventually suffers the common fate of being hit and killed by a carriage. Sonia encourages the proud Raskolnikov to make a confession, which he does. At the crossroads he bends down and kisses the earth, asking it for forgiveness.

102. Fyodor Dostoevksy, *Winter Notes on Summer Impressions* (1863), cited in Rick Allen, *The Moving Pageant: A Literary Sourcebook of London Street-Life, 1700–1914* (London: Routledge. 1998), 145–46, emphasis mine.

103. Hippolyte Taine, *Taine's Notes on England* [1872] (Fair Lawn, NJ: Essential Books, 1958), 17, 18, 29, 33, and 187, emphasis mine.

104. For Dickens's London, see "London," *Oxford Reader's Companion to Dickens,* ed. Paul Schlicke (Oxford: Oxford University Press, 1999), 348–64. For Dickens's two Londons, see Raymond Williams, *The Country and the City* (Frogmore, England: Paladin, 1975), 189–201.

105. Dickens's works are filled with night scenes. Of particular interest is his essay "Night Walks," *Art of Walking,* ed. Edward Valentine (New York: Loring & Mussey, 1934), 43–56, originally found in various editions of Dickens's *The Uncommercial Traveller* (London: Chapman & Hall, 1898). A more recent example of London night walking is Stephen Graham, *London Nights* (New York: Doran, 1926), which includes an evening visit to social center Toynbee Hall. For an introduction to other nightwalkers, see "Night Walks," Jeffrey Robinson, *The Walk: Notes on a Romantic Image* (Norman: University of Oklahoma Press, 1989), 77–87.

106. Charles Dickens, *The Old Curiosity Shop* [1841] (New York: Penguin Books, 1985), 43.

107. *Nicholas Nickleby* [1839], cited in Allen, *The Moving Pageant,* 105–6.

108. Charles Dickens, "A Nightly Scene in London," *Household Words* (January 26, 1856), 136, available in *Dickens: Selected Journalism* (London: Penguin, 1997).

109. Charles Dickens, *Oliver Twist* [serialized 1835–1837] (New York: Harper & Row, 1965), 54, 55.

110. Ibid., 59.

NOTES TO CHAPTER 7

1. For a sense of the immensity of nineteenth-century building and construction, see T. K. Derry and Trevor I. Williams, *A Short History of Technology: From the Earliest Times to A.D. 1900* (New York: Dover Publications, 1960). Also see Wolfgang Schivelbusch, *The Railway Journey* (Berkeley: University of California Press, 1986), esp. 33–44, and David Nye, *American Technological Sublime* (Cambridge, MA: MIT Press, 1994).

2. For a short overview of the "The Great Cleanup," see my chapter of that title in *Dust: A History of the Small and the Invisible* (Berkeley: University of California Press, 2000), 67–91. For an overview of the urban environment in the United States, see Martin Melosi, *The Sanitary City: Urban Infrastructure in America from Colonial Times to the Present* (Baltimore, MD: Johns Hopkins University Press, 2000), esp. 58–102.

3. Amato, *Dust,* 82–83. For studies of wastes, toilets, and bathrooms, see Lawrence Wright, *Clean and Decent: The Fascinating History of the Bathroom and the Water Closet* (London: Routledge & Kegan Paul, 1960), Reginald Reynolds, *Cleanliness and Godliness* (New York: Harcourt, Brace, 1976), J. J. Priestly, "Civilization, Water and Wastes," *Chemistry and History,* March 22, 1968, 355–63, and, more recently ,Julie Horan, *The Porcelain God: A Social History of the Toilet* (Secaucus, NJ: Carol Publishing Group, 1996), and Lucinda Lambton, *Temples of Convenience and Chambers of Delight* (New York: St. Martin's Press, 1995).

4. Asa Briggs, *Victorian Cities* (Berkeley: University of California Press, 1993), 16–17.

5. Wolfgang Schivelbusch offers an overview in *Disenchanted Night: The Industrialization of Light in the Nineteenth Century* (Berkeley: University of California Press, 1988).

6. A good essay on lighting and night life is David Nasaw's "It Begins with the Lights: Electrification and the Rise of Public Entertainment," *On the Edge of Your Seat: Popular Theater* and Film in Early Twentieth Century American Life, ed. Patricia McDonnell (New Haven, CT: Yale University Press, 2002), 45–60.

7. Cited in Donald Miller, *City of the Century: The Epic of Chicago and the Making of America* (New York: Simon & Schuster, 1996), 263.

8. For a useful survey of the place of the horse in European history, see F. M. L. Thompson, ed., *Horses in European Economic History* (Reading: British Agricultural History Society, 1983), 31–112. Other than human legs themselves the principle engine of work and pleasure, the horse still clogged the streets and killed and injured pedestrians in stunning numbers, yet, as the mounted steed, it served as the seat for the glorious commemorative statuary of the prewar leader. With 3.5 million in all of Britain and thirty million in the United States, the noisy and dung-making horse dominated the European and American city and countryside. For a note on cleaning of horse manure on the nineteenth-century streets of London, except on Sunday, see Ralph Turvey, "Street Mud, Dust and Noise," *London Journal* 21, no. 2 (1996), esp. 143. For a lengthy discussion of horse pollution and waste in the contemporary United States, see Joel Tarr, *The Search for the Ultimate Sink: Urban Pollution in Historical Perspective* (Akron, OH: University of Akron Press, 1996), 323–34.

9. For the American drive to clean itself up at home and on the streets, see Suellen Hoy, *Chasing Dirt: The American Pursuit of Cleanliness* (New York: Oxford University Press, 1995), esp. 59–71. For a general history of the articulation of the sanitary ideal, its passage from England to the United States, and its American development from colonial times to the present, see Martin Melosi, *The Sanitary City* (Baltimore, MD: Johns Hopkins University Press, 2000). For a diverse treatment of the American treatment of wastes, with a special focus on Pittsburg, see Tarr, *Search for the Ultimate Sink.*

10. For London's reaction to the pollution of the Thames in 1858 and Sir Joseph Bazalgette's building of the city's sewage system, see Stephen Halliday, *The Great Stink of London: Sir Joseph Bazalgette and the Cleansing of the Victorian Metropolis* (London: Sutton Publishing, 1999). For a general olfactory history of the nineteenth century, see Alain Corbin, *The Foul and the Fragrant: Order and French Social Imagination* (Cambridge, MA: Harvard University Press, 1986). Germ theory, which took hold in the closing decades of the century, directed public health in search of the small and invisible elements of the environment, Amato, *Dust,* 97–108.

11. For the nature of identity in a preliterate society, see Natalie Davis, *The Return of Martin Guerre* (Cambridge, MA: Harvard University Press, 1983). She also offers many insights into the nature of the early modern city in *Society and Culture in Early Modern France* (Stanford, CA: Stanford University Press, 1975).

12. For two suggestive works on the crowd in history, see George Rudé, *Ideology and Popular Protest* (New York: Pantheon Books, 1980) and E. P. Thompson's "The Moral Economy of the English Crowd of the Eighteenth Century," *Past and Present* 50 (May 1971), 605–29.

13. For one recent work showing how marching in parades, participating in celebrations, and wearing clothes and hats provided ordinary people with political identities and added volatility to street politics, see Simon Newman, *Parades and Politics of the Street: Festive Culture in the Early American Republic* (Philadelphia: University of Pennsylvania Press, 1997).

14. Simon Schama, *Fate of the Empire, 1776–2000,* vol. 3 of *History of Britain* (New York: Hyperion, 2002), 186–90.

15. For the role of execution in public drama, see Pieter Spierenburg, *The Spectacle of Suffering: Executions and the Evolution of Repression: From a Preindustrial Metropolis to the European Experience* (Cambridge, MA: Cambridge University Press, 1984).

16. David Garrioch, *The Making of Revolutionary Paris* (Berkeley: University of California Press, 2002). For his description of the patterns of Parisian life and the quality of its street life in 1700, see esp. 15–44.

17. Ibid., 1. One contemporary estimate counted Paris to have 810 streets and 23,019 houses.

18. Mark Girouard, *Cities and People* (New York: Hyperion, 1985), 179.

19. Harold Clunn, *The Face of Paris* (London: Spring Books, 1958), 3.

20. Across urban Europe, the influence of the idea-filled middle class taught simple folks to convert their riots into *jacqueries* whose primitive ideas and rampage swept the countryside like locusts, George Rudé, *The Crowd in History, 1730–1848* (New York: John Wiley & Sons, 1964), 93.

21. Garrioch, *Making of Revolutionary Paris,* 258.

22. Rudé, *The Crowd in History,* 99–100.

23. John Dalberg-Acton, *Lectures on the French Revolution* (Indianapolis, IN: Liberty Fund, 2000), 122.

24. Ibid.

25. For the pervasiveness of violence and near infinite suspicion of it, see Richard Cobb, *The Police and the People: French Popular Protest* (London: Oxford University Press, 1970), esp. 86–87.

26. For the growth of urban France, see Pierre

Sorlin, "French Society, 1840–1914: The Big Cities," *Urbanization of European Society in the Nineteenth Century,* ed. Andrew Lees and Lynn Lees (Lexington, MA: Heath, 1976), 16–27.

27. Bernard Marchand, *Paris, Histoire d'une ville (XIXe XXe siècle)* (Paris: Édition du Scuil, 1993).

28. Cited ibid., 24.

29. Ibid., 24, 25.

30. Ibid., 27.

31. Contemporary French writers Balzac, Hugo, and Sue explored the underside of Parisian life in detail, as discussed by Andrew Lees, *Cities Perceived: Urban Society in European and American Thought, 1820–1940* (New York: Columbia University Press, 1985), esp. 74–76.

32. Louis Chevalier, *Laboring Classes and Dangerous Classes in the First Half of the Nineteenth Century* (New York: Howard Fertig, 1973), 2.

33. William Langer, ed., *An Encyclopedia of World History* (Cambridge, MA: Houghton Mifflin, 1948), 630.

34. These ideas are taken from Georges Laronze, *Le Baron Haussmann* (Paris, 1932), 137–38, cited in Walter Benjamin, *The Arcades Project* (Cambridge, MA: Harvard University Press, 1999), 128.

35. Eugen Weber, *A Modern History of Europe* (New York: Norton, 1971), 793.

36. For a discussion of similar military motives underlying the building of the Ringstrasse, see Carl Schorske, *Fin-de-Siècle Vienna: Politics and Culture* (New York: Random House, 1981), esp. 25–35.

37. Donald Reid, *Paris Sewers and Sewermen: Realities and Representations* (Cambridge, MA: Harvard University Press, 1991), 30.

38. Weber, *A Modern History,* 793.

39. Schivelbusch, *The Railway,* 188. According to Paul Hohenberg and Lynn Hollen Lees, "Haussmann's plan involved three main elements: 1) decongesting the center, essentially by clearing the Île de la Cité and its bridgeheads; 2) linking the center to the inner ring of boulevards and nearby railway terminals; and 3) laying out main thoroughfares and intersections in the outer districts within the 1840s ring of fortification," *The Making of Urban Europe, 1000–1950* (Cambridge, MA: Harvard University Press, 1985), 327–28.

40. John Colson, *Paris, des origines à nos jours* (Paris: Editions Hervas, 1998).

41. Jean-Marc Léri, *History of Paris: Illustrated by the Collections of the Carnavelet Museum* (Paris: Nuit et Jour, 1994), 68–69. The "*bateau mouche*"—the riverboat service—ferried more than forty million people in 1900, while the tramway services reached seven hundred million tickets in 1930, the year it was eliminated, ibid., 69.

42. For a useful volume of extracts of literary attempts to capture the array of people and sensual impressions of the streets of nineteenth-century Paris, see Gilles Durieux, *Le roman de Paris à travers les siècles et la littérature* (Paris: Albin Michel, 2000), csp., for sounds, 203–6.

43. This is the argument of Edward Shorter and Michael Tilly, *Strikes in France: 1830–1968* (Cambridge: Cambridge University Press, 1974), esp. 343–46.

44. Langer, ed., *An Encyclopedia of World History,* 636–37.

45. Maps of France for the period 1880 to 1900 reveal the popular use of four names, indicating the advent of the new Republican era. There was *Thiers,* president of the new republic; *Gambetta,* who led the protracted war and resistance against the triumphant Germans; *Hugo,* who died in 1885; and the word *République* itself, Daniel Milo, "Street Names," *Traditions,* vol. 2 of *Realms of Memory* (New York: Columbia University Press, 1997), 363–90.

46. Maurice Agulhon, "Paris: A Traversal from East to West," *Symbols,* vol. 3 of *Realms of Memory* (New York: Columbia University Press, 1997), 541.

47. Pierre Birnbaum, *Grégoire, Dreyfus, Drancy and the Rue Copernic: Jews at the Heart of French History,* vol. 1 of *Realms of Memory* (New York: Columbia University Press, 1997), 406–9.

48. Howard Payne, *The Police State of Louis Napoléon Bonaparte, 1851–1860* (Seattle: University of Washington Press, 1966).

49. John P. McKay, *Trams and Trolleys: The Rise of Urban Mass Transport in Europe* (Princeton, NJ: Princeton University Press, 1976), 157–62, passim, and Nicholas Papayanis, "The Development of the Paris Cab Trade," *Journal of Transport History* 8, no. 1 (March 1987), 52–65.

50. McKay, *Tramways and Trolleys,* 240. France, in 1850 the most populous state in Europe next to Russia, with thirty-six million, only added three million people in the next fifty years, leaving it considerably behind Germany and roughly equal to Great Britain without Ireland, Weber, *A Modern History,* 752. Between 1870 and 1910, Great Britain grew from 26.1 million to 40.8 million, Germany went from 40.8 million to 64.9 million, and Russia, from 85.5 million to 139 million, Edward Tannenbaum, *1900: The Generation before the Great War* (Garden City, NY: Anchor Press/Doubleday, 1976), 92.

51. Impressionism, as an aesthetic, bathed the world in light. Each season beams forth. Fields burst with colorful flowers and grasses. Starry streams pour down from darkened heavens. Water scintillates and sparkles. Colorfully dressed women carry bright umbrellas and stroll paths strewn with flowers. "The impressionist sees [light] bathing everything not in dead whiteness, but in a thousand conflicting vibrations, in rich prismatic decompositions of colour," according to contemporary critic Jules Laforgue, cited in T. J. Clark, *The Painting of Modern Life: Paris in the Art of Manet and His Followers* (Princeton, NJ: Princeton University Press, 1984), 16. Even dark, grimy train stations and the interiors of cafes show color. The street in Camille Pissaro's *Street in Pontoise* (*Rue de Gisors*), 1868, is swept clean of manure and grime, literally letting the light reflect and shine. In Gustave Caillebote's *Paris, Rainy Weather* (1877), streets and squares are open, people have an abundance of room to express their individuality, and buildings, walls, lamp posts, and cobblestones reflect light and color. The impressionists' world was picturesque. It rested on the taming of space. Improved transportation permitted artists to hop in and out of town to fill their colorful palettes.

52. Stefan Zweig, *The World of Yesterday* (Lincoln: University of Nebraska Press, 1964), 3.

53. Jonas Frykman and Orvar Löfgren, *Culture Builders: A Historical Anthropology of Middle-Class Life* (New Brunswick, NJ: Rutgers University Press, 1987), 220.

54. Ibid., 220, 221–61.

55. Ibid., 187.

56. Eugen Weber, *France, Fin du Siècle* (Cambridge, MA: Harvard University Press, 1986), 68. Frykman and Löfgren provide one discussion on the spread of punctuality in *Culture Builders,* 13–41.

57. For contemporary thinkers' and artists' reactions to new technologies of speed, accelerated senses of time and diminished perceptions of distance and space, see Stephen Kern, *The Culture of Time and Space* (London: Weidenfeld & Nicolson, 1983).

58. Weber, *France, Fin du Siècle,* 60–61.

59. Ibid., 58; and his "Commonplaces: History, Literature, and the Invisible," *Stanford French Review* 4 (Winter 1980), 327–29. For those with curiosity, there is also Horan, *The Porcelain God,* and Lambton, *Temples of Convenience and Chambers of Delight.*

60. Weber, *France, Fin du Siècle,* 58.

61. Both notion of and data for France are taken from Weber, *France, Fin du Siècle,* 51.

62. Frykman and Löfgren, *Culture Builders,* 174–220.

63. Weber, *France, Fin du Siècle,* 53.

64. Frykman and Löfgren, *Culture Builders,* 55.

65. For an essay suggesting that "the interrelation of country and town is more relevant than their antagonism," see Eugen Weber, "And Man Made the Town," *American Scholar* 58, no. 1 (Winter 1988–89), 79–96. For emerging views of the countryside, see Frykman and Löfgren, *Culture Builders,* esp. 42–87.

NOTES TO CHAPTER 8

1. For a study of Nietzsche's self-searching wanderings, see David Krell and Donald Bates, *The Good European: Nietzsche's Work Sites in Word and Image* (Chicago: University of Chicago Press, 1997).

2. Jonathan Bousfield and Robert Humphreys, *The Rough Guide to Austria* (London: Rough Guides, 2001), 128.

3. Rebecca Solnit, *Wanderlust: A History of Walking* (New York: Viking, 1999), 123–24.

4. Ibid., 136. Trevelyan's 1913 essay on walking appeared in his *Clio, a Muse, and Other Essays* (Freeport, NY: Books for Libraries Press, 1968.) The particular phrase "his legs were his doctors" is cited in Jeffrey Robinson, *The Walk: Notes on a Romantic Age* (Norman: University of Oklahoma Press, 1989), 12. Walking as the way to health formed a genre of writing, represented by Bernard Macfadden, *The Walking Cure: Pep and Power from Walking—How to Cure Disease by Walking* (New York: Macfadden Publications, 1925).

5. For a guide to writings in English and short biographies of eighteenth-, nineteenth-, and twentieth-century women travelers, sojourners, missionaries, explorers, naturalists, anthropologists, and mountain climbers, see Jane Robison, *Wayward Women: A Guide to Women Travelers* (Oxford: Oxford University Press, 1990).

6. Dennis Brailsford, *Sport and Society: Elizabeth to Anne* (London: Routledge & Kegan Paul, 1969), 251.

7. A. H. Sidgwick, *Walking Essays* (London: Edward Arnold, 1912).

8. Ibid., 136.

9. R. N. Naylor and J. N. Naylor, *From John O'-Groat's to Land's End; or 1372 Miles on Foot* (London: Caxton Publishing, 1916).

10. Independent book collector and walker, Adam Sowan of Reading, England, has an extensive bibliography of walking literature. It includes 425 books, a bibliography of which he furnished me in December 2001. He supplemented his bibliography with comments on particular books, in a January 2002 letter. With a handful of items from the 1780s and 1790s and one from 1620, he recorded from three to five in the early decades of the nineteenth century until the 1860s and 1870s, which respectively produces ten and eleven books. In the first decades of the twentieth century, the number increases appreciably from eighteen in 1910 to twenty-eight in 1920 to fifty in 1930. Descending to twenty-one, twenty-five, twenty-two, and thirty-two in the four subsequent decades, the number of walking books doubled to sixty in the 1980 and rose to seventy-two in 1990. In a March 18, 2002, letter, he sent me additional insightful comments on the history of walking literature.

11. Robert Louis Stevenson does this in his charming *Travels with a Donkey* (New York: Current Literature Publishing Company, 1913).

12. Hilaire Belloc, *The Path to Rome* (1902), cited in *Shank's Mare,* ed. Ron Strickland (New York: Paragon House, 1988), 235.

13. Winston Churchill, "On Safari," *Shank's Mare,* 1.

14. Evelyn Waugh, *Ninety-two Days: A Tropical Journey* (1934), excerpt in *Shank's Mare,* 157–64.

15. Ibid., 162.

16. Paul Fussell, *Abroad: British Literary Traveling between the Wars* (New York: Oxford University Press, 1980), 65, emphasis his.

17. Ibid., 67.

18. For hiking clubs, see "Art of Walking Saved by Hiking Clubs," Fussell, *Abroad,* 29–31.

19. Derek Linton, "Youth," *Modern Germany: An Encyclopedia of History, People, and Culture, 1871–1990,* ed. Dieter K. Buse and Juergen C. Doer, vol. 2 (New York: Garland Publishing, 1998), 1103.

20. Tom Turner, *Sierra Club: One Hundred Years of Protecting Nature* (New York: Abrams, 1991), 49. For background on the creation of national parks, see Richard West Sellars, *Preserving Nature in the National Parks: A History* (New Haven, CT: Yale University Press, 1997), 7–21.

21. In her 1922 edition of *Etiquette* (New York: Funk & Wagnalls, 1922), Emily Post at scattered points made the following remarks: "No gentleman walks along the street chewing gum or, if he is walking with a lady, puffing a cigar or cigarette." A gentleman offers to carry a lady's bundles and never has her "on the left," because "a lady 'on the left' is not a lady." He only offers his arm to a lady at night, when she descends the steps of a house, travels from one building to another, and is walking a distance. "The reason is that in her thin high-heeled slippers, and when it is too dark to see her foothold clearly, she is likely to trip." Post contended, "all people in the streets, or anywhere in public, should be careful not to talk too loud. They should especially avoid pronouncing people's names, or making personal remarks that may attract passing attention or give a clue to themselves." Reasoning like the elite of old, she argued, "Do not attract attention to

yourself in public. This is one of the fundamental rules of good breeding. Shun conscious manners, conspicuous clothes [like red hair or ugly combat boots], staring at people, knocking into them, talking across anyone. . . . Do not [as the movies would increasingly have you] expose your private affairs, feelings or innermost thoughts in public. You are knocking down the walls of your house when you do." Not only houses but also whole empires and moral orders crumbled in the First World War and its aftermath.

22. George Vigarello's findings, as summarized by Alain Corbin, "Back Stage," *From the Fires of Revolution to the Great War,* ed. Michelle Perrot, vol. 4 of *History of Private Life* (Cambridge, MA: Harvard University Press, 1990), 664.

23. Ibid.

24. Dominick Cavallo. *Muscles and Morals: Organized Playgrounds and Urban Reform, 1880–1920* (Philadelphia: University of Pennsylvania Press, 1981), 1.

25. Linda Tomko, *Dancing Class: Gender, Ethnicity, and Social Divides in American Dance, 1890–1920* (Bloomington: Indiana University Press, 1999), 10.

26. Ibid.

27. Ibid.

28. In one manual, step 4-–of six steps—states, "The children are then directed to walk in normal walking tempo in single file around the room. The examiner faces the approaching line to detect and check the dynamic functioning of the feet and legs of each child," Avalclare Sprow Howland, *The Teaching of Body Mechanics in Elementary and Secondary Schools* (New York: A. S. Barnes, 1936), 18.

29. Norma Schwendener wrote, "The First World War gave countless challenges to physical education. New types of services were inaugurated in connection with war work. Physical education teachers . . . became nurse's aids and physiotherapists; or because of their knowledge of sports, games and dance, were selected as directors of recreation," *A History of Physical Education in the United States* (New York: A. S. Barnes, 1942), 154–55. For a single example of how the First World War defined physical education, see Fred Eugene Leonard, *A Guide to the History of Physical Education* (Philadelphia: Lea and Febiger, 1923).

30. George L. Mosse, *The Nationalization of the Masses: Political Symbolism and Mass Movements in Germany from the Napoleonic Wars through the Third Reich* (New York: New American Library, 1975), 161.

31. Ibid., 162.

32. Ibid., 167.

33. Ibid., 168.

34. For a brief description of parades, see "Parade," *Folklore: An Encyclopedia of Beliefs, Customs, Tales, Music, and Art* (Santa Barbara, CA: ABC-CLIO, 1997), 625–26.

35. Scott Moranda, "Maps, Markers, and Bodies: Hikers Constructing the Nation in German Forests," *The Nationalism Project,* December 1, 2002, 1, found on http://www.nationalismproject.org/pdf/moranda.pdf.

36. Ibid.

37. For a short survey of scouting, see Robert Miner, "Boy Scouts," *Encyclopedia Americana,* international ed., vol. 4 (Danbury, CT: Grolier, 1999), 384–85.

38. For the life of Baden-Powell, a London West Ender whose first youthful commitment to living a good life included realizing a world in which "all who go across the crossings shall give the poor crossing-sweepers some money," see W. S. Adams, *Edwardian Portraits* (London: Secker & Warburg, 1957), 98–146.

39. John Springhall, "English Youth Movements," *Everyman in Europe: Essays in Social History,* 3rd ed. (Englewood Cliffs, NJ: Prentice-Hall, 1990), 247. The British temperance group, the Band of Hope, similarly aimed to inculcate a new cultural identity in their young members, to facilitate the absorption of upwardly mobile working families into respectable society, Lilian Lewis Shiman, "The Band of Hope Movement: Respectable Recreation for Working Class Children," *Victorian Studies* 17, no. 1 (September 1993), 49–74.

40. Cited in Springhall, "English Youth Movements," 246.

41. When the London women's group joined a contemporary English prayer union in 1877, the organization took its name as Young Women's Christian Association.

42. Cited in the 1855 annual report, reported by Elmer Johnson, *The History of YMCA: Physical Education* (Chicago: Follett Publishing, 1979), 23.

43. Ibid., 49.

44. Ibid., 50.

45. A short overview of the spread and development of the American YMCA is found in *The Columbia Desk Encyclopedia,* 3rd ed. (New York: Columbia University Press, 1963), 2373.

46. *Salesmanship: The Standard Course of the United Y.M.C.A.* (YMCA, 1928), 22.

47. Sidney Pollard, "Factory Discipline in the Industrial Discipline," cited in Richard Golden, ed., *Social History of Western Civilization: Readings from the Seventeenth Century to the Present,* 2nd ed. (New York: St. Martin's Press, 1992), 124.

48. Steve Babson, *Working Detroit: The Making of a Union Town* (New York: Adama Books, 1984), 34–35, and Joyce Shaw Peterson, *American Automobile Workers, 1900–1933* (Albany: State University of New York Press, 1987), 22–23.

49. Once left unburied on battlefields and banished along with prostitutes from inns, the common soldier became in the course of the nineteenth and twentieth century the hero of the nation. For this transformation and the development of the cult of the fallen soldier in Europe from the French Revolution to Nazi Germany, see George Mosse, *Fallen Soldiers: Reshaping the Memory of the World War* (New York: Oxford University Press, 1990).

50. Scott Myerly, *British Military Spectacle* (Cambridge, MA: Harvard University Press, 1996), 129. For an introduction to "military ceremonies," "military music," and "vexillology," see *A Dictionary of Military History and the Art of War,* ed. André Corvisier (Oxford: Blackwell, 1994), 543–45, 844–47.

51. Prussia, which popularized the "goose step" (described in n. 67 below), responded to its defeat at the hands of France's popular revolutionary and Napoleonic armies with a national rejuvenation based on drill and physical development. More than any other individual, Berlin high school teacher and patriot Friedrich Ludwig Jahn effected a conjunction between national reform and calisthenics. His goal was nothing less than a new body and mind for the Prussian nation. To this end he formed the immensely popular *Turnverein,* gymnastic groups, which like the English public-school sports programs, simultaneously sought well-being and fellowship among young people of all classes. Ideologically fusing body and spirit, the *Turnverein* movement joined youth and nationalism. George L. Mosse, *The Nationalization of the Masses: Political Symbolism and Mass Movements in Germany from the Napoleonic Wars through the Third Reich* (New York: New American Library, 1975), 75.

52. For an introduction to the history of physical education in different nations, see Deobold Van Dalen, Elmer Mitchell, and Bruce Bennett, *A World History of Physical Education: Cultural, Philosophical, Comparative* (Englewood Cliffs, NJ: Prentice-Hall, 1953). For Sweden's important role in the dissemination of physical education, which at the time of the Napoleonic Wars fused gymnastics and literature to "develop the courage and physical prowess of Norsemen of old" in response to Russian hegemony, see ibid., 245–59.

53. For the foot life of a single northern soldier from the First Minnesota, who fought from Bull Run to Appomattox, see James A. Wright, *No*

More Gallant a Deed: A Civil War Memoir of the First Minnesota Volunteers, ed. Stephen Keilor (Minneapolis: Minnesota Historical Society Press, 2001).

54. For an examination of soldiers' loads through the ages, see William L. Ezell, "Battlefield Mobility and the Soldier's Load," www.globalsecurity.org/military/library/report/1992/EWL.htm.

55. In *Cold Mountain: A Novel,* Charles Frazier (New York: Atlantic Monthly Press, 1997) offers an epic foot journey of a southern soldier returning to his love and home in the mountains.

56. See Bruce Catton, *The Glory Road: The Bloody Route from Fredericksburg to Gettysburg* (Garden City, NY: Doubleday, 1952), 269.

57. For numbers and the stimulation of the prosthetics industry in the Civil War, see Katherine Ott, David Serlin, and Stephen Mihm, eds., *Artificial Parts, Practical Lives: Modern Histories of Prosthetics* (New York: New York University Press, 2002), 18, 26, 121, passim.

58. E. P. Thompson attributes the pacification of the working classes not just to "the productive tempo of the clock" but also to "repressive Methodism," in his *Making of the English Working Class* (New York: Vintage Books, 196), 401–12.

59. For the place of drilling, marching, and parading in the nineteenth-century British army, see Scott Hughes Myerly, *The British Military Spectacle: From the Napoleonic Wars through Crimea* (Cambridge, MA: Harvard University Press, 1996), esp. 67–87, 128–29, 166–67.

60. Although new technologies like the machine gun, barbed wire, the iron ship, and the train played a major role in the American Civil War, that conflict still can be read as essentially an infantry story—of "drills, drills, and more drills," marches, and countermarches. Soldiers carried unbearably heavy knapsacks along dusty and muddy roads across inhospitable landscapes. They wore ill-fitting boots or, in the worst of times, no shoes at all. They frequently suffered frozen feet and amputated limbs. These elements and others are found in Carlton McCarthy, *Detailed Minutiae of Soldier Life in the Army of Northern Virginia, 1861–1865* (Lincoln: University of Nebraska Press, 1993), esp. 10–55; Bell Irvin Wiley, *The Life of Billy Yank: The Common Soldier of the Union* (Baton Rouge: Louisiana State University Press, 1952), esp. 54; *The Civil War Notebooks of Daniel Chrisholm: A Chronicle of Daily Life in the Union Army, 1864–1865,* ed. W. Springere Menge and J. August Shimrak (New York: Ballantine Books, 1989), esp. 62, 135, and 141; and *All for the Union: The Civil War Diary and Letters of El-*

isha Hunt Rhodes (New York: Random House, 1992), 11.

61. Alistair Horne, "The Soldier in World War I," *The Industrial Centuries,* vol. 2 of *Everyman in Europe* (Englewood Cliffs, NJ: Prentice-Hall, 1990), 163.

62. John Keegan, *A History of Warfare* (New York: Vintage Books, 1994), 307–8.

63. For a description of the German attack on foot, see J. C. F. Fuller, *From the American Civil War to the End of World War II,* vol. 3 of *Military History of the Western World* (New York: Da Capo Paperback, 1956), 187.

64. B. H. Lidell Hart, *The Real War, 1914–1918* (Boston: Little, Brown and Company, 1930), 249.

65. Wilfred Owen, "Dulce et Decorum Est," cited in ibid., 182–83.

66. Information on Mussolini's transformation of Italy found in a booklet by the Museo di Roma in Trasvestere, for its exhibit "Roma tra le due Guerre nelle fotografie dell'instituto luce," March 2002.

67. Defined by the royal Prussian infantry in 1726, the goose step required that "the left and right foot shall be partially lifted with stiff knees and the foot will not be stamped." This *Excerziermarsch* in the tempo of 114 steps per minute came to be the characteristic *parademarsch* of the German army. The source of the popularization of the goose step was Prussia. The march in step—the special march with slow and sharp, audible steps—was brought to Germany in the eighteenth century by the troops of Karl von Hessen-Hassel. The eighteenth century Russian Army under Catherine the Great was the first of many armies to adopt the goose step. This information was supplied to me by the United States Army Military History Institute, Carlisle Barracks, Carlisle, Pennsylvania. Identified as "Marching," USAMHI RefBranch, js 1972, 1–2.

68. For the Nazis' attempt to command art and shape an entire symbolic landscape, from image of mother and work to subject of painting, design of building, and art theory, see Bertold Hinz, *Art in the Third Reich* (New York: Pantheon Books, 1979).

69. David Large, *Berlin* (New York: Basic Books, 2000), 295.

70. Ibid., 294–95.

71. Ibid., 301.

NOTES TO CHAPTER 9

1. For numbers and the stimulation of the prosthetics industry since the Civil War, see Katherine Ott, David Serlin, and Stephen Mihm, eds.,

Artificial Parts, Practical Lives: Modern Histories of Prosthetics (New York: New York University Press, 2002).

2. An example of improving surfaces is found in *Walkway Surfaces: Measurement of Slip Resistance,* American Society for Testing and Materials, ASTM Special Technical Publication 649 (Philadelphia, 1977.) The Americans with Disabilities Act, passed in 1990, voiced the government's unprecedented commitment to opening the world to all. It promoted universal accessibility by providing level sidewalks, breaks in curbing, ramps and elevators as alternatives to stairs, and lower drinking fountains and bathroom facilities.

3. George Soule, *Prosperity Decade: From War to Depression, 1917–1929,* vol. 8 of *Economic History of the United States* (New York: Harper & Row, 1947), 169.

4. Since the 1960s shoe design has taken to shoeing the fairest urban demoiselles in thick, rustic clodhoppers, lending appropriateness to one of the favorite insults we children of the late 1940s paid one another: "Ah, your mother wears combat boots."

5. For a short history of tennis shoes, athletic shoes, and sneakers, see "The Sneaker Story," *Co-Ed,* March 1985, 5, and Kathleen Low, "In the Days When Sport Shoes Weren't Fashionable," *Footwear News,* October 6, 1985, 2.

6. The sneaker had its origin in late-nineteenth-century North America, according to *The New Shorter Oxford Dictionary,* vol. 2 (Oxford: Oxford University Press, 1993), 2920.

7. But all that changed, to choose a single moment, when in 1957 the cofounders of Nike, Bill Bowerman and Phil Knight, met in Eugene, Oregon. From their encounter and their determination to produce a shoe for fitness and high athletic performance sprang up over the following decades a whole new protean industry. It mutated back and forth between sport and fitness, serving health, comfort, casual attire, and even fashion. In effect, what started as a quality athletic shoe was redesigned for all other sports, along with jogging, training, and walking (certainly a growing activity for the health conscious and sedate). Across the 1970s and 1980s an immensely competitive industry, formed by the twin American giants Nike and Reebok, made the foot and its specialized activities the object of the newest materials, technological innovation, orthopedic science, styling, and mass sales based on the endorsement of world sports superstars.

8. Adriana Di Lello, "Sneakers . . . Italian Style," *Dolce Vita Fashion,* http://www.dolcevita.it/editor/fashion/tennis/tennis.htm.

9. For the seminal importance of mining for controlling space and movement, see Lewis Mumford, *Technics and Civilization* (New York: Harcourt, Brace & World, 1962), 158.

10. For a short history of elevators, which go back at least to Roman times, see Sigfried Giedion, *Space, Time and Architecture: The Growth of a New Tradition* (Cambridge, MA: Harvard University Press, 1963), 206–9, 232–37. Preceded by a commercial platform-type elevator to hoist barrels in a mill, the safety hoist was developed by Elisha Graves Otis for New York's Crystal Palace in 1853, and he also developed a commercial elevator in an office building in lower Broadway, New York City, 1868, *Famous First Fact,* 4th ed. (New York: H. W. Wilson, 1981), 236. The hydraulic elevator was used in 1878. For a history of the elevator and skyscrapers in New York, see Peter Hall, *Cities in Civilization* (New York: Pantheon Books, 1998), 770–72. For a history of skyscrapers and elevators, especially in Chicago, see Donald Miller, *The City of the Century: The Epic of Chicago and the Making of America* (New York: Simon & Schuster, 1997), esp. 301–9.

11. For connection between the steel frame of the Eiffel Tower and Louis Sullivan's functionalism, see Jacques Barzun, *From Dawn to Decadence* (New York; Harper & Row, 2000), 601.

12. Ibid., 303.

13. With some pretension Michel de Certeau surveyed the pedestrians passing below as "the walkers, *Wandersmänner,* whose bodies follow the thick and thins of an urban 'text' they write without being able to read it," *The Practice of Everyday Life* (Berkeley: University of California Press, 1988), 93.

14. Aubrey F. Burstall, *A History of Mechanical Engineering* (Cambridge, MA: MIT Press, 1965), 386–87.

15. Jersey City made use of a rolling sidewalk in its railroad station in 1954. In 1958, a traveling sidewalk of rolling stairs was introduced to the airport at Dallas's Love Field. A two-way moving walk, consisting of three loops, totaled 1,435 feet in length. Today, downtown Hong Kong (Xianggang) boasts a half-mile-long system composed of twenty escalators and three moving sidewalks, "Urban Mass Transit," *Encyclopedia Britannica,* Encyclopaedia Britannica Premium Service, May 2, 2004, www.Britannica.com/eb/article?eu=125327.

16. For an example of designing a home around the flow of foot traffic see Donald Helper, Paul Wallach, and Dana Helper, *Architecture: Drafting and Design,* 6th ed. (Lake Forest, IL: Glencoe, 1991), esp. 89–92.

17. For safety in the home, see "Don't Let a Fall Be Your Last Trip," online brochure of the American Academy of Orthopaedic Surgeons, http://orthoinfo.AAOS.org. For U.S. Occupational Safety & Health Administration (OSHA) rules governing surfaces and stairs in the workplace on "walking/working surfaces," see http://www.osha.gov/SLTC/construction-walking/.

18. For a discussion of sitting in a chair as a learned activity and the creation of a comfortable chair as a recent historical invention, see Witold Rybczynski, *Home: A Short History of an Idea* (New York: Viking, 1986), 80–83, 96–99.

19. For a book about chairs, see Galen Cranz, *The Chair: Rethinking Culture, Body, and Design* (New York: Norton, 1998), and *Be Seated* (New York: HarperCollins, 1993); for a small part of the world of paper, see "The World and Workers of Paper," chapter 5 of Thomas J. Schlereth, *Cultural History and Material Culture* (Charlottesville: University of Virginia Press, 1992), 144–78.

20. For a set of inventions that contract and annihilate space with speed and immediacy, see David E. Brown, *Inventing Modern America from the Microwave to the Mouse* (Cambridge, MA: MIT Press, 2000): for the television, 58–61; walkie-talkies, 168–71; and personal computer, 194–97.

21. For a contemporary comparison between "new commodities and services" and "refinements in old commodities," see Stuart Chase, *Men and Machines* (New York: Macmillan, 1929), 225. Illustrative of contemporary technology's underlying commitment to end walking and lifting, see a popular four-volume juvenile series of books from pre–World War I, *The Boy Mechanic*, vol. 1, which instructs young boy inventors to invent "a sawhorse with collapsible casters," make "a portable phonograph for schools," add an extra seat to a baby carriage, put "rubber tires on wooden wheels," or turn a motorcycle into a source of power for grinding feed or cutting up firewood, or make it a delivery truck. (Chicago: Popular Mechanics, 1913), 76, 125, 143, 201, 349.

22. Jules Verne (1828–1905) is known to English readers in translation for his *Five Weeks in a Balloon* (1863), *A Journey to the Center of the Earth* (1864), *From the Earth to the Moon* (1865), *Twenty Thousand Leagues under the Sea* (1870), and *Around the World in Eighty Days* (1873).

23. Ralph Waldo Emerson, cited in *The Quotable Walker* (New York: Lyons Press, 2000), 100.

24. Yi-Fu Tuan, *Topophilia: A Study of Environmental Perception, Attitude, and Values* (New York: Columbia University Press, 1990), 89. For history of the traffic signal, beginning in United States in 1923, see Morgan, "Traffic Signal," *Inventing Modern America*, 106–11.

25. For a short history of the wheelbarrow, which may or may not have been a Chinese invention, see "Wheelbarrow," *Encyclopedia of Inventions* (New York: Galahad Books, 1977), 27–30, Henry Petroski, *The Evolution of Useful Things* (New York: Vintage Books, 1992), 225–31.

26. For an article that shows clearly how the definition of public lands is all tied up with where the wheel can go, see David G. Havlick, "Behind the Wheel: A Look Back at Public Lands," *Forest History Today,* Spring 2002, 10–20.

27. Alfred Hill, "Bearing," *Chambers Encyclopedia,* vol. 2 (Oxford: Pergamon Press, 1967), 176–78, and for a set of articles on bearings, see *Encyclopaedia Britannica* (Chicago: Encyclopaedia Britannica, 1970), 329–34. Ball bearings were first used in a weather vane in Lancaster, Pennsylvania, in 1794, *Famous First Facts,* 90. Reducing internal friction, they found their full use with the advent of powered vehicles, "Ball Bearings," *Eureka: An Illustrated History of Inventions from the Wheel to the Computer* (New York: Holt, Rhinehart and Winston, 1974), x.

28. Casters were first placed on a bedstead in 1838, *Famous First Facts,* 146. For the full array of contemporary application of small wheels, see Colson Coster Corporation's catalogue, "Casters, Wheels, Bumpers," 1998.

29. Suggesting the extent to which roads penetrate North America, five hundred thousand miles of roads have been built on America's public lands, David Havlick, "Behind the Wheel: A Look Back at Public Lands," *Forest History Today,* Spring 2002, 10.

30. The baby carriage was manufactured by Charles Burton in 1848 in New York, but because of protests about how it collided with pedestrians, "Burton moved to England, where he opened a factory and obtained orders for his perambulator from Queen Victoria, Queen Isabella II of Spain, and the Pasha of Egypt," *Famous First Facts,* 89. However, an individual baby carriage made in Paris especially for Napoleon and Marie Louise is on display at the Schönbrun's Wagenburg in Vienna. A much earlier history of the baby carriage returns us to 1733 when English architect William Kent designed for a child of the Duke of Devonshire a baby carriage in the shape of a shell to be pulled by a dog or a Shetland pony, Kristin Palm, "Baby Stroller," *How Products Are Made: An Illustrative Guide to Product Manufacturing,* vol. 4 (Detroit: Gale, 1998), 36.

31. The British Cycle & Motor Cycle Industries Association, "Bicycle," *Chambers Encyclopedia,* 306–9. For a well-illustrated history of the bicycle in the nineteenth and twentieth centuries, featuring bicycles of every size and shape, with a number of different size wheels, and combined as boats, designed for delivery and touring, and adapted in real and imagined ways for war, including even pulling and sporting guns, see Pryor Dodge, *The Bicycle* (Paris: Flammarion, 1996).

32. *Famous First Facts,* 107.

33. For the popularity of the bicycle in New York, see Stephen Longstreet, *City on Two Rivers: Profiles of New York—Yesterday and Today* (New York: Hawthorn Books, 1975), 63. After an 1878 factory sale of fifty "Columbia" bikes by Weed Sewing Machine Company of Hartford, Connecticut, bicycles took off.

34. For adaptations of the bike for mail delivery, milk haulage, and even an "amphibious machine that could be converted into a row boat" (one of which crossed the English Channel in 1883), see Geoffrey Williamson, *Wheels within Wheels: The Story of the Starleys of Coventry* (London: Geoffrey Bles, 1966), 49.

35. A new edition of the original two-volume Thomas Stevens, *Around the World on a Bicycle* (New York: Charles Scribner's Sons, 1888 & 1889) is available in paperback, with an introduction by Thomas Pauly (Mechanicsburg, PA: Stackpole Books, 2001).

36. Ibid., 6.

37. Early in the twentieth century, the Japanese—a half-century away from their startling automobile industry—replaced the rickshaw with the pedicab, a tricycle with a passenger seat, "Jinrikisha," *The Encyclopedia Americana, International Edition,* vol. 16 (Danbury, CT: Grolier, 1999), 95. A redesigned rickshaw was introduced in India to diminish air pollution by cars, scooters, buses, and trucks, in the area around the Taj Mahal, "New Cycle Rickshaw," *Whole Earth Catalog,* Summer 1991, n.p.

38. For the role of carts, roller coasters, and other wheeled vehicles at turn-of-the-century Coney Island, see John F. Kasson, *Amusing the Millions* (New York: Hill & Wang, 1978).

39. Only in 1885, Stanley Diamond continue to remark, was the gasoline engine sufficiently miniaturized so that Gottfried Daimler could install it on a bicycle, *Guns, Germs, and Steel: The Fate of Human Societies* (New York: Norton, 1999), 243.

40. For Lewis Mumford's views, see his *The Highway and the City* (New York: New American Library, 1963).

41. Philosopher José Ortega y Gasset contended in his 1930 classic, *Revolt of the Masses,* that the car created the self-satisfied "mass man," a creature who is as certain he is the goal of all past history as he is ignorant of the precarious political freedom and technological achievements that accounted for his very advent (New York: Norton, 1957), 87. At the same time, the automobile became a matter of profound personal identity: we are our cars and our cars are our lives, experiences, and dreams. Over a decade ago, social historian John Modell called my attention to the connection between individual identity and the automobile in contemporary society. Robert Karlovitz offers an "album of nostalgic automemorabilia" in *This Was Pioneering Motoring* (Seattle: Superior Publishing, 1968).

42. For a useful and engaging contemporary overview, see Sam Bass Warner, *The Urban City: A History of the American City* (New York: Harper & Row, 1972), and for the earlier evolution of Boston away from being a walking city, see his *Streetcar Suburbs: The Process of Growth in Boston, 1870–1900* (Cambridge, MA: Harvard University Press and MIT Press, 1962). American sprawl measures the automobile's transformation of walking and the walking environment. It is associated with the building of suburbs and the emerging prominence of Los Angeles, Las Vegas, Dallas, and other cities of the South and West, Tom Lewis, *Divided Highways: Building the Interstate Highways, Transforming American Life* (New York: Viking, 1997), 263. For a discussion of sprawl, those low-density dwelling and work areas that surround nearly every town of any size and those long, continuous blocks offering little architectural variety, see Andres Duany, Elizabeth Plater-Zyberk, and Jeff Speck, *Suburban Sprawl: The Rise of Sprawl and the Decline of the American Dream* (New York: North Point Press, 2000).

43. A literal counting of intersections in traditional cities and contemporary American cities and suburbs suggests how the face of the world has changed for the person on foot. Venice, Italy, has 1,500 intersections per square mile; downtown Rome, 500; Los Angeles, 160; and Irvine, California, 15, in a student workbook, *FHWA: A Course on Bicycle and Pedestrian Transportation,* pub. no. FHWA-RD-99-198 (McLean, VA: U.S. Dept. of Transportation Federal Highway Administration, 2002), 1–3. A square mile of downtown Boston contains one hundred fewer blocks than it did a century ago. Allan Jacobs, *Great Streets* (Cambridge, MA: MIT Press, 1995), 264.

44. Witold Rybczynski, *City Life: Urban Expectations in a New World* (New York: Scribner, 1995), 162.

45. For a useful study of the abstract city, see *City Signs and Lights: A Policy Study* prepared by the Boston Redevelopment Authority (Cambridge, MA: MIT Press, 1973), esp. 9–13.

46. Cited in *Famous First Facts,* 160.

47. "Automobile," *The New Encyclopedia Britannica,* vol. 1 (Chicago: Encyclopaedia Britannica, 1997), 727.

48. Claude Fischer, *America Calling: A Social History of the Telephone* (Berkeley: University of California Press, 1992), 57. For production and sale of automobile in the 1920s, see Soule, *Prosperity Decade,* 164–70.

49. For short overview of the automobile's transformation of the landscape, see Edward Relph, *The Modern Urban Landscape* (Baltimore, MD: Johns Hopkins University Press, 1987), 77–89. Also see James J. Flink, *America Adopts the Automobile, 1895–1910* (Cambridge, MA: MIT Press, 1970) and Frank Donovan, *Wheels for a Nation* (New York: Crowell, 1965).

50. Starting in 1625, with a stretch of road in Pemaquid, Maine, consisting of stones, rocks, and cobblestones, it reaches to a sixty-two-mile macadam road, the Lancaster Turnpike, that connected Lancaster and Philadelphia in 1793, and then goes on to an 1870 asphalt road in Newark, New Jersey. In 1893 eight miles of brick pavement were laid on the Wooster Pike, now U.S. Route 42, out of Cleveland, and Wayne County, Michigan, on the outskirts of Detroit, set a concrete rural road in the spring of 1909. It was one mile long, eighteen feet wide, and six and a half inches deep, *Famous First Facts,* 522.

51. Ibid., 522–23.

52. Ibid., 56–58.

53. Relph, *Modern Urban Landscape,* 78–79.

54. Ibid.

55. Charles Cheape, *Moving the Masses: Urban Public Transit in New York, Boston, and Philadelphia, 1880–1912* (Cambridge, MA: Harvard University Press, 1980), 21. Around 1870, when "cattle still grazed at 42nd Street opposite the New Grand Central Station and cattle drovers were a major source of traffic on Fifth Avenue north of 59th Street," public transit had grown as ferries, bridges, and tunnels brought surrounding population to the city center, ibid., 21. By 1870, nine ferries linked Brooklyn to New York. In 1880 an elevated railway system was completed, *New York: Old & New* (Philadelphia: Lippincott, 1903), 402.

56. For two critical surveys of New York and pedestrian traffic, see Asa Greene, "The Big City circa 1837" and Charles Dickens, "A Jaundiced View," both of which are found in *The Empire City,* ed. Alexander Klein (New York: Rinehart, 1955), 179–92.

57. George J. Lankevich, *New York City: A Short History* (New York: New York University Press, 2002), 85–86.

58. Ibid., 86.

59. For the lack of sanitary conditions in Washington, D.C., in the 1870s and after, see Constance McLaughlin Green, *Washington: Village and Capital, 1800–1878* (Princeton, NJ: Princeton University Press, 1962), 365–68. An estimate of the horse as a source of congestion and pollution in American cities in 1900 is offered in an unpublished paper by Philip Teigen, "City and Country Cousins: Changing Patterns in the Distribution of Horses and Mules in the United States, 1860–1920," delivered at the 1998 Annual Meeting of American Historians. In one instance of mechanical breakdown in New York in 1888, fifteen thousand passengers were trapped on elevated tracks, Longstreet, *City on Two Rivers,* 195. Pickpockets flourished among the El's crammed straphangers, who numbered near a million on the eve of World War I, ibid.

60. The etymology of the twentieth-century American neologism *jaywalk* (*jay,* "a stupid person," plus *walk*) has its origin, according to *Harper's Magazine* (1917), in Bostonian street talk, which "reduced a 'pedestrian who crosses the street in disregard of traffic signals' to the compact *jaywalker,*" *A Dictionary of Americanisms on Historical Principles,* ed. Mitford Mathews, (Chicago: University of Chicago Press, 1951), 900. The process by which jaywalking became a legal infraction could be traced in diverse state statutes and city laws.

61. Quotations in John Stilgoe, "*Landschaft* and Linearity," *Out of the Woods: Essays in Environmental History,* ed. Char Miller and Hal Rothman (Pittsburgh: University of Pittsburgh Press, 1997), 67.

62. Relph, *The Modern Urban Landscape,* 77.

63. Ibid., 461. The first traffic ordinances in New York (New Amsterdam), dating from 1652, dictated that "no Wagons, Carts or Sleighs shall be run, rode or driven at a gallop . . . [and] that the drivers and conductors shall walk by the Wagons, Carts, or Sleighs and so take and lead the horses [under penalty] and be responsible for all damages which may arise therefrom." Dating back to 1791, the city's first one-way traffic regulations requested "Ladies and Gentlemen" "to order their Coachmen to take up and set down with their Horse Heads to the East River to avoid confusion," ibid., 626.

64. Comprising 13 officers and 15 horses, New York's mounted patrol made 429 arrests in its first year. By 1901, it had about 700 horses and equal numbers of officers. A remnant of its former self, the mounted patrol, composed today of 145 officers and 100 horses, serves crowd control, while presenting the public with an object worthy of petting, Michael Green, *Mounted Police* (New York: Grolier, 1998), 5, 7, 9–13.

65. James Lardner and Thomas Reppetto, *NYPD: A City and Its Police* (New York: Henry Holt, 2000), 201. For the New York Fire Department, which also gained so much attention in the aftermath of September 11, and its motorization, see Paul Hashagen, *Fire Department, City of New York* (New York: Fire Safety Education Fund & New York Fire Department, 2000), esp. 33–74.

66. *Famous First Facts,* 57–58.

67. New York installed twenty-six traffic lights, which were changed by an officer in a traffic tower, *Famous First Facts,* 81.

68. Ibid., 82.

69. I derived this generalization from the Department of Public Works' examination of "Street Traffic Conditions, Saint Paul, Minnesota, 1937–1939," conducted under the auspices of Chief Engineer George Shepherd, March 1940.

70. Lewis Mumford, *The Highway and the City* (New York: Mentor Books, 1964), 44.

71. Data from exhibit "On Track: Transit and the American City," January 26–October 27, 2002, at National Building Museum, Washington, DC.

72. Nationally, driving fatalities—6,700 in the years 1913 to 1917—reached an average about 35,000 in 1930, where they remained through the early 1940s, spiraling up to an average of 55,000 by the late 1960s, a number from which they have steadily declined to 40,000 in 1996, thanks to better policing, engineering, and speed control. For this and additional data concerning automobiles, their numbers, accidents, fatalities, and pedestrians, see *Historical Statistics of the United States, Colonial Times to 1970,* part 2, section "Highway Transportation," Series Q 208–23 (Washington, DC: U.S. Bureau of the Census, 1975) and U.S. Bureau of the Census, *Statistical Abstract of the United States, 1998,* 118th ed. (Washington, DC, 2000).

73. For traffic speeds, see Paul Goldberger, *On the Rise: Architecture and Design in a Post Modern Age* (New York: Times Books, 1983), 48.

74. New York bicycle repairman Charles Howard popularized the car in San Francisco in the aftermath of the 1906 earthquake. With 3,000 dead and 225,000 homeless, the city found itself desperately needing to carry and move corpses, people, and things. Baby carriages and improvised wagons on roller skates failed. The automobile, which Howard supplied, alone sufficed, in the words of one witness, "to conquer space," Laura Hillenbrand, *Seabiscuit: An American Legend* (New York: Random House, 2001), 7.

75. In Western and Eastern Europe there were about 17 million private cars in 1957 and now there are about 200 million cars in Western Europe alone. This means that European society has had to adapt to congestion, traffic, and accidents. For instance, in 1960, Belgium had 960,000 private cars, trucks, and buses for a population of 9 million. In 1999, it had 5.7 million cars, trucks, and buses for a population of almost 10 million. Showing an improvement in traffic control and emergency medical service, as well as increased concern for drivers' well-being, Belgium had 689 lethal accidents per 10,000 cars in 1960. Society reduced this number of lethal accidents to 92 per 10,000 car accidents in 1999, according to a December 16, 2001, interview and subsequent correspondence with Antwerp journalist Jan Hertoghs, who references IRTAD (International Road Traffic and Accident Database), which can be accessed at the website of the Organisation for Economic Cooperation and Development (OECD), http://www.oecd.org.

76. For an excellent discussion of Milan's periphery and its inhabitants, commuters, and diverse users, see John Foot, *Milan since the Miracle* (New York: Oxford University Press, 2001), 135–55.

77. For conservative critic Russell Kirk's criticism of Ford Motor for having ruined the Detroit he (and the author) once innocently walked, see *Sword of the Imagination; Memoirs of a Half-Century of Literary Conflict* (Grand Rapids, MI: Erdmans, 1995), 48–49. For a study of Los Angeles—the nation's second largest city—as a place without society and in which the average driver spends seven full working days per year in traffic congestion, see Robert M. Fogelson, *The Fragmented Metropolis, 1850–1930* (Cambridge, MA: Harvard University Press, 1967). For a study that sees contemporary Los Angeles turning against commuting, see Timothy Egan, "Sprawl-Weary Los Angeles Builds Up," *New York Times,* March 10, 2002.

78. For a book on the quickening pace of modern life, see Staffan Burestam Linder, *The Harried Leisure Class* (New York: Columbia University Press, 1970). For a suggestion about the surge of disobedient foot traffic in New York, see Richard Shephard, "Why Pedestrians Play Chicken to Cross the Road," *New York Times,* March 27, 1999.

79. Through a series of cross-cultural studies of behavior regarding appointments, work, and play, Robert Levine seeks to fathom differing senses and attitudes about time. He examines pedestrian pace and willingness to stop to give information or pick up a dropped object, but does not correlate it with the history of the automobile and vehicular traffic system in a given place, *A Geography of Time* (New York: Basic Books, 1997). Also, see Paul Amato, "The Effects of Urbanization on Interpersonal Behavior," *Journal of Cross-Cultural Psychology* 14, no. 3 (Sept. 1983), 353–67.

80. For this information as well as a useful overview of Los Angeles as "the city as freeway," see Hall, *Cities in Civilization*, 815, and 803–41. Noteworthily, Charles Fletcher, a celebrated literary figure, walked to Los Angeles from Cincinnati in 1884. He went on in life to become the editor of *Land of Sunshine Magazine* and to see the invention and explosion of the most artificial metropolis, dominated by the automobile, Mike Davis, *City of Quartz: Excavating the Future in Los Angeles* (New York: Vintage Books, 1992), 24–25.

81. *The Southwest Expedition of Jedediah Smith: His Personal Account of the Journey to California, 1826–1827* (Glendale, CA: Clark, 1977), 110.

82. Quotation from Carl Degler, *Affluence and Anxiety: America since 1945* (Glenview, IL: Scott, Foresman, 1975), 190.

83. For a study of the formation by public transit of a single set of nineteenth-century American suburbs as cities without centers, see Warner, *Streetcar Suburbs*.

84. For a work that seeks to explore many of the forgotten spaces on the contemporary American landscape, see John R. Stilgoe, *Outside Lies Magic* (New York: Walker and Company, 1998).

85. Mary Battiata, "A Walk on the Wild Side," *Washington Post Magazine,* January 11, 2004, 10. For her data, she cites the Surface Transportation Project.

86. The International Council of Shopping Centers identified in its *ICSC Quarterly* (Summer 2001) 1,182 regional and super-regional malls in the United States.

87. There are more than forty-five thousand shopping centers in the United States, International Council of Shopping Centers Research, http://www.icsc.org.

88. Ibid. Also see Rybczynski, *City Life,* 206–10.

89. Mall walking even made it into the fourth edition of *The American Heritage Dictionary of Language* (Boston: Houghton Mifflin, 2001).

90. Jonathan Franzen spoke of cherished anonymity in his review "City Life," *New Yorker,* February, 19, 1996, 91.

91. For a useful introduction to the ever changing countryside, see Ervin H. Zube and Margaret J. Zube, eds., *Changing Rural Landscapes* (Amherst: University of Massachusetts Press, 1977), J. B. Jackson's journal, *Landscape,* subtitled *Human Geography of the Southwest,* and

D. W. Meinig, "Teachers," *The Interpretations of Ordinary Landscapes,* ed. D. W. Meinig (Oxford: Oxford University Press, 1979), 210–36. For the changing small towns, see the introduction and conclusion to Richard Davies, Joseph Amato, and David Pichaske's anthology *A Place Called Home* (Minneapolis: Minnesota Historical Society Press, 2003), 3–11, 375–78, passim, and for the changing environment, economy, culture, and mind, see varied sections of Joseph Amato, *Rethinking Home: A Case for Local History* (Berkeley: University of California Press, 2002).

92. For three studies of how countryside towns kept pace with the countryside, see Richard O. Davies, *Main Street Blues: The Decline of Small-Town America* (Columbus: Ohio State University Press, 1998); Joseph Amato, *Rethinking Home,* esp. 43–59, 168–84; and John Radzilowski, *Prairie Town: A History of Marshall, Minnesota, 1872–1997* (Marshall, MN: Lyon County Historical Society, 1997), 132–81.

93. Leo Dangel, "How to Take a Walk," *Home from the Field* (Granite Falls, MN: Spoon River Poetry Press, 1997), 20.

94. For a comment on the plight of malls in the 1980s, see Stilgoe, *Outside Lies Magic,* 140–41.

95. For an introduction to the New Urbanists, see Peter Calthorpe, *The Next American Metropolis: Ecology, Community, and the American Dream* (New York: Princeton Architectural Press, 1993), esp., for their tenets, 4, 43, 44. For more recent urban designs dedicated to the connection among walking, walkable streets, and the restoration of community, see Andres Duany, Elizabeth Plater-Zyberk, and Jeff Speck, *Suburban Sprawl: The Rise of Sprawl and the Decline of the American Dream* (New York: North Point Press, 2000), 273,

96. I borrowed this short summary of the New Urbanists' work from Gary Mattson, "Commitment to Community: Two Policy Paradigms," *The Small City and Regional Community,* ed. R. Shaffer and W. Ryan (Madison: University of Wisconsin Press, 2001), 273.

97. Calthorpe, *The Next American Metropolis,* 17.

98. For an article revealing conflict within the field of shoe manufacture in a society of specialized footwear, see Leah Beth Ward, "Nike Function over Fashion" *New York Times,* April 28, 2002.

99. Colin Thurbon, *Journey into Cyprus* (London: Heinemann, 1975), 7.

NOTES TO CONCLUSION

1. An example of twentieth-century peasant life continuing to move on foot is Hertha Seuberlich,

Annuzza, a Girl of Romania (Chicago: Rand, 1962). In *Jorwerd: The Death of the Village in Late-Twentieth-Century Europe* (London: Harvill Press, 1996), Geert Mak discusses the transforming of a walking village into a mere place in a riding region in the Netherlands.

2. For a contemporary study of specialized sports equipment, shoes, and associated images, see Akiko Busch, ed., *Design for Sports: The Cult of Performance* (New York: Princeton Architectural Press, 1998), 20–45.

3. For a history of explorers, see Helen Delpar, ed., *The Discoverers: An Encyclopedia of Explorers and Exploration* (New York: McGraw-Hill, 1980); for an example of how geology itself caused scientists to walk the face of the earth and the bottom of the sea, see Alexander Winchell, *Walks and Talks in the Geological Field* (New York: Chautauqua Press, 1886), 56–62; for early-nineteenth-century and subsequent exploration of the North Pole, see Mick Confrey and Tim Jordan, *Icemen* (New York: TV Books, 1992), especially chapter 1, "The Man Who Ate His Shoes," 15–33.

4. *The New Encyclopaedia Britannica,* vol. 5 (Chicago: Encyclopaedia Britannica, 1997), 921.

5. For a discussion of recent climbing and disasters on Everest, see John Krakauer, *Into Thin Air: A Personal Account of the Mount Everest Disaster* (New York: Villard, 1997).

6. Ibid. For a discussion of walking prior to the eighteenth century, see Dennis Brailsford, *Sport and Society: Elizabeth to Anne* (London: Routledge & Kegan Paul, 1969), 158–97.

7. Golf developed in the last half of the nineteenth century, with clubs, enthusiasts, fans, professionals, tournaments, and manufacturers of balls and clubs. Only in 1919 did the Royal and Ancient Club of St. Andrews form the official organization of the game. Eighteen holes of play, which became the standard round of golf, required between four and five miles of walking. In the beginning the game had a processional feel as it proceeded from hole to hole. It was partly conducted on the backs of barefooted caddies, who toted players' bags. The game was played until the twentieth century on a comparatively rough landscape, which was covered with thickets, pitted with rabbit warrens, contoured by shifting dunes, and, in some instances, even inhabited by grazing animals.

8. For an eccentric collection of individual and group walks in the United States, see Hal Borand's compilation of *New York Times* articles on walking, George Trent, ed., *The Gentle Art of Walking* (New York: Arno Press/Random House, 1971).

9. Ibid., 56.

10. Ibid., 55.

11. Historian Eugen Weber argues that the Olympic movement, like nationalism, Fauvism, Cubism, and Futurism, was an expression of "unexpended energy." He notes that "sporting life is a heroic life in a vacuum" and quotes writer Jean Giradoux's remark, "there is no contesting the liberating effect of competitive games" for an elite seeking to escape reality, "Pierre de Courbetin and the Introduction of Organized Sports in France," *Journal of Contemporary History* 5, no. 2 (1970), 3–26.

12. Scott Crawford, "Pedestrianism," *Encyclopedia of World Sport from Ancient Times to the Present,* ed. David Levinson and Karen Christensen (New York: Oxford University Press, 1999), 294.

13. Scott Crawford, "Race Walking," *Encyclopedia of World Sport,* 315.

14. Aside from different editions of the *Guinness Book of World Records,* see Hector Harold Whitlock, "Walking," *Encyclopaedia Britannica,* vol. 23 (Chicago: Encyclopaedia Britannica, 1970), 164.

15. In 1960, two British soldiers made it across the United States in sixty-six days, averaging forty-six miles a day, while a fifty-six–year-old British dietitian made it from one end to the other of Great Britain, announcing her intention to next cross the United States on foot, Trent, ed., *The Gentle Art of Walking,* 48.

16. Ibid., 50.

17. Larry Millet, "Walk Was Adventure of a Lifetime," *Pioneer Press,* June 17, 2002, 1, 5A.

18. Donald McFarlan, ed., *The Guinness Book of Records, 1992* (New York: Facts on File, 1993), 290. For one book on a world walk, see Steven M. Newman, *World Walk* (New York: William Morrow, 1989).

19. Starting in the 1930s, the Swedes awarded badges to qualified walkers. In the postwar era, the Dutch League of Physical Culture organized the Nijmegen marches, with both civilian and military categories. They lasted for four days of consecutive walking, challenging thousands of participants to cover thirty-five miles a day, Whitlock, "Walking," 64. For a book from that period, see Harry Johnson, *Creative Walking for Physical Fitness* (New York: Grosset & Dunlap, 1970).

20. Tricia O. Ortiz, "Wonju Sponsors Health and Friendship Festival," October 28, 2002, http://ima.korea.army.mil (from homepage, click category "news," then "news releases," and scroll down for Ortiz article).

21. For a discussion of overweight America, see the first in a five-part weekly series, Terry Fiedler, "The Bottom Line," *Minneapolis Star Tri-*

bune, October 12, 2003, A1, A22. For a history of fatness and beauty, read Peter Stearns, *Fat History: Bodies and Beauties in the Modern West* (New York: New York University Press, 2002).

22. Chuck Stone, "Selma to Montgomery," *National Geographic,* February 2000, 98–107.

23. In *Armies of the Night* (1968) Norman Mailer describes a rag-tag collection of seventy thousand demonstrators—comprised of college students, professors, hippies, and clergy—marching the two-plus-mile course to the Pentagon. Once there, hippies voicing the countercultural and prankster part of the antiwar movement sought to levitate the building, while earnest war protesters sought to breach the police line surrounding the building itself. A useful summary of events is found in "Levitate the Pentagon," http://www.jofreeman.com/photos/Pentagon67.html.

24. In 1989, the year the Berlin Wall came down, two million Latvians, Lithuanians, and Estonians joined hands, forming a human chain that reached 650 kilometers along the Baltic Way, to protest the fiftieth anniversary of the Molotov-Ribbentrop pact.

25. For a recent work on the battle to rove the countryside at will, see Marion Shoard, *A Right to Roam* (Oxford: Oxford University Press, 1999).

26. For "Walking the Land for our Ancient Rights Peace Walk Update," see http://lakeeyre.green.net.au/long-walk-updates-page.html. Of a multitude of peace walkers, Derek Walker Youngs continues a solo trek that at present has covered over twenty-three thousand kilometers in thirteen countries. For peace walker Derek Walker Youngs, see the Peace Walker Society website, http://www.peace-walker.com.

27. For a short history of walking, see "Zwischen Leiden und Befreiung," http://www.b_treff.com/geschi.htm, and for its rationale, see "The Society for Barefoot Living," http://www.barefooters.org. For a contemporary walk, see "Interfaith Peace Walk to Abolish Nuclear Weapons, March 24 – 30, 2002" (http://www.nevadadesertexperience.org/Peace Walk.html).

28. For Granny D's thirty-two-hundred-mile trek, see "Baird Joins 'Granny D' on Final Mile of Cross Country Walk for Campaign Finance Reform," February 29, 2000, Congressman Brian Baird homepage, http://www.house.gov/baird/prgrannyd.htm.

29. In May 1997, Ffyona Campbell confessed, as more than a few record-setting explorers and hikers have, that she had cheated on her record-breaking trek, riding a thousand miles of her North American journey at a time when she was addicted to drugs, on the brink of suicide, and pregnant. For an examination of the brouhaha surrounding her confession and an insight into the temptation to cheat for the sake of recognition by walkers, hikers, mountain climbers, and explorers, see Phillip Weiss, "If Truth Be Told They Lied," *Outside Magazine,* May 1997, 1 – 8 (online). For the curious mish-mash of subjectivity, commerce, vanity, and romance that surrounded Ffyona Campbell's walking, see her *On Foot through Africa* (London: Orion, 1994), which she dedicated "For my father and for the men who were with me."

30. For a single example, Northwest Airlines sponsored the November 2001 5th Annual Walk for Hunger Relief benefiting HungerSolutions Minnesota.

31. For information on walkathons and the March of Dimes and their activity in New York, see Lisa Napoli, "Why Walking in Circles Gets Charities Going," *New York Times,* November 17, 2002.

32. Interview with Julien van Remoortere, at his home in Ostend, December 15, 2001.

33. Karen Swenson, "A Sacred Circuit in Tibet," *New York Times,* March, 16, 2003, and Daisann McLane, "Frugal Traveler: Hiking from Tub to Tub in Rural Northern Japan," *New York Times,* October 21, 2001.

34. Paul Fussell provocatively wrote, "As long as history can remember, life has been figured as a journey, and there is nothing unique in the traditional recourse to this cliché during the 20's and 30's. But it would be hard to designate another time when it was so conventional to conceive of life specifically as a journey by *rail,*" *Abroad: British Literary Traveling between the Wars* (Oxford: Oxford University Press, 1980), emphasis his, 63.

35. Disasters and wars, as confirmed by the nightly news, return people to walking. Similar to what defeat does to an army, catastrophe returns its victims to walking. An earthquake in El Salvador in January 2001 severed roads, and to find help survivors had to take to their feet. The reversibility of walking is today seen, to take a single example, in zones of the Carpathian Mountains where the rising cost of fuel and the breakdown of the public transport established by the Soviet systems have returned people to walking former paths.

36. In a seven-to-two vote, the Court, citing the 1970 Americans with Disabilities Act, sided with disabled professional Casey Martin's right to play in a cart in professional golf tournaments sponsored by the Professional Golfer's Association. In the Court's opinion, the need to walk formed a barrier to Casey's right to full participation. Ignorant of how much the game turns on the endurance of one's legs (a four-day tournament of seventy-two holes requires walking a distance of approximately twenty miles), one judge, who probably doesn't play the game or rides in a cart, justified his ruling with an appeal to the philosophically imponderable notion "'Pure chance'" — whatever that may be! — "may have a greater impact on the outcome of elite golf tournaments than does the walking rule," cited in George Will, "Compassion's Tour in Law," *Minneapolis Star Tribune,* June 3, 2001, A27. Also, see Clifton Brown, "Martin's Case Is Settled but the Debate Continues," *New York Times,* May 30, 2001.

37. Although China, with 6 million trucks and buses and 3.6 million automobiles, has more than a 100 people per motor vehicle — compared with 1.3 people in the United States — the number of motor vehicles in China more than tripled in the 1985–2000 period, "Transportation System — China," *Encyclopedia of Modern Asia,* vol. 5, ed. David Levinson and Karen Christensen (Detroit: Thomson/Gale, 2002), 527.

38. Edward Abbey, *Desert Solitaire: A Season in the Wilderness* (New York: Ballantine Books, 1967), xii.

39. John McCollister, "Take Me Out to the Boardwalk," *Saturday Evening Post,* April 1988, 68–69.

40. For a critical feature essay on Celebration, Florida, see Michael Pollan, "Town Building Is No Mickey Mouse Operation," *New York Times,* October 29, 2000. For the inspiration of private housing aimed at designing green space and separating vehicle traffic and pedestrian walkways, first realized in Radburn, New Jersey, see Evan McKenzie, *Privatopia: Homeowner Associations and the Rise of Residential Private Government* (New Haven, CT: Yale University Press, 1994), 9.

41. For a single example, in "Walking to Work," family physician Tim Rumsey recounts the diversity he experienced in one of St. Paul's oldest neighborhoods during his five years of walking through it on the way to work, Curt Brown, "The Pulse of Neighborhood," September 10, 2000, E1, 4.

42. Minneapolis Mayor Rybak and St. Paul Mayor Kelly's commitment to walking and biking was on full display at a September 2002 walking conference in St. Paul, Laurie Blake, *Minneapolis Star Tribune,* September 8, 2002, 3B.

43. Cited in editorial in *Minneapolis Star Tribune,*

January 6, 2002, 20A. In effect, Mayor Rybak quoted the conclusion of Jane Jacobs's *Death and Life of Great American Cities* (New York: Random House, 1961).

44. In contrast to Lewis Mumford and others, Jacobs's ideal walking city makes room for trucks, buses, and automobiles. She argues that "we blame [them] too much" rather than the city planners who have failed to defend walkers and meet the true needs of a city, ibid., 7, 20–25, 338.

45. An example of the medical glance at the child is Andrew Chong, *Is Your Child Walking Right? Parents' Guide to Little Feet* (Wheaton, IL: Wheaton Resource, 1986).

46. A range of articles appeared on the U.S. Defense Department's support of research at the Georgia Institute of Technology, which, with a high rate of success, can identify individual walks. Widely reprinted and quoted was an AP article by Michael Sniffen, "Telling the Way We Walk," May 21, 2003.

47. To offer a single example, in Sukababo, Indonesia — a village of 832 people who live on less than fifty cents a day — the nearest telephone is more than three miles away, Wayne Arnold, "Hook Up Rural Asia, Some Say, and Poverty Can Be Mitigated," *New York Times,* January 19, 2001.

48. Naturalist and writer Dan Flores concludes his *Caprock Canyonlands* (Austin: University of Texas Press, 1990), remarking on "the symbiotic grip our toes and terra firma have on one another," 175.

49. Paul C. Adams, "Peripatetic Imagery and Peripatetic Sense of Place," *Textures of Place,* ed. Paul C. Adams, Steven Hoelscher, and Karen E. Till (Minneapolis: University of Minnesota Press, 2001), 201.

50. I argue about the connection of locale, locality, and place in *Rethinking Home: A Case for Local History* (Berkeley: University of California Press, 2002), 1–15.

51. John Burns, "A Nation at War: Tumult, Cheers, Tears and Looting in Capital Streets," *New York Times,* March 4, 2003, late ed., A1.

52. James Hillman, "Perambulate to Paradise," *Utne Reader,* March–April 2000, 86.

53. A recent fashion of walking labyrinths, popular in the European past, started up in the 1990s. With eighteen hundred now in the nation and dozens recently installed in San Francisco Bay Area spas, parks, churches, schools, and teen centers, we see how walking continues to be a source of renewal, therapy, and self-knowledge in a riding society, *San Francisco Chronicle,* February 28, 2003, E6.

Acknowledgments

THE WRITING OF *On Foot* has been a long journey, and, as with most such endeavors, my gratitude is great and diverse. My first thanks go to my wife, Cathy, who now and then threw out an idea and listened more than her fair share as the price of living with someone whose passion is to turn insights into books. From the nearby nursing home, my mother got her two cents in on this book up to the very end, when in fall 2002 she died at age ninety.

At the Southwest Minnesota State University, my colleagues at the Center for Rural and Regional Studies helped along the manuscript in many ways. My son, Anthony, and Geoff Cunfer supplied a variety of insights focused on the differences among walking in the mountains and on flat and wet lands and the nature of travel and exploration in early U.S. history. Center members Jan Louwagie, Janet Timmerman, Donata DeBruyckere, Nancy Torner, and Margaret Barker made a variety of contributions to the book, from providing ideas, moving shelves of books and files, and correcting errors to simply offering good-natured encouragement. Center assistant Nancy Brown pointed out that walking and carrying were largely inseparable activities for early humanity.

Student assistant Christie Kubat organized the project's mushrooming and unruly file folders and successfully wrote, out of my materials, a first draft on early American walking. Esvary Devi Jaya-balan entered corrections in an early draft. Student Richard May, fresh out of a career in military service, provided me with the army drill manual, and called my attention to the Nijmegan marches organized by the Dutch League of Physical Culture. Jody Grismer helped pre-pare the index. Student Darlene Guse rescued me on a few occasions from my own computer ignorance.

University colleagues from outside the Center for Rural and Re-gional Studies also made contributions. Historian Lloyd Peterson pro-vided me with materials on the way walking dominated the plight of the Civil War soldier. Poet Philip Dacey enlightened me about Walt Whitman, while writer David Pichaske generously provided me with a crucial anthology of walking and gave an early draft of the manu-script a first full copyedit. University physical therapist Dan Snobl and community therapist Ritch Mjelde clarified for me the mechanics of walking. Music instructor William Taylor explained to me why it is difficult to get marching bands in step.

Southwest Minnesota State University librarians JoAnn Robasse, Mara Wiggins, Mary Jane Striegel, Kathleen Ashe, Sandra Fuhr, Sandy Hoffbeck, and Dicksy Howe/Noyes met my research needs. Shawn Hedman, director of computer services, kept my computer up and running. Library workers Nancy DeRoode and Connie Stensrud supplied me with an array of materials, many of which came from the University of Minnesota Wilson Library, whose ref-erence librarians have across the last three decades made me feel I have a second research home there. I also received a friendly wel-come at the adjacent Elmer L. Andersen Building, where Rudi Vecoli, director of the Immigrant Archives, and the staff of the So-cial Welfare History and YMCA Archives, especially David Klaassen, helped me greatly with my research. Additional materials were sup-plied by the downtown Minneapolis public library; the Marshall, Minnesota, city library; the Minnesota Historical Society; and the Guildhall Library in London.

Museums provided a wealth of valuable material, particularly the Amsterdam Historical Museum in the Netherlands, the London Mu-seum of Transport, the Minnesota Science Museum, the Museo di Roma, the Musée Carnevalet in Paris, and the Museum of London.

With profound apologies to those I have forgotten to acknowledge, I express my sincere thanks to Andrea Antonini, Eric Davenport, Bradley Dean, Ralph Gakenheimer, Dan Giles, Adrien Greenwood, Jan Hertoghs, Jean and Mark Larson, William Leonard, Robert Levine, C. Paul Martin, Tom Martin, Nomura Masichi, John McGrath, Jay Ohlsen, Carl Pansaerts, John Radzilowski, Thaddeus Radzilowski, Paul Rehkamp, Jeffrey Russell, Gijs Schilthuis, Phil Schuyler, Joe Sheridan, Peter Stearns, Kevin Stroup, Stephen and Caroline Tonsor, Julien van Remoortere, Scott Vick, Laura Dassow Walls, and Stephen Wolter. I also thank in particular Eugen Weber, who always gives me cause to think, and Adam Sowan, who generously shared a wealth of materials on modern English walkers.

The transformation of the manuscript into a book was truly aided by three individuals. Phil Freshman significantly improved the first draft of this work. Edward Knappman, my agent, continually nudged the manuscript along in the right direction. New York University Press editor Debbie Gershenowitz enthusiastically accepted it and asked for significant—and at points what seemed daunting—revisions that helped fashion the manuscript into as good a book as it could be. Of course, I exempt her, the press's fine copyeditor Emily Wright, and supportive managing editor Despina Papazoglou Gimbel, and all the others to whom I have expressed gratitude from the errors and shortcomings of this work, which, in all truth, went as far as this old caddie could go.

Index

Carriages, 75, 77, 94, 126, 180, 186, 191, 235–36, 256; aristocratic prestige, 76; like automobile of earlier era, 86; in colonial Boston, 127; on parade in the Baroque city, 85–86; in Russia, 293n. 105; speed in 1820s and 1830s, 293n. 19; travel in eighteenth-century Europe, 97–100; types and places, 290n. 46. *See also* Carts; Horses; Promenading and strolling

Cars: car culture, 248; car vs. walking, 18, 239–41; in China, 271, 318n. 37; compared to horses, 58–59; creator of a new environment, 240; definer of new cities, 240; definer of the status of its driver and rider, 240; diminish walking, 270–71; displace walkers, horses, and carts, 157; distinguish walkers and riders, 241; expander of the suburbs, 240; first drivers of, 239; inimical to pedestrians and walkers, 239–40, 244, 246, 247, 254; increase pace of urban life, 247; in Latin America, 271; invention of, 239; maker of new life styles, 241; mass production and popularity, 241–43; popularization in San Francisco, 314n. 74; ratio to population, 246; regulation of speed and drivers, 245; traffic control, 245–46; transformer of the countryside, 240, 251–52

Carts, 30, 31, 39, 98, 126, 157, 186, 189, 191, 235–36, 313n. 63

Catlin, George, painter, 138

Chairs and sitting, 37, 43, 72, 76–77, 81–82, 127–28; in contemporary homes and offices, 233; sitting vs. walking in contemporary world, 233; superior to walking, 10–11

Chapman, Charlie, 227

Chapman, John, a.k.a. Johnny Appleseed, 137

Chariots, 30, 31

Chartist movement, 185

Chesterfield, Lord, 90

Chimborazo, 116

Chivalry, origins tied to mounted warrior, 59–60

Churchill, Winston, African walker, 206

Cities and towns: Baroque, 84–87; European origins and tie to commerce, 63–64; in the Middle Ages, 61–64; as source of modern walker, 167

City ordinances regulating walkers, streets, crowds, and traffic: in the Middle Ages, 67–68; modern regulations, 182–83, 209

Civil War, 219–221, 309n. 60; amputees and prosthetic devices, 221; importance of boots and shoes, 221

Cleanliness and sanitation, 159, 166, 182, 191–92, 200, 289n. 118

Clothing fashions, aristocratic, 87–89. *See also* Walking apparel

Coleridge, Samuel Taylor, 106–107, 154

Commune of 1871, 195

Commuting and commuters, 95, 123–24, 157–58, 162, 167–68, 169–70, 171–72, 198–99, 272

Compostella trail, 286n. 50. *See also* St. James of Compostella

Congestion: in London, 159, 161, 169; in Middle Ages, 66; in New York, 243–45; in Paris, 109–10, 186; in Rome, 36–37

Conrad, Joseph, 8

Contemporary design, diminishes walking, 231–33

Control of urban streets, 228; battle for streets in aftermath of World War I, 210; in colonial Boston, 127; during French Revolution, 187–89; Mussolini shapes Rome, 225–26; Napoleon suppresses crowd, 189; Nazis fashion Berlin, 226–27; overview of modern history, 179–81, 183–85. *See also* Nationalism

Cook, Captain James, British explorer, 11

Coronado, Francisco Vásquez de, 131

Countryside, the United States: end of walking, 251–52; Main Street decline, 252–53

Crime and police: London, 165–66; New York, 243, 244–45, 313n. 64; Paris, 192

Cripples, lame, 65

Crowds and mobs, 179, 180, 181–83, 184–85, 196, 204; in colonial Boston, 127; governments fight crowds and revolutions, 189–90; in New York, 243; in Paris, 184–96; roving bands in the Middle Ages, 68–69; street battles in the United States and Europe, 1968, 265; traffic laws, 183–84; unregulated in the Middle Ages, 66. *See also* French Revolution; Traffic

Crusades, 57–61, 287n. 75

Curie, Marie, 155

Curie, Pierre, 155

Custine, Marquis de, 99

Dance, 23–24, 35, 57, 78, 81–82, 92

Dangel, Leo, 252

Darwin, Charles, 117

Defoe, Daniel, 86–87

Della Casa, Giovanni, 91

Denecourt, Claude François, tourist entrepreneur, 120

De Quincy, Thomas, 154

De Soto, Hernando, 131

Detroit, 242, 314n. 77

Dickens, Charles, 154, 163; *Bleak House*, 163; *David Copperfield*, 88; *Dombey and Son*, 170; *Household Words*, 177; *Nicholas Nickleby*, 176; *Old Curiosity Shop*, 176; *Oliver Twist*, 177; visits New York, 243

Domestication, 26–27

Mosse, George, 214, 215
Motion pictures: teach walking, 210–11; Hollywood films, 15. *See also* Mauss, Marcel
Mountain climbing, 38, 118, 258–59; Mt. Everest, 259
Mountains, 118–19; their reappraisal, 295n. 65
Mounted warriors, 28, 47, 57–61, 131
Mount Everest, 118
Muir, John, 117, 144, 277; creator of Yosemite Park, 208
Mumford, Lewis, 84–85, 86, 161, 239, 246

Napoleon I, 189
Napoleon III, 192–93
Nationalism: teacher of body movement and walking, 212–13, 219; intensified efforts for war, 214; Fascism and Nazism, 214
National Socialist Germany, 226, 243; anti-Semitism, 226; Berlin, its streets and walkers made ready for the 1936 Olympics, 226–27; control of the streets, 226; parades, processions, and marching, 225
Natural sciences, botany, and geology, 111, 113–14, 115, 116–17, 122, 143–44, 146, 148–49
Naturfreunde, 215
Newell, Robert, 107
Newman, Steven, four-year traversing of twenty countries and five continents, 262
New urbanists. *See* Reinventing walking places
New York: city ordinances related to walking environment, 245; conditions of streets, 243–44; mobs and crimes, 243; police, 243, 244–45, 313n. 64
Nicollet, Joseph N., explorer, 138
Nietzsche, Friedrich, 205
Nijmegen marches, 316n. 19
Nomads, 24–27, 29
North American Indians, 12, 13; travelers on foot, 129; use of animals, 129; walking pace, 132

Olympics, 316n. 11; Greek, 38; in 1896, 260; in 1906, 261
Oñate, Don Juan de, 131
Orthopedists, podiatrists, and physical therapists, 5–6
Otto, Nickolaus, 239
Ötzi man, 24
Owen, Wilfred, 224
Oxford, 67

Pack animals, 47–48; camels, 31; donkeys, 5, 31
Parades, marches, and drills, 17, 35, 79–80, 85–86, 203–4, 209–19; foot soldiers, 219; in the French Third Republic, 195; to Gettysburg, 220; in step, 284n. 50; March on Rome, 225; May Day, 215; military indoctrination, 219;

role of drills and marching for infantry in the Civil War, 309n. 60; of Sherman's Army, 219; socialism, 215–16; of Stonewall Jackson, 220; training of Roman soldiers, 35. *See also* Goose step
Paris, 153; Baroque, 85, 86, 91–92; changing condition of the streets, 194–95; cleaned up, 197, 200; comparison with eighteenth-century London, 158–59; crime, 192; disease, 192; foot traffic, 195; growth in nineteenth century, 193–94; in the Middle Ages, 66, 67–68; Paris vs. London, 181, 190–91; people march to Versailles, 188; popular street protest in nineteenth-century Paris, 195–96; sanitation and health, 192; sidewalk cafes, 194; street conditions, 90–91, 186, 191–92; struggle to control crowds, 184–96; tourists, 194; traffic, 186–87, 191, 194; transportation, 194
Pastoralism, 28
Paths and trails, 26–27, 28–30, 75, 134; animal trails, 26; Appalachian Trail, 258; hiking, 258–59; in the Middle Ages, 50–51; Natchez Trace, 133; in North America, 129–30, 132; Oregon Trail, 138–39
Pavement, 67, 158–59, 181. *See also* Surfaces
Peary, Robert, American explorer, 122
Peddlers, 133–34, 183; streets of London, 156–57, 160, 164
Pedestrians, 17; appearance of, 199–200, 212–13, 217–18; as city walkers, 167, 179, 180, 182; created by vehicular traffic, 245, 247; internalized new order of time and movement, 183, 198–99; London, 159–62, 165–66; nicknames, 158; origin of the word, 123; pedestrians vs. carriages, 86, 161; plight in North American suburbs, cities, and countryside, 253; polite, 209; relation to commuting, 123–24; teachers of manners, gestures, and movements, 211–19; transformed into commuters, 272
Penn, William, and son Thomas Penn, 129–30
Pennant, Thomas, 104
Pennsylvania Road, 140–41
Pentagon identifies individual walks, 4, 275
Pepys, Samuel, 94, 292n. 78
Pereira, Tomas Carlos, ten-year journey on foot around five continents, 262
Peripatetic, 7
Peripatetic, The (1793), 106
Perry, Lewis, 144
Persia, 34
Physical education, gymnastics, and calisthenics, 212–14, 307n. 29; Turnverein, 308n. 51
Pilgrimages and pilgrims, 40, 51; clothing of, 53, 54; Compostella trail and its pilgrims, 53–54, 286n. 50; in the Middle Ages, 51–55; in Rome, 51, 54

Travel: Aristocratic, eighteenth century, 93; colonial North America, 125–30; early modern Europe, 74; in eighteenth-century, 97–100; in Europe around 1300, 62–63; exploration vs. travel vs. tourism, 121; foot travel, in early modern Europe, 75–76; foot travel, as a universal necessity in the Middle Ages, 47–48; increasing speeds at end of eighteenth century, 95–97; ordeals of, Alexander the Great's Army, 32–33; ordeals of, Greeks retreating from Persia, 31–32; reasons improved at end of eighteenth century, 114; recreational, Rome, 38; Roman, 33–34, 38–39; Roman ship travel, 33, 40; the traveling court, 47. *See also* Tourism

Travel guides, 54; Baedeker, Karl, 120; in Rome, 39

Trevelyan, G. M., 205

Umbrella, 89–90; manners and styles, 291n. 63; umbrella vs. parasol, 291n. 62

Urban life, diverse and quickening pace, 247–48

Urban lighting, 171–72, 182, 197

Urban walking, 171, 150–51, 158–59, 208–10; etiquette, 209; neighborhood, 208; styles and fashions, 208

Vaca, Alvar Núñez Cabeza de, 131

Vagrancy, vagabonds, and beggars, 55, 68–69, 99, 157, 183, 288nn. 107, 112, 292n. 3

Valdes, Peter, 55–56

Valéry, Paul, 123

Vegetius, 35

Verne, Jules, 234

Versailles, 78–79

Vienna, 197–98; Ringstrasse, 193

Wagner, Richard, 154

Wagon travel, 138–39

Walden Pond, 144–45

Walkathons, 267–68

Walker, nineteenth-century slang, 165

Walkers, 14–15; beach and boardwalk, 119–20, 145–46; Chinese trackers, 34; city, 12, 13, 105–6, 162–63, 164, 200–202, 251–52; city visitors, 69–70, 244, 313n. 60; country, 13–14, 105–6, 200–202, 204–5, 251–52; differentiation in eighteenth-century, 100; eighteenth-century, 106–107; eighteenth-century fashion, 290n. 28; English as fast pedestrians, 157–58; ethnic, 14; *flâneurs*, 123–24, 173–75; Hmong, 13; inferiority of, 42–43; Kalahari of Africa, 25; the Mardudjara of Australia, 25–26; middle-class walkers, leisure and means to go to the countryside, 204–5; movie stars, 211; North American eclipse of backcountry walkers, 150–51; pavement, 158; primitives,

25–26; slave, 14; types of urban walkers, 208; the unemployed of London, 170–71; *walker*, as a pejorative, 165. *See also* Commuting and commuters; Medieval walkers; Pedestrians; Riding vs. walking; Urban walking

Walking: act of inferiority, 72, 76; act of penance, 51, 52; African, 21; animal power, 27–28; an antidote against being fat, 263; on the battlefield, 222–24; Chinese, 34; as a choice, 73, 103–4, 111, 129, 171; in churches, 69; city, 153; city, Berlin, 226–27; city, dangers and difficulties of, 164–65; city, London, 162–63; city, New York, 244–45; city, Paris, 193–94; class differentiation, 71–73; class and status, 10–12, 16–17; in colonial North America, 125–30, 132–33; conditions in countryside around 1900, 200–201; in courts, 77–79; in defense of commons, 105, 266; definition of, 6–7; diminished indoors, 232–34; displaced in the United States, 128–29, 151; displacement of, equals demise of place, 150–52; diversity of, in the Middle Ages, 68–70; early civilization, 20–21; eclipse of, in nineteenth-century Europe, 157; eclipse of, in the United States, 149–52; end of, 269; in Europe in 1300, 62–63; fashionable, 15, 76, 86–87; as a gesture, 4–5; Greek, 8–9; increasingly the exception across much of the world, 254; indispensable, 223–24, 274–76; Japanese (*namba*), 8; labyrinth, 318n. 53; as a leisure activity, origins, 101–2; male and female, 25, 87–88, 91–92, 212–13; mall, 250; as means of claiming ownership, 129–30; as means to explore and settle North America, 130–41; as means of fitness and health, 262, 263, 272; as means of self renewal, 276–78; middle-class walks and travels, 90–93, 201–202; migrant, 100; as necessary and efficient, 31, 42–44, 100, 105, 121, 153–54, 169, 199, 200–201, 257–58, 270, 275–76; New England, 14; new speeds, 200; night (noctambulation), 165; in nineteenth-century Europe, 153–57; North American Indian, 12, 13; Old Testament and New Testament, 10, 44; origins of, 19–23; pace, 31, 33, 199; pace of middle-class London walker, 164; pace of Roman army, 35; pace, varying in different cities, 79; peasant, 158; peasant vs. aristocratic and upper class, 80, 88, 100, 211; planned, 273–74; prehistoric North America, 27–28; in public, 14; recreational, 106–7, 197, 201–202; refinement of, 72, 73, 76–78; as related to road and way, 62–63; riding does away with, 269–71; Romantic, 106–7, 123–24; in service of causes, 214–15, 207–8; shaped to fit terrain, 24; source of empathy for other walkers, 45;

taught by institutions, 212–13; turn-of-the-century, 200; types at beginning of nineteenth century, 123–24; unnecessary, senselessness of, 106, 107, 252, 254, 271; urban, 37–38; vs. wandering, 101–2; as way to knowledge, 148; working-class, 156–57, 194, 199

Walking apparel: Baroque, 87, 92; medieval, 40, 44, 50, 53–54; Roman, 39. *See also* Shoes and footwear

Walking Purchase Treaty (Delaware), 129–30

Walking sticks, staffs, and canes, 39, 45–46, 53, 89; symbol of power and uses, 284n. 65

Walking tours, 268–69

Wallace, Anne, 279n. 2, 293n. 10

Wandering Jew, medieval myth of, 45

War and war footing, 219–21, 222–24, 226–27

Waugh, Evelyn, British novelist, 206–7

Way of the cross, 46

Weber, Eugen, 96, 155, 193, 197

Wheeled cannons, 84, 85

Wheels: all-terrain vehicles, 239; baby carriages, 211, 237, 311n. 30; ball bearings, 311n. 27; casters and coasters, 236; jeeps, 237; miscellaneous vehicles, 239; for rolling objects, 235–37; superiority of foot to wheel in the Middle Ages, 48–49; triumphs over foot, 229, 232, 235–38. *See also* Bicycle

Wilderness Road, 134

Wilson, Edward O., 122

Woodruff, William, memoirist, 156–57

Wordsworth, William, 104–5, 106, 123, 154

World War I: foot soldiers, 220–24; tanks, 223–24; wounded, 224

Xenophon, 31

Young, Arthur, 97, 99

Young Men's Christian Association (YMCA), 215, 216–17

Zweig, Stefan, 197–98

About the Author

Joseph A. Amato is Professor Emeritus of History and Rural and Regional Studies at Southwest Minnesota State University. Amato has authored fifteen books, including *Rethinking Home: A Case for Local History* (2002), *Dust: A History of the Small and Invisible* (2000), *Golf Beats Us All: And So We Love It* (1999), *The Great Jerusalem Artichoke Circus: The Buying and Selling of the Rural American Dream* (1993), and *Victims and Values: A History and Theory of Suffering* (1990).